The LINUX® Network

The LINUX® Network

Fred Butzen and
Christopher Hilton

IDG Books Worldwide, Inc.
An International Data Group Company

Foster City, CA ◆ Chicago, IL ◆ Indianapolis, IN ◆ New York, NY

The LINUX® Network

Published by
IDG Books Worldwide, Inc.
An International Data Group Company
919 E. Hillsdale Blvd., Suite 400
Foster City, CA 94404
www.idgbooks.com (IDG Books Worldwide Web site)

Library of Congress Catalog Card No.: 98-071852

ISBN:1-55828-589-X

Printed in the United States of America

10 9 8 7 6 5 4 3 2 1

1B/QY/QX/ZY/FC

Distributed in the United States by IDG Books Worldwide, Inc.

Distributed by Macmillan Canada for Canada; by Transworld Publishers Limited in the United Kingdom; by IDG Norge Books for Norway; by IDG Sweden Books for Sweden; by Woodslane Pty. Ltd. for Australia; by Woodslane (NZ) Ltd. for New Zealand; by Addison Wesley Longman Singapore Pte Ltd. for Singapore, Malaysia, Thailand, Indonesia, and Korea; by Norma Comunicaciones S.A. for Colombia; by Intersoft for South Africa; by International Thomson Publishing for Germany, Austria, and Switzerland; by Toppan Company Ltd. for Japan; by Distribuidora Cuspide for Argentina; by Livraria Cultura for Brazil; by Ediciencia S.A. for Ecuador; by Ediciones ZETA S.C.R. Ltda. for Peru; by WS Computer Publishing Corporation, Inc., for the Philippines; by Unalis Corporation for Taiwan; by Contemporanea de Ediciones for Venezuela; by Computer Book & Magazine Store for Puerto Rico; by Express Computer Distributors for the Caribbean and West Indies. Authorized Sales Agent: Anthony Rudkin Associates for the Middle East and North Africa.

For general information on IDG Books Worldwide's books in the U.S., please call our Consumer Customer Service department at 800-762-2974. For reseller information, including discounts and premium sales, please call our Reseller Customer Service department at 800-434-3422.

For information on where to purchase IDG Books Worldwide's books outside the U.S., please contact our International Sales department at 650-655-3200 or fax 650-655-3297.

For information on foreign language translations, please contact our Foreign & Subsidiary Rights department at 650-655-3021 or fax 650-655-3281.

For sales inquiries and special prices for bulk quantities, please contact our Sales department at 650-655-3200 or write to the address above.

For information on using IDG Books Worldwide's books in the classroom or for ordering examination copies, please contact our Educational Sales department at 800-434-2086 or fax 317-596-5499.

For press review copies, author interviews, or other publicity information, please contact our Public Relations department at 650-655-3000 or fax 650-655-3299.

For authorization to photocopy items for corporate, personal, or educational use, please contact Copyright Clearance Center, 222 Rosewood Drive, Danvers, MA 01923, or fax 978-750-4470.

ABOUT IDG BOOKS WORLDWIDE

Welcome to the world of IDG Books Worldwide.

IDG Books Worldwide, Inc., is a subsidiary of International Data Group, the world's largest publisher of computer-related information and the leading global provider of information services on information technology. IDG was founded more than 25 years ago and now employs more than 8,500 people worldwide. IDG publishes more than 275 computer publications in over 75 countries (see listing below). More than 90 million people read one or more IDG publications each month.

Launched in 1990, IDG Books Worldwide is today the #1 publisher of best-selling computer books in the United States. We are proud to have received eight awards from the Computer Press Association in recognition of editorial excellence and three from *Computer Currents'* First Annual Readers' Choice Awards. Our best-selling *...For Dummies®* series has more than 50 million copies in print with translations in 38 languages. IDG Books Worldwide, through a joint venture with IDG's Hi-Tech Beijing, became the first U.S. publisher to publish a computer book in the People's Republic of China. In record time, IDG Books Worldwide has become the first choice for millions of readers around the world who want to learn how to better manage their businesses.

Our mission is simple: Every one of our books is designed to bring extra value and skill-building instructions to the reader. Our books are written by experts who understand and care about our readers. The knowledge base of our editorial staff comes from years of experience in publishing, education, and journalism — experience we use to produce books for the '90s. In short, we care about books, so we attract the best people. We devote special attention to details such as audience, interior design, use of icons, and illustrations. And because we use an efficient process of authoring, editing, and desktop publishing our books electronically, we can spend more time ensuring superior content and spend less time on the technicalities of making books.

You can count on our commitment to deliver high-quality books at competitive prices on topics you want to read about. At IDG Books Worldwide, we continue in the IDG tradition of delivering quality for more than 25 years. You'll find no better book on a subject than one from IDG Books Worldwide.

John Kilcullen
CEO
IDG Books Worldwide, Inc.

Steven Berkowitz
President and Publisher
IDG Books Worldwide, Inc.

Eighth Annual Computer Press Awards ➤1992

Ninth Annual Computer Press Awards ➤1993

Tenth Annual Computer Press Awards ➤1994

Eleventh Annual Computer Press Awards ➤1995

IDG Books Worldwide, Inc., is a subsidiary of International Data Group, the world's largest publisher of computer-related information and the leading global provider of information services on information technology. International Data Group publishes over 275 computer publications in over 75 countries. More than 90 million people read one or more International Data Group publications each month. International Data Group's publications include: **ARGENTINA:** Buyer's Guide, Computerworld Argentina, PC World Argentina; **AUSTRALIA:** Australian Macworld, Australian PC World, Australian Reseller News, Computerworld, IT Casebook, Network World, Publish, Webmaster; **AUSTRIA:** Computerwelt Osterreich, Networks Austria, PC Tip Austria; **BANGLADESH:** PC World Bangladesh; **BELARUS:** PC World Belarus; **BELGIUM:** Data News; **BRAZIL:** Annuário de Informática, Computerworld, Connections, Macworld, PC Player, PC World, Publish, Reseller News, Supergamepower; **BULGARIA:** Computerworld Bulgaria, Network World Bulgaria, PC & MacWorld Bulgaria; **CANADA:** CIO Canada, Client/Server World, ComputerWorld Canada, InfoWorld Canada, NetworkWorld Canada, WebWorld; **CHILE:** Computerworld Chile, PC World Chile; **COLOMBIA:** Computerworld Colombia, PC World Colombia; **COSTA RICA:** PC World Centro America; **THE CZECH AND SLOVAK REPUBLICS:** Computerworld Czechoslovakia, Macworld Czech Republic, PC World Czechoslovakia; **DENMARK:** Communications World Danmark, Computerworld Danmark, Macworld Danmark, PC World Danmark, Techworld Danmark; **DOMINICAN REPUBLIC:** PC World Republica Dominicana; **ECUADOR:** PC World Ecuador; **EGYPT:** Computerworld Middle East, PC World Middle East; **EL SALVADOR:** PC World Centro America; **FINLAND:** MikroPC, Tietoverkko, Tietoviikko; **FRANCE:** Distributique, Hebdo, Info PC, Le Monde Informatique, Macworld, Reseaux & Telecoms, WebMaster France; **GERMANY:** Computer Partner, Computerwoche, Computerwoche Extra, Computerwoche FOCUS, Global Online, Macwelt, PC Welt; **GREECE:** Amiga Computing, GamePro Greece, Multimedia World; **GUATEMALA:** PC World Centro America; **HONDURAS:** PC World Centro America; **HONG KONG:** Computerworld Hong Kong, PC World Hong Kong, Publish in Asia; **HUNGARY:** ABCD CD-ROM, Computerworld Szamitastechnika, Internetto online Magazine, PC World Hungary, PC-X Magazin Hungary; **ICELAND:** Tolvuheimur PC World Island; **INDIA:** Information Communications World, Information Systems Computerworld, PC World India, Publish in Asia; **INDONESIA:** InfoKomputer PC World, Komputek Computerworld, Publish in Asia; **IRELAND:** ComputerScope, PC Live!; **ISRAEL:** Macworld Israel, People & Computers/Computerworld; **ITALY:** Computerworld Italia, Macworld Italia, Networking Italia, PC World Italia; **JAPAN:** DTP World, Macworld Japan, Nikkei Personal Computing, OS/2 World Japan, SunWorld Japan, Windows NT World, Windows World Japan; **KENYA:** PC World East African; **KOREA:** Hi-Tech Information, Macworld Korea, PC World Korea; **MACEDONIA:** PC World Macedonia; **MALAYSIA:** Computerworld Malaysia, PC World Malaysia, Publish in Asia; **MALTA:** PC World Malta; **MEXICO:** Computerworld Mexico, PC World Mexico; **MYANMAR:** PC World Myanmar; **NETHERLANDS:** Computer! Totaal, LAN Internetworking Magazine, LAN World Buyers Guide, Macworld Netherlands, Net, WebWereld; **NEW ZEALAND:** Absolute Beginners Guide and Plain & Simple Series, Computer Buyer, Computer Industry Directory, Computerworld New Zealand, MTB, Network World, PC World New Zealand; **NICARAGUA:** PC World Centro America; **NORWAY:** Computerworld Norge, CW Rapport, Datamagasinet, Financial Rapport, Kursguide Norge, Macworld Norge, Multimediaworld Norge, PC World Ekspress Norge, PC World Nettverk, PC World Norge, PC World ProduktGuide Norge; **PAKISTAN:** Computerworld Pakistan; **PANAMA:** PC World Panama; **PEOPLE'S REPUBLIC OF CHINA:** China Computer Users, China Computerworld, China InfoWorld, China Telecom World Weekly, Computer & Communication, Electronic Design China, Electronics Today, Electronics Weekly, Game Software, PC World China, Popular Computer Week, Software Weekly, Software World, Telecom World; **PERU:** Computerworld Peru, PC World Profesional Peru, PC World SoHo Peru; **PHILIPPINES:** Click!, Computerworld Philippines, PC World Philippines, Publish in Asia; **POLAND:** Computerworld Poland, Computerworld Special Report Poland, Cyber, Macworld Poland, Networld Poland, PC World Komputer; **PORTUGAL:** Cerebro/PC World, Computerworld/Correio Informático, Dealer World Portugal, Mac*In/PC*In Portugal, Multimedia World; **PUERTO RICO:** PC World Puerto Rico; **ROMANIA:** Computerworld Romania, PC World Romania, Telecom Romania; **RUSSIA:** Computerworld Russia, Mir PK, Publish, Seti; **SINGAPORE:** Computerworld Singapore, PC World Singapore, Publish in Asia; **SLOVENIA:** Monitor; **SOUTH AFRICA:** Computing SA, Network World SA, Software World SA; **SPAIN:** Communicaciones World España, Computerworld España, Dealer World España, Macworld España, PC World España; **SRI LANKA:** Infolink PC World; **SWEDEN:** CAP&Design, Computer Sweden, Corporate Computing Sweden, Internetworld Sweden, it.branschen, MaxiData Sweden, MikroDatorn, Natverk & Kommunikation, PC World Sweden, PCaktiv, Windows World Sweden; **SWITZERLAND:** Computerworld Schweiz, Macworld Schweiz, PCtip; **TAIWAN:** Computerworld Taiwan, Macworld Taiwan, NEW ViSiON/Publish, PC World Taiwan, Windows World Taiwan; **THAILAND:** Publish in Asia, Thai Computerworld; **TURKEY:** Computerworld Turkiye, Macworld Turkiye, Network World Turkiye, PC World Turkiye; **UKRAINE:** Computerworld Kiev, Multimedia World Ukraine, PC World Ukraine; **UNITED KINGDOM:** Acorn User UK, Amiga Action UK, Amiga Computing UK, Apple Talk UK Computing, Macworld, Parents and Computers UK, PC Advisor, PC Home, PSX Pro, The WEB; **UNITED STATES:** Cable in the Classroom, CIO Magazine, Computerworld, DOS World, Federal Computer Week, GamePro Magazine, InfoWorld, I-Way, Macworld, Network World, PC Games, PC World, Publish, Video Event, THE WEB Magazine, and WebMaster; online webzines: JavaWorld, NetscapeWorld, and SunWorld Online; **URUGUAY:** InfoWorld Uruguay; **VENEZUELA:** Computerworld Venezuela, PC World Venezuela; and **VIETNAM:** PC World Vietnam.
5/7/98

Credits

ACQUISITIONS EDITOR
Laura Lewin

DEVELOPMENT EDITOR
Barbra Guerra

TECHNICAL EDITOR
Kevin Reichard

COPY EDITORS
Bill McManus
Carolyn Welch
Nicole Fountain

PROJECT COORDINATOR
Tom Debolski

BOOK DESIGNER
Jim Donohue

COVER DESIGN
©mike parsons design

GRAPHICS AND
PRODUCTION SPECIALISTS
Stephanie Hollier
Jude Levinson
Anderas Schueller

QUALITY CONTROL SPECIALISTS
Mick Arellano
Mark Schumann

GRAPHICS TECHNICIANS
Linda J. Marousek
Hector Mendosa

ILLUSTRATORS
Fred Butzen
Christopher Hilton

PROOFREADER
Mary C. Barnack

INDEXER
Fred Butzen

About the Authors

Fred Butzen is a technical writer, database designer, and programmer. He worked as a technical writer for Mark Williams Company and in that capacity was the principal author of the manual for the Coherent operating system (a precursor to Linux).

   Christopher Hilton is a programmer and consultant who specializes in networked applications that run in the UNIX environment.

To Anne: All ways true, true always.
— F.B.
For Raymond Hilton
— C.H.

Preface

The 1990s has with good reason been called the *decade of the Internet*. The advent of a publicly accessible network over which computers can exchange information around the world at little or no cost has radically changed the way we manage information. This change has affected all enterprises that work with information from schools to research laboratories and from hospitals to direct-mail marketers.

One of the most important effects of the Internet revolution is that it empowers people. A solitary person cannot accomplish much, but the Internet helps a person who has a good idea and a flair for organization to find like-minded people and work with them, even though they may never meet in the flesh.

One such person is a young Finnish programmer named Linus Torvalds. In the late 1980s, he announced on an Internet newsgroup that he had written a clone of the UNIX operating system's kernel (that is, the central program that is the heart of the operating system), and he invited other programmers to join him to help build a fully featured clone of UNIX. UNIX has been the operating system of choice for engineers and serious computer programmers for nearly 25 years, so interest in this project was keen. Soon, what had been the part-time project of a solitary programmer in Finland became an international movement that has involved hundreds of volunteer programmers from nearly every country in the world. The fruit of their work is the Linux operating system, a fully featured robust clone of UNIX that is available for free. Linux is the gift of a community of talented and generous programmers from around the world — a community that is united not by an accident of geography but by shared interest and choice expressed through the medium of the Internet.

The Audience for This Book

Networking and the Internet led to the creation of Linux, and networking lies at the heart of the Linux system. However, networking remains a technology that is unfamiliar to many people who want to use it. For many people, networking remains a tantalizing possibility: they know that networking computers would increase the efficiency with which they work and would broaden the range of work that they could do, but they do not know how to set up networking for themselves. Consultants and off-the-shelf packages are both too expensive and too limiting.

It is for these people that we have written *The LINUX Network*.

The LINUX Network is a primer. It is written for the computer user who has little or no experience in setting up a network. You do not need programming experience to read *The LINUX Network* with profit (although programming experience certainly would not hurt). *The LINUX Network* will take you from the ABCs of networking through setting up your own network and grafting it onto the Internet. The discussions are fully illustrated with examples you can use with your own Linux system.

We have designed *The LINUX Network* to help enterprises that will benefit from networking:

◆ Elementary schools and secondary schools, both private and public

◆ Nonprofit organizations

◆ Researchers and scientists

◆ Small businesses

◆ Church and volunteer organizations

◆ Individuals who want to acquire a new skill, or who simply want to learn about the new networking technology

Not to mention, of course, people who find the idea of building an intranet in their homes to be "really cool."

If you are willing to invest sweat equity in your computer system, *The LINUX Network* can help you to learn networking, and so bring the benefits of networking to your enterprise.

The Structure of This Book

The LINUX Network is organized into four parts:

◆ *Part I — An Introduction to Networking.* In this part, we discuss the ABCs of networking: what a network is, what the Internet is, and what the TCP/IP protocols are. If you are new to networking, this part will teach you the terminology and theory you need to work with networking intelligently.

◆ *Part II — Installing Networking.* In this part, we describe how to install networking hardware onto your Linux machine, how to configure your Linux system to use networking, and how to connect your Linux system to the Internet via either an existing Ethernet intranet or via modem connection to an Internet service provider.

◆ *Part III — Creating an Intranet.* In this part, we discuss how to use Ethernet to wire together two or more machines into a local network, or *intranet*. We also discuss how to configure a Linux machine so that it can provide services to other machines across your intranet and how to configure a Linux machine to act as a gateway to the Internet for all other machines on your intranet.

◆ *Part IV — Advanced Topics.* In this part, we discuss some advanced networking topics. These include how to configure Linux and Windows 95 so they can provide services to each other across your intranet, and network security — letting friends in and keeping foes out.

As you can see, *The LINUX Network* progresses from elementary topics to the sophisticated in a step-by-step fashion. The discussion of each topic consists of the following:

◆ Theory, clearly explained — including how this topic fits into the subject of networking, and why it may interest you

◆ The most common uses of a tool or feature and its most commonly used options

◆ A meaty example that you can use as a model for configuring your own system or intranet

◆ References to places where you can obtain more information

If you are a beginner, you can read the book straight through, following the configuration instructions as you go. Or, if you have some experience with networking, you can concentrate on the chapters that particularly interest you and skip the others.

Version of Linux to Use

This book is designed to teach you how use the Linux operating system to set up and run a TCP/IP network. The CD-ROM included with this book holds a copy of the Slackware release of Linux. You can use it either to install Linux onto your PC or to extract individual packages or files. However, it is beyond the scope of this book to teach you how to install Linux on your PC.

If you have not yet installed Linux, we suggest you purchase *Linux: Configuration & Installation*, second edition, edited by Patrick Volkerding, Kevin Reichard, and Eric F. Johnson (New York, MIS:Press, 1997). This book comes with release 3.2 of Slackware Linux, which is built around release 2.0.29 of the Linux kernel (one of the most recent of the stable releases of Linux). It will walk you through what can be the difficult the process of installing and configuring the basic Linux system.

The LINUX Network is designed to be used with Slackware Linux release 3.2. We have tried to make the descriptions and examples in this book to be as general as possible. Unfortunately, versions of UNIX vary in how they implement some networking commands, and even different versions of Linux will vary a bit from one another. If you are using a version of Linux other than Slackware 3.2, you probably will find *The LINUX Network* to be helpful, but we cannot guarantee that every example and configuration file will work on your system.

A Note about Acronyms

It is a fact of life that the talk about computers involves an inordinate number of acronyms. This is one reason books about computers are so impenetrable to beginners. Unfortunately, *The LINUX Network* is no exception; the terminology of networking is filled with acronyms, and we must use them.

However, we will decipher the acronyms we use as we introduce them. We hope that our explanations will help newcomers to learn not just what these acronyms say, but what they *mean,* and so help a little light to penetrate the murk that surrounds any discussion of computer networking.

Icons Used in This Book

You will find the following icon used in this book:

This icon signals a cross reference to another section in the book where you will find additional information on the topic.

A Final Thought

We have tested and re-tested the descriptions in this book to ensure their accuracy; however, despite our best efforts, this book may still contain errors. If you have any questions or complaints about *The LINUX Network*, please mail your inquiries and expostulations, as well as your jeremiads, philippics, and panegyrics (the last most welcome) to linuxnet@lepanto.com.

Regards, and we hope you enjoy *The LINUX Network.*

Acknowledgments

The figures in this book were drawn using **xfig**, running under the Linux operating system. Linux screen shots were taken using **xv**, that most wonderful of shareware packages.

We wish to thank Hal Snyder, MD, Robert Meister, John Dennison, Martin Butzen, Bob Wilber, Tom Welsh, Velica Huston, Calvin Berkins, Lee Williams, James Driver, and Tony Bailey, who reviewed portions of this book as it was in preparation, and who helped both to improve the clarity of the book and purge it of science fiction. The errors and ambiguities that remain in this book are the responsibility of the authors alone.

Finally some personal notes:

I would like to give special thanks to my wife Sanju for her patience and support while I was writing this book. I would also like to thank Jim Bilotta, Steve Levine, and everyone else at LHR-ITS for their help while I juggled this book and a very active programming project. Finally I would like to thank Susan Elconin Feinberg, John Smith, Toni Giammatti, and Elizabeth Lubin. It wasn't obvious to me at the time but I now realize that what you were trying to teach me was very important. — C.H.

We wish to thank our former colleagues at Mark Williams Company for their help and encouragement. You know who you are! — F.B. and C.H.

Contents at a Glance

Contents

Part IV   Advanced Topics

Part I

An Introduction to Networking

Chapter 1

A Networking Primer

IN THIS CHAPTER

- ◆ What is a network?
- ◆ What is TCP/IP?
- ◆ Networking hardware and protocols
- ◆ Networking software

IN THIS CHAPTER, we begin with the basics: by describing what a *network* is. In particular, we explain how the *TCP/IP* protocols work. The Internet is built using the TCP/IP protocols, and these protocols are the foundation of networking for the UNIX operating system and operating systems modeled after UNIX, including Linux.

This chapter offers only background information: we do not actually start working with your Linux system until the next chapter. However, if you are new to networking – or if you have used networking but have never studied how a network works – we urge you to read this chapter before you plunge into the details of installing and running networking on your Linux system. If you take a little time to grasp the theories behind networking, you probably will find that many of the descriptions that follow are much easier to understand: instead of being "magic," you will see these descriptions as aspects of a larger pattern whose design you understand.

What Is a Network?

Because this is a book about computer networking, we offer a definition of network that applies specifically to computers: *A* network *is a group of computers that can exchange data without human supervision.*

This definition has two important points:

- ◆ In a network, computers *exchange data.* Usually, one computer requests a service from another computer that fulfills the request (the so-called *client-server architecture*); but the exchange may take other forms as well.

◆ In a network, the exchange is *unsupervised*. Although the exchange of data may be initiated by a human being (say, a user who types a command at her keyboard), the computers are programmed to handle the details of the exchange of data on their own.

Moving data from one computer to another is relatively easy – for example, by using a floppy disk (the so-called "sneakernet"); but wiring the computers together and programming them to do the exchange on their own – that is the hard part. So, how do you teach computers to do this?

Before we answer this question, we must first answer another question: just what must two entities do to exchange data over a wire? And to answer *this* question, let's look at a method that two entities – in this case, human beings – have used for many years to exchange data over a wire: the telephone call.

Example of Data Exchange: the Telephone Call

For most of us, making a telephone call is as familiar as lifting a fork or putting on a shirt. We do not think much about it – we just do it. Now, however, consider exactly what steps you take when you make a telephone call:

1. You decide whom to call.

2. You find that person's telephone number – or, to be more exact, the number of the telephone that is at the same location as that person. If you do not remember that person's number, you either look it up in a printed telephone book, or you call Directory Assistance and the operator finds it for you.

3. You lift the receiver and wait for the dial tone.

4. When you hear the dial tone, you dial the number. You wait to hear the ringing sound. If you do not hear it within a short time, you hang up and dial again; likewise, if you hear the busy sound, you hang up and try again later.

5. The telephone system interprets the number you dial into the physical address of the telephone you are calling. The system makes the connection with that physical telephone, rings the instrument, and sends the ringing sound to your instrument, to tell you that it is ringing the telephone that you are calling.

6. When you hear the ringing sound, you wait for the telephone to be answered. If the telephone is not answered within a few rings, you hang up and try again later.

7. When a person answers the telephone, you and that person introduce yourselves to each other. If you are calling a friend or relative, the two of you may simply recognize each other's voices. If you are calling a stranger, you formally introduce yourself.

8. After all these preliminaries to establish contact with the person with whom you wish to speak, you and the person whom you called begin to converse. The rules of the conversation will vary, depending upon your relationship with the person you are calling and the reason why you called him. For example, if you are calling a friend, the conversation is informal, in part because you and your friend already know a great deal about each other. If, however, you are calling a stranger to transact business (say, to sell him aluminum siding), the conversation is formal: you state your business, ask him how he is today, and proceed with a script that is carefully prepared to conduct the business most efficiently.

9. If a problem arises during your conversation – such as excessive noise on the line – you may ask the other person to repeat herself. Likewise, if the other person is giving you instructions, she may ask you to repeat them, to ensure that you understood what she said.

10. When the conversation has concluded, you and the person you are calling say "Good-bye," to signal that the conversation is at an end. You both then hang up the telephone, to break the physical connection between you.

What a Network Must Do

As you can see from the preceding description of a simple telephone call, performing a task over a network involves quite a few elements.

In this section, we discuss these elements one by one; but before we do that, we must define a very important term.

WHAT IS A PROTOCOL?

Many of the preceding steps involve a protocol. A *protocol* is a set of rules that dictate what to do in a given situation.

For example, diplomats have a protocol for each of the many situations they may encounter – a protocol for when they present their credentials, one for when their home country declares war on the country in which they are stationed, and so forth. They follow these protocols to help ensure that no misunderstanding occurs as they do their work.

Likewise, much of the work of setting up and running a network involves protocols. Computer programmers love protocols, because only by following a carefully designed set of rules can two computers – which are, after all, incredibly stupid creatures – perform any sort of useful work. Arguably, the hardest part of building a network is writing protocols that are *robust* – that is, do not overlook situations or mislead machines – yet work efficiently.

Much of this book describes protocols to you. This may seem tedious, but it is important. After all, protocols articulate the rules by which computers communicate with each other *without human supervision* – which is the goal of building a network.

That being said, let's now return to our telephone example and see just what a network needs so that two entities can exchange data.

HARDWARE

To begin, networking involves *hardware*: the wires that connect the entities that exchange data, and the instruments that translate data into impulses that can be sent over those wires.

In a telephone call, the hardware need not concern you very much – after all, that's what you pay your telephone bill for. In networking, however – and particularly in an intranet, which we discuss in Part III of this book – you string the wire and plug in the connectors, so hardware is rather important.

ADDRESSING

Next, networking involves *addressing* – finding a way to send the data to the physical device that interests you, and to that device alone.

In a telephone call, each telephone instrument is identified by a unique number: its country code, area code, and its local number, plus (in some instances) its extension. To make a call, you must find the number of the telephone instrument you need to call, and then pass that number to the telephone system by dialing it into your telephone instrument.

In a computer network, each box is also identified by a unique number; however, this is complicated by the fact that no computer equivalent of a telephone company exists to assign numbers to boxes. Addressing is one of the most important topics in computer networking, and we discuss it throughout the rest of this book.

NAME RESOLUTION

Because people are not particularly good at remembering numbers, a telephone number is stored by the name of the person who owns it. To find the telephone number to dial, you must somehow *resolve* the name of the person with whom you wish to speak into the number of the telephone instrument she uses.

Thus, networking involves *name resolution* – translating a name into the number that identifies a physical device.

Several ways exist to resolve a name. You can retrieve the number from a local storage area, or *cache*, of numbers (that is, your memory or a pocket address book). If you have never dialed the number before (and therefore do not have it in a cache), you can use one of the telephone company's services to resolve a person's name into her telephone number: you can look it up in a telephone directory, or you can call Directory Assistance.

Computer networks also store addresses under mnemonic names. You can store the name of a computer system and its corresponding address in a cache (the computer equivalent of your pocket address book). Or, a computer analogue of Directory Assistance exists that a computer can interrogate to turn a name into a numeric address.

Name resolution is also an important topic in computer networking, and one that we discuss at several points in this book.

COMMUNICATION PROTOCOLS

Next, during a telephone call, the telephone system uses special sounds to communicate with you and help you make your call. These sounds include the dial tone, the ringing sound, and the busy signal. These sounds help you to communicate with the telephone network itself – to enter the information the telephone network needs to complete your call, and to react appropriately to error situations (for example, when the line is busy).

Thus, a network needs *communication protocols* – a way for a computer to communicate with the network itself.

When you make a telephone call, some of these communication protocols talk to you; others are internal to the telephone system – for example, the protocol that records and times your call, so the telephone company can bill you for it.

Communication protocols are also an important part of computer networking. We discuss them at some length in this book.

TRANSMISSION CONTROL PROTOCOLS

When two people converse, whether on the telephone or in person, they use a well-defined set of signals to control the passing of information from one person to another. Which signals they use will vary, depending upon the type of conversation they are having, and the circumstances under which it is being held. For example, in an informal conversation between friends in a noisy bar, the protocol may be as simple as cupping your hand behind your ear to signal that you cannot hear your friend, or saying "Uh huh" every few seconds to indicate that you hear and understand her, or pausing every few seconds to see whether your friend is still paying attention; whereas, when the conversation is between a customer and a salesperson, the salesperson may repeat the customer's order verbatim, and explicitly ask the customer to confirm that the details are correct.

Computers also use well-defined techniques to control the transmission of data. The term for such a technique is *transmission control protocol*.

Later in this chapter, we describe the most commonly used transmission control protocols. You don't have to study them in detail – this is something that a computer network handles on its own – but at least knowing these protocols exist and how they work is very helpful.

APPLICATION PROTOCOLS

Finally, when you do "connect" with the person with whom you want to speak, other protocols govern just how you and that person talk with each other. These protocols depend upon the nature of the information being exchanged: one protocol applies when you are calling to ask a friend out to lunch, whereas another protocol applies when you are trying to sell aluminum siding to a stranger.

Thus, a network needs *application protocols*. These govern the actual exchange of information once the two machines are connected, depending upon the type of information to be exchanged.

One interesting point is that application protocols do not depend on communication protocols. For example, the telephone system in Europe uses a different communication protocol – a different set of sounds, in other words, to communicate with you when you make a call – but once you finally connect to the person with whom you want to speak, the rules that govern how you speak with that person remain the same.

Much of this book concerns application protocols. Once you have set up your network, it largely runs itself (after all, the whole point of having a network is to enable your computers to exchange data without your supervision); but you will be continually adding new tasks for the network to perform – and each of those new tasks involves learning and configuring new application protocols.

From Telephones to Computers

Networks are pretty much alike, because they all involve *hardware*, and they all must perform the tasks of *addressing, name resolution, transmission control*, and executing *application protocols*.

The next step is to see how these tasks are performed when computers, rather than people, are exchanging data.

HOW PROTOCOLS FIT TOGETHER

As you've probably noticed in our discussion of networking so far, a hierarchy exists for the tasks that a network must perform. After all, you cannot begin a telephone conversation with another person until you pick up the telephone, dial her telephone number, and make the connection with her telephone.

Earlier, we discussed the term *protocol*, and how important protocols are to building a network. In fact, the engineers who designed the computer networks that currently are in use have also designed a *master protocol* – a protocol that describes how networking protocols fit together. (They have also devised a protocol for writing new protocols, which we discuss a little later in this chapter.) So, your first task in understanding how a network works is to look at this "protocol of protocols," so you can see how all the networking protocols fit together.

THE NETWORKING STACK   The protocol of protocols is usually described as a *stack*, because diagrams of it show the constituent protocols stacked one on top of another, much like the layers of a layer cake. The layers of the stack are set hierarchically: the highest layer is the protocol with which a human user interacts, whereas the lower layer is the protocol that controls the transmission of electrical signals through silicon and copper.

We should, in fact, speak of networking *stacks*, because many of them exist. Each stack was devised by a different organization, and each stack layers its cake a little differently. Here, we discuss two of the most common protocol stacks: the Open Systems International (OSI) stack, and the Advanced Research Projects Agency (ARPA) stack.

The OSI model of networking was devised by the International Standards Organization (ISO), and has been adopted by many organizations as their official model. The OSI model has seven tiers, from the *application* tier at the top, to the *physical* tier at the bottom.

The ARPA model was devised in the 1960s by the Advanced Research Projects Agency of the U.S. Department of Defense. The ARPA model has only four tiers, from *application* at the top, to *network-access* at the bottom. This model has not been supported officially in the way that the OSI model is supported; however, the ARPA model is the basis for the TCP/IP set of networking protocols, and, in turn, TCP/IP is the foundation of the Internet and of the networking used by the Linux operating system. (We define TCP/IP in much more detail later in this chapter.) In other words, the OSI model is the *de jure* standard for networking, but the ARPA model is the *de facto* standard.

No book on networking would be complete without a diagram of the OSI and ARPA stacks; so, Figure 1-1 provides this diagram, and shows how the stacks compare with each other.

We include the diagram of the OSI stack for reference, because it is frequently mentioned in books and articles on networking. However, this diagram is peripheral to networking as implemented under Linux, so we do not discuss it further.

The ARPA stack has four tiers:

1. *Application* – This tier is where the application protocols are implemented. Again, many application protocols exist – one, in fact, for each application that you want to run.

2. *Host-to-host* – This tier is where the transmission control protocols are implemented. We say *protocols*, because networking uses many such protocols. We describe the most important protocols a little later in this chapter.

3. *Internet* – This tier is where the name resolution and addressing protocols are implemented.

4. *Network-access* – This tier is where the communication protocol is implemented – where the rules that comprise the communication protocol are translated into a program that can be run on a computer.

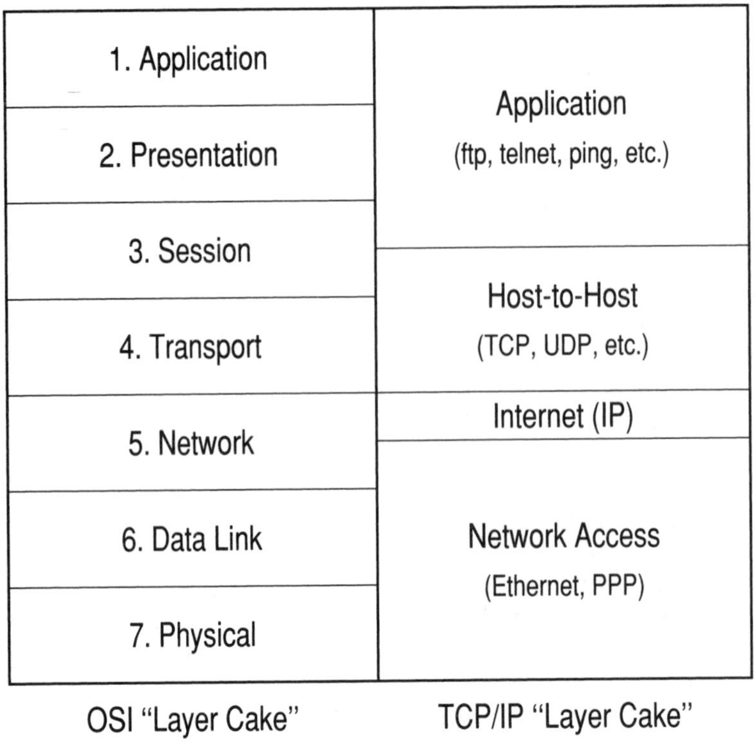

1. Application	**Application** (ftp, telnet, ping, etc.)
2. Presentation	
3. Session	**Host-to-Host** (TCP, UDP, etc.)
4. Transport	
5. Network	**Internet (IP)**
6. Data Link	**Network Access** (Ethernet, PPP)
7. Physical	

OSI "Layer Cake"   TCP/IP "Layer Cake"

Figure 1-1: The OSI and ARPA "layer cakes"

Now, you may be asking why the tiers are stacked on top of each other, and whether the order in which the tiers appear in the stack is important.

To answer the first question: The diagram in Figure 1-1 shows the parts of networking as a stack to indicate that each of the parts of networking work pretty much independently of the other parts. Often, each part is implemented as a program unto itself. Networking operates by having these pieces exchange data with each other. The advantages to this way of implementing a program – of this *architecture* – are very great. Further, the diagram shows the tiers stacked on top of each other in order to represent how data is passed among the parts of the networking software: when a computer is transmitting data, the data is passed from the user (at the top of the stack) to the hardware (at the bottom); however, when the computer is receiving data, the data is passed in the opposite direction, from the hardware at the bottom of the stack to the user at the top.

To answer the second question, the order in which the tiers appear is very important, because each tier receives data from the tier immediately above it (when transmitting data) or below it (when receiving data). For example, when a machine is transmitting data, the host-to-host tier receives data from the application tier and passes it down to the Internet tier; however, when the machine is receiving data, the host-to-host tier receives data from the Internet tier and passes it up to the application tier. This passing of data up and down the stack will be clearer when we explore some examples later in this chapter.

Although the ARPA stack may seem to be just an abstraction, in fact, it is quite helpful to understanding just how networking works, both on the Internet and under Linux. We hope you take the time to commit the ARPA diagram to memory — it consists of only four elements, after all — because you will find it quite helpful as you read further in this book.

INFORMATION HIDING   We need to make one last point regarding stacks, which is very important: Each tier in the stack is concerned solely with doing its own work. No tier knows anything about what any other tier is doing, nor does it care.

This approach greatly simplifies the task of building a network, for it means that software engineers can break the very complex task of networking into a set of small, discrete parts, each of which can be designed, built, tested, and debugged individually. This, in turn, means that the bits that comprise a given tier can be replaced without affecting how the other tiers work. This is particularly important for the network-access tier: this tier may be accessing many different types of hardware via many different types of interfaces — Ethernet, parallel ports, serial ports, and so on. The stack design lets a network work with all different kinds of hardware, without having to modify any of the other tiers in any way whatsoever, which clearly is a great advantage in making a network both robust and easily extended to new types of hardware. We discuss this at greater length later in the chapter.

CLIENT-SERVER ARCHITECTURE   We must add one last clause to our definition of a network. The exchange of data among computers is not a monologue, with one machine talking and one or more just listening. Rather, the exchange of data is a conversation, usually between two machines.

The conversation almost always involves one machine requesting a service from another machine, and the other machine executing the request and returning data to the requester. In this conversation, the requester machine is called the *client*, and the machine that executes the client's request is called the *server*. Thus, the dialogue between machines is called *client-server architecture*.

The terms *client* and *server* actually refer to programs that a computer is running (also called *processes*), rather than to physical machines; and the client and server processes may actually both be running on the same computer. However, in most instances, the client process is running on one computer and the server process is running on another computer, so this distinction need not worry you at this point.

Like most conversations, the conversation between client and server has a formal structure. On Linux and most other operating systems that use the ARPA model for networking, the conversation's structure follows the structure of the ARPA stack, previously described – which should not come as a surprise. As we mentioned a little earlier, data moves up and down the ARPA stack: outgoing data moves from the application (and the user who is running the application) at the top of the stack to the hardware at the bottom; incoming data moves in the opposite direction, from the hardware at the bottom to the application at the top. The conversation between client and server runs up and down the ARPA stacks on the respective machines. Figure 1-2 shows the structure of the conversation between client and server.

As you can see, the conversation is initiated in the application tier on the client side. The client always initiates the conversation, and so sets the rules of the conversation – the server always responds to a request from a client, and replies by using the rules set by the client. (We discuss this at greater length a little later in this chapter.) The data is passed down the stack on the client side, is transmitted to the server, and then is passed up the stack to the server's application tier. The server's application tier performs the service requested by the client and builds a data set to return to the client. The server's reply is passed down the stack on the server, is transmitted to the client, and then is passed up the stack on the client side to the client's application tier, which reads and interprets the reply.

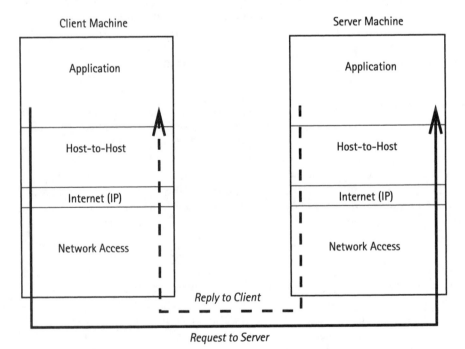

Figure 1-2: Client-server architecture

The server's reply will vary, depending upon the type of conversation carried on between the client and server. In some instances, the server's reply simply acknowledges that it received the client's transmission; in other instances, the server may return a large mass of data (such as a Web page). The type of conversation is dictated by the type of application that is exchanging data. Each application speaks to other applications of the same type; for example, a Web client (or *browser*) talks with a Web server, whereas a mail client talks with a mail server. The conversation between the client and server for a given type of application is always governed by a protocol that is written specifically for that type of application. Much of this book is spent describing the protocols of the conversations that are carried on between the clients and servers of particular types of applications.

Thus concludes the definition of what a network is. Next, we move on to the type of network that is used by the Internet (and by Linux): TCP/IP.

Review

To summarize what we have said so far:

◆ A *network* is the hardware and software that lets computers exchange data without human supervision.

◆ Networking software implements *protocols*, which are sets of rules that govern how computers behave in a given situation.

◆ A network consists of hardware plus software that performs the following tasks: addressing, name resolution, communication with the network, transmission control, and applications. How each task is performed is described by a protocol.

◆ *Protocols of protocols* describe how all other protocols fit together.

◆ Networking on the Internet, and on the Linux operating system, is built around the ARPA protocol, which has four tiers. From top to bottom, these tiers are: *network-access, Internet, host-to-host,* and *application*.

◆ Networking consists of a conversation between clients and servers: clients request services from servers, and servers execute the clients' requests and return data to them.

So much for theory – now we begin to discuss just how networking is implemented for real on the Internet, and on your Linux machine.

What Is TCP/IP?

TCP/IP is a term that has appeared a few times in this chapter, and that appears many more times before this book is finished, because TCP/IP is one of the most important concepts in networking.

TCP/IP is an acronym for *Transmission Control Protocol/Internet Protocol*. TCP and IP are, in fact, two of the key protocols of the set of protocols with which the Internet is built.

In this section, we introduce the TCP/IP protocols – what they are intended to do, and some details about how they do it.

The Origins of TCP/IP

At this point, we discuss briefly the origins of the TCP/IP suite of protocols. This may seem to be a side-step, but in fact, it is not: TCP/IP was created to fulfill a specific set of requirements, and if you have some idea of what those requirements are, you have a better grasp of why TCP/IP is designed as it is, and why it works the way it does.

The TCP/IP suite of protocols is the result of research performed in the 1960s and 1970s by the U.S. Department of Defense's Advanced Research Projects Agency (ARPA) – later renamed the Defense Advanced Research Projects Agency (DARPA). The Pentagon wanted to build a system to connect computers at its military bases and key research establishments. The network it wanted to build had to meet numerous criteria, of which the most important was that the network had to be able to function during a nuclear war.

Nuclear holocaust may seem an odd basis for designing a computer network, but such is the origin of the Internet. To be able to survive a nuclear war, a network must meet two criteria:

- ◆ The network must be totally *decentralized* – no key central installation must exist whose destruction by the enemy would knock out the entire network.

- ◆ The network must be fully *redundant* – data must be able to get from site A to site B even if an indefinite number of randomly selected sites are destroyed.

In addition, the Pentagon's proposed network had to meet two other criteria:

- ◆ The software had to be *multiprocessing* – it had to be able to converse with multiple other machines simultaneously.

◆ The software had to work *asynchronously* – the sending machine and receiving machine had to work independently of each other. If this concept is unclear to you, think of synchronous transmission as being like two FAX machines: data must be sent from one machine to the other in a particular order, and one machine cannot send until the other FAX machine signals that it is ready to receive. Asynchronous transmission, however, is like sending data through the mail: you write the data onto paper, pop it into the mailbox, and then go off and do something else until the reply arrives, whenever that might happen to be. The advantage of working asynchronously is that two machines do not have to be directly in contact with each other in order to exchange data – they can communicate through one or more intermediary machines.

In 1968, ARPA hired the firm of Bolt, Beranek, and Newman (BBN) to design its first networking hardware and software. The prototype network, called ARPANET, connected four sites.

Over time, ARPA gradually added new nodes to its network; meanwhile, researchers began to piggyback their own applications onto ARPANET, so that they could exchange files and logins. After it shook the kinks out of ARPANET, the Defense Department created other networks: MILNET, to connect military installations in the United States, and MINET, to connect installations in Europe.

By 1980, the core set of protocols now known as TCP/IP had been written and published. At about the same time, the Pentagon funded BBN to implement the TCP/IP protocols under the Berkeley dialect of the UNIX operating system – and this is a story in itself.

The UNIX operating system was created at AT&T Bell Laboratories in the 1970s – UNIX and TCP/IP were born almost simultaneously – and thanks to a quirk in U.S. antitrust laws, UNIX was given for free to U.S. universities. Berkeley UNIX was created at the University of California at Berkeley, and was at that time the most popular dialect of UNIX in academic computer-science circles. It offered numerous attractive features, particularly its use of *sockets* to pass information among programs. (Please take note of the term *sockets* – you will encounter it often in this book.)

Thus, the Department of Defense's decision to implement its TCP/IP networking under Berkeley UNIX gave colleges and universities throughout the United States a freely available body of software for networking their computers – and this was while universities were becoming strongly interested in networking their machines. Arguably, the Berkeley implementation of TCP/IP is one of the most successful bodies of software ever written, and Berkeley TCP/IP remains the basis of the software used to run the Internet – including the TCP/IP networking under the Linux operating system.

Early in the 1980s, the National Science Foundation (NSF) used Berkeley TCP/IP to create its Computer Science Network (CSNET) to link universities in the U.S., and later created NSFNET to link a number of supercomputers. Thereafter, TCP/IP networking proliferated, and has grown into the huge, loosely knit network known as the Internet.

A few years ago, the federal government privatized the Internet. Control of the main Internet network — the Internet's *backbone* — was turned over to a consortium of major communications companies. What is not yet clear is how privatization will affect the direction of the Internet's evolution, or how a privatized Internet will cope with the serious problems that it confronts in the next few years, but this process will be most interesting to watch, and to participate in.

Why TCP/IP?

Other protocols for computer networking have been written over the years. However, none of these protocols has come close to TCP/IP's popularity. What is so special about TCP/IP that it should become the basis for the global computer network that is called the Internet? Several good reasons exist:

◆ *The TCP/IP protocols had the support of the federal government.* At a time when research into computer networking was prohibitively expensive, the government — and, in particular, the Pentagon — had the resources to do the job right. Further, the fact that the Pentagon mandated that TCP/IP be the basis for its networks immediately made TCP/IP attractive to software vendors.

◆ *The TCP/IP protocols are in the public domain.* Because it was created by the federal government, the TCP/IP protocols belong to the people of the United States. This gives software vendors a standard that they can support without giving a rival company an unfair advantage.

◆ *TCP/IP implementation is freely available.* The Berkeley UNIX code that implements TCP/IP is copyrighted, but it is freely available, without license or royalty. This means that even people who give software away for free, such as the Linux movement, can implement TCP/IP networking without the tremendous overhead of writing all their own code from scratch.

◆ *The Internet has no central authority.* The fact that TCP/IP was written with a nuclear war in mind meant that the TCP/IP network has no central authority whose destruction would cripple the network. This means that no central authority controls the Internet and that the network can grow in an *ad hoc* manner: nobody can forbid a machine being attached to the Internet. Whenever you dial into an Internet provider and plug your machine into its network, you grow the Internet to include your machine. And before this book is finished, we show you how you can grow the Internet to include other machines that are plugged into your computer.

◆ *The Internet does have central coordination.* Although no central authority grants or denies participation in the Internet, central agencies *do* exist that coordinate such tasks as handing out addresses, granting domain names, and running the backbone of the network. This "federalist" approach to managing the Internet – where the central authority provides coordination, but leaves the task of governing the network to the local people in each region – has proven to be extremely successful.

◆ *The TCP/IP protocols are well designed.* This should become clear as you proceed through this chapter, and through this book. Some features of TCP/IP networking – particularly the way that the Internet performs name resolution – simply are superior to any proprietary scheme that any private vendor has devised.

This list is far from exhaustive, but should give you an idea of why TCP/IP has been so successful. Hopefully, this idea will become even clearer as you proceed through this book.

The Internet Today

The Internet is a publicly accessible computer network that is based on the TCP/IP protocols. The Internet, as you probably have heard, now extends around the globe; however, the core of its activity is in the United States.

In this section, we discuss the current structure of the Internet. This may seem like a digression, but it really isn't – for two reasons. First, throughout this book, we use terms that come from the Internet; and you need to be introduced to this gaggle of acronyms in its proper context. Second, the ultimate goal of this book is to help you set up and configure TCP/IP networking so that your Linux system can plug itself into the Internet and join the global network; so you might as well know just what it is that you are plugging into.

ACCESSING THE PHYSICAL INTERNET

Until recently, the Internet was run by the federal government, which had responsibility for running the physical network and providing central coordination. However, a few years ago, the Internet was privatized, and is now run by private or semipublic groups.

The physical Internet now consists of a *backbone* of high-speed telephone lines that are run by a consortium of major communications companies. The extent of the backbone changes yearly, but it has access points in most major metropolitan centers of the United States. Access from countries outside the U.S. is provided through high-speed land lines or satellite hookup.

Internet service providers (ISPs) purchase access to the backbone, and then resell their access to companies and individual customers. These customers can access their ISP through various means: high-speed dedicated telephone lines (T1s and the like), digital telephone connections (ISDNs), or voice telephone lines (that is, via modems).

Depending upon its agreement with its ISP, a company can resell its Internet access to other groups or individuals. And these groups or individuals, in turn, can then sell or give access to other groups and individuals. So, in this way the Internet spreads throughout the world.

THE NETWORK INFORMATION CENTER (NIC)

The Internet is largely a self-governing entity – no body of law governs the operation of the Internet, and no central Internet agency can enforce rules, apart from the TCP/IP protocols themselves. Rather, the Internet is governed by *custom*: individuals choose to adhere to protocols (that word again, but now in the diplomatic sense rather than the computer sense) in order to make the enterprise work. However, a few groups do coordinate the operation of the Internet. Two of the most important groups are the Network Information Center (NIC) and the Internet Engineering Task Force (IETF), which are described briefly next.

Earlier, we mentioned that addressing and domain-name resolution are two of the tasks that a network has to perform. The Internet has a system of addressing and domain-name resolution, which we describe later in this chapter. At the risk of getting ahead of ourselves, we must mention that the NIC has two major responsibilities: to oversee the assignment of *Internet addresses*, and to oversee the assignment of *domain names*. This coordination is important to the smooth operation of the Internet, as you will see when we discuss these topics.

THE INTERNET ENGINEERING TASK FORCE (IETF)

The Internet Engineering Task Force (IETF) is the group that coordinates the adaptation of most standards for the Internet at large. Like the NIC, the IETF was originally established by the U.S. Department of Defense, but now is a private, volunteer group.

The process of adapting a standard involves the circulation of a document called a *Request for Comment* (RFC). Each proposed RFC is assigned its own number, and then is circulated for public comment. A period of comment is followed by a new draft that responds to comment. After several drafts (the details of which need not concern you here), the proposed standard is either adopted or rejected.

Some RFCs describe application-level protocols; other RFCs deal with more basic issues, such as those RFCs that propose ways to extend the number of Internet addresses available (discussed later in the chapter). Other RFCs are housekeeping documents, such as the RFC that lists all RFCs. Occasionally, we refer to an RFC by number. At the end of this chapter, we give sources from which you can obtain copies of RFCs for yourself.

How TCP/IP Works

To this point, we have discussed what a network is and what protocols are; we also have given a brief introduction to that extended implementation of the TCP/IP protocols known as the Internet.

Now we begin to explore how TCP/IP works: what parts comprise it, how each part works, and how the parts fit together. Some of what follows is rather technical. None of the technical material is essential to being able to operate networking, and if you skip it, you will still be able to use the rest of this book. However, you will find that much of the rest of this book is more comprehensible if you make an effort to grasp the technical details that are presented here.

This section covers a great deal of ground. However, this section provides a blueprint for the rest of this book. Once you grasp what is in this section, the rest of the book will simply be filling in the details.

WHAT IS A DATAGRAM?

The first point to understand about networking is that a network does not transport data in a continuous stream, like a hose carrying water. Rather, a network ships data from one machine to another in the form of discrete messages, called *datagrams*. (In certain contexts, these discrete messages are called *frames* or *packets*; we explain the difference a little later in the chapter.)

A datagram is not just a blob of data. Rather, its structure is carefully dictated by the TCP/IP protocols, and in fact reflects the structure of the ARPA stack that we previously described. Recall that the ARPA stack has four tiers: *application, host-to-host, Internet,* and *network-access*. The application tier is the highest (the closest to the user), and the network-access tier is the lowest (closest to the networking hardware).

When TCP/IP networking software builds a datagram, it passes the outgoing datagram down the stack. As the datagram proceeds down the stack, each tier adds its own tier-specific data to the datagram. When TCP/IP software reads an incoming datagram, it passes the datagram up the stack. As the datagram proceeds up the stack, each tier reads and interprets the information written by the corresponding tier of the host that transmitted the datagram – that is, the receiver's network-access tier reads the data written by the transmitter's network-access tier, the receiver's Internet tier reads the data written by the transmitter's Internet tier, and so on.

The data generated by the application tier is the core of the datagram – that data, after all, describes the work that the user wants to perform.

The data added by the host-to-host, Internet, and network-access tiers is specific to the task that that tier performs in networking. Each of these three tiers adds its data in the form of *headers* and *trailers* – data appended to the beginning and end (respectively) of the datagram as received from the tier above it.

The structure should be clear if you think of a datagram as resembling an ordinary letter:

◆ The data generated by the application tier is equivalent to the letter itself — it contains the message being carried by the network.

◆ When the datagram is being transmitted, the host-to-host, Internet, and network-access tiers each puts its own electronic "envelope" around the datagram.

◆ When the datagram is being received, the host-to-host, Internet, and network-access tiers each reads, interprets, and removes the "envelope" written by the corresponding tier on the transmitting host.

You can think of the transmission of a datagram as being similar to putting a letter into a succession of envelopes, and the reception of a datagram as being similar to reading and removing those envelopes one by one.

Now, after all of these preliminaries, let's stroll down the four tiers of the ARPA stack to see what happens in each tier.

APPLICATION TIER

As we mentioned earlier, the application tier is the highest tier in the ARPA stack. On the client machine, this is the tier that actually interacts with the user; on the server machine, this is the tier that executes the requests of the client machine.

Many protocols inhabit this tier — in fact, one protocol for each task that a user may want to perform. As mentioned earlier, much of this book is spent presenting the protocols that can be used in this tier.

The following are a few examples of the protocols that occupy the application tier:

◆ *telnet* — Log into the server machine and type commands into it directly. The telnet protocol often is used to implement terminal-emulation programs.

◆ *ftp* — The *File Transfer Protocol*. As its name implies, ftp is used to copy files from one machine to another.

◆ *pop* — The *Post Office Protocol*. This protocol downloads a batch of mail from one machine to another.

◆ *smtp* — The *Simple Mail Transfer Protocol*. This protocol is used to upload or download a single mail message.

◆ *http* — The *Hypertext Transfer Protocol*. This protocol downloads Web pages and images from one machine to another. Undoubtedly, this is the most popular protocol nowadays.

These are just a few examples of the more popular applications.

We discuss ftp and telnet at greater length in Chapter 4; pop and smtp are examined in Chapter 5; http is covered in Chapter 7.

HOST-TO-HOST TIER

As we mentioned earlier, the host-to-host tier in the ARPA stack implements the network's transmission control protocols. These protocols ensure that the data received by the receiving machine is a true copy of the data sent by the transmitting machine.

TCP/IP, in fact, implements a number of transmission control protocols. Each protocol is designed to perform a specific type of networking task. The program on the application tier chooses which transmission control protocol it wants to manage the transfer of its data; some applications that can interact in a variety of ways with the recipient machine will select one or another transmission control protocol, depending on the task it needs to perform at a given moment.

Three transmission control protocols are used most commonly:

◆ *Transmission Control Protocol* (TCP) – The TCP manages the disassembly of a mass of data into a stream of datagrams, and its reassembly on the receiving machine. Most applications use this protocol to ship their data from one machine to another. This is the protocol from which TCP/IP gets the TCP. The name of this protocol, unfortunately, does lend itself to ambiguity; however, in this book we try to make it clear to you when we speak of the *Transmission Control Protocol* in particular, and the class of transmission control protocols in general.

◆ *User Datagram Protocol* (UDP) – This protocol uses a single datagram to send a simple message from one machine to another. It usually is used for networking housekeeping tasks.

◆ *Internet Control Message Protocol* (ICMP) – Systems use this protocol to send control messages to each other.

The following sections discuss each protocol in turn.

TCP – BREAKING AND REASSEMBLING DATA INTO DATAGRAMS   TCP is the transmission control protocol that an application uses when it needs a *reliable connection* with the host to which it is transmitting data. The application needs to transfer a stream of datagrams, and it needs to know for certain that each of the datagrams is received undamaged.

An application will select this protocol either to transfer a mass of data that is too large to fit into a single datagram, or to let a client application and its server counterpart carry on a conversation.

For example, assume the sending machine wants to send a large file to the recipient machine. For the sake of efficiency, most machines set a limit on the maximum size of a datagram – usually 1.5K. If the file is several megabytes, the sending machine uses the TCP protocol – or, to be more precise, the software that implements the TCP protocol – to break the file into a series of datagrams, and send the datagrams in a stream to the recipient machine. The recipient machine then uses its TCP software to reassemble the datagrams into the complete file on its end.

Because the sender is transmitting a stream of datagrams to the recipient, the TCP protocol requires that the transmitting host and the recipient host engage in a well-defined conversation, as follows:

1. Before the transmitter sends data, it sends a datagram to the recipient host, asking the recipient whether it is ready to receive data.

2. If it is ready, the recipient sends an acknowledgment to the transmitter, and prepares to receive data.

3. When it receives the recipient's acknowledgment, the transmitter prepares and transmits the stream of datagrams.

4. When the recipient receives one of the transmitter's datagrams, it sends a datagram back to the transmitter, acknowledging that it received the datagram in question.

5. If the transmitter does not receive the recipient's acknowledgment within a set period of time, it retransmits the datagram. When networks are running slowly and acknowledgment may be delayed, TCP uses an elaborate algorithm to help ensure that networks do not become further clogged with multiple retransmissions of the same datagram.

6. When the transmission is complete, the transmitter sends a special datagram that tells the recipient that the transmission is finished. The recipient acknowledges, and the two machines close this transmission session.

AN EXAMPLE OF TCP IN ACTION   If you have used a Web browser, you may have noticed that when you're downloading a Web page, you see a series of messages on the browser's message line, something like the following:

1. Connect: Looking up host

2. Connect: Host www.*whatever*.com acknowledges.

3. Reading file *something-or-other*.

4. XX% of YYYK downloaded.

5. Document done.

The preceding messages briefly describe a TCP session between your machine (the recipient) and the Web server (the transmitter), and have the following corresponding meanings:

1. Your browser requests a file of data – in this case, a Web page.

2. The transmitting host acknowledges your request.

3. The transmitting host opens a TCP stream between itself and your machine.

4. The transmitter sends a stream of datagrams to your machine. Occasionally, transmission may slow to the point where it appears to be stalled, and then pick up again.

5. The transmission of the file is complete; your machine and the sending machine close down the TCP stream.

You will see this series of messages multiple times when you download a Web page, because each element in a Web page – the text, as well as each image, animation, and sound-bite – is a separate file, and requires its own TCP stream between your machine and the Web server.

One last note: networking software is *multitasking* – TCP software can manage multiple streams of datagrams simultaneously. This is why you may see all of a Web page's pictures slowly appearing simultaneously as the page is downloaded.

We discuss the role TCP plays in the Web in Chapter 7, when we discuss how to set up a Web server on your machine.

STRUCTURE OF THE TCP HEADER   TCP is a complex protocol, but its internal structure is worth looking at, because this structure illustrates numerous interesting features of how data is transmitted over a network. Figure 1-3 shows the structure of a datagram once the TCP header has been added.

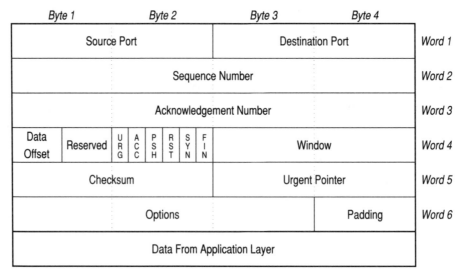

Figure 1-3: Structure of the TCP header

The TCP header is 24 bytes long; the 24 bytes are numbered 0 through 23, and are organized into six, 4-byte *words*. (In the literature of networking, bytes often are called *octets* – the reason being that TCP/IP defines a byte as having 8 bits, whereas some of the machines being networked when TCP/IP was first created did not use 8-bit bytes. Nowadays, practically every machine uses an 8-bit byte, so we use the more familiar word *byte* instead of *octet*.) The following list describes the fields of the TCP header. This may seem overly technical to you at first, but it really isn't too technical – and this exercise helps illustrate some of the important features of TCP/IP networking:

♦ *Source Port* – As mentioned earlier, when a host transmits a datagram, the TCP tier receives its data from the application tier; when a host is receiving a datagram, the TCP tier passes data to the application tier. TCP uses *ports* to identify the application from which a datagram is coming, and the application to which a datagram is going.

♦ The TCP software assigns a unique *source port* number to all the datagrams in a given conversation, to distinguish a given conversation from all the other conversations that it is carrying on.

◆ *Destination Port* — The destination port identifies the application to which a datagram is being sent. TCP/IP uses a system of *well-known ports* to identify applications. For example, a Web server is always accessed through port 80, whereas the mail receiver is always accessed through port 25. We discuss ports and well-known ports at greater length later in this chapter.

◆ *Sequence Number* — As previously mentioned, communication between hosts on a network is *asynchronous* — sending datagrams across a network is rather like sending a series of letters through the post office, in that the sender and the recipient are not necessarily in direct communication with each other. And like a series of letters sent through the post office, no guarantee is given that a series of datagrams will be received in the order in which they are sent. The sequence number indicates a datagram's place in a series of datagrams. The receiving host uses this number to reassemble a series of datagrams into the body of data that the transmitting host wants to transmit.

◆ *Acknowledgment Number* — This number helps to keep the transmitter and the receiver coordinated with each other.

◆ *Data Offset* — This field indicates where in the datagram the actual data content begins.

◆ *Reserved* — This is reserved for some future use.

◆ *Flags* — These flag special conditions. For example, the URG field flags whether this datagram holds an urgent message.

◆ *Window* — This field indicates the number of bytes that the recipient machine is ready to process. This field is set by the recipient host; in effect, this is the field in which the recipient host tells the transmitting host that it is ready to receive and process more data.

◆ *Checksum* — The recipient host uses this value to check whether a datagram was garbled in transmission.

Urgent Pointer, Options, and Padding fields usually are not used.

This concludes your brief introduction to the TCP transmission control protocol. As you can see, TCP is an important part of managing the transmission of data over a network. We will be returning to these concepts again and again as you proceed through this book.

UDP – SEND A SINGLE DATAGRAM MESSAGE   Another important transmission control protocol is the *User Datagram Protocol* (UDP).

UDP is much simpler than TCP: UDP is designed to send a single datagram message from one machine to another, rather than a stream of datagrams. Also, unlike TCP, a machine is not expected to reply to a UDP (although many applications that use UDP to communicate with another machine expect to receive a UDP datagram in reply to a UDP datagram). Rather, the sending machine sends the UDP datagram; if it does not receive a reply within a given period of time, it assumes that the datagram was not received, and it then either sends another datagram or fails, depending upon what its protocol determines is the best action to take.

STRUCTURE OF THE UDP HEADER   Figure 1-4 shows the internal structure of a UDP datagram.

Byte 1	Byte 2	Byte 3	Byte 4	
Source Port		Destination Port		Word 1
Length		Checksum		Word 2
Data From Application Layer				

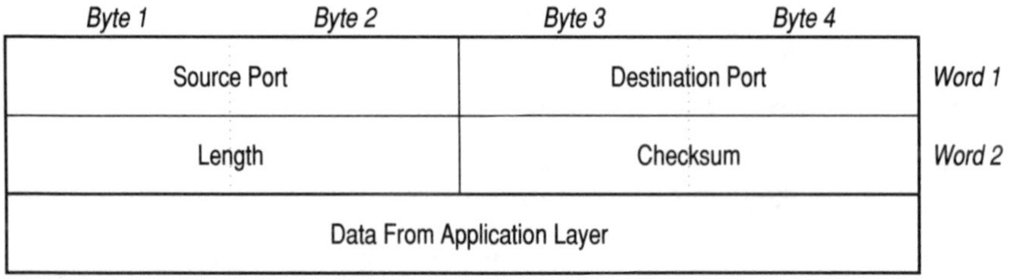

Figure 1-4: Structure of a UDP datagram

As you can see, a UDP datagram is much simpler than a TCP datagram. A UDP datagram's header is only 8 bytes long, and holds only the source port, destination port, message length, and a checksum field. This simplicity and efficiency are what make UDP attractive for certain types of jobs: machines can exchange information without having to go through the bother and overhead of establishing a TCP stream.

ICMP – SEND A CONTROL MESSAGE   The Internet Control Message Protocol (ICMP) is used to carry control messages across the Internet. These messages control the way that Internet hosts communicate with each other, and in most instances, applications do not use ICMP datagrams. Numerous control messages are defined for ICMP; of these, the following three are used most commonly:

◆ *ICMP_ECHO_REQUEST* — Request that a system send a message in reply. The command ping transmits a stream of these messages, as demonstrated shortly.

◆ *ICMP_ECHO_REPLY* — The ICMP message that is sent in reply to an ICMP_ECHO_REQUEST message.

◆ *ICMP_REDIRECT* — A host transmits an ICMP message when it wants to correct another host's routing table. Consider the example of an intranet that has three hosts on it: *fasthost*, which has a fast connection to the Internet, *slowhost*, which has a slow connection to the Internet; and *localhost*, which does not have its own connection to the Internet. By default, localhost routes all of its datagrams to the Internet through fasthost, to take advantage of that host's fast connection to the Internet. However, if for some reason fasthost's connection to the Internet is broken (say, a wire is cut somewhere) and it can no longer forward datagrams to the Internet, it sends an ICMP_REDIRECT message to localhost, telling localhost to route its datagrams to the Internet through slowhost.

ICMP, unlike the TCP or UDP datagrams, does not assign port numbers to its datagrams. This affects how some Linux software functions, as explained in Chapter 8 within the discussion of IP masquerading. An example of an application that uses ICMP is given later in this chapter — the command ping.

CONCLUSION   This concludes the discussion of the protocols that can be used in the host-to-host tier. Other protocols are also used in this tier; however, they are specialized, and you probably will never have to deal with them.

All the protocols in the host-to-host tier exchange information with the Internet tier; thus, the next sections step down the ARPA stack to the Internet tier.

INTERNET TIER

Once the transmission control software in the host-to-host tier has finished doing its work with a datagram, it passes the datagram to the tier below it — the *Internet tier*.

Unlike the host-to-host tier, which uses multiple protocols, the Internet tier uses only one protocol. This protocol's job is straightforward, yet extremely important: it tells each datagram where to go. This process may seem simple, but really it is not.

To grasp what this tier must do, we must first examine how Internet addressing works. We first introduce how an Internet address is structured; then we introduce Internet routing.

STRUCTURE OF AN IP ADDRESS   The Internet Protocol (IP) assigns a unique number, or *IP address*, to each interface that is exchanging information across the Internet. This is analogous to the unique number that the telephone company assigns to every telephone that is plugged into the telephone network. By assigning each interface its own number, the Internet Protocol ensures that every interface can send datagrams to any other host — in theory at least, and to a large extent, in practice as well.

For the sake of accuracy, we must elaborate upon two terms that are used in this definition of Internet Protocol:

◆ *Unique number* — In theory, every IP address addresses one and only one interface. However, in practice, an IP address may be used by multiple interfaces. Numerous techniques are used to permit more than one interface to use a single Internet address; these techniques include *masquerading* and *aliasing*. For simplicity, the descriptions in this chapter assume that each IP address is used by only one interface; however, please remember that this may not necessarily be so. We go into this in more detail in Chapter 8, when we describe how to set up *IP masquerading* on your Linux machine.

◆ *Interface* — Please note that this does not say "host." A given host may have multiple interfaces on it, and therefore multiple IP addresses. For simplicity, most descriptions in this chapter assume that each host has only one interface on it; however, please remember that the situation may be more complex than that. We return to this subject later in this chapter, when we discuss the network-access tier.

An IP address is 32 bits (4 bytes) long. Normally, an IP address is written using "dot" format, with the 4 bytes of the address separated by periods (dots). For example, the IP address of the main computer at the White House is 198.137.241.30; and the IP address of the main computer at Microsoft Corporation is 131.107.1.7. Each of the four numbers in an IP address, because it is 1 byte long, can hold any value between zero and 255; however, some numbers are reserved for special uses.

ADDRESSES VERSUS DOMAIN NAMES   If you have cruised the World Wide Web or other domains within the Internet, you probably have noticed that names like www.whitehouse.gov are sometimes called *addresses*. Actually, this is a misnomer: the White House's *address* is 198.137.241.30, whereas www.whitehouse.gov is its *domain name*. The address is how your computer finds the White House's computer; the domain name is a mnemonic, to help you remember the White House's computer.

One of the most important jobs performed on the Internet is transforming, or *resolving*, domain names into their corresponding IP addresses. We discuss this topic at length later in this chapter; for now, just note that a domain name is simply a synonym for an IP address, and that computers use IP addresses to communicate with each other.

Who assigns addresses?

As we mentioned earlier, IP addresses are handed out by the Network Information Center (NIC), an agency that helps manage the Internet (insofar as it is managed at all).

Assigning IP addresses is one of the most important tasks that the NIC performs; after all, only by having a central authority that assigns addresses can we avoid having more than one host using the same address – and the chaos that would cause.

Actually, saying that the NIC assigns IP addresses is a bit misleading; rather, the NIC assigns IP *network* addresses. In effect, the NIC assigns a block of addresses to an authority that runs a local network, and that authority doles out IP addresses to the individual hosts on its network. This system works well: the NIC retains control of IP addresses, and ensures the uniqueness (and therefore, the integrity) of the addresses, without having to micromanage the assignment of addresses to the millions of individual machines that are plugged into the Internet.

So, just what is a "network address"? That is the next topic.

Classes of networks

As you may have guessed by now, IP addresses are not just a clutch of numbers that are assigned willy-nilly. The set of IP addresses is carefully structured. Some addresses are reserved for special purposes (described shortly) and the remaining addresses are organized into blocks, or *classes*, of networks. The classes of networks differ mainly in the number of bits within the 32-bit IP address that each gives to the network itself and the number of bits each has remaining to address hosts within the network: the fewer bits that must be used to address the network itself, the more that are available to address individual hosts, and therefore the more hosts that the network can address.

The IP protocol defines three main classes of networks:

◆ *Class A* – These networks use 7 bits to address the network, and 24 bits to address the individual hosts on the network. Each class A network can address up to 16,777,216 hosts; therefore, the NIC assigns a class A network only to extremely large networks, such as the federal government or huge private organizations like IBM. Any IP address whose first number is between 1 and 127 is on a class A network. As you can see, a very limited number of such network addresses are available – after setting aside a few IP addresses reserved for special purposes, only 125 such network addresses are available on the Internet.

◆ *Class B* – These networks use 16 bits to address the network, and 16 bits to address the individual hosts on the network. Each class B network can address up to 65,536 hosts; therefore, the NIC assigns a class B network only to large organizations, such as major universities or corporations. Any IP address whose first number is between 128 and 191 is on a class B network: 16,382 class B network addresses are available on the Internet.

◆ *Class C* – These networks use 24 bits to address the network, and 8 bits to address the individual hosts on the network. Each class C network can address up to 256 hosts; therefore, a class C network address is assigned to small organizations, such as local Internet providers and other small companies. An IP address whose first number is between 192 and 223 is on a class C network: 2,097,150 class C network addresses are available on the Internet.

A company may be assigned more than one IP network address. For example, a large Internet service provider (ISP) may have several class C addresses assigned to it, and the ISP, in turn, uses the IP addresses to give Internet access to its customers. (We'll discuss ISPs at greater length in Chapter 2.)

Special or reserved addresses

The following IP addresses are set aside for special purposes:

◆ *Class D addresses* – These addresses have a first number that is between 224 and 239, and are used for multicasting.

◆ *Class E addresses* – These addresses have a first number that is between 240 and 255, and are reserved by the Internet for its own uses.

◆ *Private addresses* – The Internet reserves the following three sets of IP addresses for private, nonconnected networks:

   ■ Class A network 10.0.0.0

   ■ Class B networks 172.16.0.0 through 172.31.0.0

   ■ Class C networks 192.168.1.0 through 192.168.255.0

   Companies and private individuals can use any of these addresses for a private Internet, or *intranet*. The drawback is that hosts can use these addresses only to communicate with other hosts on its private network – it cannot use the IP address to communicate with other hosts on the Internet. However, ways around this exist, as we show you in Chapter 8.

◆ Addresses 0.0.0.0 and 255.255.255.255. These are used for special purposes on local networks, as we describe later.

The Internet is running out of addresses

As we noted earlier, an IP address is 32 bits (4 bytes) long. Addresses are organized into classes, and some addresses are reserved for special purposes. If you add up the number of addresses available in each class, you get the following:

♦ Class A = 125 unique networks, each of which can address 16,777,216 hosts

♦ Class B = 16,382 unique networks, each of which can address 65,536 hosts

♦ Class C = 2,097,150 unique networks, each of which can address 256 hosts

♦ Total = 2,113,658 unique networks, addressing a total of 3,724,410, 368 hosts

The Internet can address more than 3.7 billion unique hosts; however, it can address only 2.1 million unique networks. This number of hosts is enormously large (approximately one unique IP address for every two people on earth), but the number of networks is much smaller. Two million is still an enormously large number, even in the computer domain, in which (it seems) a million is the basic unit of measurement; and in 1981, when the IP addressing scheme was first devised (and only 43 networks were in existence throughout the world), 2 million must have seemed inexhaustible. However, the explosive growth of the Internet over the last five years – thanks in large part to the invention of the World Wide Web – has consumed most of the available addresses. By the time you read this book, all 2.1 million Internet network addresses may be in use already.

Obviously, this is a serious problem. The IETF is considering proposals to deal with the problem, most of which involve replacing the Internet Protocol with an updated protocol that allows for many more addresses. However, agreeing on which protocol to adopt is a difficult question, and even when the IETF adopts a new protocol, implementing the new protocol and installing the new bits onto every networked computer in the world will be a long, difficult job. So the Internet Protocol and its limitations will be with us for some time to come.

This is not a problem that users should sit up nights worrying about. However, you should be aware that the Internet Protocol will be changing in the near future, and that these changes will affect how networking operates on your Linux machine.

In the meantime, a number of schemes have been designed to help work around the limitations on the number of IP addresses. Most such schemes let multiple machines use a single IP address. In Chapter 8, we show you how to use such a method, called *IP masquerading*, to hook several machines into the Internet through a single IP address.

ROUTING   So far, we have described a TCP/IP network as if it involved only two hosts – the host that was transmitting a datagram, and the host that was receiving it. However, a network can involve many hosts: the sending host, the recipient host, and an indefinite number of hosts that stand between the sender and the recipient and pass along the datagrams from the sender to the recipient.

The hosts that stand between the sender and the recipient pass a datagram from one another, in turn, until it arrives at its intended destination – rather like a row of fans at a baseball game passing a hot dog from hand to hand until it has traveled from the vendor to the person who bought it. For example, when host `myexample`
`.com` sends a datagram to host `whitehouse.gov`, the datagram passes through 13 intermediary sites, one after another. This may seem very inefficient. However, a datagram can be sent from `myexample.com` to `whitehouse.gov`, and a reply datagram sent from `whitehouse.gov` back to `myexample.com`, in less than two-tenths of a second – despite one of the connections being via a modem. Thus, inefficient or not, the system does work well.

So, you may be asking, who or what figures out the route a datagram must take in order to travel from one host to another?

To answer that question, first recall that the Internet is designed to be decentralized. No central host exists through which all datagrams are routed, nor a central system that holds every route from one host to another. Rather, information about how to get from one machine to another is stored throughout the Internet.

A *route* is not information that is stored on a host: a host must figure out a route on the fly. *Routing* is the Internet's term for the "black art" of figuring out the route a datagram must take to travel from its sender to its intended recipient.

Routing is raised at this time because most of the work that the software in the Internet tier does is to examine datagrams – whether generated on the local host or received from another host – and figure out the host to which it should forward the datagrams. Given that millions of hosts exist on the Internet, any of which can communicate with any other, this task is very complex; the fact that the Internet works as well as it does is something of a marvel.

When you connect your Linux system to the Internet, you have to maintain some routing information on your system. This job can be simple or it can be quite complicated, depending upon how many hosts your Linux system will be serving. Maintaining routing information is one of the most important tasks you will have to perform. We deal with this topic in some depth in Chapters 3, 8, and 12.

STRUCTURE OF THE IP HEADER   Now that IP addresses have been discussed, and the topic of routing has been introduced, we return to our discussion of datagrams – and, in particular, of what the Internet tier of networking software adds to a datagram.

The Internet tier attaches its own header to each datagram. This header is 24 bytes long. Figure 1-5 shows a diagram of this header.

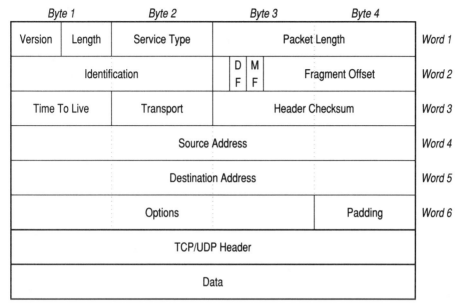

Figure 1-5: Structure of the IP header

The fields in the Internet tier's header are as follows:

◆ *Version* and *Length* — These are flags that indicate the version of the Internet Protocol being used, and the length of the header. This byte is always set to a value of 69.

◆ *Service Type* — This flag usually is set to zero.

◆ *Packet Length* — This indicates the total length of the datagram (packet).

◆ *Identification* — This gives the identifying number that the Internet tier applies to this datagram.

◆ *Flags* and *Fragment Offset* — These fields, along with the Identification field, help to manage *fragmentation of datagrams* — that is, when a site that lies between you and the remote host must break a datagram into pieces because the datagram is too large for it to handle. (Datagram fragmentation is discussed shortly.)

◆ *Time To Live* – When the Internet tier handles a packet, it sets this field to a maximum value. Every time the Internet tier on another system handles this datagram – either to pass it to an application or to forward it to another system – it decrements this value by one. When the value of this field reaches zero, the Internet tier throws the datagram away. This is to prevent infinite loops from occurring, in which an improperly addressed datagram circulates forever around the Internet.

◆ *Transport* – This gives a code that identifies the protocol of the host-to-host tier that generated this datagram. A value of 6 in this field indicates that this is a TCP datagram, whereas a value of 17 indicates that this is a UDP datagram. The Internet layer on the receiving host uses this information to forward the datagram to the appropriate software on the host-to-host tier.

◆ *Header Checksum* – This allows the Internet tier's software to verify that the header wasn't damaged in transit. As you can see, the Internet tier and the host-to-host tier use separate checksums.

◆ *Source Address* – The IP address of the machine that is transmitting this datagram.

◆ *Destination Address* – The IP address of the machine to which this datagram is being sent.

DATAGRAM FRAGMENTATION AND REASSEMBLY   As we noted earlier in this section, most machines that handle a datagram simply read its address and then forward it – either to the machine to which it should go, or to another machine that is along the route.

The chain of machines that handle a datagram may involve many kinds of hardware and many different implementations of TCP/IP software. Thus, not all of the machines can handle datagrams of the same size: some may be able to handle only datagrams that are very small.

So, what occurs when a host forwards a datagram that is too large to another host for that second host to handle? The Internet layer handles this through a mechanism called *datagram fragmentation*.

As its name implies, datagram fragmentation breaks a datagram into two or more pieces, and then forwards each piece to the next host, which reassembles them. The flags field and the fragment-offset field in the Internet tier's header indicate whether a host has fragmented a datagram, and if so, just where in the original datagram a given fragment must go.

Please note that datagram fragmentation does not affect in any way how the TCP protocol splits a file of data into datagrams. As far as the Internet tier is concerned, each datagram is whole and complete – it doesn't care that a given datagram may be only part of a much larger mass of data.

This concludes the introduction of the Internet tier and its software. We return to this tier throughout this book; in particular, we go in depth into the subject of routing – this "black art" that is one of the most difficult and most important parts of configuring a TCP/IP network.

NETWORK-ACCESS TIER
So far, we have examined the top three tiers in the ARPA stack:

- The application tier, which is the tier that interacts with the user.

- The host-to-host tier, which organizes the data received from the user into datagrams.

- The Internet tier, which routes a datagram to its destination.

We must descend one more tier to reach the bottom of the ARPA stack: the *network-access tier*. This tier contains the software that connects the other tiers with the hardware that actually transports the bits from one host to another.

The network-access tier, in fact, consists of multiple *interfaces*. Each interface provides a means of communicating with another host. An interface links a host's IP address – which is a *logical address* – with the *physical address* of the serial port, Ethernet card, or fiber-optic port to which bits must be shipped in order to ship a datagram physically to another host.

TYPES OF INTERFACES Later in this chapter, we introduce the protocols (Ethernet, SLIP, and PPP) with which your host will communicate with other hosts. However, at this point, one idea that you must remember is that every interface is either of two types – a *broadcast* interface, or a *point-to-point* interface:

- A *broadcast* interface is like a CB radio: the conversation takes place on a shared medium, and anyone in range and on the same channel can receive the conversation. Ethernet is a broadcast interface with a protocol that determines when a workstation can broadcast, and what to do if two workstations try to broadcast at the same time. The Ethernet protocol also determines which datagrams a workstation will listen to. It's as if CB radio had a protocol that said "to share this channel, we will preface all messages with the intended recipient's name, and we won't pay attention to messages that aren't for us or to the group in general."

- A *point-to-point* interface is like a closed-circuit telephone line: you can only speak to the one host that is at the other end of the wire. At first glance, point-to-point links appear useless. However, if the host at the other end of the wire can then relay your messages to other systems, a point-to-point link can be extremely useful.

Broadcast interfaces tend to be media-intensive: after all, each machine on the network is talking to all the other machines on the network, all of the time. For this reason, broadcast networks tend to be small in scope – spanning a single building or department.

Point-to-point interfaces are not media intensive, and usually require only a pair or two of wires or a single channel on a piece of fiber-optic cable. However, they tend to be slower than broadcast links.

When we build a network, we will use both broadcast and point-to-point interfaces to connect to machines on both a local network and on other networks throughout the Internet.

IP ADDRESS OF AN INTERFACE   Earlier in this chapter, when we discussed IP addresses, we noted that a host can have multiple interfaces, each of which can have its own IP address. Your host can actually have multiple interfaces on its network-access tier, each of which has its own IP address. The Internet tier's software uses an interface's IP address both to recognize incoming datagrams and as the source IP address for outgoing datagrams.

When an application asks the kernel to create an interface, the application tells the kernel the IP address to assign to the interface. The kernel then uses this IP address to identify your host to every other host with which it communicates via that interface. It also uses this IP address to check the datagrams it receives via this interface, and to recognize datagrams that are addressed to itself.

For example, consider a host that has two interfaces: interface 1, which has IP address 192.168.1.1, and interface 2, which has IP address 192.168.1.2.

When our host transmits datagrams via interface 1, it writes IP address 192.168.1.1 into the IP header's source field. Other hosts that receive datagrams from our host via Ethernet use IP address 192.168.1.1 to reply to our host. Likewise, when our host transmits datagrams via interface 2, it writes IP address 192.168.1.2 into the IP header's source field. Other hosts that receive datagrams from our host via PPP will use IP address 192.168.1.2 to reply to our host.

When our host receives a datagram from interface 1, it checks the destination IP address. If the destination IP address is 192.168.1.1, our host recognizes the datagram as being addressed to itself, and therefore passes it up to the host-to-host tier for further processing. If, however, the destination address is not 192.168.1.1, the host recognizes that the datagram is intended for another host, and forwards it to that host.

In Chapter 3, we discuss the varieties of interfaces that are available under Linux, and how you can *activate* an interface and assign it an IP address.

ROUTING   The fact that a host can have multiple interfaces raises one other problem: how the software on the Internet tier knows which interface to use to send a datagram to another given host?

For example, suppose that a host has two interfaces: interface 1, which communicates with local hosts via Ethernet, and interface 2, which communicates with an Internet service provider via PPP. Now, suppose that a program on the application tier has created a datagram that is to go to the host with IP address 192.168.39.1. How does the software on the Internet tier know to which interface on the network-access tier it should direct the datagram – the Ethernet interface or the PPP interface?

The answer, briefly, is that the host uses a *routing table* to connect destination IP addresses with interfaces. The routing table defines which IP addresses go to which interfaces. It can also establish a default interface – that is, the interface to which the IP tier should direct datagrams when it cannot figure out where they should go.

In Chapter 3, we discuss the network-access tier at greater length. We describe how you can activate an interface, and how you can manage the routing table on your Linux machine.

EXAMPLES OF TCP/IP IN USE

So far, we have discussed TCP/IP networking in the abstract. Although TCP/IP networking is well designed, you may find some of what we've discussed so far to be confusing. To help make matters clearer, this section gives two examples of TCP/IP in use. In each example, we walk up and down the tiers of TCP/IP, to show how TCP/IP makes the magic of networking happen.

In one example, a human being at host myexample.com pings the main computer at the White House. In the other example, the human being at myexample.com sends a mail message to a friend at Microsoft Corporation. Figure 1-6 shows a diagram of these examples. You may want to look carefully at this figure, as we refer to it frequently during our explanation of these examples.

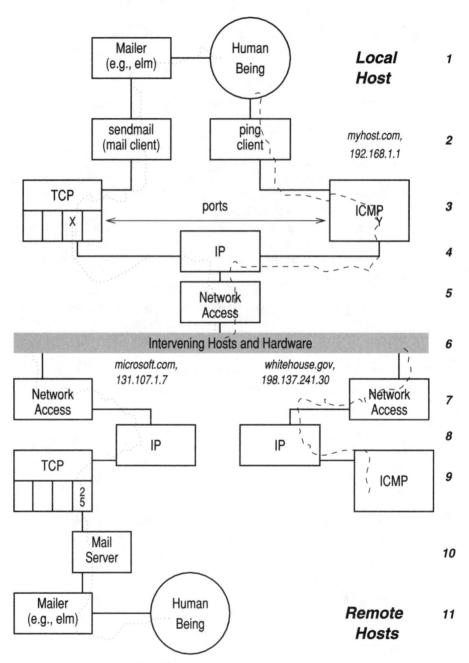

Figure 1-6: Two examples of TCP/IP in use

We discuss first the example of pinging a remote site, and then the example of sending a mail message.

PINGING A REMOTE SITE   The program `ping` sends a datagram to another host; the other host then sends one back. The `ping` program commonly is used to check whether another host is "on the air." The right side of Figure 1-6 shows how a user on host `myexample.com`, which has the IP address 192.168.1.1, pings host `whitehouse.gov`, which has IP address 198.137.241.30. Please note, by the way, that the IP address 192.168.1.1 is one of the reserved IP addresses, and therefore will not actually work on the Internet; we use it here just for purposes of this example.

Figure 1-6 marks the events in the example with numbers that run down its right side. The dashed line traces the route that data flows through the network, as follows:

1. The human being . . .

2. . . . invokes a `ping` application program. This program, or *client*, is part of the application tier.

3. The `ping` client forms a mass of data, which it passes to the ICMP transmission control software on the host-to-host tier. ICMP builds a datagram that includes the message `ICMP_ECHO_REQUEST`.

4. The ICMP software then passes the datagram it built to the software on the Internet (IP) tier. This tier figures out the IP address of the target host, and the address of the host to which the datagram should be forwarded (if the local host does not have a direct connection to the remote host). The Internet tier then adds its own header to the datagram.

5. The IP software then forwards the datagram to the network-access tier. The software on this tier figures out how to physically access the host to which the datagram is being sent (whether modem by serial port, or to an Ethernet address, or whatever), and invokes resources in the Linux kernel to send the data there.

6. If the ICMP datagram is being sent over the Internet, an indefinite number of hosts can handle the datagram before it arrives at its destination host. This indefinite set of hosts is sometimes called the *Internet cloud*. Tracing the passage of a datagram through the Internet cloud is possible, and Chapter 3 shows you how to do it; but in most instances, you will not know what hosts are handling your datagrams, nor will you care.

7. When the datagram arrives at the host to which it is addressed, it is physically read by the software on that host's network-access tier.

8. The software on the network-access tier forwards the datagram to the software on the Internet tier. This software determines that the datagram is intended for this host. It checks the checksum field on the IP header to ensure that the datagram was not damaged in transmission. It then reads the destination address field and confirms that the datagram is intended for host `whitehouse.gov`. The transport field says that this datagram is to be handled by UDP on the host-to-host tier, so the IP software forwards it to that software.

9. When the ICMP software receives the datagram from the Internet tier, it checks the ICMP message in the datagram to see what it should do. In this instance, we have sent it an `ICMP_ECHO_REQUEST` message; therefore, the ICMP software builds a datagram that holds the message `ICMP_ECHO_REPLY` and returns it to the host that originated the request.

The next example is a little more complex.

SENDING A MAIL MESSAGE   In this example, our user host `myexample.com` sends a mail message to a friend who works at Microsoft Corporation. The diagram for this example runs down the left side of Figure 1-6. The dotted line traces the movement of datagrams through the network. Again, the numbers on the right margin of Figure 1-6 mark the steps in executing the example, as follows:

1. The human user on our local host, `myexample.com`, invokes a *mail user agent* (MUA), such as *elm* or *mail*, and writes a mail message.

2. The MUA hands the completed mail message to a *mail transfer agent* (MTA) – in this instance, *sendmail*. We discuss electronic mail in detail in Chapter 5; in brief, however, an *MUA* helps a user to compose or read mail, whereas an *MTA* sends the mail message to its proper destination, be that a mailbox on the local host, another host that is connected via another networking system (such as UUCP), or another host that is connected via TCP/IP networking. Because the MTA interacts with the networking software on our system, the MTA, not the MUA, occupies the application tier of this example. (This is true under UNIX and Linux; other operating systems, such as Windows NT, do not necessarily separate the MUA and the MTA.)

3. The MTA sendmail determines that host `microsoft.com` must be accessed via TCP/IP networking (that is, via the Internet) and therefore forwards the mail message to the host-to-host software. The MTA knows that electronic mail uses the TCP protocol rather than UDP, and thus forwards it appropriately. The TCP software does the following:

- It sends special datagrams to the corresponding TCP software at `microsoft.com`, and establishes a connection with it. Part of establishing a connection is *negotiating* aspects of how data will be exchanged, such as the size of each datagram. The TCP software addresses each datagram to port 25 on the recipient machine, because port 25 is the well-known port for software that implements the *Simple Mail Transfer Protocol* (SMTP), which is the usual method for transmitting a single mail message over the Internet.

- The TCP software then takes the mail message and splits it into a set of datagrams. The number of datagrams depends upon the size of the message and the datagram size that it negotiated with `microsoft.com`.

- The TCP software listens for the TCP software at `microsoft.com` to acknowledge that each datagram was received safely. If a datagram is lost or damaged in transmission, the TCP software retransmits that datagram.

- When `microsoft.com` acknowledges that the entire mail message has been received safely, the TCP software on each host closes the connection between them.

4. The TCP software passes each datagram of the mail message to the software that comprises the Internet tier. The IP software determines the address of the host to which the datagram is being sent, and the address of the host to which it should be sent or forwarded.

5. When the IP software has finished its work with a datagram, it forwards the datagram to the software that comprises the network-access tier. This tier determines how to physically transmit the data to the host that must handle the datagram next.

6. The Internet "cloud" then forwards the datagram among themselves until it finally arrives at host `microsoft.com`.

7. The network-access tier at `microsoft.com` physically receives and processes each incoming datagram, and then forwards it to the software on the Internet tier.

8. The Internet tier uses the checksum field in the IP header to confirm that the datagram was not damaged in handling. It checks the destination address in the IP header to confirm that the datagram is intended for `microsoft.com`. The transport field says that this datagram is to be handled by TCP on the host-to-host tier, so the IP software strips the IP header from the datagram and forwards the datagram to that software.

9. The TCP software on the receiving machine establishes a reliable connection with the TCP software on the transmitting machine, as previously described. For each datagram that comprises the mail message, the TCP software does the following:

- It checks the checksum in the TCP header to ensure that the datagram was not damaged in handling.

- If a datagram was received intact, the TCP software sends the transmitting host a datagram that confirms the datagram's safe receipt. However, if the datagram was damaged in transmission, the TCP software sends the transmitting host a datagram that indicates that this datagram was damaged in transmission, and requests a retransmission.

- The TCP software strips the TCP header from the datagram.

- The TCP software assembles the datagrams to re-create the mail message as it was originally transmitted.

- The TCP software then forwards the reconstituted mail message to the server that is plugged into port 25. This is always the mail server, as port 25 is a well-known port that is reserved for software that implements the SMTP protocol.

10. The server that has implemented the SMTP protocol comprises the application tier on the receiving machine. It reads the message and processes it. We have spoken of "a" mail message; however, transmitting mail via SMTP involves a dialogue of messages that are exchanged by the MTA (sendmail) on the transmitting host and the mail server on the receiving machine. Each such message goes through steps 3 through 9 in this example. (We walk you through this dialogue in Chapter 5.)

11. Finally, when the mail server has completed its dialogue with the MTA on the transmitting host, it writes the completed mail message into the mailbox of the user to whom it is addressed. The user can use an MUA to read the mail message.

And that is how a mail message is transmitted over the Internet. As you can see, this process has many steps, but each step is relatively simple and well-defined. The rest of this book does nothing more – and nothing less – than explore one detail or another of the process illustrated in these examples.

One last point: although we are discussing networking under Linux, TCP/IP has the same design regardless of the operating system under which it is implemented, be it Linux or (in the case of microsoft.com) Windows NT. In Chapter 9, we show this in detail, when we discuss how to connect Linux and Windows 95 via TCP/IP.

REVIEWING TCP/IP PROTOCOLS

In this section, we introduced the TCP/IP protocols. These protocols are the blue-print from which the Internet is built.

We examined the origin of TCP/IP, and how the Internet was originally designed to be a decentralized network that could survive a nuclear attack.

We then looked at how the Internet is governed, and how two agencies in par-ticular — the NIC and the IETF — help to manage the Internet's resources, and chart its future direction.

Then we looked at how TCP/IP works internally. We introduced the concept of a *datagram*, which is a bundle of data that is placed in an electronic "envelope" and "mailed" from the transmitting machine (or *host*) to the recipient host. Then we walked down the four tiers of the ARPA model, and looked at what TCP/IP does in each tier:

- ◆ The *application tier*, which is where the applications live that interact with the user.

- ◆ The *host-to-host tier*, which is where the data to be transmitted is packaged into datagrams for transmission — and correspondingly, where datagrams are received and unpackaged for use. This tier uses numerous different protocols, depending on the type of connection to be made with the recipient machine; the three most commonly used protocols are the *User Datagram Protocol* (UDP), the *Transmission Control Protocol* (TCP), and the *Internet Control Message Protocol* (ICMP). The TCP protocol is where the "TCP" of TCP/IP comes from.

- ◆ The *Internet tier*, which reads the address of the host to which a datagram is being sent, and figures out how to get it there. We discussed the structure of an IP address, and introduced the subject of *routing* — which we discuss at length throughout this book.

- ◆ The *network-access tier*, which takes an IP address and translates it into a physical address to which bits can be sent. This tier also exchanges datagrams with the hardware.

Finally, we concluded this section by walking through two examples: pinging a machine, and sending a mail message from one host to another.

In the next section, we discuss one of the most important aspects of TCP/IP net-working: how a network translates domain names like `whitehouse.gov`, which are used by humans, into IP addresses like 198.137.241.30, which can be used by machines.

Domain Names

In the previous section, we mentioned how each host that is plugged into the Internet has a unique IP address. To review the features of an address quickly:

◆ An IP address is 32 bits (4 bytes) long.

◆ An IP address is almost always printed using dot notation, in which the 4 bytes of the address are separated by a period (for example, 192.168.1.1). The periods, however, are not themselves part of the address – they are just used to make the address easier for humans to read.

◆ Addresses comes in classes, depending upon how many bytes are used to address the network and how many are used to address the hosts plugged into the network. Class A uses 1 byte for the network and 3 bytes for the local hosts, class B uses 2 bytes for the network and 2 bytes for the local hosts, and class C uses 3 bytes for the network and 1 byte for the local hosts.

◆ Some addresses are reserved: some for use by local networks that are not plugged into the Internet, others for administrative purposes.

Although the TCP/IP protocols themselves use only the IP address to find a host on the Internet, the Internet has a system by which each host can also be given a unique name – a name that is easier for human beings to remember than is a 4-byte IP address. Such a human-friendly name is called a *domain name*.

In this section, we first describe the system with which the Internet manages domain names; then we describe the Internet's system for transforming domain names back into the IP addresses that TCP/IP software needs to do its work.

STRUCTURE OF A DOMAIN NAME

The Internet does not assign names at random to hosts. Rather, a well-defined procedure exists for selecting and registering a domain name: the Internet's *Domain-Name System* (DNS).

The DNS defines a structure for a domain name, rather like that of an IP address:

◆ A *top-level* domain, which gives the domain's general class: whether it is an educational site, a commercial site, or whatever.

◆ A *second-level* domain, which gives the name of the individual domain. Usually, this names a network, although it may only name an individual machine.

◆ A *host* name, which is an optional name that names an individual host that resides within the domain.

The elements of a domain name are written separated by periods. Unlike an IP address, they are read from right to left, with the top-level domain being rightmost in the name. For example, in the name thor.myexample.com, the top-level domain is com, the secondary-level domain is myexample, and the host name is thor.

Two additional points must be made about domain names:

- A final period '.' is the root of a domain name, just as a backslash '/' is the root of the Linux file system. Thus, just as /usr/local/foo is the relative path name and /usr/local/foo is an absolute path name, so too thor.myexample.com is a relative domain name and thor.myexample.com. (note the final '.') is the absolute domain name. In almost every instance, you will use a relative domain name; however, software that resolves domain names does distinguish between absolute and relative domain names, so do not be surprised if you see a domain name that terminates in a period.

- Domain names are *not* case-sensitive. That is, the name myexample.com and the name MYEXAMPLE.COM and the name Myexample.Com are exactly the same. Different applications use different conventions for handling domain names: some write them in all uppercase letters, some write them in all lowercase letters, and some use mixed cases, but all forms are equivalent.

We now discuss each element of a domain name in a little more detail.

TOP-LEVEL DOMAINS   When the DNS was designed in 1983, it defined seven top-level domains, shown in Table 1-1.

TABLE 1-1 PRINCIPAL TOP-LEVEL DOMAINS

Domain Name	Definition
.com	Commercial domains
.edu	Educational institutions
.gov	Federal government sites, excluding the military
.int	International organizations
.mil	Military sites
.org	Miscellaneous organizations, often not-for-profit

With the exception of .int, these top-level domains apply only to the United States.

In addition, the DNS defines a national top-level domain for nearly every nation on earth. For example, the national top-level domain for the United States is .us, and France's is .fr. This list of top-level domains is too long to reproduce here; however, at the end of this chapter, we give sources where you can find them listed.

SECOND-LEVEL DOMAINS   As we noted earlier, a domain name is, in effect, a synonym for an IP address: a domain name gives the IP address in a form that is easily remembered by humans. For this reason, second-level domains cannot just be used willy-nilly: they must be registered. Registration ensures that the name of a given second-level domain is unique throughout the Internet, and lets the fact that a given IP address is associated with a given domain be disseminated throughout the Internet.

Naturally, a second-level domain name must be unique within its top-level domain. For example, only one second-level domain myexample can exist within top-level domain .com; however, another second-level domain myexample can exist within top-level domain .edu, and a third second-level domain myexample can exist within top-level domain .us.

The NIC is one of the agencies that can register secondary-level domains for the seven top-level domains in the preceding list. In theory, this applies only to the United States; however, many foreign networks have also chosen to register with the NIC under a top-level domain. In Chapter 2, we show you how to register a domain for yourself, should you want to do so.

Within a national top-level domain, a country has the authority to structure second-level domain names as it wants. In the United States, second-level domain names describe the state and community in which a network physically resides. For example, if domain myexample were located in Chicago, Illinois, its domain name would be myexample.chi.il.us, where the secondary-level domain name chi.il describes the facts that myexample resides in Chicago, and that Chicago is in the state of Illinois. This rule, however, often is bent, even by government agencies. Other nations have different policies; for example, Australia mirrors the seven principal top-level domain names, so myexample in Australia could have the domain name myexample.com.au. (At the end of this chapter, we cite a reference that gives you detailed information about how the .us domain is structured.)

Each country also defines its own method for registering second-level domain names for its national domain. In the United States, each locality has a local authority that can register the second-level domains that reside in that locality. For example, in Chicago, the network administrators at the University of Chicago have the authority to register second-level domain names for the local domain chi.il.us.

OTHER LEVELS OF DOMAINS   The Internet gives administrators of a second-level domain the right to organize their domain as they wish, in order to best serve their needs.

Thus, a large second-level domain (such as, say, ibm.com) can be broken into an indefinite number of third-level domains (for example, vnet.ibm.com). These third-level domains may be broken into fourth-level domains, and in rare cases, fourth-level domains may be broken into fifth-level domains.

Again, each domain name must be unique within its higher-level domain; thus, only one vnet.ibm.com can be used; however, having a third-level domain named vnet.myexample.com is perfectly legal, as the "name spaces" for myexample.com and ibm.com are entirely separate.

A domain going beyond a third level is unusual, but the Internet protocols give a domain the power to do so, as its needs require.

HOSTS' NAMES   A domain name registers a domain, rather than the hosts that are part of that domain. If you think of a domain as being equivalent to a network, you won't be too far off the mark.

As with a network, the administrators of the domain have the responsibility for managing the individual hosts that reside within the domain. The administrators must assign a name to each host, and each host's name must follow these rules:

◆ It must be unique within its domain.

◆ It cannot be more than 24 characters long.

◆ It must consist only of alphabetic characters, numerals, and the hyphen character.

Host names do not need to be registered with any higher-level authority. The administrators of the local network must ensure that datagrams addressed to a given local host are routed correctly to that host.

In Chapters 6 and 7, we describe how to ensure that datagrams addressed to a given local host are routed correctly to that host.

EXAMPLE OF THE DNS IN ACTION   The networking command whois sends a message to the InterNIC, and requests information about a given domain. For example, the command

```
whois whitehouse.gov
```

retrieves the following information from the InterNIC:

```
[rs.internic.net]
Executive Office of the President USA (WHITEHOUSE-HST)
  WHITEHOUSE.GOV                          198.137.241.30
Whitehouse Public Access (WHITEHOUSE-DOM)
  WHITEHOUSE.GOV
```

As you can see, this shows that the domain `whitehouse.gov` has the IP address 198.137.241.30. This information is disseminated throughout the Internet, so that any system that wants to contact the White House's site can find its IP address. In the next section, we describe how this dissemination is performed.

CHANGES ARE COMING   The InterNIC's policy for registration had been on a first-come, first-serve basis — whoever requested a second-level domain name got it. The InterNIC did not attempt to determine whether a person had the right to register a given name.

As the Internet has grown in popularity, the registration of a second-level domain name has created some problems, particularly for names being registered in the `.com` top-level domain. For example, some unscrupulous individuals registered names of corporations or other copyrighted material, and attempted to extort money from the corporations in return for relinquishing the registration they possessed. This has involved the InterNIC in lawsuits, and other unpleasantness.

Also, the system of seven top-level domains is clearly inadequate. In 1983, putting all commercial sites into a single top-level domain may have been acceptable, because the Internet in those days consisted primarily of governmental and academic users. Nowadays, however, the `.com` top-level domain is growing enormously — so much so that finding a new secondary-level domain name within it is difficult.

Some groups and individuals have also chafed at the way InterNIC has handled requests for registration, and its policy of charging $50 per year for maintaining a domain's registration.

As a result, the system of registering secondary-level domain names is being restructured. New agencies will be taking up this task, and the suite of top-level domains is being redefined. As of this writing, the situation has not settled sufficiently for us to describe it in any detail, but you should be aware of the fact that change is coming.

ALTERNATIVE DOMAIN-NAME SYSTEMS   So far in this chapter, we have spoken of the InterNIC as if it were a governmental agency, and its domain names as if they were the only possible set of domain names. However, the InterNIC's authority is established by custom rather than by law. There is no reason why another agency could not set up its own system of top-level domain names, and let users register their secondary-level domain names under them; and if it can persuade enough users to use its service instead of the InterNIC's, then it would become the standard.

In fact, a group that calls itself the AlterNIC has already set up its own set of top-level domain names, and is soliciting registrations. In effect, this is an "alternate universe" of domain names, which is parallel to that managed by the InterNIC. AlterNIC is a long way from displacing the InterNIC as the principal agency for registering domain names, but its set of top-level domain names is interesting. It may well be that in the future, Internet users will have the choice of registering a domain with any number of agencies – and Internet systems may have to check all of them to look up a domain name.

For more information on the AlterNIC, see its Web page, at URL `http://www.alternic.net`.

DOMAIN-NAME SERVICE (DNS)

One of the most important features of TCP/IP networking is the mechanism by which it translates domain names into IP addresses. This method is called *Domain-Name Service*, also known by the acronym DNS.

Here we have an example of "acronym collision," where one acronym has two different meanings — in this case, "DNS" can mean "Domain-Name System" or "Domain-Name Service." Hopefully, which DNS we are referring to will be clear from the context.

Experienced Internet administrators tend to spend a lot of time grumbling about DNS – its limitations, its problems, its deficiencies. However, a comparison of the Internet's DNS with any other networking protocol's method for resolving domain names shows that DNS is like democracy: it's the worst possible system, except for all the others.

We describe DNS in detail in Chapters 7 and 8; in this chapter, we just give you an overview of DNS, so that you can see how it fits into the scheme of TCP/IP networking as a whole.

In brief, DNS translates human-readable names into IP addresses. Simply put, the computer looks up the numbers so that you don't have to.

DISTRIBUTION OF DOMAIN NAMES   As we noted earlier, the Internet is decentralized: no central system holds all domain name and IP addresses for all hosts on the Internet. Rather, domain names and IP addresses are organized into a hierarchy of domain-name servers, each of which services what is termed a *zone* of domains.

Each domain-name server knows the names and IP addresses of the domains in its zone. It also knows the names of the domain-name servers in its zone, and the name (but *not* the IP address) of each domain that each domain-server serves. The InterNIC requires that each domain be served by at least two domain-name servers; in this way, if a domain-name server goes down, another domain is still reachable.

The zones are organized as follows:

◆ The InterNIC maintains a root machine that gives the name and IP address of the domain-name servers for each of the top-level domains (.com, .edu, and so on).

◆ Each domain-name server for a given top-level domain holds the name and IP address of each domain-name server in its domain, and the name of each domain that the domain-name server serves.

◆ Each domain-name server within a top-level domain holds the name and IP address of each domain in its zone. As we mentioned earlier, a domain must be served by more than one domain-name server, which means that zones may overlap to a certain extent. Usually, this server is the *gateway* system that gives the domain's machines access to the Internet.

◆ If a secondary-level domain is broken into third-level domains, each third-level domain probably is served by its own domain-name server.

◆ The name and IP address of a local host is registered with the domain-name server of the domain in which it resides. For example, host thor, which is part of the domain myexample.com, has its name and IP address registered with the domain-name server that services myexample.com.

This configuration is complex, but it has several important advantages:

◆ The fact that no central domain-name server exists means that the breakdown of any one system can't stop traffic across the entire Internet. Nor does one central system exist that can bottleneck traffic across the entire Internet.

◆ Work for maintaining information about the Internet is distributed across the entire Internet. Thus, as more systems are added to the Internet, more resources become available to manage information about those hosts.

◆ The task of finding the IP address of a host can be performed hierarchically: the local server maintains information about local hosts — and since most datagrams are addressed to local hosts rather than remote ones, the local domain-name server can resolve inquiries for IP addresses, which is faster and much more efficient than having such an inquiry processed by some remote, central server.

Now that we've briefly discussed how domain names are distributed throughout the Internet, we'll walk through how IP software translates a domain name into an IP address.

HOW DNS WORKS   DNS actually consists of a library of code that looks up domain names. This code is called the *resolver*. The resolver is built into your Linux system's TCP/IP software, and it is invoked for every application that needs to look up a domain name.

The easiest way to explain how DNS works is to show it in action, so here's an example. Suppose a user at the domain `myexample.com` wants to find more information about the book *The Linux Database* by Fred Butzen and Dorothy Forbes (New York, MIS:Press, 1997). To do so, she could use Netscape to view the MIS:Press Web site. Our inquisitive user will type in the Universal Resource Location (URL) of the MIS:Press Web site, which is `http://www.mispress.com`. (If you do not know what a URL is, or what `http` means, don't worry — we discuss these terms when we introduce browsers in Chapter 4.) As you can see, embedded within the URL is the name of the MIS:Press Web-server host, `www.mispress.com`.

As we noted earlier, the datagrams going out onto the Internet use IP addresses, not domain names. Therefore, Netscape has a copy of the resolver built (or *linked*) into it, so that it can translate the name `www.mispress.com` into that host's IP address and "talk" with that host.

To translate the name `www.mispress.com` into that host's IP address, the resolver goes through several steps, as follows:

1. The resolver usually first checks the `hosts` file on its local host (although it may be configured to check another source first). The `hosts` file holds the domain names and IP addresses of frequently accessed hosts. (This file usually can be edited by a host's administrator, to help the resolver work most efficiently.) Under Linux, this file is named `/etc/hosts`.

2. Under Linux (and most other operating systems), the networking software *caches* (stores in a temporary log) the name and IP address of every site that it has communicated with recently. Therefore, the resolver first checks the cache on the local host to see whether `myexample.com` has contacted `www.mispress.com` recently. This is the easiest and most efficient way to find this information.

3. If the host name `www.mispress.com` is not in the cache on `myexample.com`, the resolver checks the domain name `mispress.com`. Because the name does not end with a dot, ".", the resolver first tries to append the domain name of the local host onto the end of the name of the requested host, and then tries to look up the concatenated host name in your local domain. For example, if a user is at `myexample.com`, the resolver will try to find host `mispress.com.myexample.com` in your local domain. It takes this step because most domain-name lookups that the resolver has to perform are within the local domain, so this optimization often works.

4. If the resolver cannot find a host named `mispress.com` within `myexample.com`'s own domain-name space, it assumes that `mispress.com` lies outside the local domain; it therefore must search the Internet's domain-name servers to find this site. The first step in this process is to find the address of a domain-name server for the top-level domain `.com`. The resolver takes the name `mispress.com` and appends a "." to it, to turn it into a *Fully Qualified Domain Name* (FQDN), and then sends a query to the root servers at the InterNIC to find the correct name-server for this site. Many such servers exist; one is `A.ROOT-SERVERS.NET`, whose IP address is 198.41.0.4.

5. Once the resolver has found the IP addresses of a domain-name server for the top-level domain `com.` domain, it picks one IP address and asks it for the server that holds information about `mispress.com`. The resolver sends a query to `A.ROOT-SERVERS.NET` and asks it about `mispress.com`; the resolver replies that host `ORIGIN.HEPCATS.COM`, whose IP address is 207.111.17.2, knows about `mispress.com`, and can tell us its IP address.

6. The resolver now knows that it should ask server `ORIGIN.HEPCATS.COM` for information about domain `mispress.com`. So, the resolver asks that server about `www.mispress.com`; `ORIGIN.HEPCATS.COM` replies that the IP address of `www.mispress.com` is 207.111.17.4.

At this point, the resolver has done its work: we now know the IP address of `www.mispress.com`. Netscape can now send datagrams to the Web server at `www.mispress.com`.

This concludes our description of DNS, and also concludes our introduction to the TCP/IP protocols. We hope that this admittedly brief overview helps you make sense of the many, seemingly arbitrary details that follow in this book. The next section discusses the hardware with which networking is implemented.

Reviewing TCP/IP Networking

In this section, we introduced TCP/IP networking, which is the networking protocols and software with which the Internet is built.

We also discussed the history and origin of the Internet and the agencies that manage it.

We then walked down the four tiers of TCP/IP networking:

1. The *application tier*, which provides the data to be networked (for example, a mail message).

2. The *host-to-host tier*, which takes the data produced by a program on the application tier, and packages it into datagrams for transmission to the host for which it is being sent.

3. The *Internet tier*, which receives a datagram from the host-to-host tier, figures out the address to which the datagram should be sent, and sends it on its way.

4. The *network-access tier*, which receives a datagram from the Internet tier, figures out how to physically send the datagram to the correct IP address, and sends it on its way.

We gave two extended examples of TCP/IP in action: of one host pinging another host, and of one host sending a mail message to another host.

Finally, we discussed the Internet's Domain-Name System, which is how the Internet distributes information that links a given domain name to its IP address.

In the next section, we introduce the hardware with which networking is implemented.

Networking Hardware and Protocols

In this section, we introduce the hardware on which networking is implemented.

This chapter provides a general discussion of hardware. We discuss the actual installation and configuration of hardware in Chapter 2.

In brief, two types of hardware exist upon which networking is implemented: Ethernet and serial lines (that is, modems). We discuss each in turn.

Before we begin, one point of terminology. So far, we have spoken of data being organized into units called *datagrams*. The term *datagram* applies to the way that TCP/IP organizes data. Hardware protocols, however, handle data organized by many networking protocols: not only TCP/IP, but also OSI, DECNET, Novell Network, AppleTalk, and so on. So, when we discuss how data is organized by hardware protocols, we speak of data being organized into units called *frames*. It may seem to be hairsplitting to use a different term, but in fact it is not: if you read further into the literature of networking, you will encounter these terms used in specific circumstances, and if you know under what circumstances each term applies, it will lend precision to your reading.

And now on to our discussion of hardware: first Ethernet, and then serial lines.

Ethernet

Ethernet is one of the older networking technologies. It is the networking hardware of choice: it is fast, reliable, and inexpensive.

In this section, we'll briefly introduce Ethernet hardware, and then discuss how Ethernet transmits information, and then describe the Linux software with which you can work with Ethernet.

HARDWARE

Ethernet is implemented by a card that is plugged into your PC. Ethernet cards come in a great variety of speeds, internal formats, and prices; however, almost every Ethernet card can talk with almost every other one (exceptions do exist, of course).

Chapter 2 explains how to install an Ethernet card into your Linux box and configure it. For now, we'll discuss not the cards themselves, but how they are connected.

Ethernet hardware comes in several "flavors." Each flavor uses a different kind of cable to transmit bits from one computer to another. Two types of Ethernet are commonly used in homes and offices:

◆ *Thin coaxial* – Uses a lighter coaxial cable to transmit bits. It is also called *thin-coax* or *10base-2* Ethernet.

◆ *Twisted pair* – Uses an 8-strand copper cable that resembles a serial-port cable. It is also called *10base-T* Ethernet.

We discuss each type of Ethernet in turn.

THIN COAX   Thin coax uses a thin-coaxial cable to connect computers. Each end of the cable is terminated by a 50-ohm terminator, and a computer is connected to the cable through a socketed T-connector.

With thin-coax Ethernet, the computers are strung out in a line, like charms on a charm bracelet. The maximum length of the coaxial cable that connects all the computers is 185 meters. For networks that extend over more than 185 meters, a device called a *repeater* can be inserted into the network, to repeat and amplify the data being sent over the cable. Figure 1-7 shows the schema of a thin-coax network.

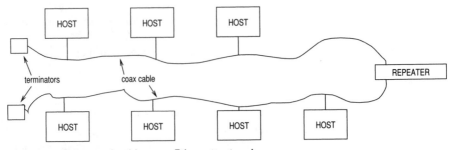

Figure 1-7: Schema of a thin–coax Ethernet network

Thin coax has a number of advantages and disadvantages, as shown in Table 1-2.

TABLE 1-2 ADVANTAGES AND DISADVANTAGES OF THIN COAX

Advantages	Disadvantages
It can support a relatively long cable run (more than 300 feet).	Throughput is limited to 10 megabits per second (Mbps). This probably isn't a problem in a small intranet, but it may become a problem in business settings.
Because it uses shielded coaxial cable, it is largely immune to electrical noise. This may be a consideration for an intranet in your home, if you want your network to work correctly while someone else is running a vacuum cleaner or television set.	If the cable is broken or disconnected, the entire network goes down. This complicates fault diagnosis.
It is inexpensive: the only equipment needed (beside the Ethernet cards themselves) is some cheap coaxial cable and connectors.	Because machines are connected to one long cable, thin-coax Ethernet is not suitable for connecting machines scattered throughout a locale — snaking one cable around so that it reaches each machine is simply too difficult.

If you are connecting a group of machines that are near each other — say, within the same room or along a single bench — then thin-coax Ethernet is worth considering. However, for more complex configurations, you should consider twisted-pair Ethernet, which we describe next.

TWISTED PAIR   Twisted-pair Ethernet uses ordinary 8-strand ribbon cable to connect machines. The cable is terminated with an RJ-45 connector. This connector closely resembles the plug used on your telephone, except that it has eight wires instead of four.

Unlike thin-coax Ethernet, in which the computers are connected to a single long strand of cable, twisted-pair Ethernet uses a spoke-and-hub configuration, in which each machine is plugged directly into a special device, called (not surprising) an *Ethernet hub*. Figure 1-8 shows the schema of a twisted-pair Ethernet network.

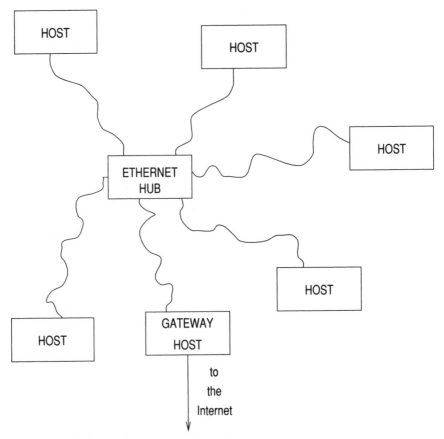

Figure 1-8: Schema of a twisted-pair Ethernet network

The number of machines that can be plugged into the hub is limited only by the number of ports on the hub. Multiple hubs can be linked, or *daisy-chained*, to supply more ports if needed.

It is common for twisted-pair Ethernet ports to be run through walls, like telephone cables, and even terminated in the same wall outlets as a telephone jack. When many ports are cabled simultaneously, the wires to the individual outlets often are bundled together, and then punched down onto a *terminating block*. Patch cables plugged into the terminating block then run to the hub.

A single strand of twisted-pair cable cannot exceed 90 meters (approximately 300 feet). This is more than adequate for nearly every office or home.

Like thin-coax Ethernet, twisted-pair Ethernet has its advantages and disadvantages, as shown in Table 1-3.

TABLE 1-3 ADVANTAGES AND DISADVANTAGES OF TWISTED-PAIR ETHERNET

Advantages	Disadvantages
Twisted pair offers better throughput than thin coax: Cat 3 can run at speeds up to 10 Mbps; Cat 5 can run at up to 100 Mbps (although the equipment is more expensive).	Twisted-pair cabling is unshielded. Thus, it does not work well in noisy environments.
Twisted pair's hub-and-spoke layout is easier to manage in most situations, particularly when machines are scattered through an office or home.	It is more expensive than thin-coax Ethernet: hubs cost about $10 to $50 per port, depending on how many "bells and whistles" are built into it. (However, you can use twisted-pair Ethernet to link two machines, without using a hub — we'll show you how in Chapter 2.) If you're planning to wire an entire office, you need to buy a pin block and harmonica, ribbon cable, connectors, and probably a crimping tool as well (for attaching connectors onto cable).

Twisted-pair Ethernet is much more flexible and convenient to maintain than is thin-coax Ethernet. Further, if the connection to a single machine is broken, the rest of the network can continue to operate; whereas if the cable in a thin-coax network is broken, the entire network goes down. If you are networking the machines in an office, or networking machines that are in different rooms of your home, twisted-pair Ethernet is almost certainly the way to go.

OTHER TYPES OF ETHERNET   Two other types of Ethernet are also in common use. These are not used within homes or offices, but are used to carry data into them, where twisted-pair or thin-coax Ethernet can be used to distribute the data. These types are *thick-coaxial* Ethernet, and *fiber* Ethernet, which are described next briefly, in case you should encounter them.

Thick-coaxial Ethernet uses a heavy coaxial cable to transmit bits. It is also called thick-coax or 10base-5 Ethernet. Thick-coaxial cable is used by cable-television companies to carry their signals; so if you purchase cable-modem Internet service from a cable company, thick-coax Ethernet may be used to carry the data into your home or office. Thick-coax Ethernet has all the advantages of thin coax, plus much higher throughput.

Fiber Ethernet uses a fiber-optic circuit to carry data. Fiber optics allow very long runs (over 2,000 meters) and is completely immune to electrical interference. It also offers extremely high throughput. However, fiber optics is also extremely expensive. Fiber Ethernet is used only to carry data into an office that consumes enormous amounts of data.

ETHERNET PROTOCOLS

Ethernet, like the graphical user interface (GUI) and object-oriented programming (OOP), was created at the Xerox Palo Alto Research Complex (PARC) in the early 1970s. (How Xerox managed to create so many extraordinary breakthroughs in computer technology, yet profit so little from them is amazing; but this story is beyond the scope of this book.) The word *Ethernet*, in fact, is a trademark of Xerox Corporation (which is why we always capitalize it), although it is widely used as a common noun to name an entire class of data-transmission devices.

An Ethernet network works on a set of simple principles:

◆ Every Ethernet card in the world has a unique address that is burned into it by its manufacturer. The Institute for Electrical and Electronics Engineers (IEEE) is responsible for doling out blocks of Ethernet addresses to manufacturers.

◆ All Ethernet devices plugged into the network simultaneously listen to the network and can transmit to it.

◆ Only one frame can be on the network's "wire" at any one time. If more than one Ethernet device attempts to transmit a frame simultaneously, a *frame collision* results; this situation is rather like when both parties on a Speakerphone speak at the same time − because both are using the same channel to communicate, neither can be heard. When this happens, both devices wait a random period of time, and then attempt to transmit again.

◆ When a device transmits a frame onto the network, it stamps the frame of the address of the Ethernet card to whose computer it is intended.

◆ Every Ethernet device on the network reads the frame and checks its address. If the frame is addressed to a given device, it reads and processes that frame; otherwise, the device ignores the frame.

So much for the principles of Ethernet. Now we look at the Ethernet frame itself.

THE ETHERNET FRAME   A discussion of the layout of an Ethernet frame includes some bad news and some good news:

◆ The bad news is that two competing standards for Ethernet frames actually exist: the original, "classic" Ethernet, and Ethernet as described by IEEE standard 802.3.

◆ The good news is that the software that reads Ethernet frames knows how to recognize and interpret both types of frames, so the fact that two competing standards exist will not present a problem to you − in most instances at least.

You probably will never work on this level, so going into detail as to how the standards differ isn't necessary. However, to illustrate the structure of an Ethernet frame, Figure 1-9 gives the layout of a "classic" Ethernet frame.

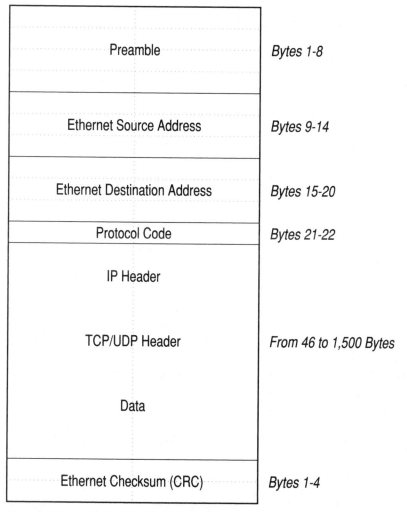

Figure 1–9: Layout of a "classic" Ethernet frame

♦ The 8-byte preamble is used to synchronize the Ethernet devices. It contains no information of interest to you.

♦ The 6-byte address of the Ethernet device to which the frame is being transmitted. A special address indicates that a frame is intended for all hosts on a network; we discuss in the next section when and why this special address is used.

♦ The 6-byte address of the Ethernet device from which the frame was transmitted.

♦ The 2-byte code that indicates the networking protocol of the data within the frame — that is, whether the frame holds a TCP/IP datagram, a Novell Network packet, an AppleTalk packet, or whatever.

♦ The data itself. This can range from 46 to 1,500 bytes long. If the frame contains a TCP/IP datagram, the data section includes the datagram's IP head and TCP or UPD header.

♦ Finally, the CRC (*cyclic redundancy check*) field holds data that the receiving device uses to confirm that the frame was received intact.

One more topic needs to be discussed before concluding this brief introduction to Ethernet: Ethernet addressing.

ADDRESSING   As we mentioned earlier, each Ethernet card has a unique 6-byte address burned into it by its manufacturer. This address has nothing to do with the IP address assigned to any given host on a TCP/IP network — those addresses are assigned by either the InterNIC or a local network administrator and, in fact, can be changed easily. So how does a network figure out that a host with a given IP address should be accessed through a given Ethernet address?

The solution to this problem is built into TCP/IP itself. This process has two steps: first, each host must figure out for itself what IP address it has, what the address is on its Ethernet card, and then connect the two. Then, the host must tell other hosts on the network that its IP address must be accessed through the particular Ethernet address on its card. We discuss each task in turn next.

Figuring out your own addresses

The TCP/IP software on your Linux system has code built into it that lets you tell it that your machine has a particular IP address and a particular Ethernet address. The IP address is stored in a special file. The Ethernet address either can be given to the Linux kernel through a special command that is executed when you boot your Linux machine, or you can let the Linux kernel *autoprobe* your Ethernet card and figure out the card's Ethernet address on its own.

Autoprobing works with most, but not all, brands of Ethernet card. In some instances, a host may have two Ethernet cards in it, which is the case when the host is acting as a *gateway* that connects two separate TCP/IP networks. In this instance, you have to tell the Linux kernel explicitly the IP address that you want to have associated with a given Ethernet address.

This process sounds complex, but actually it is quite simple. We discuss it at length in Chapter 3. Also, we discuss gateways in Chapter 8.

Telling addresses to other hosts

Recall from the introduction to the TCP/IP protocols that the bottom tier of the TCP/IP stack manages access to the physical network. This tier uses two protocols to exchange Ethernet addresses: the *Address Resolution Protocol* (ARP) and the *Reverse Address Resolution Protocol* (RARP).

ARP, as its name implies, resolves a remote host's IP address into the address of the Ethernet card that connects that host to the local network. (By the way, "ARP" has nothing to do with ARPA – the U.S. Department of Defense's Advanced Research Projects Agency, which originally created the TCP/IP protocols. This is just another example of acronym-collision within the terminology of networking.)

When a host needs to learn the hardware address of a another host on the network, it broadcasts an ARP datagram to all hosts on the network. In the case of an Ethernet network, it uses the special hardware address that addresses a frame to every Ethernet device on the network. The ARP datagram gives the hardware address and the IP address of the transmitting host, and the IP address of the host whose hardware address the transmitting host wants to learn. The intended target host then writes its hardware address into the ARP datagram and returns it to the inquirer host. The inquirer host then stores this information in a cache, and then uses this information to send data to that remote host.

A related protocol is the Reverse Address Resolution Protocol (RARP). This protocol is used by a device that does not known its own IP address, such as a Hewlett-Packard JetDirect box (which connects a LaserJet printer to an Ethernet network) or a network computer or X terminal (which does not have a hard disk, and so has no way to store its own IP address or the IP addresses of other machines on the network). The inquirer device builds a RARP datagram that contains its own hardware address, and then broadcasts the datagram to every other host on the network. A special host, called the *server host*, holds the hardware address and IP address of the device; the server host writes the inquirer host's IP address into the RARP datagram, and then returns the datagram to the inquirer.

This concludes our brief introduction to Ethernet. We discuss Ethernet networking at greater length in Chapter 2, when we describe how to install an Ethernet card in your Linux workstation, and in Chapter 6, when we describe how to use Ethernet to build an intranet.

Serial Lines

The other usual method for networking Linux machines is through serial ports —
particularly, through a serial port that is connected to a modem.

HARDWARE

A *serial port* is a port that transmits bytes *serially* — one after the other, like water
flowing through a host, rather than bundled into frames, as with Ethernet hardware. This design lets serial communication work reliably, even over noisy connections, like a telephone line; however, it does mean that communication through a
serial port is much slower than through Ethernet.

(Please note that when we speak of a *serial port*, we mean a port that is physically built into your computer. This is not the same thing as the ports used by the
host-to-host tier of the TCP/IP software: those ports are *virtual* — they are implemented only in software, and are used only to help organize the information that
flows over a TCP/IP network.)

The only practical use of networking through a serial port is when that serial
port has a modem plugged into it that is used to connect your machine into an
Internet provider's network. In Chapter 2, we discuss at length how to set up serial
ports on your machine, how to install a modem, and how to configure it for networking. Connecting two Linux machines through their serial ports and letting
them communicate via TCP/IP is possible; however, the performance will be quite
poor, and the alternative — namely, Ethernet — is so inexpensive that we will not
discuss this alternative further.

PROTOCOLS

When we earlier introduced Ethernet, we described an Ethernet frame and how it
carries information over the hardware. The Ethernet frame is defined by the
Ethernet protocols themselves. The software in the TCP/IP network-access tier simply implements this predefined frame and uses it to communicate over the Ethernet
hardware.

Matters are different with serial ports: Serial ports communicate with a stream of
bytes instead of frames. Thus, the TCP/IP protocols must themselves define how
bytes that flow through a serial port are organized into frames. In fact, two
commonly used protocols exist for organizing serial bits into frames: the *Serial
Line Internet Protocol* (SLIP) and the *Point-to-Point Protocol* (PPP). We discuss each
in turn.

SLIP AND CSLIP   SLIP is a very simple protocol: to build a frame, SLIP simply
fixes a magic character of hexadecimal value 32 (in decimal, 50) at the end of a
TCP/IP datagram, to indicate that the datagram has finished. Should a byte with
value 50 occur within a datagram, the SLIP software prefixes it with another magic
value, to indicate that this is not the end of the datagram.

Compressed SLIP (CSLIP) increases the flow of data through the serial port by compressing the datagram's headers. Actually, it does not exactly compress the headers — rather, it deletes from the headers information that the recipient machine already knows.

SLIP is generally regarded as being obsolete. The fact that a SLIP frame does not include a checksum limits its usefulness. However, some Linux networking software uses SLIP internally; in particular, the `diald` daemon (which automatically dials your modem when your system detects a datagram that needs to be uploaded to your Internet provider's machine) uses SLIP to manage its activity. We discuss this further when we introduce `diald` in Chapter 8.

PPP   PPP is a protocol that was devised to replace SLIP. It defines a frame that overcomes some of the limitations of SLIP, as shown in Figure 1-10.

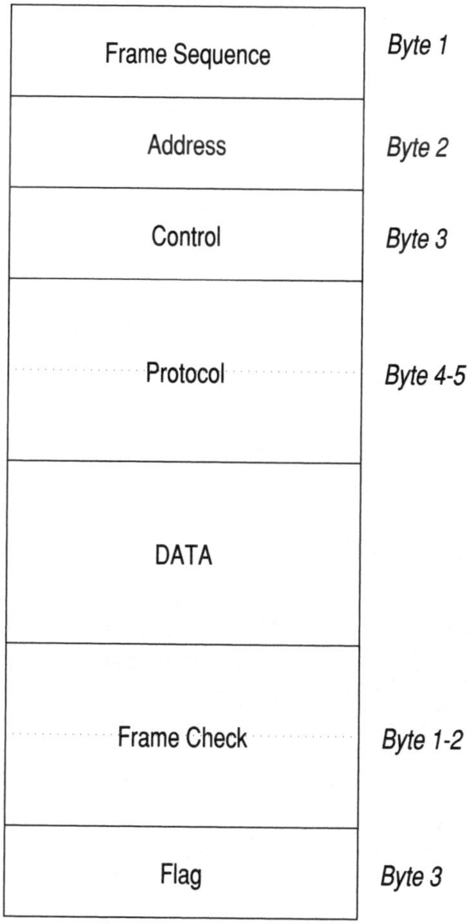

Frame Sequence	*Byte 1*
Address	*Byte 2*
Control	*Byte 3*
Protocol	*Byte 4-5*
DATA	
Frame Check	*Byte 1-2*
Flag	*Byte 3*

Figure 1-10: Layout of the PPP frame

The PPP frame contains the following fields:

◆ *Frame Sequence* — A single-byte field that always holds the number 126.

◆ *Address* — A single-byte field that is always set to the number 256.

◆ *Control* — A single-byte field that is always set to the number 3.

◆ *Protocol* — A 2-byte field that holds a "magic number" that identifies the control protocol of the datagram that the frame contains. For example, a value of 33 indicates that the frame contains an Internet (TCP/IP) datagram. This value lets the PPP software that receives this frame forward the frame's datagram to the appropriate networking software.

◆ *Data* — This field holds the data; in the case of TCP/IP, the datagram (including the headers appended to the data by the tiers of the TCP/IP software) is stored in this field. The data field can be of an indefinite length; by default, the maximum size of this field is 1,500 bytes.

◆ *Frame Check* (FCS) — This field holds a checksum that is calculated from the contents of the other fields in the frame (not including the Frame Sequence field). The PPP software on the host that reads a PPP frame uses this checksum to determine whether a frame was garbled in transmission; this is particularly important when transmitting data over telephone lines, which can be quite "dirty."

◆ *Flag* — Finally, a PPP frame concludes with a 1-byte field that always holds the number 126.

The PPP protocol also describes the conversation that two hosts perform when they begin to exchange frames.

This concludes our introduction to the protocols for transmitting data over serial lines. We discuss this topic in much greater length in Chapter 2.

Reviewing Networking Hardware

In this section, we introduced networking hardware.

Two types of hardware are most commonly used to network computers: Ethernet and serial ports. Ethernet is the preferred hardware for networking computers that are in the same locale; serial ports and modems are used to connect a machine to a remote host — usually, an Internet service provider.

Networking software for Ethernet uses the frame that the protocols that define Ethernet describe for that system. However, TCP/IP itself defines two different protocols for organizing the bits that flow through a serial port into frames: the Serial Line Internet Protocol (SLIP) and the Point-to-Point Protocol (PPP). The latter is more sophisticated and preferred; however, SLIP is still used, usually for internal purposes.

Networking Software

To conclude our networking primer, we discuss how TCP/IP networking is implemented under the Linux operating system.

This section gives an overview of how Linux implements TCP/IP. We discuss this topic at much greater length in Chapter 3, when we describe how to install and configure networking software on your Linux system.

For simplicity, we discuss how Linux implements each tier of the TCP/IP stack. Our discussion goes from the bottom up – that is, beginning with the network-access tier, and working up to the application tier.

Network-Access Tier

The network-access tier interacts with hardware to transport datagrams from one host to another. In practice, this means transporting datagrams over serial lines via the SLIP or PPP protocols, or over Ethernet using the standard Ethernet protocol.

The implementation of this tier has two aspects:

◆ *Modules* that implement the protocols used by this tier

◆ *Drivers* that let the Linux kernel interact with the hardware on your machine

We discuss each aspect in turn.

MODULES
The software programs that implement the PPP, SLIP, and Ethernet protocols are implemented as modules. These modules are compiled and linked into the Linux kernel. In Chapter 3, we show how to do that.

The Ethernet module also manages the linking of the Ethernet device (and its address) with your Linux box's IP address.

The PPP and SLIP modules include software for conversing with a remote host, to establish a connection with the Internet. This includes managing *dynamic IP addresses* – that is, when an Internet service provider (ISP) assigns an IP address to your host when you dial into the ISP.

DRIVERS
Each variety of hardware has its own way to interact with your computer: its own timings, its own "magic values," and its own set of registers. Your Linux kernel uses a special software module, called a *driver*, to talk with a particular type of hardware.

Linux comes with drivers for practically every kind of hardware available on your computer. These include drivers for serial devices (and thus, for modems), and drivers for nearly every variety of Ethernet cards.

When you compile your Linux kernel, you have to tell the configuration script just what hardware you have. We show you in Chapter 3 how to do this.

Internet and Host-to-Host Tiers

The software for the Internet tier and the protocols on the host-to-host tier are implemented as modules that are compiled and linked into the Linux kernel.

The program that builds the Linux kernel includes these modules automatically when you tell it that you want to use TCP/IP networking. At the risk of sounding repetitious, we discuss in Chapter 3 how to do this.

Application Tier

The application tier assembles the content that is transmitted over the network. Given that many different kinds of data are transmitted over a network – Web pages, mail messages, terminal emulation, file transfers, and so on – this tier consists of many programs. However, the programs can be assembled into either of two categories.

- ◆ *Clients* – A client is a program that initiates an exchange of data over a network. The transaction may be the transmission of a mass of data from one host to another, such as when a mail message is transmitted from one host to another; or the transaction may be a request for data, as when a Web browser requests a Web page from a remote host. Often – though not always – a client also interacts with a human user.

- ◆ *Servers* – A server is a program that services requests from clients. What a server does depends upon the application protocol that it implements. Some protocols require that the server receive and process a mass of data; for example, receive and process a mail message. Other protocols require that a server fulfill a request; for example, return a requested Web page.

Much of this book discusses how to configure and run clients and servers. We'll discuss each in turn briefly.

CLIENTS

Clients are standalone programs that are invoked either by a user or by a program that the user is using. A Web browser, for example, interacts directly both with a user and the network. On the other hand, a mailer like elm or pine interacts with the user, but invokes a mail router like sendmail or smail to forward mail to the appropriate host or mailbox. The mail router then determines how the mail is to be transmitted: over a TCP/IP connection, a UUCP connection (UUCP being an obsolete form of networking that was once commonly used on UNIX systems), or some other form of transmission.

We discuss clients throughout this book, particularly in Chapter 4.

SERVERS

Servers often are implemented as a *daemon* – a program that runs continually and that "listens" for a given event. In the case of a program that works over a network, a daemon listens to a well-known port, as previously described.

Given the proliferation of networking programs, having a daemon for each application would be difficult to manage. For this reason, a master daemon has been invented: the `inet` daemon. This daemon listens to all sockets – or to all the ports you tell it to listen to. When it "hears" a datagram arriving on a given port, it invokes the appropriate server and lets it handle the incoming data. In this way, you can have one daemon managing your network services.

We discuss daemons and `inet` in much more detail in Chapters 3 and 7.

Summary

This chapter gives a brief primer on networking. In this chapter, we discussed the following:

- What a *network* is, and the tasks it must perform. To illustrate, we discussed a network that practically everyone has used: the telephone system.

- What a *protocol* is, and why it is important to have a well-defined set of rules for performing a given networking task.

- What the *TCP/IP* family of protocols are, and how they are used as the basis of the global computer network called the Internet.

- What the Internet is, how it operates, and who manages it.

- What the TCP/IP "layer cake" is, and what each tier does: the *application tier*, the *host-to-host tier*, the *Internet tier*, and the *network-access tier*.

◆ Which hardware is used to implement networking, and the protocols that are used to manage the flow of data over those devices.

◆ Finally, how TCP/IP networking is implemented under the Linux operating system.

Part II

Installing Networking

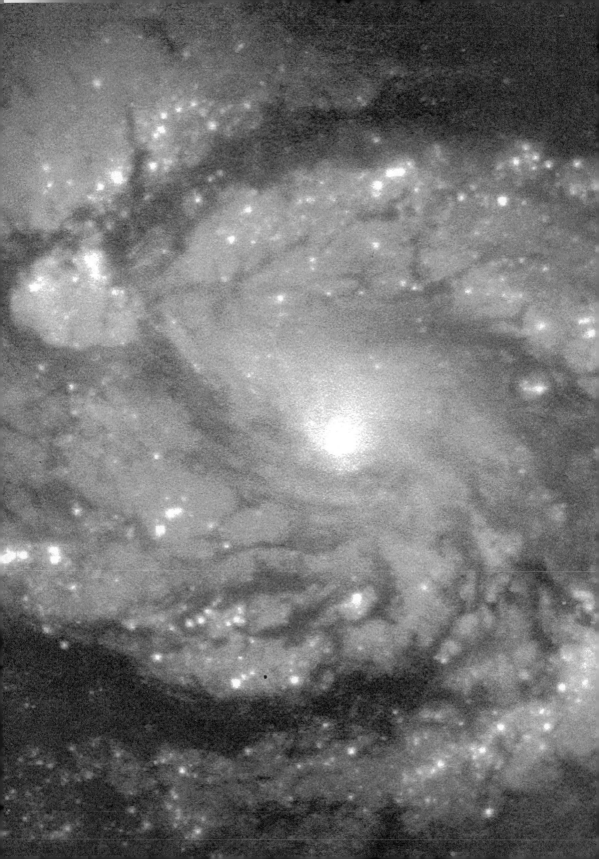

Chapter 2

Adding Networking to Your Linux System Hardware

IN THIS CHAPTER

- ◆ Installing hardware
- ◆ Selecting an Internet service provider

IN CHAPTER 1, we presented the theory and design of TCP/IP networking, which is the basis for the Linux operating system's implementation of networking. Now the time has come to start turning theory into reality on your Linux workstation.

This chapter and Chapter 3 together present the basics of adding networking to your Linux workstation. As we explained in the introduction to Part II, we assume that at this point in your exploration of networking, you have a single Linux workstation that you want to attach to an existing network. This existing network may be either the Internet, which you access via a modem connection to an Internet service provider, or a local intranet that you access through Ethernet. You need to know the basic information presented in this chapter and Chapter 3, even if you intend to perform more-sophisticated networking, such as building your own intranet.

In this chapter, we discuss how to install the following hardware, which your Linux box will use to communicate with the network:

- ◆ A modem to connect with an Internet service provider
- ◆ An Ethernet card to connect with a local intranet

At the end of this chapter, we discuss some of the details of selecting an Internet service provider.

Installing Hardware

In this section, we discuss how to install networking hardware into your Linux workstation. We cover three major topics:

◆ How to allocate your computer's resources to the devices you add to it

◆ How to install a modem onto your system

◆ How to install an Ethernet card into your system

System Resources

As you probably are aware, the IBM PC (from which most personal computers descended) was designed over 15 years ago. This design, called *ISA*, has worn remarkably well, given its age. However, the ISA PC's design has various limitations that can make adding new peripheral devices difficult. In particular, the ISA PC has limited numbers of DMA channels and interrupts, and limited memory for buffers. If you are fortunate enough to be using a PCI-based personal computer, which is a later, more sophisticated design than ISA, you do not have to deal with the problem of allocating system resources. However, if you have a standard ISA PC, then you must assign your machine's resources carefully: every peripheral device must receive the resources it needs, and no two peripheral devices can use the same resource.

In the rest of this section, we discuss what these resources are, and how you can manage their allocation.

INTERRUPTS

An *interrupt* is a channel by which the computer's central processing unit (CPU) communicates with another physical device. Each peripheral device must have its own interrupt, so the CPU can communicate with the device, without interfering with other peripheral devices. Some peripheral devices, such as an SCSI interface card, can parcel out information received via one interrupt among numerous physical devices; most physical devices, however, need their own interrupt.

An ISA PC has 16 *interrupt channels* (or *IRQs*) built into it. Each IRQ is assigned a number, from 0 through 15. Table 2-1 gives the standard assignment of IRQs.

TABLE 2-1 PC INTERRUPTS

IRQ	Assignment
0	System timer
1	Keyboard controller

Continued

IRQ	Assignment
2	Second IRQ controller
3	Serial port 1 (COM2)
4	Serial port 2 (COM1)
5	Line printer 2 (LPT2)
6	Floppy-disk controller (controls two disks)
7	Line printer 1 (LPT1)
8	Real-time clock
9	Redirected IRQ2
10	Unused
11	Unused
12	Motherboard (PS/2) mouse port
13	Mathematics coprocessor
14	Hard-disk (IDE) controller 1 (controls two disks)
15	Hard-disk (IDE) controller 2 (controls two disks)

As you can see from this table, few IRQs are available for peripheral devices. If your machine uses a serial mouse rather than a bus mouse, then that frees up an IRQ for your use; likewise, if you rejumper to your system's peripheral-controller card so that it uses only one parallel port, that frees up a another IRQ. Still, if you add a sound card, standalone CD-ROM device, and Ethernet card, you pretty much have exhausted the interrupts available on your machine.

Most peripheral devices can be configured to use one of a limited number of IRQs. The need to select a device that uses a particular IRQ may limit the equipment that you can use.

To assign the IRQs for your peripheral devices, we suggest that you create on paper a chart of your system's resources, as follows:

1. Write down the available IRQs, from 0 through 15. For each IRQ, write down the peripheral device in your Linux workstation that now uses it. If you are not sure, use Table 2-1 to help you. When you finish, you will know which IRQs have been used and which are available.

2. For each peripheral device that you intend to install, write down the IRQs that it can take.

3. Compare the available IRQs with the IRQs recognized by each peripheral device that you will be installing. Assign available IRQs to devices. When you assign an IRQ, be sure to add it to your list of IRQ assignments.

You may have to juggle the IRQs used by your peripheral devices. You may also have to remove some unused peripheral devices – for example, the second parallel port.

PORT ADDRESSES

The vast range of port addresses makes it impossible to provide a chart similar to that for interrupts. At the same time, the vast range simplifies the problem somewhat, because finding an unassigned port for a given device is easier.

Large ranges of ports are available that are not assigned to commonly installed PC hardware. Most card manufacturers have done a good job of fitting their cards into these ranges of ports.

In the case of I/O ports, your biggest problem is making sure that you do not reuse a port that you have assigned to another card. To avoid this, we again suggest that you write on paper the port addresses used by all hardware on your machine. This information is found in the documentation that comes with your hardware. Then you can chart the ports that are used by each peripheral device you want to install, and assign ports to each device.

BUFFER ADDRESSES

The range of memory addresses for buffers is also restricted. When IBM designed the PC, it reserved the range of addresses from 640K to 1024K for expansion-card memory buffers. An expansion card must map into this area all RAM (random-access memory) buffers and ROM (read-only memory) BIOSs (basic input/output systems) that it needs for control. For example, an SVGA video card typically reserves addresses 640K to 704K for graphics RAM, 704K to 768K for text RAM, and 768K to 800K for the video BIOS. This leaves 224K for ROMs and RAM buffers.

The limited amount of buffer space can become a problem if you want to add several devices that use large amounts of buffer space – for example, an SCSI card, a network card, and a multiport serial card.

Again, your best approach to solving any conflicts over RAM involves understanding the resources you have and the resources that you need.

To begin, prepare a table (like the tables you prepared for IRQs and port addresses) that shows how buffer addresses are already allocated on your machine. This will show you how much buffer memory is available for peripherals.

Then, consult the documentation that comes with your peripheral cards. Jot down the buffer addresses that can be used for each card; then, assign buffers to each card. You may have to reconfigure one or all of your devices – either by rejumpering them or by using their configuration programs – to ensure that each card uses the buffer space that you have allocated to it.

This process of allocating resources on paper may seem tedious to you. However, we guarantee that some attention to planning, before you start installing hardware, will save you all manner of difficulty in the future.

CONFIGURING CARDS

Once you have assigned on paper the resources you will be assigning to each peripheral card, you must configure the card itself to use those resources.

Some peripheral cards can be configured by using *jumpers*. Jumpers are literally switches on the card that you close or leave open by inserting or removing *jumper caps*. Jumpers are used on most types of controller cards, such as the card that controls your hard disk. However, most modern peripheral devices (particularly Ethernet cards and internal modems) are configured through a configuration program, which probably runs only under MS-DOS. Thus, to configure your peripheral cards, you probably have to boot MS-DOS on your computer. Hopefully, you still have an MS-DOS boot disk available so that you can boot MS-DOS on your machine.

Newer Plug-and-Play cards can be configured with the Linux ISAPNP package. Currently, however, this package is experimental, so we caution users to avoid cards that are exclusively Plug-and-Play.

PLUGGING IN A CARD

If you have never plugged a card into a PC bus, you are well advised to ask an experienced friend or colleague to show you how to do it. If you have no such experienced friend or colleague, then keep the following points in mind:

1. Before you open up your computer, shut down Linux; then turn off your computer and unplug it.

2. When pressing the card into its slot, make sure that it is lined up correctly; then press down on the card, firmly but gently, until it snaps into the slot. The motherboard may flex *slightly* as you press the card into its slot.

3. Make sure that the card is pressed all the way into its slot. You can tell when it is all the way in, because the L-shaped metal strip at the back end of the card will be pressed flush with the metal strip that runs along the back of the machine.

4. When you are certain that the card is seated properly in its slot, screw down the card's metal strip to the chassis. This step is important, because this strip grounds the card. If you do not screw it down, it will not be grounded properly, and an electrical problem may short out your motherboard.

5. Make sure that you have retrieved any screws or other metal bits that may have dropped into the machine as you installed the card.

After the card is in place, replace the lid of your computer and screw it down before you plug in your machine and power it up again.

This concludes our discussion of topics that are common to all cards. We now move on to discuss in detail two varieties of networking devices: modems and Ethernet cards.

Installing a Modem

The word *modem* is a contraction of the term *modulator/demodulator*. In brief, a modem is a device that translates digital data into analogue signals that can be transmitted over a telephone line, and translates analogue signals back into digital data when receiving information.

The speed with which a modem can transmit data is measured in thousands (kilo) of bits per second (Kbps). Please note that bits per second should be divided by eight to get the maximum bytes per second that a modem can transmit; thus, a 28.8 Kbps modem can transmit a maximum of approximately 3,500 bytes per second. Given the overhead of transmission and of the networking protocols, the actual amount of useful data that a 28.8 Kbps modem can transmit in a second is considerably less than 3,500 bytes.

Currently, 56 Kbps modems are becoming popular. Unfortunately, these modems use two competing – and mutually exclusive – protocols. Before you buy one of these modems, make sure that your ISP supports the device you want to buy.

Finally, a class of modems called *winwave* or *mwave* modems are available. These modems do not use a serial port. However, you should avoid these devices because, currently, no Linux driver has been written for them.

INTERNAL VERSUS EXTERNAL   Modems come in two varieties: internal and external. The *internal* modem is a card that you plug directly into a slot in your computer's motherboard. The *external* modem is a little box that plugs via a cable into one of your machine's serial ports.

Each type of modem has its advantages and disadvantages:

◆ *Internal modem* – Generally $10 to $20 cheaper than an external modem. An internal modem does not require an external power supply, nor does it take up space on your desk. However, to install it, you must open your computer and plug the modem into the motherboard. The internal modem does not have a bank of lights, so it is harder to tell what the modem is doing or what its state is. Finally, because an internal modem is, in effect, another serial port that you are installing into your machine, you have to execute some specific commands to avoid having it conflict with your existing serial ports.

◆ *External modem* – More expensive than the internal modem. An external modem takes up space on your desk, and it requires a separate power supply, which means having one more cable snaking around your desk, and one more power outlet you must find. However, installation is easy – you just plug it into a serial port – and it presents no chance of conflicts with your existing serial hardware. Finally, most modems have a bank of lights that describe its state and what it's doing. These lights make diagnosing what the modem is doing much easier.

You should select the type of modem that best suits your needs and pocketbook. If price is not your paramount consideration, and you want simplicity of installation and configuration, then get an external modem. However, if you don't mind a more complex installation, and saving a few dollars is important to you, then the internal modem is the way to go.

Remember, too, that both types of modem require a telephone outlet nearby.

We also suggest that if you are going to use your modem frequently, you should consider installing a telephone line that is dedicated to the modem. If you are setting up your computer at home, having a second telephone line is almost a necessity. You should consider this when calculating the cost of your Internet connection.

As we mentioned, modems work through your Linux system's serial ports. Therefore, before we talk about installing the modem, we must backtrack a bit and discuss how Linux manages serial ports.

SERIAL PORTS

A *serial port* is a character device that transmits a stream of bytes serially. Because the modem works through a serial port, your serial hardware – and your configuration of the serial ports – seriously affect how well your modem works.

HARDWARE   All serial ports use a chip called a *universal asynchronous receiver and transmitter*, or UART. The industry-standard UART is manufactured by National Semiconductor. Numerous models of National UARTs are used by manufacturers: some use the less-expensive National 16450 UART, but to get acceptable performance from modern, high-speed modems, you must use a serial port that has a National 16550 UART, or a later model.

A few other companies manufacture UARTs. However, these usually are designed to emulate one of the National Semiconductor UARTs, and serial hardware that use these manufacturers' UARTs state in their documentation which National Semiconductor part it is emulating.

In years past, parallel ports, serial ports, and disk controllers each had their own peripheral card. Now they commonly are all combined into one controller card. Check the card's documentation; if your controller card does not use or emulate the National Semiconductor 16550 UART (or later model), then you should either replace the card or purchase an internal modem (which has its own UART). If your computer has serial ports built into the motherboard, check the documentation and see which UART the motherboard uses. If it does not use or emulate the 16550 or a later-model UART, then you should consider getting an internal modem. After all, spending hundreds of dollars purchasing Internet service and a high-speed modem, only to have its performance strangled by a cheap UART, doesn't make sense.

DEVICE NAMES   An IBM-style PC can support up to four serial ports, named COM1 through COM4.

When you install an internal modem, part of the configuration is to tell the modem which serial port to use. This cannot conflict with an existing serial port — for example, you cannot have two devices identified as COM2.

Under Linux, the special files through which the serial ports are accessed are named (rather confusingly) /dev/cua0 (for serial port COM1) through /dev/cua3 (for serial port COM4).

ASSIGNMENT OF INTERRUPTS   As stated in our earlier discussion of interrupts, serial port COM1, by default, is assigned IRQ 4, and serial port COM2 is assigned IRQ 3.

For historical reasons, no standard IRQs are assigned to serial ports COM3 and COM4. Rather, COM3 is assigned the same interrupt as COM1, and COM4 the same interrupt as COM2; and operating systems are expected to manage these ports through a technique called *polling*.

Linux does not support polling. Therefore, if you add a third serial port to your system — usually by adding an internal modem — you must find a free IRQ for that third port, and then use the command setserial to tell the Linux kernel which IRQ that third serial port uses.

The lesson is that, if possible, you should avoid adding a third serial port to your system. If you are using an internal modem, and one of the existing serial ports on your system is idle, you should (if possible) turn it off, usually by jumpering its controller, and then configure the internal modem to take the place of the device you have turned off. Jumpers are described later in the chapter.

MUX CARDS   A MUX card is a multiport serial card. With a MUX card, you can plug a bank of modems into your Linux system.

The Linux kernel supports a large variety of popular MUX cards — as you will see in the next chapter, when we discuss how to reconfigure the Linux kernel. If you intend to run more than one modem into your Linux system (perhaps to support dial-in as well as dial-out), then you should consider a MUX card. See the references at the end of this chapter for sources of more information.

INSTALLING AN EXTERNAL MODEM

When you boot your Linux system, the kernel's serial-port driver configures COM1 and COM2 automatically. Installation of an external modem is simple: plug it into a serial port. You probably will have to supply a cable with the appropriate number of pins and appropriate sex on each side.

To test whether your system is communicating with the modem, type the following command:

```
echo AT > /dev/cuan
```

where *n* is the number of the device, from 0 (COM1) through 3 (COM4). When you execute this command, you should see a light blink on the modem. If nothing happens, check the following:

- ◆ You are using the correct serial device.

- ◆ The modem's DIP switches are correctly set for the port. (For details on setting the DIP switches, see the manual that came with your modem.)

- ◆ The cable is secure and the modem is turned on.

Once you have guaranteed that you can communicate with the modem, we suggest that you use command `setserial` to reset the serial port to its highest possible speed:

```
/bin/setserial /dev/cuan baud_base 115200 spd_vhi
```

where *n* is the number of the port's device, from 0 (COM1) through 3 (COM4). Argument `baudbase 115200` sets the base baud rate for the port to 115200, which is the maximum that can be processed by the 16550 UART. Argument `spd_vhi` ensures that the port is always opened at the maximum speed, regardless of the speed at which the application opens the port.

We suggest that you write this command into file `/etc/rc.d/rc.local`, so that the serial port is set automatically when you reboot your Linux system.

For details on `setserial`, see its main page.

INSTALLING AN INTERNAL MODEM

Installing an internal modem is more complicated than installing an external modem. We walk you through this process in this section.

SELECTING AN IRQ As we mentioned earlier, installing an internal modem is, in effect, the same as installing another serial port into your machine. Finding a free IRQ for this third serial port may be a problem.

For this reason, if one of the serial ports on your computer is unused, you may want to rejumper its controller card so that the port is disabled. That will free up that COM port and its IRQ for use by the internal modem.

If you cannot disable a serial port, you must find an IRQ that is not in use and that is usable by your internal modem. (Most internal modems are designed to use no more than three or four possible IRQs. To find the IRQs supported by your internal modem, see its documentation.) This may require some shuffling of IRQs among your existing peripheral devices, to free up an IRQ that can be used by the modem.

CONFIGURE THE CARD   Most internal-modem cards can be configured by running a custom-configuration program. This program, naturally, runs only under MS-DOS, so you probably have to boot DOS on your machine to run this program.

The configuration program varies quite a bit from one manufacturer to another. Most programs, however, ask you for the following information:

◆ The number of the serial port you are assigning to this device. If the modem is taking the place of another serial port that you have disabled, enter that COM port (either COM1 or COM2); otherwise, enter COM3 or COM4.

◆ The IRQ to use. Enter the IRQ you selected for this device.

◆ The base address for that IRQ. Select the default value.

As we described earlier, if you are setting the serial port to COM3 or COM4, you have to use the command `setserial` to reset the port's IRQ. To do so, use the following form of `setserial`:

```
/bin/setserial /dev/cuan irq I baud_base 115200 spd_vhi
```

As before, *n* gives the number of the serial port (remember, `/dev/cua2` is for COM3, and `/dev/cua3` is for COM4). Option `irq` indicates that you are resetting the IRQ of this port. *I* gives the number of the IRQ to which you are resetting the port.

Please be careful when you are using this command. If you set the IRQ to that which is already used by another device, you will lock up your Linux system.

ENABLING A MODEM FOR DIAL-IN

You may want to set up your modem so that users can dial in as well as dial out. This is called *enabling* the port.

Before you think about letting people dial into your machine from the outside world, you must take at least some rudimentary steps to protect your system against intruders. Make sure every account is protected by a password, and that each user's password is not an obvious one. This particularly applies to the account for the superuser `root`. For more information on security, see Chapter 10.

To enable a serial port on your Linux system, you must first tell your modem to answer the telephone for an incoming call. To do so, use the following command:

```
echo "ATS0=1" | /dev/ttySn
```

The string ATSO=1 is the standard modem instruction that tells it to answer the telephone on the first ring. *n* is the number of the serial port, from 0 (COM1) through 3 (COM4). (Under Linux, the devices /dev/ttyS0 through /dev/ttyS3 are used for incoming traffic on the serial ports.)

Next, you must tell edit file /etc/inittab to turn on the program agetty to "listen" to the port. The standard version of this file contains the following entries:

```
#d1:12345:respawn:/sbin/agetty -mt60 38400,19200,9600,2400,1200
 ttyS0 vt100
#d2:12345:respawn:/sbin/agetty -mt60 38400,19200,9600,2400,1200
 ttyS1 vt100
```

If your modem is plugged into serial port COM1, uncomment the line that begins d1 (that is, remove the pound sign (#) from the beginning of it); if the modem is plugged into serial port COM2, uncomment the line that begins d2. If your modem uses serial ports COM3 or COM4, do the following:

1. Copy the line that begins with d2.

2. Change the d2 to d3 or d4, as appropriate.

3. Change ttyS1 to ttyS2 or ttyS4, as appropriate.

4. Uncomment the line.

5. To bring your change into effect, reboot your system.

For details on inittab and agetty, see their respective manual pages.

We suggest, by the way, that you investigate by using the command mgetty to manage your dial-in ports. mgetty offers various features that are quite useful, including support for FAX modems.

This concludes our discussion of modems. We now move on to discuss how to install an Ethernet card into your Linux system.

Installing an Ethernet Card

In Chapter 1, we introduced Ethernet, including how it works and how it can be configured to suit a variety of media. In particular, we discussed the differences between Ethernet that uses thin-coaxial cable as its connection medium (called *thin-coax* Ethernet), and Ethernet that uses 8-strand copper cable as the medium (called *twisted-pair* Ethernet).

In this section, we discuss some of the issues that relate to selecting and installing an Ethernet card.

SELECTING A CARD

Ethernet equipment comes in a wide variety of price ranges and types. The choices can be bewildering. The equipment to buy depends upon your needs and the network to which you are connecting your machine.

If you are connecting your machine to an existing network, then you should purchase the card recommended by that network's administrator.

However, if you are setting up a small intranet in your home or office, you should consider purchasing an inexpensive "clone" card, such as one that clones the popular Novell NE2000 card. The performance of such cards is not as good as the more expensive name-brand cards, but you probably will find it to be sufficient for your purposes.

If you are connecting your card to a thin-coax network, you should, if possible, purchase a card that has both thin-coax and twisted-pair connections. This helps ensure that if you upgrade your network to twisted-pair, you will not have to scrap your cards.

INSTALLING A CARD

Installing an Ethernet card is relatively straightforward, compared with installing an internal modem.

As with a modem or serial device, you must allocate system resources to the Ethernet card: interrupt, port address, and memory buffer. To see which resources can be used by the card, check the documentation that comes with it. You have to consult your records to see which resources are available on your system. If no match exists between the resources available on your system and those that can be used by the Ethernet card, you may have to do some reconfiguration of your existing cards, in order to free an IRQ or port that can be used by your card.

Older Ethernet cards can be configured through jumpers. However, most current cards require that you run a configuration program under MS-DOS. For details, see the documentation that came with your card.

This concludes our discussion of how to install networking hardware. The rest of this chapter discusses a related topic: how to shop for an Internet service provider.

Frame Relay

Frame relay is another method of moving data from one point to another, such as from your local network to an ISP. It is a service that is purchased from the telephone company.

To summarize how frame relay works, it exchanges data in the manner that the telephone company uses. The telephone company allocates 64K of bandwidth for any telephone conversation between two switches. In frame relay, the telephone company uses its digital codes and a method of encapsulation that carries data to create a virtual circuit between two points served by their switches. This virtual circuit has a guaranteed minimum bandwidth on it. Frame relay is cheaper than a dedicated line because no wire is pulled or connected, and because the telephone company does not guarantee the route that your packets will take over its network.

To run frame relay, you need a frame relay card inside your Linux box, or you can use a frame relay-to-Ethernet router. The discussion of setting up a frame relay card is beyond the scope of this book. If you are interested in frame relay, we recommend that you purchase a frame relay-to-Ethernet router.

If you want more information on how the telephone company encodes data moved over telephone lines, see the sidebar on 56 Kbps modems in this chapter.

Selecting an Internet Service Provider

Now that you have installed your hardware, one other task remains that you must consider – at least if you are going to use a dial-up connection for the Internet: selecting the Internet service provider that will connect you to the Internet.

An *Internet service provider* (ISP) is a company that provides access to the Internet. Basically, this company has purchased Internet access in bulk from a telephone company, via one or more high-speed connections, and now offers access via one or more computers running server software, and a bank of modems and telephone lines. Customers can dial into the ISP's computer, connect with it via PPP or SLIP, and then gain access through that computer to the entire Internet.

ISPs vary wildly, from a couple of kids with a PC in their basement, to corporate giants like Ameritech. The number and variety of services you can obtain, both from ISPs and from your local telephone company, also vary greatly from one region of the United States to another.

If you live in a major technology center, such as San Francisco or Chicago, you have a great variety of vendors and services to choose among. However, if you live in rural Wyoming (for example), your choices are considerably fewer.

You should pick an ISP carefully, because switching from one ISP to another is difficult and expensive. When you switch, you can (at the very least) count on your e-mail being interrupted, and you have to pay set-up fees. The costs of connecting to the Internet can also vary greatly from one provider to another. So, shopping carefully for an ISP is worth your while.

In this section, we discuss some of the questions you should ask ISPs as you shop for Internet service. We also discuss whether you should obtain your own Internet domain, and if so, how you can get one.

Catalogue Your Needs

Before you begin shopping, you should catalogue what you need:

- What kind of modem do you have – 56 Kbps or 28.8 Kbps?

- Do you want your own domain?

- How much connectivity do you need – a few minutes a day, several hours, or a continual connection? Be sure to use high estimates: once you get your system onto the Internet, you probably will use it much more than you expect – at least at first.

- Do you want a login account on the provider's machine? This is helpful, for several reasons:

  - If you cannot connect to the Internet for any reason, you have another route by which you can access the Internet, and communicate with your ISP.

  - Most ISPs that give you a login account let you set up a personal Web page in that account. This lets you set up your Web page, should you want one, without the hassle (and risk) of setting up an HTTP daemon on your machine.

As we were writing this book, two 56 Kbps modem quasi-standards were available on the marketplace: X2 from US Robotics (now 3Com) and K56 Flex from Rockwell. With two mutually incompatible quasi-standards battling in the marketplace and 56 Kbps not being as large a step as the numbers suggest, it was a safe bet to wait for the market to declare one standard the winner before upgrading. At this point in time, however, a standard has been decided upon; so in our opinion, a 56 Kbps modem is now a worthy upgrade.

From the outside you can treat a 56 Kbps modem just like any other modem by setting your serial baud rate at four times the transmission rate of the modem, or its highest setting, to allow for compression. You may be interested in the magic that makes a 56 Kbps modem work, however. A 56 Kbps modem is really a 33.6 Kbps analogue modem with the ability to receive digital signals directly from the telephone company's switch when the wiring between them will permit it. With a 33.6 Kbps modem, data is sent onto the telephone line as a series of analogue tones. These tones are received by the telephone company's switch and sampled into a set of digital signals by a process called analogue-to-digital (A/D) conversion. The resulting digital signals are sent to your ISP's switch, converted back from digital to analogue and sent on the telephone line that connects to this modem.

For 33.6 Kbps and slower modems, this process happens to data transmitted in either direction. However, 56 Kbps modems are a hybrid. In one direction they are analogue, like a regular 33.6 Kbps modem. In the other direction, they are digital devices capable of using most of the digital signals that the telephone company uses to send data between its switches. The telephone company uses 8-bit samples gathered at a rate of 8,000 samples per second to digitize communications between switches. This maps to 64,000 distinct digital signals per second between switches for each connection. The telephone network is designed to carry digitized voice communications, not raw digital data, so tones that are too close to each other to distinguish on a noisy telephone line are eliminated. This reduces the transmission bandwidth to 56 Kbps. Furthermore, some tones would not normally occur in a voice communication, and would require more power to transmit than the FCC's power limitation for voice telephony. These tones are also eliminated, restricting the real transmission bandwidth of a 56 Kbps modem to 53 Kbps. The way 56 Kbps modems are designed, your uplink to your ISP's modem is analogue and limited to 33.6 Kbps. If your telephone wiring will allow it, your downlink from your ISP is digital, so you can receive at up to 53 Kbps.

Whether or not you can use this technology depends upon the quality of the telephone wiring to your computer. If you are in an area where you can use this technology at all, it works well enough that you will notice a difference in download speed. And with the price of 56 Kbps modems less than $120, you cannot really go wrong, because at worst a 56 Kbps modem will perform exactly the same as a 33.6 Kbps modem. However, if are considering upgrading a 33.6 Kbps modem and you really want to know whether or not you can use a 56 Kbps modem, you can test your line using a service set up by 3Com. To do this from a terminal emulator (such as minicom), dial the 3Com Line Test facility at 1-888-877-9248. Answer no or yes to use graphics as appropriate (use no if you cannot tell) and log in using a first name of "LINE" and a last name of "TEST". Your telephone line will be tested for 56 Kbps compatibility and you'll know if it's time to run out to the computer store.

Talk with the ISP

Once you have cataloged what you need from your ISP, check your local Yellow Pages or other business directory, make a list of the local providers, and then talk with each one that looks promising. When you talk with the ISP's representative, you should ask her the following questions:

RELIABILITY

The most important questions concern the reliability of the ISP. You should ask the ISP:

◆ How long have you been in business?

- ◆ What are your hardware resources?

- ◆ What are your resources for connecting to the Internet?

- ◆ What are your resources for dialing in?

- ◆ How frequently do your dial-up customers run into busy signals? (Do not expect an ISP to answer this question candidly; you may want to poll your friends or your local computer society.)

SERVICES

The following questions concern whether the ISP can do what you need done. You should ask the ISP:

- ◆ Do you have a point of presence (POP) in my local telephone exchange? (This is very important: If the ISP does not have a POP in your telephone exchange, you may have to make a long-distance or a metered call to connect to it, which will run up your telephone bill very quickly. Tell the ISP your telephone number; if it does not have a POP within a local telephone call of you, or if it does not know, then you should look elsewhere.)

- ◆ Do you support PPP connectivity? (If not, you won't be able to use that ISP.)

- ◆ Do you have any experience working with Linux or UNIX? (This is not an iron-clad requirement, but it certainly is helpful if your ISP knows about UNIX and can help you with UNIX/Linux-related problems.)

- ◆ Do I get a login account on your server machine? (Some ISPs include a login account as a standard part of their package; others charge extra for it. The login account is helpful, though not a requirement.)

- ◆ Can you manage a domain for me? By managing a domain, we mean the following:

  - ▪ Apply to the InterNIC for a domain name for you. Route to your machine all mail sent to your domain.

  - ▪ Will you give me a static IP address, or do you assign IP addresses dynamically? (Most ISPs charge extra for a static IP address. Linux handles either quite smoothly.)

  - ▪ What sort of technical support do you offer? Is somebody in the office all the time, or do you answer the telephone only during business hours?

- Do you support other forms of connectivity besides modems, such as ISDN and frame-relay services? (You may not want to purchase these services at this time, but it is good to know that the ISP is up-to-date technologically.)

FEES AND CHARGES

Now comes crunch time: how much does the ISP charge? Check the following:

◆ What is the set-up fee for a new account?

◆ What sort of service plans do you offer? (Plans offered by ISPs will vary wildly: some offer unlimited connectivity for a flat fee per month; others offer metered connectivity; some mix the two – you get a set amount of connect time as part of your fee, with any connect time above that amount being metered and charged extra. You should select the plan that best meets your needs, based on your estimate of your connect time.)

◆ How much will I have to prepay my bill? (Unlike the telephone company, which bills for service you have already used, many ISPs require that you pre-pay your bill for upcoming time. Many also charge by the quarter (three months), but some offer a discount if you prepay for longer periods of time. Payment policy varies greatly from one ISP to another; for example, the larger ISPs, such as AT&T and MCI, do not prebill or charge by the quarter. Check what the ISP's policy is in this regard.)

◆ If I want my own domain, how much do you charge to do the paperwork and set it up for me? (You can do some of the paperwork yourself, but the ISP must provide some information, and they will charge you for it.)

◆ If I have a 56 Kbps modem, do you charge extra for supporting that equipment?

◆ If I want a vanity Web page on my login account, do you charge extra for that?

NOW CHOOSE

Once you narrow down the candidates to the ISP that provides the service you need at a price you can afford, check out that ISP: ask your friends or the local computer society whether that ISP provides good, reliable service. You may want to check with your local Better Business Bureau to see whether complaints have been registered against the company; however, Internet users tend to be a touchy lot, so you should take such complaints with a grain of salt.

If the ISP still looks attractive to you, give it a call and sign up.

Obtaining Domains and Addresses

You can even obtain your own Internet domain, if you want.

Having a domain of your own presents some advantages and some disadvantages. The advantages include the following:

♦ If you have a small business, or if your work is associated with the computer industry, your own domain ensures that you have a presence on the Internet.

♦ If you switch ISPs, you can reestablish your domain with the new ISP. This means that people can continue to send you electronic mail, without learning a new address for you.

The disadvantages principally relate to cost:

♦ The InterNIC charges $50 a year to maintain a domain, and demands a prepayment of $100 for the first two years.

♦ You need your ISP's cooperation to register your domain, and most ISPs charge a fee for this service. The usual charge is $50, but some charge more or less than that.

If you decide that the benefits of having a domain are worth the costs, you will find that obtaining a domain of your own is relatively easy.

SELECTING A DOMAIN NAME

Your first task is to select the domain's name. Most domains are, in fact, subdomains of the .com (as described in Chapter 1). A domain name can be no more than 15 characters long, and can include all alphabetic characters, numerals, and the hyphen (-).

For example, the following are some good domain names: myexample.com, microsoft.com, major-site.com, 3com.com.

The following domain names are not acceptable: thisisanextremelylongdomain name.com, my.domain.com, or 12345.com.

The InterNIC will not let you use any of George Carlin's seven words that you can't say on radio, but InterNIC's criteria are broad—some say too broad, as suggested by domains like kiddieporn.com, kidsex.com, and boyrape.com. (We are not making these up. The Internet, unfortunately, has become the global pornography superhighway.)

Once you pick your domain name, you must check whether that domain name is already taken by somebody else. The easiest way to check is to go to a Linux or UNIX machine that is connected to the Internet, and type the command whois, followed by the name of the domain you want to use. If the domain is already claimed by someone else, the InterNIC will tell you so. For example, if you type the command

```
whois whitehouse.gov
```

you see:

```
[rs.internic.net]
Executive Office of the President USA (WHITEHOUSE-HST)
 WHITEHOUSE.GOV

 198.137.241.30
Whitehouse Public Access (WHITEHOUSE-DOM)
 WHITEHOUSE.GOV
```

If the domain has not already been claimed, the InterNIC reports that it cannot find a reference to that domain in its database. For example, if you type the command `whois foobar.gov`, you see

```
[rs.internic.net]
No match for "FOOBAR.GOV".
```

and the InterNIC replies that this domain is not known.

If the domain you select has already been claimed by someone else, you must select another name.

Another way to check domain names is to access the InterNIC's Web page at `http://www.internic.net`. The Web page gives access to a form that lets you access the `whois` database a little more easily.

By the way, do not use a registered trademark or corporate name as your domain name. When the Internet first became known to the business world, some individuals registered corporate names as private domains, and then attempted to sell the domain names to those corporations. Some corporations paid, but others sued both the InterNIC and the individuals involved. So be warned: if you use a corporate name or registered trademark as a domain name, you probably will find yourself involved in a lawsuit.

REGISTERING A DOMAIN

To register a domain with the InterNIC, you must fill out a standard form with the InterNIC. This form can be obtained from URL:

```
ftp://rs.internic.net/templates/domain-template.txt
```

Or you can find the form on the InterNIC's Web page, `http://www. internic.net`, and fill it out interactively. The form is as follows:

```
[ URL ftp://rs.internic.net/templates/domain-template.txt ]
 [ 09/95 ]
******************* Please DO NOT REMOVE Version Number
   *********************
Domain Version Number: 2.0
*************** Please see attached detailed instructions
   *****************
******** Only for registrations under ROOT, COM, ORG, NET, EDU, GOV
   ********
0.    (N)ew (M)odify (D)elete....:
1.    Purpose/Description........:
2.    Complete Domain Name.......:
Organization Using Domain Name
3a.   Organization Name..........:
3b.   Street Address.............:
3c.   City.......................:
3d.   State......................:
3e.   Postal Code................:
3f.   Country....................:
Administrative Contact
4a.   InterNIC Handle (if known)......:
4b.   Name (Last, First).........:
4c.   Organization Name..........:
4d.   Street Address.............:
4e.   City.......................:
4f.   State......................:
4g.   Postal Code................:
4h.   Country....................:
4i.   Phone Number...............:
4j.   E-Mailbox..................:
Technical Contact
5a.   InterNIC Handle (if known)......:
5b.   Name (Last, First).........:
5c.   Organization Name..........:
5d.   Street Address.............:
5e.   City.......................:
5f.   State......................:
5g.   Postal Code................:
5h.   Country....................:
5i.   Phone Number...............:
5j.   E-Mailbox..................:
Billing Contact
6a.   InterNIC Handle (if known)......:
6b.   Name (Last, First).........:
6c.   Organization Name..........:
6d.   Street Address.............:
6e.   City.......................:
6f.   State......................:
6g.   Postal Code................:
6h.   Country....................:
6i.   Phone Number...............:
6j.   E-Mailbox..................:
Primary Name Server
7a.   Primary Server Hostname....:
```

```
7b.   Primary Server Netaddress..:
Secondary Name Server(s)
8a.   Secondary Server Hostname..:
8b.   Secondary Server Netaddress:
Invoice Delivery
9.    (E)mail (P)ostal...........:
```

Most of the entries are self-explanatory. The two most problematic entries are 7a and 7b. As mentioned in Chapter 1, the InterNIC requires that every domain have at least two connections to the Internet, and questions 7a and 7b ask for the names or IP addresses of the primary and secondary hosts that will pass data to your machine. Your ISP has to give you this information – which is why it must participate in registering your domain.

If you want, you can submit an incomplete form – that is, fill in all the information except questions 7a and 7b. This will register your domain name for you, so that nobody else can grab it. Later, your ISP's technical person can update the form and complete it for you.

However, if you are not in a rush, you might prefer to let your ISP fill in the form for you – after all, you will be paying it to do this for you, so you might as well get your money's worth.

If you change ISPs, for whatever reason, the new ISP will have to update your domain's registration to include the names of the new systems that will be routing datagrams to your machine. Your new ISP will charge you for performing that task.

This concludes our discussion of registering a domain name.

Summary

In this chapter, we discussed topics that relate to installing or managing networking hardware in your Linux workstation. These include the following:

- ◆ How to allocate resources on an ISA-bus PC

- ◆ How to install Ethernet cards, serial port, and modems into a PC

- ◆ How to select an Internet service provider

- ◆ How to apply for your own Internet domain

Chapter 3

Adding Networking Software to Your Linux System

IN THIS CHAPTER

- ◆ Adding networking to your Linux kernel
- ◆ Configuring the network
- ◆ Elementary troubleshooting
- ◆ Autodialing

AT THIS POINT, you have installed the networking hardware onto your Linux system — the modem or Ethernet card that physically runs networking.

In this chapter, we show you how to compile networking into your Linux system's kernel, and how to configure it. Then we test it, and debug it if necessary.

Although the people who created Linux have taken great pains to make the installation and configuration of the networking software as simple and as robust as possible, installing it is still a painstaking task. Please pay careful attention to the directions in this chapter.

In this chapter, we discuss the following topics:

- ◆ *How to recompile the Linux kernel* — Most important networking software is built directly into the Linux kernel. This section gives a step-by-step description of how to recompile the Linux kernel, in case you never have done this before.

- ◆ *How to perform elementary configuration* — This chapter tells you how to turn on networking when you boot your Linux system, and how to tell the networking software what to do when it is running.

- ◆ *How to write PPP scripts* — If you are using Point-to-Point Protocol (PPP) to communicate with your Internet service provider (ISP), then you have to write some scripts that tell the PPP software how to dial the modem

93

and connect with the provider. This is a rather complex task, and can be confusing for the new Linux user; in this chapter, we show you how to write such scripts, and also give you examples of scripts.

◆ *How to monitor your network* – This section describes the basic steps you can take when something isn't running as it should.

◆ *How to install autodialing* – Linux comes with a package that dials the telephone and makes a connection whenever you want to interact with a host on the Internet. This feature, while not necessary to running networking on your system, is a great convenience – especially if you are running an intranet, as we describe in Part II of this book. In this section, we describe how to set up and configure autodialing on your Linux system.

That being said, let's get to work.

Adding Networking to Your Linux Kernel

The *kernel* is the master program of the Linux operating system. The kernel provides resources to all other programs that you run under Linux, and manages all other programs as they run. The kernel has built into it code that performs certain specialized tasks, including TCP/IP networking. The kernel also includes special modules, called *drivers*, that manage physical devices. The kernel must contain a driver not only for each class of device (e.g., SCSI interfaces or sound cards), but often for each brand of device as well – because different brands of the same type of device often work in radically different ways.

It would be possible to include in the Linux kernel all possible code and all possible drivers. However, such a kernel would be extremely large – probably too large to run, and certainly so large that just running the kernel would drain most of your computer's resources. While the generic kernel that was installed as part of the installation process may work for you, it may contain drivers for hardware that you don't have. Therefore, the administrator of a Linux system should configure and compile a kernel to match the system that he is running. This kernel should include code to run all of the tasks that he wishes to support (such as networking), but nothing else; and it should include drivers for all of the hardware on his system – but only for that hardware, and nothing else.

Linux, unfortunately, cannot sense all of the hardware on your system and automatically configure itself for that hardware; instead, you must tell it what hardware you have. Further, Linux has no way to read your mind and discover what tasks you want to perform – again, you must tell it what you want to do. This task of telling Linux what code you want included in the kernel is called *configuring* the kernel.

In this section, we describe how to recompile your Linux kernel to include networking software. If you are a newcomer to Linux and have never rebuilt a kernel before, don't panic! We walk you through the entire process of configuring and compiling a Linux kernel. Rebuilding the kernel is a painstaking task, but you can do it even if you are a newcomer to Linux, as long as you are careful.

Preparations

The following are some tasks that you must perform *before* you start to configure your kernel.

INSTALL KERNEL SOURCES

To compile a kernel, you first must install the kernel sources onto your Linux system. Your release of Linux should include a full set of sources. If you did not install kernel sources when you installed Linux onto your system, check the documentation that came with your release, and follow its directions for installing kernel sources. (If you are not sure whether sources are installed onto your system, look in directory /usr/src/linux, which is the usual directory for storing kernel sources. If you see stuff in this directory, then you have the kernel sources.) If the release of Linux that you are using does not include kernel sources, or if a friend just installed a binary system onto your machine, we suggest that you consult with the person who installed Linux onto your system or with your local Linux guru and obtain a set of sources that are appropriate for the release of Linux that you are running.

As we noted in the introduction to this book, you must be running Linux release 2.0 or higher to use all of the software described in this book. If you are running a release of Linux older than release 2.0, you will still be able use this book, but some of the things we discuss won't be present or will not work; and we strongly suggest that you consider upgrading your system to the newest stable release.

The compiled kernel sources require about 35 megabytes of disk space; so make sure that you have at least that much disk space available before you install the kernel sources.

INSTALL CONFIGURATION FILE

If you are using the Slackware release of Linux for which this book is written, you need to obtain one additional file: the configuration file for the version of the kernel that you are running. The configuration file, which is always named .config, describes how your kernel is configured (not surprisingly). To find the configuration file for your kernel, do the following:

1. su to the superuser root.

2. Make sure that directory /cdrom exists. If it does not, use the command mkdir to create it.

3. Place your Slackware disk 1 into your CD-ROM drive; then mount it by typing the following command:

```
mount /dev/cdrom -t iso9660 /cdrom
```

4. Once you have found the directory for the kernel you are running, use command cd to enter it. Then type the following command:

```
cp .config /usr/src/linux
```

5. This will copy the configuration file .config for the kernel you are running into the directory that holds your Linux sources. Linux will then use this configuration file as its default when you rebuild your kernel. This will greatly improve your chances of rebuilding the kernel successfully.

HARDWARE LIST

The next step is rather more difficult: Take a piece of paper and write down information about the hardware in your system:

♦ *CPU:* Intel 80386, Intel 80486, Pentium, or a clone CPU.

♦ *Disk Controller:* Are you using an IDE controller? If so, what make and model is it? In particular, what chipset does it use?

♦ *CD-ROM:* Do you have a CD-ROM? If so, is it an ATAPI drive that is plugged into an IDE controller card? Or does it use a SCSI interface? Or does your CD-ROM uses a custom interface card? In this last instance, note the manufacturer and model of your CD-ROM, and the interrupts and ports that it uses.

♦ *SCSI Card:* Does your system have a SCSI interface card? (If you don't know, then your system probably does not have one.) If so, what company manufactured the card? What is the card's model number? What interrupt and ports does the card use?

♦ *SCSI Devices:* If your system has a SCSI card, what devices are plugged into it – disk, CD-ROM, tape?

♦ *Tape Devices:* Does your system have a tape drive? If so, what interface does it use – floppy-disk controller, ATAPI interface, SCSI interface? What company manufactured it? What is its model number?

♦ *Bus Mouse:* Does your system use a bus mouse? If so, what company manufactured the mouse? What mouse interface standard does it use (Microsoft or Logitech)?

♦ *Ports:* Does your system have a parallel port? Does it have serial ports? If so, how many of each does it have?

- ◆ *MUX Card:* Does your system have a multi-port serial card? (If you are not sure, then it does not.) If it does, what is the card's manufacturer and model?

- ◆ *Ethernet:* Does your computer have an Ethernet card installed into it? If so, who manufactured the card? What is its model number? What interrupts and ports does the card use? One point is especially important: many cheap "clone" cards emulate a popular brand-name card; in particular, the Novell NE-2000 card is emulated by "clone" Ethernet cards. If your card emulates another type of card, note the make and model of the card that it emulates.

If you are unsure on any of these points, check the documentation that came with your computer.

READ THIS SECTION

One last point: we strongly suggest that you read this section all the way through *before* you begin to configure your kernel.

If necessary, make notes directly into this book — preferably in red — to remind yourself of the hardware you have and the Linux features you want to use.

That being done, we are now ready to configure your kernel.

Configuring the Kernel

To configure a kernel, Linux uses scripts that run under the UNIX utility make. We use the config system of configuration scripts, partly because it is simple, and partly because it is common to all releases of Linux.

The script config uses a question-and-answer approach: it asks you a question, and you type y (for "yes") or n (for "no"). Some questions offer a third option, m; this is equivalent to y, but tells the system to implement that option as a module rather than building it into the kernel. (You will see in a moment what a *module* is.) If you need help with a given question, type ? and the script will display a brief explanation of what the question means.

Each question has a unique identifier that is in parentheses; for example, CON-FIG_FIREWALL is the identifier for whether or not you want to use a firewall on your system. (We discuss firewalls in Chapter 8.) If you look in file /usr/src/linux/.config, you will see that the configuration file consists of a set of these identifiers, some of which are commented out (that is, prefixed with a # character) and others are followed by =y (for "yes,") or =m (for "implement as a module"). We refer to each question by its identifier, to help you navigate through this process.

Each question is followed by the possible answers in square brackets. The default answer appears first, and is capitalized. The default answers are drawn from your

.config file — that is, the file used to build the kernel you are now running. To select the default answer, just press the Enter key. For example, consider the question:

```
Enable loadable module support (CONFIG_MODULES) [Y/n/?]
```

This question asks you whether you want your kernel to support loadable modules. CONFIG_MODULES is the identifier for this question. The possible answers are y for yes, n for no, or ? for help. To select the default answer (in this case, Y), press the Enter key. If you type ?, you see the following:

```
Kernel modules are small pieces of compiled code which can be
inserted in or removed from the running kernel, using the
programs insmod and rmmod. This is described in the file
Documentation/modules.txt. Modules can be device drivers, file
systems, binary executable formats, and so on. If you think that
you may want to make use of modules with this kernel in the future,
then say Y here. If unsure, say Y.
```

Unfortunately, if your finger slips and you type the wrong answer, there is no easy way to back up and answer a question again. If you make a mistake, your only recourse is to type control-C to abort configuration, and start over again. The point is: *Think before you type, then type carefully.*

We describe each question used by the configuration script that comes with the default Slackware release of Linux. If you are not using Slackware, the configuration script that you use may differ slightly from what you see below: one or more questions may be missing; further, you may see a few additional questions. For information on these questions, type ? at the question's prompt.

In this section, we describe how to configure a kernel that will contain all code required by the rest of this book. At the end of this section, we describe how to compile a kernel that is used by an ordinary host on your intranet — one that does not interact with the Internet.

BEGINNING CONFIGURATION

That being said, let's get started. To begin, cd to directory /usr/src/linux, then su to the superuser root. Then, to begin configuration, type the command:

```
make config
```

The first output you see on your screen is:

```
rm -f include/asm
( cd include ; ln -sf asm-i386 asm)
/bin/sh scripts/Configure arch/i386/config.in
#
# Using defaults found in .config
#
```

```
*
* Code maturity level options
*
```

This is followed immediately by the first question:

```
Prompt for development and/or incomplete code/drivers
  (CONFIG_EXPERIMENTAL) [Y/n/?]
```

Answer y to this prompt, because some of the code that we want to use (in particular, IP masquerading) is officially regarded as being experimental – or was, at the time this book was written.

MODULES

The next few questions concern modules. A *module* is a small, self-contained chunk of kernel code that is stored in a file. A module is loaded into the kernel only when it is needed; otherwise, it is left in its file, where it is not consuming memory. The first question asks whether you want to use modules:

```
Enable loadable module support (CONFIG_MODULES) [y/n/?]
```

Answer y here: modules are useful in their own right, and a number of the networking subsystems that we want to use are implemented as modules.

```
Set version information on all symbols for modules
  (CONFIG_MODVERSIONS) [y/n/?]
```

This option asks whether to store the version of a module within the module itself. This is useful only if you wish to use modules that are imported from outside the Linux kernel source tree. Unless you have a pressing reason not to, answer n to this question.

```
Kernel daemon support (e.g. autoload of modules) (CONFIG_KERNELD)
  [y/n/?]
```

This tells the kernel to include code that lets it load and unload modules automatically, instead of your having to do it by hand. Answer y.

GENERAL SETUP

The next set of questions concerns the general configuration of your Linux kernel.

```
Kernel math emulation (CONFIG_MATH_EMULATION) [y/n/?]
```

Linux can emulate code generated by mathematics hardware. The Intel 80387 co-processor performs mathematics processing, and mathematics circuits are built into the Intel i486DX and Pentium chips, as well as similar parts made by AMD and

Cyrix. Intel 80386 and 80486SX chips do not have mathematics circuits in them. If your machine does not have mathematics hardware, you must answer y to this question. If your machine does have mathematics hardware, this code will do no harm, but it will make the kernel about 45 kilobytes larger than it need be. If you know that you are running a machine with mathematics hardware, type n; if you are not sure, type y.

```
Networking support (CONFIG_NET) [y/n/?]
```

Type y to this question – otherwise why would you be reading this book?

```
Limit memory to low 16MB (CONFIG_MAX_16M) [y/n/?]
```

This tells the kernel to use special code that maps kernel routines to the low 16 megabytes of memory. This helps to work around some problems seen with buggy motherboards. If you have 16 megabytes of RAM or less, or if your machine appears to run correctly, type n; if you experience random problems and have more than 16 megabytes of RAM, type y.

```
PCI bios support (CONFIG_PCI) [y/n/?]
```

Type y if your machine has a PCI bus; otherwise, type n. If you are not sure, check the documentation that came with your computer. If you type y to this question, you will then be asked:

```
PCI bridge optimization (experimental) (CONFIG_PCI_OPTIMIZE) [y/n/?]
```

This is experimental, but will speed up your kernel. Type y.

```
System V IPC (CONFIG_SYSVIPC) [y/n/?]
```

This enables UNIX System-V style interprocess communication. If you are not sure what this is, let us simply say that it is a good thing and is required by many applications. Type y.

```
Kernel support for a.out binaries (CONFIG_BINFMT_AOUT) [Y/m/n]
```

This option lets your kernel run programs in the old, a.out format. (Linux switched to ELF format a number of releases ago.) This option is very useful, and hardly increases the size of the kernel at all; answer y.

```
Kernel support for ELF binaries (CONFIG_BINFMT_ELF) [Y/m/n/?]
```

This option lets your kernel run programs in the ELF format, which is the format now used by Linux. Answer y.

```
Kernel support for JAVA binaries (CONFIG_BINFMT_JAVA) [Y/m/n/?]
```

This option lets your kernel run Java applications directly. This will speed the execution of Java *applications*, but not of Java *applets*, which are mini-programs downloaded from the World Wide Web. As more programs are distributed in Java format, this will become more useful; but at present, it is a luxury. Answer n, unless you are absolutely certain that you will want to run Java programs directly through your kernel.

```
Compile kernel as ELF - if your GCC is ELF-GCC (CONFIG_KERNEL_ELF)
   [y/n/?]
```

This option compiles the kernel itself into ELF format, which is now the default Linux binary format. Answer y.

```
Processor type (386, 486, Pentium, PPro) [Pentium]
```

Enter the type of processor in your machine. This lets your kernel take advantage of some of the special tricks built into the more advanced processors. If you are not sure, type 386 — your kernel will run a little slower on a more advanced chip than it would otherwise, but at least you will be certain that it will run.

CONFIGURATION OF BLOCK DRIVERS

The next step is to select and configure the drivers for block devices. A *block device* is one that reads blocks of data at once, rather than one byte at a time. These devices principally are storage devices, such as hard disks, floppy disks, and CD-ROMs. At this point, you will start to refer to the hardware list that you prepared earlier.

The first question is:

```
Normal floppy disk support (CONFIG_BLK_DEV_FD) [Y/m/n/?]
```

This compiles support for floppy-disk drives into your kernel. Answer y.

IDE DRIVES   The next set of questions asks about support for IDE devices. File /usr/src/linux/Documentation/ide.txt describes IDE devices, and explains how Linux supports them.

```
Enhanced IDE/MFM/RLL disk/cdrom/tape support (CONFIG_BLK_DEV_IDE)
   [Y/n/?]
Please see Documentation/ide.txt for help/info on IDE drives
```

This compiles support for IDE controller cards into your kernel, in addition to support for obsolete MFM and RLL devices. Practically all machines built since 1995 use an IDE controller, to control hard disks, serial ports, parallel ports, and floppy-disk drives. Unless you know that your machine does not use an IDE drive, answer y.

If you answered n to question CONFIG_BLK_DEV_IDE, you will see the question:

```
Old harddisk (MFM/RLL/IDE) driver (CONFIG_BLK_DEV_HD_ONLY) [Y/n/?]
```

This asks whether you want to use the older Linux driver for IDE devices, instead of the newer IDE driver. If you have very old IDE equipment or have very limited amounts of RAM available on your system, answer y to this question; otherwise, you should answer y to question CONFIG_BLK_DEV_IDE.

If you answered y to question CONFIG_BLK_DEV_IDE, you will see the following series of questions:

```
Use old disk-only driver on primary interface (CONFIG_BLK_DEV_HD_
    IDE) [N/y/?]
```

This option tells the kernel to use an older driver. This driver includes support for MFM or RLL drives, and does not support ATAPI CD-ROMs. This option is useful only if (1) you have more than one disk controller in your machine, and (2) the primary controller is MFM or RLL. If you don't know how many controllers you have, or if you don't know what an MFM or RLL device is, answer n.

```
Include IDE/ATAPI CDROM support (CONFIG_BLK_DEV_IDECD) [Y/n/?]
```

This option asks (1) whether you have a CD-ROM device in your machine, and (2) that CD-ROM uses an ATAPI interface. The ATAPI interface plugs the CD-ROM directly into the IDE controller, so that it works like a second hard-disk drive. If you are unsure, check the documentation that came with your computer or CD-ROM device; most newer computers use the ATAPI interface for their CD-ROM devices. Answer y if your CD-ROM uses the ATAPI interface, n otherwise.

```
Include IDE/ATAPI TAPE support (CONFIG_BLK_DEV_IDETAPE) [N/y/?]
```

Answer y if your machine has an ATAPI tape drive, n if it does not. If you do have an ATAPI tape drive, check the documentation file ide.txt (cited above) for more information on how to configure this device.

```
Support removable IDE interfaces (PCMCIA) (CONFIG_BLK_DEV_IDE_
    PCMCIA) [N/y/?]
```

If your device has a removable IDE interface – i.e., one that lets you swap disks in and out without turning the machine off – then answer y. If you do not have a removable IDE disk drive, or if you are not sure, answer n.

```
CMD640 chipset bugfix/support (CONFIG_BLK_DEV_CMD640) [Y/n/?]
```

This option includes code to deal with the bugs in the CMD640 disk-controller chip. If you are certain that you do *not* have a CMD640 controller on your machine, answer n; otherwise, answer y. If you answer y to this question, you will then see the following question:

```
CMD640 enhanced support (CONFIG_BLK_DEV_CMD640_ENHANCED) [Y/n/?]
```

This option includes code to enhance the performance of the CMD640 controller chip. In some instances, these enhancements are already implemented in hardware. Answer y.

If you earlier said that you had a PCI machine, you will see the following two questions:

```
RZ1000 chipset bugfix/support (CONFIG_BLK_DEV_RZ1000) [Y/n/?]
```

The RZ1000 is another IDE controller chip that is commonly used in PCs. This option includes code to detect it, and correct a number of bugs in how it works. If you are certain that your machine does *not* use the RZ1000 controller chip, answer n; otherwise, answer y. Please note that including code for more than one type of controller chip will not cause the kernel to hang or otherwise misbehave.

```
Intel 82371 PIIX (Triton I/II) DMA support (CONFIG_BLK_DEV_TRITON)
  [Y/n/?]
```

This option includes code to speed the performance of the Intel 430 FX PCI chipset. If you are certain that your machine does *not* use this chipset, answer n; otherwise, answer y. Including the code even if you do not have the chipset on your machine will make your kernel a little larger, but otherwise will not cause the kernel to misbehave.

Regardless of whether or not you said you had a PCI machine, you will see the following questions:

```
Other IDE chipset support (CONFIG_IDE_CHIPSETS) [N/y/?]
```

If you answer y to this question, the configuration script will ask you if you want to add code that enhances Linux support for various IDE controller chipsets. Unlike the earlier questions for the CMD640 and RZ1000 chipsets, this code does not fix bugs; rather, it speeds up performance. Please note that most of these options require that you pass the kernel special command-line options when you boot it. If you know what your IDE controller's chipset is and are knowledgeable enough to configure the kernel's boot parameters, answer y; otherwise, answer n.

If you answered y to the previous question, you will see the following questions:

```
ALI M14xx        support (CONFIG_BLK_DEV_ALI14XX) [N/y/?]
DTC-2278         support (CONFIG_BLK_DEV_DTC2278) [N/y/?]
Holtek HT6560B   support (CONFIG_BLK_DEV_HT6560B) [N/y/?]
PROMISE DC4030   support (EXPERIMENTAL) (CONFIG_BLK_DEV_PROMISE)
  [N/y/?]
QDI QD6580       support (CONFIG_BLK_DEV_QD6580) [N/y/?]
UMC 8672         support (CONFIG_BLK_DEV_UMC8672) [N/y/?]
```

Answer y to the chipset that applies to your machine. See the document ide.txt (cited above) for details on the boot parameter you must pass to the kernel to invoke the special driver code.

This concludes the questions that relate to IDE devices.

ADDITIONAL BLOCK DEVICES   Now, the configuration script asks some questions about miscellaneous block devices on your machine:

```
Loopback device support (CONFIG_BLK_DEV_LOOP) [Y/m/n/?]
```

This asks whether you want to use a *loopback* device, which lets you mount a file as a file system. This is a specialized usage that is not needed by most users; if you are unsure what a loopback device is, answer n.

```
Multiple devices driver support (CONFIG_BLK_DEV_MD) [Y/n/?]
```

This option includes code that lets you combine several partitions on a hard disk into one. This is a specialized usage that most users will never need. If you are not sure whether you need this or not, answer n.

If you answered y to the previous question, you will see the following questions:

```
Linear (append) mode (CONFIG_MD_LINEAR) [Y/m/n/?]
RAID-0 (striping) mode (CONFIG_MD_STRIPED) [Y/m/n/?]
```

If you are seeing these questions, we assume that you are knowledgeable in the subject of multi-device accessing, and know what form of accessing you want. Answer y to the mode that you prefer to use.

All users will see the following question:

```
RAM disk support (CONFIG_BLK_DEV_RAM) [Y/m/n/?]
```

A RAM disk is a chunk of memory that is set aside and has a file system written into it. Applications can then read files from the RAM disk, just like they read files

from any other physical device. In the past, RAM disks were used to hold a minia-
ture version of the kernel during booting, or to hold temporary files during compilation; nowadays, however, RAM disks are not used frequently. Answer n unless
you are certain that you will use an application that requires a RAM disk.

If you answered y to the previous question, you will see the following:

```
Initial RAM disk (initrd) support (CONFIG_BLK_DEV_INITRD) [Y/n/?]
```

This tells the kernel to build a RAM disk as part of its initialization process. For
details, see documentation file initrd.txt. If you are not sure, answer n to this
question.

Finally, all users will see the following question:

```
XT harddisk support (CONFIG_BLK_DEV_XD) [Y/n/?]
```

This includes code to support very, very old IBM XT hard disks. Answer n unless
you are certain that you have one of those disks in your machine.

This concludes the questions for block devices.

NETWORK CONFIGURATION

The next set of questions ask you what "flavors" of networking you want your kernel to support. As we've noted earlier, the standard form of networking supported
under Linux is TCP/IP networking; however, Linux supports other varieties as well,
including IPX networking (which is used by Novell networks) and packet-radio networking. We assume that you are interested only in TCP/IP networking, but these
other varieties of networking are available for you to explore.

The first questions ask about general configuration:

```
Network firewalls (CONFIG_FIREWALL) [Y/n/?]
```

This asks whether you want to install a firewall between your host and the
Internet. A *firewall* is code that examines TCP/IP datagrams and ensures that they
are coming from, or going to, an approved host. We discuss firewalls in Chapter 8.
Answer y, because we use the firewall later in this book.

```
Network aliasing ( CONFIG_NET_ALIAS) [Y/n/?]
```

This option includes code to support aliasing. *Aliasing* lets you attach more than
one network address to an interface. This will not enlarge your kernel significantly,
and it is very useful for advanced projects; therefore, answer y to this question.

```
TCP/IP networking (CONFIG_INET) [Y/n/?]
```

Answer y.

```
IP: forwarding/gatewaying (CONFIG_IP_FORWARD) [Y/n/?]
```

This option asks whether your machine will be forwarding datagrams from other hosts. Answer y, because this is required for IP masquerading, which we discuss in Chapter 8.

```
IP: multicasting (CONFIG_IP_MULTICAST) [Y/n/?]
```

Broadcasting is when you send a datagram to all hosts on your intranet. *Multicasting* is broadcasting to multiple intranets simultaneously. Answer y, unless you know that you have no need to do this.

```
IP: firewalling (CONFIG_IP_FIREWALL) [Y/n/?]
```

This turns on IP-specific firewall code. Answer y.

```
IP: firewall packet logging (CONFIG_IP_FIREWALL_VERBOSE) [Y/n/?]
```

This asks you whether you will want to log what the firewall does. Output of logging is handled by the logging daemon, which we describe later in this chapter. Answer y.

```
IP: masquerading (EXPERIMENTAL) (CONFIG_IP_MASQUERADE) [Y/n/?]
```

Answer y. We discuss IP masquerading in Chapter 8.

```
IP: transparent proxy support (EXPERIMENTAL)
 (CONFIG_IP_TRANSPARENT_PROXY) [Y/n/?]
```

A *transparent proxy* lets your network set up a local server that acts as a proxy for distant systems. Local applications can interact with the proxy, as if they were talking to a remote system. Unless you know you will use this feature, answer n.

```
IP: always defragment (CONFIG_IP_ALWAYS_DEFRAG) [Y/n/?]
```

This tells the IP tier always to reassemble fragmented datagrams before forwarding them. Answer y, because this is required by IP masquerading.

```
IP: accounting (CONFIG_IP_ACCT) [Y/n/?]
```

This option includes code that lets you view statistics about the datagrams that pass through your machine. Answer y.

```
IP: optimize as router not host (CONFIG_IP_ROUTER) [Y/n/?]
```

Answer n, unless you expect that most of the datagrams your machine handles will be generated by other machines on an intranet that you will be setting up.

```
IP: tunneling (CONFIG_NET_IPIP) [Y/m/n/?]
```

Tunneling is a technique whereby datagrams for one protocol are embedded within datagrams for another. This has certain specialized uses; which will not be discussed in this book.

If earlier you answered y to question CONFIG_IP_MULTICAST, you will see the following question:

```
IP: multicast routing (EXPERIMENTAL) (CONFIG_IP_MROUTE) [Y/n/?]
```

This implements MBONE, which is a method of broadcasting datagrams over multiple networks simultaneously. If you do not know what MBONE is, you do not need this option; therefore, answer n.

If earlier you answered y to question CONFIG_NET_ALIAS, you will see the following question:

```
IP: aliasing support (CONFIG_IP_ALIAS) [Y/m/n/?]
```

This feature lets your host give multiple IP addresses to a single hardware interface. This feature is useful if you have a sophisticated Internet service, or for using virtual hosts with the Apache Web server. Answer n.

The following questions concern some networking issues that are of a very narrow interest. They are prefixed by the comment it is safe to leave these untouched, which is good advice: you should accept the defaults for all of them.

```
IP: PC/TCP compatibility mode (CONFIG_INET_PCTCP) [N/y/?]
```

This includes some code that supports the PC/TCP implementation of telnet. Answer n, unless yours is one of the rare intranets that still uses the PC/TCP application.

```
IP: Reverse ARP (CONFIG_INET_RARP) [N/y/m/?]
```

We discussed RARP briefly in Chapter 1. In most instances, RARP is used on networks that use specialized TCP/IP devices, such as Hewlett-Packard's JetDirect Ethernet printer interface device. If your intranet uses such a device, answer y; otherwise, answer n.

```
IP: Disable Path MTU Discovery (CONFIG_NO_PATH_MTU_DISCOVERY)
 [N/y/?]
```

Normally, TCP/IP networking discovers the maximum transmission unit (MTU) through trial-and-error, by starting out with large packets and shrinking them if a problem is encountered during transmission. This is called *MTU discovery*. However, some software does not work if you turn on this feature. This option lets you turn off MTU discovery; answer n unless you know for certain that you must support software that is broken by MTU discovery.

```
IP: Drop source routed frames (CONFIG_IP_NOSR) [Y/n/?]
```

This tells the kernel to drop datagrams that are *source routed* – that is, that record a path all the way back to the source host. Such datagrams introduce security problems; so answer y to this question.

```
IP: Allow large windows (CONFIG_SKB_LARGE) [N/y/?]
```

This option increases the amount of data your network can have buffered. Answer n unless your machine has more than 16 megabytes of RAM, and has a high-speed connection to the Internet.

The next few questions concern networking protocols other than TCP/IP.

```
The IPX protocol (CONFIG_IPX) [Y/m/n/?]
```

This option lets you add support for Novell NetWare networks to your Linux kernel. Novell support is beyond the scope of this book; answer n.

```
Appletalk DDP (CONFIG_ATALK) [Y/m/n/?]
```

This option lets you add support for AppleTalk networks to your Linux kernel. AppleTalk support is beyond the scope of this book; answer n.

```
Amateur Radio AX.25 Level 2 (CONFIG_AX25) [Y/n/?]
```

This option lets you add support for packet-radio networks to your Linux kernel. Packet-radio support is beyond the scope of this book; answer n.

```
Bridging (EXPERIMENTAL) (CONFIG_BRIDGE) [Y/n/?]
```

This option lets you add support to Ethernet bridging. *Bridging* lets you install two Ethernet cards into your machine, and have the machine automatically pass datagrams between each Ethernet card's intranet. You probably will not need this option, so answer n.

```
Kernel/User network link driver (CONFIG_NETLINK) [Y/n/?]
```

This option lets you interact directly with some parts of the networking software. This is particularly useful if you are developing new networking software. Answer n.

This concludes the section on general networking configuration. We answer some TCP/IP-specific questions later in the configuration process. Next, we configure support for SCSI devices.

SCSI DEVICES

A SCSI interface is a type of computer interface that supports peripheral devices, such as disks, tapes, and CD-ROMs. It is used by many computer manufacturers, in particular makers of UNIX workstations (such as Sun), and by Apple's Macintosh line of computers. SCSI devices tend to offer higher performance than IDE devices (although IDE devices have improved greatly in recent years). By adding a SCSI interface to your machine, you can add up to seven SCSI peripheral devices to your computer. All seven devices, it should be noted, consume only one interrupt on your system's bus.

The next set of questions lets you configure support for SCSI devices. Although the configuration of SCSI devices is beyond the scope of this book, we describe this to help new Linux users configure a kernel successfully.

The first question asks you whether you want to support SCSI devices at all:

```
SCSI support (CONFIG_SCSI) [Y/m/n/?]
```

Answer y to this question if you have a SCSI interface card in your machine, or if you have an Iomega ZIP drive plugged into your machine's parallel port. If you do not have a SCSI interface card or an Iomega ZIP drive in your machine, answer n and skip ahead to the next section.

The next three questions ask you about the type of devices your SCSI interface has. Answer y to each type of device that applies:

```
SCSI disk support (CONFIG_BLK_DEV_SD) [Y/m/n/?]
SCSI tape support (CONFIG_CHR_DEV_ST) [Y/m/n/?]
SCSI CD-ROM support (CONFIG_BLK_DEV_SR) [Y/m/n/?]
```

The next question asks whether the SCSI code should probe each device for multiple logical unit numbers (LUNs):

```
Probe all LUNs on each SCSI device (CONFIG_SCSI_MULTI_LUN) [Y/n/?]
```

Most SCSI devices have only one LUN; answer n unless you are certain that your SCSI device uses multiple LUNs.

The next question asks about verbose reporting:

```
Verbose SCSI error reporting (kernel size +=12K) (CONFIG_SCSI_
  CONSTANTS) [Y/n/?]
```

Answer y. This increases the size of the kernel by 12 kilobytes, but it returns error messages that can be read and interpreted by human beings.

The next set of questions asks you what type of SCSI adapter you have. Answer y to the SCSI card you have; answer n to all the rest. Please note that adding support for more than one SCSI card will not harm your kernel, but it will make the kernel unnecessarily large. A few devices require that you answer some extra specific questions. We do not describe these here; for help with these specialized questions, type ? at the prompt.

```
7000FASST SCSI support (CONFIG_SCSI_7000FASST) [Y/m/n/?]
Adaptec AHA152X/2825 support (CONFIG_SCSI_AHA152X) [Y/m/n/?]
Adaptec AHA1542 support (CONFIG_SCSI_AHA1542) [Y/m/n/?]
Adaptec AHA1740 support (CONFIG_SCSI_AHA1740) [Y/m/n/?]
Adaptec AHA274X/284X/294X support (CONFIG_SCSI_AIC7XXX) [Y/m/n/?]
AdvanSys SCSI support (CONFIG_SCSI_ADVANSYS) [Y/m/n/?]
Always IN2000 SCSI support (CONFIG_SCSI_IN2000) [Y/m/n/?]
AM53/79C974 PCI SCSI support (CONFIG_SCSI_AM53C974) [Y/m/n/?]
BusLogic SCSI support (CONFIG_SCSI_BUSLOGIC) [Y/m/n/?]
DTC3180/3280 SCSI support (CONFIG_SCSI_DTC3280) [Y/m/n/?]
EATA-DMA (DPT, NEC, AT&T, SNI, AST, Olivetti, Alphatronix) support
  (CONFIG_SCSI_EATA_DMA) [Y/m/n/?]
EATA-PIO (old DPT PM2001, PM2012A) support (CONFIG_SCSI_EATA_PIO)
  [Y/m/n/?]
EATA ISA/EISA/PCI (DPT and generic EATA/DMA-compliant boards)
  support (CONFIG_SCSI_EATA) [Y/m/n/?]
Future Domain 16xx SCSI support (CONFIG_SCSI_FUTURE_DOMAIN)
  [Y/m/n/?]
Generic NCR5380/53c400 SCSI support (CONFIG_SCSI_GENERIC_NCR5380)
  [Y/m/n/?]
NCR53c406a SCSI support (CONFIG_SCSI_NCR53C406A) [Y/m/n/?]
IOMEGA Parallel Port ZIP drive SCSI support (CONFIG_SCSI_PPA)
  [Y/m/n/?]
PAS16 SCSI support (CONFIG_SCSI_PAS16) [Y/m/n/?]
Qlogic FAS SCSI support (CONFIG_SCSI_QLOGIC_FAS) [Y/m/n/?]
Seagate ST-02 and Future Domain TMC-8xx SCSI support
  (CONFIG_SCSI_SEAGATE) [Y/m/n/?]
Trantor T128/T128F/T228 SCSI support (CONFIG_SCSI_T128) [Y/m/n/?]
UltraStor 14F/34F support (CONFIG_SCSI_U14_34F) [Y/m/n/?]
UltraStor SCSI support (CONFIG_SCSI_ULTRASTOR) [Y/m/n/?]
```

This concludes the section on support for SCSI devices. The next block of questions lets you configure networking devices, including Ethernet devices.

NETWORK DEVICES
The first question asks you whether you want your kernel to support network devices:

```
Network device support (CONFIG_NETDEVICES) [Y/n/?]
```

Answer y.

The next question asks about dummy devices:

```
Dummy net driver support (CONFIG_DUMMY) [Y/m/n/?]
```

A *dummy* device lets a SLIP or PPP interface connect to a non-existent IP address. This is used by some useful software, in particular the `diald` daemon, which we describe later in this chapter; therefore, answer y.

```
EQL (serial line load balancing) support (CONFIG_EQUALIZER)
[Y/m/n/?]
```

This option balances the load between multiple serial-line interfaces. Answer y only if you will have multiple modem or serial-line connections running at once; otherwise, answer n.

```
DLCI support (EXPERIMENTAL) (CONFIG_DLCI) [Y/m/n/?]
```

Frame relay is a type of dedicated network connection or leased line. We discuss frame relay in Chapter 2. Connecting your Linux system directly to a frame-relay line is beyond the scope of this book. You can utilize frame relay and this book by purchasing a dedicated frame relay to Ethernet router. If you have done this, the frame relay to Ethernet router will handle the conversion of packets between your Ethernet and your frame-relay connection, so you should answer n.

```
PLIP (parallel port) support (CONFIG_PLIP) [Y/m/n/?]
```

Parallel-port IP (PLIP) is a method of networking two machines through their parallel ports. It enjoyed some popularity in years past, but is obsolete now that inexpensive, reliable Ethernet cards have become available. Answer n.

```
PPP (point-to-point) support (CONFIG_PPP) [Y/m/n/?]
```

This option includes support for the Point-to-Point Protocol (PPP), which we described in Chapter 1. Answer y.

```
SLIP (serial line) support (CONFIG_SLIP) [Y/m/n/?]
```

This option includes support for the Serial Line Internet Protocol (SLIP). This protocol has been superceded by PPP; however, you should answer y because SLIP is used by the `diald` daemon, which we describe later in this chapter.

The next three questions ask how to configure SLIP. Because we will not be using SLIP to connect to a remote host, these options are not needed: answer n to each:

```
CSLIP compressed headers (CONFIG_SLIP_COMPRESSED) [Y/n/?]
Keepalive and linefill (CONFIG_SLIP_SMART) [Y/n/?]
Six bit SLIP encapsulation (CONFIG_SLIP_MODE_SLIP6) [Y/n/?]
```

The next question asks about packet-radio interfaces:

```
Radio network interfaces (CONFIG_NET_RADIO) [Y/n/?]
```

This adds support for radio interfaces. Radio interfaces are very rare, and are beyond the scope of this book; therefore, answer n.

ETHERNET CARDS   The next set of questions ask about Ethernet devices:

```
Ethernet (10 or 100Mbit) (CONFIG_NET_ETHERNET) [Y/m/n/?]
```

If you have added an Ethernet card to your Linux machine, answer y.

The following questions ask you to identify the type of Ethernet card you have. These questions are in groups: first, cards by major manufacturers; then miscellaneous ISA cards; then PCI and on-board controllers; and finally pocket adapters.

Cards by Major Manufacturers

The questions ask about major manufacturers of Ethernet cards. If you see the manufacturer of your card, answer y; otherwise, answer n.

First, you will be asked whether you have a card manufactured by 3COM:

```
3COM cards (CONFIG_NET_VENDOR_3COM) [Y/n/?]
```

If you answer y, you will be asked to select the model of 3COM card you are using:

```
3c501 support (CONFIG_EL1) [Y/m/n/?]
3c503 support (CONFIG_EL2) [Y/m/n/?]
3c505 support (CONFIG_ELPLUS) [Y/m/n/?]
3c507 support (CONFIG_EL16) [Y/m/n/?]
3c509/3c579 support (CONFIG_EL3) [Y/m/n/?]
3c590 series (592/595/597) "Vortex" support (CONFIG_VORTEX)
  [Y/m/n/?]
```

Next, you will be asked whether your card was manufactured by AMD or PCnet:

```
AMD LANCE and PCnet (AT1500 and NE2100) support (CONFIG_LANCE)
  [Y/n/?]
```

If you answer yes, you will see:

```
AMD PCInet32 (VLB and PCI) support (CONFIG_LANCE32) [Y/n/?]
```

Next, you will be asked whether your card was manufactured by Western Digital or SMC:

```
Western Digital/SMC cards (CONFIG_NET_VENDOR_SMC) [Y/n/?]
```

If you answer y, you will be asked to select the appropriate model of card:

```
WD80*3 support (CONFIG_WD80x3) [Y/m/n/?]
SMC Ultra support (CONFIG_ULTRA) [Y/m/n/?]
SMC 9194 support (CONFIG_SMC9194) [Y/m/n/?]
```

Other ISA Cards
The next set of questions asks about miscellaneous ISA cards:

```
Other ISA cards (CONFIG_NET_ISA) [Y/n/?]
```

If you have not yet seen your Ethernet card on this list, answer y. If you answer y, you will see the following questions; answer y only to the question that names the type of Ethernet card you have:

```
AT1700 support (EXPERIMENTAL) (CONFIG_AT1700) [Y/m/n/?]
Cabletron E21xx support (CONFIG_E2100) [Y/m/n/?]
DEPCA, DE10x, DE200, DE201, DE202, DE422 support (CONFIG_DEPCA)
  [Y/m/n/?]
EtherWORKS 3 (DE203, DE204, DE205) support (CONFIG_EWRK3) [Y/m/n/?]
EtherExpress 16 support (CONFIG_EEXPRESS) [Y/m/n/?]
EtherExpressPro support (CONFIG_EEXPRESS_PRO) [Y/m/n/?]
FMV-181/182/183/184 support (CONFIG_FMV18X) [Y/m/n/?]
HP PCLAN+ (27247B and 27252A) support (CONFIG_HPLAN_PLUS) [Y/m/n/?]
HP PCLAN (27245 and other 27xxx series) support (CONFIG_HPLAN)
  [Y/m/n/?]
HP 10/100VG PCLAN (ISA, EISA, PCI) support (CONFIG_HP100) [Y/m/n/?]
ICL EtherTeam 16i/32 support (CONFIG_ETH16I) [Y/m/n/?]
NE2000/NE1000 support (CONFIG_NE2000) [Y/m/n/?]
NI5210 support (CONFIG_NI52) [Y/m/n/?]
NI6510 support (CONFIG_NI65) [Y/m/n/?]
SEEQ8005 support (EXPERIMENTAL) (CONFIG_SEEQ8005) [Y/n/?]
SK_G16 support (CONFIG_SK_G16) [Y/n/?]
```

EISA, PCI, or On-Board Controllers
The next set of questions ask about EISA, PCI, and on-board controllers:

```
EISA, VLB, PCI and on board controllers (CONFIG_NET_EISA) [Y/n/?]
```

If you have not seen your Ethernet card among those listed so far, answer y. If you answer y, you will see the following questions; answer y only to the question that names the type of Ethernet card you have:

```
Ansel Communications EISA 3200 support (EXPERIMENTAL)
  (CONFIG_AC3200) [Y/m/n/?]
Apricot Xen-II on board ethernet (CONFIG_APRICOT) [Y/m/n/?]
DE425, DE434, DE435, DE450, DE500 support (CONFIG_DE4X5) [Y/m/n/?]
DECchip Tulip (dc21x4x) PCI support (CONFIG_DEC_ELCP) [Y/m/n/?]
Digi Intl. RightSwitch SE-X support (CONFIG_DGRS) [Y/m/n/?]
Zenith Z-Note support (EXPERIMENTAL) (CONFIG_ZNET) [Y/n/?]
```

Pocket Adapters
The next set of questions ask about pocket adapters:

```
Pocket and portable adaptors (CONFIG_NET_POCKET) [Y/n/?]
```

Pocket adapters are Ethernet adapters that plug into a machine's parallel port. In years past, these were popular in laptop computers, although they are less so nowadays. Answer y if your machine uses such an adapter; otherwise, answer n.

If you answered y to the previous question, you will be asked what kind of pocket adapter you have. Answer y to the question that names the pocket adapter you use; answer n to the others:

```
AT-LAN-TEC/RealTek pocket adaptor support (CONFIG_ATP) [Y/n/?]
D-Link DE600 pocket adaptor support (CONFIG_DE600) [Y/m/n/?]
D-Link DE620 pocket adaptor support (CONFIG_DE620) [Y/m/n/?]
```

This concludes the configuration of Ethernet adapters.

MISCELLANEOUS NETWORKING ISSUES   The section on networking hardware concludes with a few additional questions.

First, the script asks whether you are using a Token Ring card:

```
Token Ring driver support (CONFIG_TR) [Y/n/?]
```

Token Ring is a proprietary IBM networking protocol, which it uses instead of Ethernet. Answer y if you have such a card in your Linux system; otherwise, answer n. If you answer y, you will be asked:

```
IBM Tropic chipset based adaptor support (CONFIG_IBMTR) [Y/m/n/?]
```

Answer y if your Token Ring card uses this chip set.
Next, config asks are you using DEC FDDI:

```
FDDI driver support (CONFIG_FDDI) [Y/n/?]
```

FDDI stands *for fiber distributed data interface*. FDDI is a 100-Mb-per-second network standard based on fiber-optic cable and token ring technologies. If you have an FDDI card in your Linux system, answer y; otherwise, answer n. If you answer y, then you will be asked:

```
Digital DEFEA and DEFPA adapter support (CONFIG_DEFXX) [Y/m/n/?]
```

Answer y if you have such an adapter; otherwise, answer n.

Finally, you will be asked if you have an ARCnet card in your machine:

```
ARCnet support (CONFIG_ARCNET) [Y/m/n/?]
```

ARCnet is yet another networking protocol that is being displaced by Ethernet. If you have such a card in your Linux system, answer y; otherwise, answer n. If you answer y, you will be asked how to configure the ARCnet interface:

```
Enable arcOe (ARCnet "Ether-Encap" packet format) (CONFIG_ARCNET_
  ETH) [Y/n/?]
Enable arcOs (ARCnet RFC1051 packet format) (CONFIG_ARCNET_1051)
  [Y/n/?]
```

Answer y to the interface or interfaces you wish to use.

And with that, the configuration script has finished with configuring networking hardware.

ISDN DEVICES   The next block of questions ask about adding ISDN support to your kernel. First, you will be asked:

```
ISDN support (CONFIG_ISDN) [Y/m/n/?]
```

Answer y if you have ISDN; otherwise, answer n and skip to the next section.

config next asks you some detailed questions about how you want ISDN support configured:

```
Support synchronous PPP (CONFIG_ISDN_PPP) [Y/n/?]
```

Answer y only if your Internet service provider supports synchronous PPP. Otherwise, answer n. If you answer y, you will see the following two questions:

```
Use VJ-compression with synchronous PPP (CONFIG_ISDN_PPP_VJ) [Y/n/?]
```

Enable compression of headers. Answer y, but only if your Internet service provider supports compression.

```
Support generic MP (RFC 1717) (CONFIG_ISDN_MPP) [Y/n/?]
```

This question asks whether you want to bundle multiple ISDN connections, thus speeding through-put. Answer y if you expect to have multiple ISDN connections; otherwise, answer n.

Next, you will be asked about ISDN audio:

```
Support audio via ISDN (CONFIG_ISDN_AUDIO) [Y/n/?]
```

With appropriate software and drivers, this would let you use your Linux system as a telephone answering machine. For details, see documentation file isdn/ README.audio.

The following questions ask what type of ISDN card you have. Answer y to the question that names the type of card you have, n to all other questions:

```
ICN D support (CONFIG_ISDN_DRV_PCBIT) [Y/m/n/?]
Teles/2B and 4B support (CONFIG_ISDN_DRV_ICN) [Y/m/n/?]
PCBIT-NICCY1016PC/Creatix support (CONFIG_ISDN_DRV_TELES) [Y/m/n/?]
```

This concludes the configuration of ISDN.

CD-ROM DEVICES

The following set of questions apply if your computer has a standalone CD-ROM device – that is, a CD-ROM device that uses neither an ATAPI interface nor a SCSI interface.

First, you will be asked:

```
Support non-SCSI/IDE/ATAPI CDROM drives (CONFIG_CD_NO_IDESCSI)
[Y/n/?]
```

If your machine does not have a CD-ROM device, or if its CD-ROM device uses an ATAPI or SCSI interface, answer n and skip to the next section. Otherwise, answer y and read on.

The following describes the standalone CD-ROM devices for which drivers have been written. Answer y only to the question that names your machine's CD-ROM device. A few types of CD-ROM devices require some detailed information from you:

```
Aztech/Orchid/Okano/Wearnes/TXC/CyDROM  CDROM support (CONFIG_AZTCD)
  [Y/m/n/?]
Goldstar R420 CDROM support (CONFIG_GSCD) [Y/m/n/?]
Matsushita/Panasonic/Creative, Longshine, TEAC CDROM support
  (CONFIG_SBPCD) [Y/m/n/?]
Mitsumi (standard) [no XA/Multisession] CDROM support (CONFIG_MCD)
  [Y/m/n/?]
Mitsumi [XA/MultiSession] CDROM support (CONFIG_MCDX) [Y/m/n/?]
Optics Storage DOLPHIN 8000AT CDROM support (CONFIG_OPTCD) [Y/m/n/?]
Philips/LMS CM206 CDROM support (CONFIG_CM206) [Y/m/n/?]
Sanyo CDR-H94A CDROM support (CONFIG_SJCD) [Y/m/n/?]
```

```
Soft configurable cdrom interface card support (CONFIG_CDI_INIT)
 [Y/n/?]
Sony CDU31A/CDU33A CDROM support (CONFIG_CDU31A) [Y/m/n/?]
Sony CDU535 CDROM support (CONFIG_CDU535) [Y/m/n/?]
```

This concludes configuration of CD-ROM devices.

FILE SYSTEMS
The next section asks you what type of file systems you want your Linux kernel to support.

```
Quota support (CONFIG_QUOTA) [Y/n/?]
```

Some systems with many users may want to limit the amount of disk space that any single user can use — in other words, set a *quota* on a user's disk usage. This option lets you add support for quotas to your Linux kernel. Answer y only if you are certain you need quotas; otherwise, answer n.

```
Mandatory lock support (CONFIG_LOCK_MANDATORY) [Y/n/?]
```

This option adds file locking to the Linux kernel. This option is useful only if applications know how to use it. Answer n.

```
Minix fs support (CONFIG_MINIX_FS) [Y/m/n/?]
```

Support the file system for the Minix operating system. Answer n unless you know that you will need to read Minix file systems.

```
Extended fs support (CONFIG_EXT_FS) [Y/m/n/?]
```

The extended file system is an early form of the Linux file system. Answer n.

```
Second extended fs support (CONFIG_EXT2_FS) [Y/m/n/?]
```

This is the standard Linux file system. Answer y.

```
xiafs filesystem support (CONFIG_XIA_FS) [Y/m/n/?]
```

XIA is an obsolete file system that is seldom, if ever, seen any more. Answer n.

```
DOS FAT fs support (CONFIG_FAT_FS) [Y/m/n/?]
```

The DOS FAT file system is the basic type of file system used by the MS-DOS and Windows line of operating systems. Answer y.

```
MSDOS fs support (CONFIG_MSDOS_FS $CONFIG_FAT_FS) [Y/m/n/?]
```

This option adds support for the MS-DOS file system. In all probability you will need this, if only to read an MS-DOS floppy disk. If your machine has both MS-DOS and Linux on it, this option will also let you mount the MS-DOS partition and use Linux tools to read and write into it. Answer y.

```
VFAT (Windows-95) fs support (CONFIG_VFAT_FS $CONFIG_FAT_FS)
  [Y/m/n/?]
```

This option adds support for the Windows 95 file system. Answer y.

```
umsdos: Unix like fs on top of std MSDOS FAT fs (CONFIG_UMSDOS_FS
  $CONFIG_MSDOS_FS) [Y/m/n/?]
```

This lets you build Linux files within an MS-DOS file system. Answer n unless you truly need to do such a thing.

```
/proc filesystem support (CONFIG_PROC_FS) [Y/m/n/?]
```

Answer y. The proc file system is a special, virtual file system: every process running on your machine is described as a file. This makes it very easy to get information about the status of a process. In addition, a number of applications depend upon the proc file system.

```
NFS filesystem support (CONFIG_NFS_FS) [Y/m/n/?]
```

This option adds support for the network file system (NFS) to the kernel. Answer y if you will be using NFS to interact with other Linux or UNIX systems on your local network; otherwise, answer n. We discuss NFS in Chapter 7.
  If you answer y to the previous question, you will be asked:

```
Root file system on NFS (CONFIG_ROOT_NFS) [Y/n/?]
```

This asks whether you want to export the root file system via NFS. You would do this if your intranet was supporting one or more diskless workstations. Most users will not need to do so; answer n.
  If you answer y to the previous question, you will be asked:

```
BOOTP support (CONFIG_RNFS_BOOTP) [Y/n/?]
```

Let the machine to which you export the root file system use the bootp protocol to discover your machine's IP address.

```
RARP support (CONFIG_RNFS_RARP) [Y/n/?]
```

Let the machine to which you export the root file system use the RARP protocol to discover your machine's IP address. We discussed RARP in Chapter 1.

```
SMB filesystem support (to mount WfW shares etc..) (CONFIG_SMB_FS)
 [Y/m/n/?]
```

This option lets you mount an SMB resource as a file system. In Chapter 9, we discuss networking Windows 95 with Linux. If you will be interacting with a machine that runs Windows 95 or Windows for Workgroups on your intranet, answer y; otherwise, answer n.

If you answered y to this question, you will then be asked:

```
SMB Win95 bug work-around (CONFIG_SMB_WIN95) [Y/n/?]
```

The Windows 95 SMB server is buggy; this option includes a work-around for the problem. Answer y.

If much earlier you had answered y to CONFIG_IPX, you will be asked:

```
NCP filesystem support (to mount NetWare volumes) (CONFIG_NCP_FS)
 [Y/m/n/?]
```

This option lets you export some or all of your file system to a Novell NetWare client. Answer y if you wish to do this.

The next question asks about the ISO-9660 file system.

```
ISO9660 cdrom filesystem support (CONFIG_ISO9660_FS) [Y/m/n/?]
```

The ISO-9660 file system is the file system used on CD-ROMs. Answer y.

```
OS/2 HPFS filesystem support (read only) (CONFIG_HPFS_FS) [Y/m/n/?]
```

Answer n unless you expect that you will have to to work with the OS/2 file system.

```
System V and Coherent filesystem support (CONFIG_SYSV_FS) [Y/m/n/?]
```

System V is the commercial, orthodox implementation of UNIX released by AT&T Bell Laboratories. Coherent was a commercial clone of System-V UNIX; it is gone, but not forgotten. Both use the same file system. Answer n unless you have some old Coherent or SCO disks lying around that you will want to read.

```
Amiga FFS filesystem support (EXPERIMENTAL) (CONFIG_AFFS_FS)
 [Y/m/n/?]
```

Answer n, unless you know you will be working with disks created on an Amiga.

```
UFS filesystem support (read only) (CONFIG_UFS_FS) [Y/m/n/?]
```

UFS is the file system used by Berkeley UNIX and the operating systems descended from it, including SunOS. This option lets you mount and read UFS disks – though not write to them. Answer n unless you will need to read Berkeley UNIX media.

If you answer y to the previous question, you will be asked two additional questions:

```
BSD disklabel (FreeBSD partition tables) support
 (CONFIG_BSD_DISKLABEL) [Y/n/?]
```

Answer n, unless you need to read Free BSD media.

```
SMD disklabel (Sun partition tables) support (CONFIG_SMD_DISKLABEL)
 [Y/n/?]
```

Answer n, unless you need to read SunOS media.

This concludes configuration of the file systems. Now, we move on to configuring character devices.

CHARACTER DEVICES

A *character device* is a device that reads data as a stream of bytes rather than in blocks. These devices include serial ports, parallel ports, mice, and miscellaneous devices, e.g., an uninterruptable power supply (UPS).

The following questions let you configure character devices.

```
Standard/generic serial support (CONFIG_SERIAL) [Y/m/n/?]
```

Answer y.

```
Digiboard PC/Xx Support (CONFIG_DIGI) [Y/m/n/?]
```

A MUX card lets you plug an entire bank of serial ports into your Linux system. You would use this if, for example, you were supporting a BBS with a bank of telephone lines coming into it. Digiboard is a brand of MUX card. Answer n unless you know that your machine contains such a card.

```
Cyclades async mux support (CONFIG_CYCLADES) [Y/m/n/?]
```

Answer n unless you know that your machine contains a Cyclades MUX card.

```
Stallion multiport serial support (CONFIG_STALDRV) [Y/n/?]
```

Answer n unless you know that your machine contains a Stallion multiport serial card.

If you answered y to the previous question, you will be asked two additional questions:

```
Stallion EasyIO or EC8/32 support (CONFIG_STALLION) [Y/m/n/?]
```

Answer n unless you have one of the cards listed here.

```
Stallion EC8/64, ONboard, Brumby support (CONFIG_ISTALLION)
[Y/m/n/?]
```

Answer n unless you have one of the cards listed here.

```
SDL RISCom/8 card support (CONFIG_RISCOM8) [Y/m/n/?]
```

Answer n unless you know that your machine contains this card.

```
Parallel printer support (CONFIG_PRINTER) [Y/m/n/?]
```

Answer y if you intend to use your parallel port to drive a printer. If your machine has only one parallel port and you intend to use it to support parallel-port IP (PLIP) or an Iomega ZIP drive, answer n.

```
Mouse Support (not serial mice) (CONFIG_MOUSE) [Y/m/n/?]
```

Answer y if your machine has a bus mouse rather than a serial mouse.

If you answered y to the previous question, you will then be asked which type of bus mouse your system uses; answer y to the question that names the type of mouse you use, and answer n to all other questions:

```
ATIXL busmouse support (CONFIG_ATIXL_BUSMOUSE) [Y/m/n/?]
Logitech busmouse support (CONFIG_BUSMOUSE) [Y/m/n/?]
Microsoft busmouse support (CONFIG_MS_BUSMOUSE) [Y/m/n/?]
PS/2 mouse (aka "auxiliary device") support (CONFIG_PSMOUSE)
[Y/m/n/?]
```

The next question asks about some miscellaneous character devices:

```
Support for user misc device modules (CONFIG_UMISC) [Y/n/?]
```

Answer n, unless you need this feature to test a device driver that you are developing.

```
QIC-02 tape support (CONFIG_QICO2_TAPE) [Y/m/n/?]
```

Answer y if you have a tape drive that uses the QIC-02 protocol. If you have a tape drive but are unsure what protocol it supports, check its documentation before you answer this question.

If you answered y to the previous question, you will be asked the following question:

```
Do you want runtime configuration for QIC-02 (CONFIG_QICO2_DYNCONF)
[Y/n/?]
```

There are two ways to configure a QIC-02 tape drive: by editing header file /usr/src/linux/include/linux/tpqic02.h, which configures the drive once and for all; or by preparing a configuration file named qic02conf, which lets you configure the drive at run-time. Answer y or n, depending upon which method you prefer to use.

The next question asks about floppy tape:

```
Ftape (QIC-80/Travan) support (CONFIG_FTAPE) [Y/m/n/?]
```

Answer y if your machine has a floppy-tape drive that uses the QIC-80 protocol.

```
Advanced Power Management BIOS support (CONFIG_APM) [Y/n/?]
```

Advanced Power Management (APM) is the system built into laptop computers and newer ATX-style workstations. Answer y if you are configuring such a system and you wish to use such laptop features as suspend/resume and the power saving modes of your display – and you are certain that your laptop meets APM standards. Otherwise answer n.

If you answered y, then you will be asked some questions concerning how you want to configure APM on your machine:

```
Ignore USER SUSPEND (CONFIG_APM_IGNORE_USER_SUSPEND) [Y/n/?]
Enable PM at boot time (CONFIG_APM_DO_ENABLE) [Y/n/?]
Make CPU Idle calls when idle (CONFIG_APM_CPU_IDLE) [Y/n/?]
Enable console blanking using APM (CONFIG_APM_DISPLAY_BLANK) [Y/n/?]
Power off on shutdown (CONFIG_APM_POWER_OFF) [Y/n/?]
```

Answer y to invoke the options that you want.

The following option asks about watchdog timers:

```
Watchdog Timer Support (CONFIG_WATCHDOG) [Y/n/?]
```

A *watchdog timer* is a system process that lets a system check its own operation: opening a watchdog file and then failing to write to it for more than one minute results in the system being rebooted automatically. This lets the machine reboot itself automatically should the kernel be locked up in any way. Answer n unless you are sure you need this feature.

If you answer y to this option, you will be asked a few additional questions:

```
Disable watchdog shutdown on close (CONFIG_WATCHDOG_NOWAYOUT)
[Y/n/?]
```

This option does not let you disable the watchdog timer once it is turned on.

```
WDT Watchdog timer (CONFIG_WDT) [Y/m/n/?]
```

This is a brand of watchdog card. Answer y if you are sure your machine contains this type of card. If you answer y, you will be asked some questions about how you want the card configured; we do not discuss them here.

```
Berkshire Products PC Watchdog (CONFIG_PCWATCHDOG) [Y/m/n/?]
```

This is a brand of watchdog card. Answer y if you are sure your machine contains this type of card.

Finally, you will be asked whether you want real-time clocks:

```
Enhanced Real Time Clock Support (CONFIG_RTC) [Y/n/?]
```

A *real-time clock* lets you open a device that reads your computer's real-time clock directly. Answer y if you think you will need this feature; otherwise, answer n.

This concludes the configuration of character devices.

SOUND CARDS
The next section asks you whether you wish to configure a sound card:

```
Sound card support (CONFIG_SOUND) [Y/m/n/?]
```

Given that the subject of sound cards is far beyond the scope of this book, we suggest that unless your Linux kernel already has been configured successfully to run sound, you answer n to this question. Once you have a kernel that supports networking properly, you can return and configure the sound driver.

KERNEL HACKING
The final section asks you whether you want to perform kernel hacking:

```
Kernel profiling support (CONFIG_PROFILE) [Y/n/?]
```

Kernel profiling builds a special device that tells you how much time the kernel spends executing various procedures. Answer n unless you seriously intend to hack the Linux kernel.

And with that, configuration is finished.

CONFIGURING AN ORDINARY HOST
The directions we gave above will configure a kernel that works for a *gateway* machine: this machine will be able to speak to an outside network, via either Ethernet or a PPP link over a modem — and it will be able to transfer to the outside

network the datagrams that it receives from other machines on a local Ethernet-based intranet. In Part III of this book, we describe how to build an intranet and how to configure your gateway machine so that every machine on the intranet can use it to interact with hosts in the outside world.

However, if you are not interested in building an intranet – that is, you want your Linux workstation just to interact with the outside by itself, rather than providing services to other machines – then you should answer n to the following configuration questions:

```
IP: forwarding/gatewaying (CONFIG_IP_FORWARD) [Y/n/?]
IP: firewalling (CONFIG_IP_FIREWALL) [Y/n/?]
IP: masquerading (EXPERIMENTAL) (CONFIG_IP_MASQUERADE) [Y/n/?]
IP: always defragment (CONFIG_IP_ALWAYS_DEFRAG) [Y/n/?]
IP: accounting (CONFIG_IP_ACCT) [Y/n/?]
```

Compiling and Installing

Now that the kernel is configured, you must set the dependencies within the kernel and clean out old object modules. Type:

```
make dep
make clean
```

To compile the kernel, type:

```
make zImage
```

Now, go and get something to eat: this will take a while.

You may see some problems with compilation or with linking. In particular, you may see a message that includes the phrase out of memory. This message indicates that you tried to build a kernel that was too big for your machine to link, given its available physical memory. If this occurs, you must go back, reconfigure the kernel, and drop some options to make the kernel smaller.

INSTALLATION

To install the newly compiled kernel, first su to the superuser root. Then, install the modules you may have compiled by typing:

```
make modules_install
```

Now, move the newly compiled kernel binary to the root file system:

```
cp /usr/src/linux/arch/i386/zImage /testkernel
```

The next step is to configure lilo, which is the program that actually loads the kernel into memory. Use your favorite text editor to add the following lines to the end of file /etc/lilo.conf:

```
image = /testkernel
  root = /dev/device
  label = testkernel
  read-only
```

Be sure to indent each line after the one that begins image.

device names the physical device on which your root partition is mounted, for example /dev/hda1. If you are unsure which physical device holds the root partition, type command mount and look for an entry of the form:

```
/dev/hda1 on / type ext2 (rw)
```

Directory / (that is, a slash all by itself) is the directory on which the root file system is mounted. The root file system is always mounted on this directory; therefore, by looking for the physical device mounted on directory /, you will find the physical device that holds the root file system.

Once you have edited lilo.conf, type command lilo. lilo re-reads the configuration file, and reconfigures itself.

Now, make sure that all other users have logged off your system; then use command reboot to reboot the system.

When your system starts to come up, you will see the prompt:

```
lilo
```

Press the left Shift key; you will see the rest of the prompt, followed by a :. Type newkernel. lilo will boot the new kernel.

If all goes according to plan, you will now be running a Linux kernel that now contains all of the code you need to run TCP/IP networking.

TEST THE KERNEL
In general, if the kernel boots, it works; so if your kernel comes up when you reboot Linux, then we can proceed.

If the kernel does boot, then type the following command to see if networking is actually functioning:

```
ping 127.0.0.1
```

The IP address 127.0.0.1 is the "loopback" address — that is, the IP address at which a host would address itself. If all goes well, you will see something like the following:

```
64 bytes from 127.0.0.1: icmp_seq=0 ttl=255 time=0.500 ms
64 bytes from 127.0.0.1: icmp_seq=1 ttl=255 time=0.518 ms
64 bytes from 127.0.0.1: icmp_seq=2 ttl=255 time=0.553 ms
```

Type control-C to kill the ping command.

If you see this, then congratulations! TCP/IP networking is installed and is working in your machine's Linux kernel. At this point, you are not yet attempting to communicate with another host, but it does mark a major milestone on getting networking running on your Linux machine.

IF SOMETHING GOES WRONG

If the newly compiled kernel does not boot, check for error messages on the console, and jot them down. Your Linux system probably also copied the error messages into file /usr/adm/syslog. You should then reboot your system, using your old kernel — that is, the one you had been using before you compiled this new one.

If the error message points to a particular portion of the kernel, then try reconfiguring the kernel excluding that portion of code, and try again.

If problems persist, see the *Linux Kernel HOWTO* for tips on commonly seen errors and how to debug them. Directions on how to obtain this document appear at the end of this chapter.

If you're having problems with a particular portion of code — say, a particular device does not work — see the contents of directory /usr/linux/Documentation for documentation on the various Linux sub-systems. These documents will give you details about how to compile and configure Linux sub-systems, especially drivers; and they refer to other, more-detailed sources of information.

This concludes our discussion of how to build a Linux kernel that supports networking. Next, we discuss how to configure networking on your Linux machine, and get it running.

Configuring Networking

Now that you have compiled the networking software into your Linux kernel, we discuss how to turn on networking. This discussion has four parts:

◆ *Configuration files*, which hold information that networking programs use as they run.

◆ *Configuration commands*, which link IP addresses with interfaces.

◆ *Networking scripts*, which hold the commands that configure networking, and invoke the daemons that perform networking tasks. They are executed automatically when you boot your Linux system.

◆ *PPP scripts*, which let you turn on a PPP connection to an Internet provider.

We discuss each part in its turn.

If your Linux system is connecting to an existing intranet, you do not need to read the discussion of PPP scripts. If, however, you are setting up your Linux system to dial into an Internet service provider, then you should read all four of these sub-sections.

Configuration Files

Much network configuration is performed by entering information into configuration files that are kept in directory `/etc`:

◆ `/etc/hosts` — This file gives the names and IP addresses of the hosts with which your machine will interact frequently.

◆ `/etc/services` — This file identifies the networking services that your host will offer, and maps them to ports on your machine.

◆ `/etc/protocols` — This file identifies the TCP/IP protocols implemented under Linux.

◆ `/etc/HOSTNAME` — This file holds the name of your Linux machine.

◆ `/etc/inetd.conf` — This file configures the `inet` daemon: it tells the daemon what ports to listen to, and what command to invoke when it receives on each given port.

◆ `/etc/host.conf` — This file configures some selected aspects of how the host interacts with its network. In particular, we use this file to set how the host retrieves domain-name information.

◆ `/etc/resolv.conf` — This file identifies the hosts from which this host will retrieve domain-name information.

We discuss each file in turn.

/etc/hosts

`/etc/hosts` is a text file that holds a database of the host names and IP addresses of hosts with which your system will interact frequently. Your Linux system reads this database to convert a commonly used host name into its IP address.

`/etc/hosts` has the following format:

```
dotted.IP.address      primary.hostname [nickname ... ]
```

Therefore, the entry in `/etc/hosts` for machine `baldur` on a local intranet may be:

```
192.168.1.3      baldur.myexample.com baldur
```

/etc/hosts is used primarily to give key IP addresses, such as the addresses of other hosts on your intranet and the IP address of your Internet service provider.

As it comes out of the system, this file probably names only the loopback host. You should insert the following entries into this file:

◆ One entry for each host on your intranet, should your Linux workstation be plugged into one.

◆ An entry for your Internet service provider, or other gateway to the Internet. You will get this information from your ISP when you register with them.

NICKNAMES   The format of /etc/hosts lets you set one or more *nicknames* to each host. This is useful in several ways.

First, a nickname lets you type a shorter version of a host name. For example, the entry given above sets the nickname baldur for host baldur.myexample.com; thus, you can type baldur instead of the more cumbersome baldur.myexample.com each time you want to refer to this machine.

Second, a nickname can be used as an *alias* with which you can tell every machine on your intranet where to obtain a particular service. This means that you will not have to reconfigure every host should you decide to move a service from one machine to another.

For example, network myexample uses one machine, named thor, as the primary server for mail and news. The network administrator inserted the following entry into /etc/hosts to give a descriptive nickname to each service that that machine provides:

```
192.168.1.1.   thor.myexample.com devbox mailhost.myexample.com \
               mailhost news.myexample.com newshost
```

The system administrator then distributes a copy of /etc/hosts to every machine on her intranet. Every machine can then use the nickname mailhost to pick up mail, and the name newshost to pick up mail.

If the load on the server later becomes too large, the network administrator can set up a new mail or news server, then modify /etc/hosts as follows:

```
192.168.1.1     thor.myexample.com devbox
192.168.1.50    mailhost.myexample.com mailhost
192.168.1.51    newshost.myexample.com newshost
```

By distributing a copy of /etc/hosts thus modified, the other hosts on the intranet can continue to request mail and news from mailhost and newshost, respectively, without having to be aware of the fact that they are now talking to different machines.

This is a useful system for small intranets — say, three or four hosts. However, the larger the intranet is, the more frequently this file will need to be changed, and the more difficult it is to distribute an updated copy to each host on the intranet. The Internet's domain-name service (DNS) solves this problem, as we see in Chapter 6, when we describe how to set up and configure DNS on an intranet.

/etc/services

`/etc/services` names the networking services that your Linux host provides to other hosts on the Internet, and identifies the port and host-to-host protocol used by that service. This file uses the following format:

```
service-name IP-port/udp|tcp
```

For example, the `telnet` service has the following entries in `/etc/services`:

```
telnet      23/tcp
telnet      23/udp
```

Port 23 is the well-known port for `telnet`. Please note that this entry reserves port 23 for `telnet` under both the TCP and the UDP host-to-host protocols, even though `telnet` does not use the UDP protocol. This reflects the policy of the IANA, which is to assign both the TCP and UDP ports to a service that used either.

Ports less than 1,024 are considered *reserved*. This means that a program cannot bind the port unless it is run by, or `setuid` to, the superuser `root`.

If you wish to add a comment to this file, the comment format is the same as other UNIX configuration files and scripts: a comment begins with the pound sign '#' character and continues to the end of the line.

Your Linux system has a copy of `/etc/services` that names all of the standard network services that Linux supports. You will rarely, if ever, need to modify this file; this will occur only if you are assigning a port for a custom purpose (for example, a custom interface to a database server), or to add a new application to your Linux system. In Chapter 9, we give an example of modifying `/etc/services` to add a server that lets your Linux system interact with a Windows 95 system.

/etc/protocols

File `/etc/protocols` names the TCP/IP protocols that your system recognizes, and assigns a number to each of them. You will never need to modify this file, but you will may need to look at it from time to time.

/etc/hostname

File `/etc/HOSTNAME` holds your Linux machine's name. For example, if you named your machine `foobar.com`, then the contents of `/etc/HOSTNAME` should read:

```
foobar.com
```

You should have named your computer when you installed Linux onto it. If the name was not set at that time, or if you wish to change its name after you have installed Linux, all you have to do is edit this file.

/etc/inetd.conf

The program `inetd` is your host's *super server*. `inetd` is a daemon that listens to multiple ports simultaneously. When a datagram arrives on one of the ports to which it is listening, `inetd` invokes the program that should handle the datagrams on this port, then hands over the connection to that program. Thus, instead of having many daemons running simultaneously on your system, each listening to one port, you have one daemon listening to many ports. This reduces overhead on your system: when no services are being used, there is only one daemon running and accepting connections.

File `inetd.conf` configures `inetd`. In particular, it names the ports to which `inetd` should listen, and the server that `inetd` should invoke to handle traffic on each given port.

Your Linux system comes with a version of `inetd.conf` that handles the standard Linux networking tasks. However, over time you may need to modify `inetd.conf`. For example, you may wish to have `inetd` manage a server that had previously been run independently as a daemon; or you may wish to change the server that `inetd` invokes to process a given connection.

FORMAT OF inetd.conf   Each line in `inetd.conf` describes how `inetd` manages one service. Each line has seven fields, as follows:

```
service_name socket_type protocol flags user server_name arguments
```

We discuss each field in turn:

- *service_name* — The service name comes from file /etc/services, which we described above. `inetd` looks up the service's entry in /etc/services to find the well-known port for the service. In some special cases, the service name can also be the name of an RPC service. RPC is remote-programs services that was designed by Sun Microsystems. A discussion of RPC is beyond the scope of this book, but we mention them here so that you will recognize the RPC services named in /etc/inetd.conf.

- *socket_type* — A *socket* is the type of connection that the Linux kernel uses internally to read datagrams from a port. A socket must be one of the following types:

  - stream — A stream socket. Such a socket is used for the TCP host-to-host protocol.

- ■ dgram — A datagram socket. Such a socket is used for the UDP host-to-host protocol.

- ■ raw — A raw socket.

- ■ rdm — A reliably delivered message.

- ■ seqpacket — Sequenced packet data. The socket is almost always of type stream or, less frequently, of type dgram.

- ◆ *protocol* — The protocol must be a valid protocol name, as set in file /etc/protocols. This is always either tcp or udp. RPC services are entered as rcp/tcp and rcp/udp.

- ◆ *flags* — This is either wait or nowait, which refers to disposition of the socket after inetd hands it to the server. Datagram (UDP) services use the wait flag; this is because the listening socket gets handed to the server so the server can process the inbound data. Connection-oriented (TCP) services use the nowait flag; this is because the Linux kernel can queue connection requests to inetd for these services.

- ◆ *user* — This names the user that the service will be run as. Normally this will be either root or nobody; however, a special application (e.g., uucp) may require that it be run as some other user.

- ◆ *server_name* — This gives the full path name of the server that processes the datagrams read on this port.

- ◆ *arguments* — This gives the arguments, if any, that inetd passes to the server when it invokes it.

For example, the following gives the entry in inetd.conf for telnet:

```
telnet  stream  tcp     nowait  root    /usr/sbin/tcpd  in.telnetd
```

- ◆ telnet names the service, as set in file /etc/services. When we look up this service's entry in /etc/services, we see that it is linked to port 23 (which is the well-known port for the TELNET protocol).

- ◆ stream indicates that the kernel uses a stream socket to connect to this service's port.

- ◆ tcp names the host-to-host protocol used by this service.

- ◆ nowait flags that a no-wait connection is used for this service, as is usual for a connection-oriented protocol like TCP.

- ◆ root indicates that the server must be run under the identity of the superuser.

- ◆ /user/sbin/tcpd gives the path name of the server to process telnet datagrams. tcpd is a program that implements a number of the most common server protocols, including telnet, finger, and ftp.

- ◆ in.telnetd is the argument passed to tcpd. In this instance, the argument informs tcpd that it is to run as a telnet server.

/etc/host.conf

File /etc/host.conf configures a number of aspects of a host. The directive that interests us at present is order, which sets the order in which the host interrogates sources of domain-name information.

Edit file /etc/host.conf so that directive order reads as follows:

```
order hosts, bind
```

This tells the host first to read file /etc/hosts for domain-name information, then use the bind package to retrieve the domain-name information from a domain-name server.

We assume that you are not yet running DNS, so it is important that the order of lookup be hosts first, then bind. If you do not, any traffic with one of the hosts on your local intranet will trigger a DNS query to your ISP's server, and so dial a connection with your ISP.

In Chapter 8, we discuss how to set up DNS on your own, and how to modify this file to use the DNS service that you set up.

/etc/resolv.conf

File /etc/resolv.conf identifies the host or hosts from which this host receives domain-name service. This information is set by the directive nameserver, which has the following syntax:

```
nameserver ip.address
```

where ip.address gives the IP address of the machine that will be providing domain-name service to your intranet. To get this address, talk with the person who administers the network from which you will be receiving name-resolution services.

For the present, we assume that you have *not* set up domain-name service (DNS) on your intranet, and therefore you will be looking up addresses from file

/etc/hosts. In this case, *ip-address* should be the address of your local machine. In Chapter 8, when we discuss how to set up DNS, we show you how to modify this file to use the domain-name service you have set up on your intranet.

This concludes our discussion of configuration files. Next, we discuss the commands you will use to configure networking on your system.

Network Configuration Commands

The configuration files discussed above hold information that is read by networking software as it runs. Once these files are set up properly (and most of them came correctly configured "out of the box"), you can move on to our next topic: how to configure networking within your Linux kernel – or to be more precise, how to configure networking *interfaces* on your system.

INTERFACES

You may recall from Chapter 1, when we discussed the ARPA module for networking, we described how the network-access tier has multiple *interfaces*:

◆ Each interface gives access to a physical means of transporting data to another host.

◆ Each interface is either of two types: a *broadcast* interface, which talks with multiple hosts simultaneously; or a *point-to-point* interface, which talks with exactly one other host.

◆ A host assigns an IP address to each of its interfaces. The host uses this IP address to identify itself to the other hosts with which it communicates via that interface.

◆ A host uses a *routing table* to decide which interface it should use to communicate with a given host.

HOW INTERFACES ARE CREATED

Ethernet interfaces generally are created when you boot your Linux system. The Ethernet software in your Linux kernel probes for the Ethernet card, and creates interface eth0 when it finds the card. For example, the following boot-time messages indicated that the kernel's NE2000 driver found an NE2000 Ethernet card and created an interface to it:

```
ne.c:v1.1 9/23/94 Donald Becker (becker@cesdis.gsfc.nasa.gov)
NE*000 ethercard probe at 0x340: 00 40 05 22 bf 0f
eth0: NE2000 found at 0x340, using IRQ 5.
```

PPP interfaces, on the other hand, are created by the PPP daemon pppd as they are needed.

An Ethernet interface is static — it's created once and remains unchanged. PPP interfaces are dynamic: pppd creates them as they are needed, and removes them when they are no longer being used. In either case, there will be only one interface to each physical device on your system — one Ethernet interface for each Ethernet card, and no more than one PPP interface for each modem.

NAMING AN INTERFACE

The name of an interface consists of a root that identifies the networking-tier module to be used, followed by a number that identifies it uniquely. The names use the following roots:

- ♦ ppp — An interface to the PPP module; e.g., ppp0 or ppp1.

- ♦ sl — An interface to the SLIP module; e.g., sl0 or sl1.

- ♦ eth — An interface to the Ethernet module; e.g., eth0 or eth1.

- ♦ lo — The interface to the loopback module. A Linux machine will have only one such interface.

Interface Configuration Commands

There are two principal networking commands you will use to configure interfaces:

1. ifconfig, which assigns an IP address to an interface. This is called *activating* an interface.

2. route, which tells your kernel the interface to use in order to communicate with a given IP address. This is called *routing*.

We discuss each in turn.

If you are plugging your Linux system into an existing intranet through an Ethernet card, you must use both of these commands to establish networking on your system. If, however, you will be dialing into an ISP and connecting via PPP, you will not use either of these commands to configure your system (the PPP daemon pppd will handle these tasks for you); however, you would be well advised to read these sub-sections anyway, as we use both ifconfig and route to set up more sophisticated networking configurations later in this book.

ifconfig

Command ifconfig *activates* an interface. You can use it with many different types of interfaces, including Ethernet and PPP; however, in practice you will use ifconfig only to *activate* the interfaces to the Ethernet and the loopback devices.

The syntax of ifconfig is:

```
ifconfig interface IP_address [broadcast address] [netmask mask]
```

where:

◆ *interface* names the physical interface. As we mentioned earlier, this usually will be an interface to an Ethernet card: if you have one Ethernet card in your machine, it will be eth0; if you have two Ethernet cards, it will be eth0 or eth1. We assume that your machine holds only one Ethernet card; and in this case, interface eth0 is automatically set up by the driver for your Ethernet card when you boot your Linux system.

◆ *IP_address* gives the IP address you have assigned to your machine. If you are plugging your Linux machine into an existing network, this address may be assigned to you by your network's administrator.

◆ broadcast *address* gives the "magic address" that will be used to broadcast a message to every machine on your network. This argument is not required.

◆ netmask *mask* gives the mask for the class of your local network, as we described in Chapter 1. If you are on a class-A network, *mask* is 255.0.0.0; if you are on a class-B network, it is 255.255.0.0; if you are on a class-C network, it is 255.255.255.0.

For example, let's say your Linux host uses IP address 192.168.1.1 to communicate with an Ethernet-based intranet. If you're using the standard subnet mask for your class of network, you can skip the broadcast and netmask options and just connect the address to Ethernet interface eth0 as follows:

```
/sbin/ifconfig eth0 192.168.1.1
```

If you want to be explicit, you would do it this way:

```
/sbin/ifconfig eth0 192.168.1.1 netmask 255.255.255.0 broadcast
 192.168.1.  255
```

Other Activation Commands

ifconfig is not the only command that can activate an interface. In particular, we use two other commands to activate interfaces:

1. pppd – This command creates an interface to the PPP module.

2. diald – This daemon creates an interface to the SLIP module.

We give examples of these commands later in this chapter.

ifconfig IN DIAGNOSTIC MODE

You can also invoke `ifconfig` with option `-a` to list the addresses and characteristics of each network interface configured into the kernel. When you do so, it returns output that resembles the following:

```
lo          Link encap:Local Loopback
            inet addr:127.0.0.1  Bcast:127.255.255.255  Mask:255.0.0.0
            UP BROADCAST LOOPBACK RUNNING  MTU:3584  Metric:1
            RX packets:3330 errors:0 dropped:0 overruns:0
            TX packets:3330 errors:0 dropped:0 overruns:0

eth0        Link encap:10Mbps Ethernet  HWaddr 00:40:05:22:BF:0F
            inet addr:192.168.39.1  Bcast:192.168.39.255
   Mask:255.255.255.0
            UP BROADCAST RUNNING MULTICAST  MTU:1500  Metric:1
            RX packets:49564 errors:0 dropped:0 overruns:0
            TX packets:48249 errors:0 dropped:0 overruns:0
            Interrupt:5 Base address:0x340

sl0         Link encap:Serial Line IP
            inet addr:192.168.0.1  P-t-P:192.168.0.2  Mask:0.0.0.0
            UP POINTOPOINT RUNNING  MTU:1500  Metric:1
            RX packets:0 errors:0 dropped:0 overruns:0
            TX packets:2079 errors:0 dropped:0 overruns:0

ppp0        Link encap:Point-Point Protocol
            inet addr:207.241.63.123  P-t-P:207.241.63.126
   Mask:255.255.255.0
            UP POINTOPOINT RUNNING  MTU:1500  Metric:1
            RX packets:31 errors:0 dropped:0 overruns:0
            TX packets:35 errors:0 dropped:0 overruns:0
```

Interface `lo` is the interface to the loopback device. This usually is set up when you boot your Linux machine, as we describe later in the chapter. The other interfaces are to the Ethernet device `eth0`, the SLIP device `sl0`, and the PPP device `ppp0`.

For each interface the output lists the following:

> `inet addr` — The IP address linked to the interface. In the case of Ethernet interface `eth0`, this is the hobbyist IP address with which this host communicates with its intranet. In the case of the `ppp0` interface, it is the IP address assigned to the host by the ISP.
>
> `Bcast` — The broadcast address.
>
> `Mask` — The network mask.

A summary of the interface's status:

- ◆ TX packets — A summary of the datagrams transmitted.
- ◆ RX packets — A summary of the datagrams received.

For the Ethernet interface eth0, the output also gives the unique hardware address (HWaddr) burned into the Ethernet card at the factory, and the interrupt and the base address that the Ethernet card uses.

This concludes our introduction to the command ifconfig. We return to it later in the chapter, when we discuss how to write the scripts that actually turn on networking.

ROUTE

As we described in Chapter 1 (when we discussed the network-access tier of the ARPA networking model), the Linux kernel uses its routing table to determine which interface accesses a given host. The command route lets you — or to be precise, the superuser root — manipulate the Linux kernel's routing tables. With it, you can add entries to the routing table, delete entries from it, or modify entries within it.

SYNTAX route is a powerful command with a complex syntax. The following gives an abbreviated syntax for route:

```
/sbin/route [[add|del] [-net|-host] target gw gateway \
[netmask netmask] [dev interface]]
```

where:

> add — Tell route to add an entry to the routing table.
>
> del — Tell route to delete an entry from the routing table.
>
> net target — The target address refers to a network.
>
> host target — The target address refers to a host.
>
> gw gateway — The address of the gateway host.
>
> netmask netmask — The mask for this class of network.
>
> dev interface — The interface to use.

When route is invoked without any arguments, it prints a summary of the kernel's routing table.

EXAMPLE OF CONFIGURATION

In this example, we set up routing information for a Linux system that has the following configuration:

- ◆ A local intranet, whose hosts communicate with each other via Ethernet.

- ◆ A gateway machine on the intranet that forwards datagrams from all hosts on the intranet to another network.

If you are connecting your Linux system via Ethernet to an intranet, you will use this configuration, or one very much like it.

In this example, we assume the following:

- ◆ The intranet uses the class-C hobbyist network address 192.168.1.0. Because it's a class-C network, the netmask is 255.255.255.0, the network part of the address is 192.168.1, and the host part comes after the last period.

- ◆ Your host has IP address 192.168.1.1.

- ◆ Host 192.168.1.100 is a gateway that is configured to forward datagrams to another network (and by extension, to the Internet itself).

Now, let's connect your system to the intranet.

ifconfig COMMAND You would first use ifconfig to connect the host's IP address with Ethernet interface eth0, as follows:

```
/sbin/ifconfig eth0 192.168.1.1 netmask 255.255.255.0 broadcast
  192.168.1.255
```

We described this command earlier.

route COMMANDS Next, you need to use the command route to tell the kernel how to route to send datagrams to hosts on the intranet, as follows:

```
/sbin/route add -net 192.168.1.0 netmask 255.255.255.0 dev eth0
```

This tells route to add an entry to the kernel's routing table that routes all datagrams to any host on network 192.168.1.0 to the Ethernet interface eth0. Strictly speaking, the argument netmask 255.255.255.0 is not needed, because route knows that any network whose IP address begins with 192 is a class-C network. Further, the argument dev eth0 probably isn't necessary, as the kernel in most instances can deduce the interface to use by examining the IP address linked to each device, and from the entries already in its routing table; but it does no harm to name the interface explicitly (assuming that you name the correct interface).

Finally, you must route to the gateway host all datagrams bound for hosts outside the intranet:

```
/sbin/route add default 192.168.1.100 dev eth0
```

This names the host with IP address 192.168.1.100 as the *default* host. Your Linux kernel will forward to that host all datagrams that its routing table does not explicitly describe how to route. In Chapter 6, we show you how to configure the gateway host, so that it will be able to forward to the Internet datagrams that it receives from the other machines on your intranet.

If a host on our intranet needs to communicate with a host that is not on our local network, and if the default route is through an Ethernet interface, the kernel creates an Ethernet frame with the following attributes:

♦ The Ethernet destination address is that of the default gateway.

♦ The source IP address is that which the command ipconfig has linked with Ethernet interface eth0.

♦ The destination IP address of the host to which you wish to send the datagram.

The gateway host will receive the datagram, then forward it along its way.

As complicated as it sounds, this is it. Once you execute these commands, your Linux machine is now completely set up and ready to go.

Networking Scripts

Now that we have introduced the configuration commands ifconfig and route, the time has come to put it all together, and write some scripts that will turn on networking for you.

Under Linux, networking commands are kept in files /etc/rc.d/rc.inet1 and /etc/rc.d/rc.inet2. Your Linux system came with these files set to some reasonable default; however, you will need to modify these files in order to get networking up and running on your Linux system, so we look at them in some detail here.

rc.inet1

File rc.inet1 holds the configuration information for networking. In this file you set up all of your interfaces. The following gives a working copy of this file:

```
#! /bin/sh
#
# rc.inet1     This shell script boots up the base INET system.
#
# Version:     @(#)/etc/rc.d/rc.inet1  1.01    05/27/93
#
HOSTNAME=`cat /etc/HOSTNAME`
```

```
# Attach the loopback device.
/sbin/ifconfig lo 127.0.0.1
/sbin/route add -net 127.0.0.0 netmask 255.0.0.0 lo
# IF YOU HAVE AN ETHERNET CONNECTION, use these lines below to
  configure the
# eth0 interface. If you're only using loopback or SLIP, don't
  include  the
# rest of the lines in this file.
# Edit for your setup.
IPADDR="192.168.1.1"        # REPLACE with YOUR IP address!
NETMASK="255.255.255.0"     # REPLACE with YOUR netmask!
NETWORK="192.168.1.0"       # REPLACE with YOUR network address!
BROADCAST="192.168.1.255"   # REPLACE with YOUR broadcast address, if
  you
                            # have one. If not, leave blank and edit
  below.
GATEWAY="192.168.1.1"       # REPLACE with YOUR gateway address!
# Uncomment the lines below to configure your Ethernet card.
#/sbin/ifconfig eth0 ${IPADDR} broadcast ${BROADCAST} netmask
  ${NETMASK}
#if [ ! $? = 0 ]; then
#  echo "Error: the Ethernet card was not initialized properly"
#fi
# Uncomment these to set up your IP routing table.
#/sbin/route add -net ${NETWORK} netmask ${NETMASK} dev eth0
#if [ ! ${GATEWAY} = "" ]; then
# /sbin/route add default gw ${GATEWAY} netmask 0.0.0.0 metric 1 dev
  eth0
#fi
# End of rc.inet1
```

As it is currently set up, this script initializes two interfaces:

♦ The loopback interface lo

♦ The Ethernet interface eth0

If your machine does *not* have an Ethernet card, you do not have to do anything to this script. However, if you do have an Ethernet card, you must make two changes to the script:

♦ Set addressing variables.

♦ Uncomment configuration commands.

We discuss each in its turn.

SET VARIABLES   If your system has an Ethernet card, you must set the following addressing variables:

- ◆ IPADDR – This gives the IP address you are assigning to this interface.

- ◆ NETMASK – This is your network mask. The networking drivers will combine this with your IP address to derive the address of the network to which you are connected. If your local network's administrator has given you a netmask, then use that. Otherwise, stick with the standard scheme, as follows:

    - ■ Class A IP address (0.0.0.0 through 127.255.255.255) – Use netmask 255.0.0.0

    - ■ Class B IP address (128.0.0.0 through 191.255.255.255) – Use netmask 255.255.0.0

    - ■ Class C IP address (192.0.0.0 through 223.255.255.255) – Use netmask 255.255.255.0

- ◆ NETWORK – Here we need the network part of the address. Again, your intranet's network administrator can provide you with this information. If you are your site's system administrator, then you will again do well to stick to the standard, as follows:

    - ■ Class A IP address (0.0.0.0 through 127.255.255.255) – Set the last three numbers to zero.

    - ■ Class B IP address (128.0.0.0 through 191.255.255.255) – Set the last two numbers to zero.

- ◆ Class C IP address (192.0.0.0 through 223.255.255.255) – Set the last number to zero.

    For example, IP address 192.168.1.1 is a class C address, because it's between 192.0.0.0 and 223.255.255.255. In a class C address, the network is the first three numbers from our address; thus, to represent the network, we set the last (fourth) number to zero: 192.168.1.0.

- ◆ BROADCAST – This is the address that our software can use to talk to every machine connected to the same physical network as this machine. The broadcast address is formed by taking the network address and replacing all zeros with 255. For example, IP address 192.168.1.1 is a class C address, because it's between 192.0.0.0 and 223.255.255.255. Thus, its network address is 192.168.1.0 and its broadcast address is 192.168.1.255.

◆ GATEWAY — Set this variable to the address of the machine through which this host can contact the rest of your intranet (if it's made up of several networks) or the Internet. In this example, the gateway machine in the intranet we described above has IP address 192.168.1.100. Note that the router has two IP addresses (one with which it communicates with the intranet, and the other with which it communicates with the Internet), but you must use the address of the interface with which the gateway machine communicates with the intranet.

UNCOMMENT CONFIGURATION COMMANDS   If your machine has an Ethernet card, your next task is to uncomment the parts of the script that configure the hardware.

First, uncomment – that is, remove the initial pound sign '#' from lines:

```
#/sbin/ifconfig eth0 ${IPADDR} broadcast ${BROADCAST} netmask
 ${NETMASK}
#if [ ! $? = 0 ]; then
#  echo "Error: the Ethernet card was not initialized properly"
#fi
```

These lines turn on the ifconfig command to activate the interface eth0. They also check whether the interface was activated properly; and print an error message if it was not.

Next, uncomment the following lines:

```
#/sbin/route add -net ${NETWORK} netmask ${NETMASK} dev eth0
#if [ ! ${GATEWAY} = "" ]; then
#  /sbin/route add default gw ${GATEWAY} netmask 0.0.0.0 metric 1 dev
 eth0
#fi
```

These commands add the network and gateway to your Linux kernel's routing table, as we described earlier.

rc.inet2

File /etc/rc.d/rc.inet2 starts up the various daemons that provide the standard services on a Linux network. Basically, this is a shell script that tests for the existence of the daemon, then invokes the daemon. The following excerpts the part of the script that starts the daemon inetd to illustrate the structure of the script:

```
# Start the INET SuperServer
if [ -f ${NET}/inetd ]; then
  echo -n " inetd"
  ${NET}/inetd
else
  echo "no INETD found.  INET cancelled!"
  exit 1
fi
```

As it comes out of the box, this script turns on all necessary networking services. At various times during this book, we ask you to modify this script so that one or another networking feature that we are adding will be turned on automatically when you boot your Linux system.

TURNING ON NETWORKING

This has been a long preamble: compiling a new kernel, checking configuration files, learning about the commands ifconfig and route, and checking and modifying scripts rc.inet1 and rc.inet2. Now you are ready to turn on networking. To do so, simply reboot your Linux system.

When the system has rebooted, you should now have networking up and running.

If your system has an Ethernet card in it and you are talking with an intranet, then you should be on the air now. If, however, you plan to connect to an Internet service provider via PPP, then we have one more obstacle to overcome – writing a script to dial your ISP's machine, make connection with it, and turn on PPP. We discuss this next.

Configuring PPP

The Point-to-Point Protocol (PPP) is a protocol for transferring information over a serial link from one point to another. PPP is designed to address the deficiencies of the Serial Line Internet Protocol (SLIP) by specifying the means by which the participants in a link can authenticate each other, and negotiate the IP address that both sides of the link will use.

We introduced PPP in some detail in Chapter 1. You may wish to review this discussion; however, you do not need to know even this much detail to use PPP to connect your Linux workstation to another network.

PARTS OF PPP

We can divide Linux's implementation of PPP into three parts:

◆ *The physical interface* – the serial port and the modem that are plugged into it

◆ *The kernel interface* – the PPP line discipline and network interfaces

◆ A daemon to control operation of the link – pppd

The rest of this section discusses the kernel interface, and how to configure the daemon pppd.

THE KERNEL INTERFACE   The Linux kernel's PPP interface is handled by a kernel driver that provides the PPP line discipline and provides an interface for routing. To include this code in your Linux kernel, you must have answered y to the question

```
PPP (point-to-point) support (CONFIG_PPP) [Y/m/n/?]
```

when you configured your Linux kernel.

Including the PPP module also automatically includes the line-discipline module, so if you have configured the PPP interfaces, you should be all set.

You can test for the presence of PPP by running the following code at a command prompt:

```
pppd
```

If PPP is correctly configured on your system, you should see something like the following:

```
~=FF}#=CO!}!}!} }7}!}$}%=DC}#}%=C2#}%}%}
```

The gibberish that the command returns indicates that your kernel is ready for PPP. After about a minute, the `pppd` will give up and return control you to a command prompt.

If, however, you see a message saying that the PPP line discipline is not present, then your kernel does not contain support for PPP. We suggest you return to the beginning of this chapter, review the sections on configuration and booting, and make sure that the Linux kernel you have booted contains support for PPP.

pppd – THE PPP CONTROL DAEMON   The operation of PPP on your Linux system is controlled by the daemon `pppd`. `pppd` and gives you a way to activate an interface to the PPP code that is built into your Linux kernel.

`pppd` – or, to be more exact, the PPP interface that `pppd` activates – serves two purposes: it can be used as a server, to handle requests from other systems that wish to connect to your sytem via PPP; and it can be used as a client, to request PPP services from another system. Because the same program activates interfaces for two very different purposes, its options can be a little confusing; we try to clarify them for you as we discuss `pppd`.

The configuration of `pppd`, and thus of the kernel's PPP interface, is performed through instructions that you write into files. The rest of this section concerns these files, and the instructions you write into each.

pppd CONFIGURATION FILES

The following files are used to help configure `pppd` in directory `/etc/ppp`:

- `options`
- `options.*`
- `chap-secrets`
- `pap-secrets`

- ip-up

- ip-down

- ppp-on-dialer

The following files are used to help configure pppd in directory /usr/sbin:

- ppp-on

- ppp-off

The following files are used to help configure pppd in each user's home directory:

- .ppprc

The rest of this section discusses how to configure each of these files in turn.

FILES OPTIONS, OPTIONS.*, AND .ppprc   These files contain the master configuration for the PPP daemon pppd.

File options is read by all configurations. File options.*device* is read when PPP is invoked for a given *device*.

When the user invokes pppd, it reads information in the following order:

- First, pppd reads file /etc/ppp/options.

- Then, pppd reads file .ppprc from the user's home directory.

- Then, pppd reads the options on its command line.

- Finally, pppd reads file /etc/ppp/options.*device*.

This order is important. As a rule, the information in these files can be seen by any user on your system, but only the system administrator can write into them. We recommend that you use the following commands to set the ownership and permissions on these files:

```
chown root:root /etc/ppp/options*
chmod 644 /etc/ppp/options*
```

pppd runs setuid in normal operation — that is, assumes the privileges of the superuser root, regardless of the user who invokes it. This is because pppd manipulates the kernel's routing table, and root privilege is required to do this. Because pppd runs as root, you can be more paranoid and narrow the permissions on file options, like this:

```
chmod 600 /etc/ppp/options
```

This means that only the superuser root will be able to read this file.

Two options that you may wish to keep from your users are defaultroute and proxyarp. Adding a default route to your system or a proxyarp entry could be a dangerous thing. If you set the flags -defaultroute or -proxyarp in file options, neither can be overridden in later files, such as .ppprc or from the command line.

File .ppprc is available to each user whom you want to be able to establish a PPP link. Each user can modify her .ppprc to suit her individual needs.

The copy of options included with Linux is well configured. This file also includes extensive comments that describe each option in detail. If you want to modify options, we suggest that you save a backup copy of it — calling it, say, options.save — before you modify it.

The following sub-sections describe the flags within options that you will have to consider modifying.

Authentication Options

The following options concern authentication — that is, how your ISP can confirm that it is really talking with you, rather than another system that is merely pretending to be you. File options lets you set the following PPP options to help manage authentication:

- ◆ auth — This option tells pppd to use authentication by either the Cryptographic Handshake Authentication Protocol (CHAP) or the Password Authentication Protocol (PAP) when a client is being established with the server. CHAP and PAP resemble authentication through ordinary logins and passwords, but offer two major advantages: they are more secure than ordinary logins, and they let clients bypass having to write a script that mimics interactive login onto your ISP's system. Take note of the PAP and CHAP options — we return to them later.

- ◆ +chap — If authentication is requested, require authentication by CHAP. This option helps to control the type of authentication used for the connection. If you strongly prefer one type of authentication over the other, then using the option auth and either the option +pap or +chap will give you what you want.

- ◆ -chap — Forbid authentication by CHAP. This option helps to control the type of authentication used for the connection. If you will be authenticating yourself to a server, using this option can force PAP authentication.

- ◆ login — Use your Linux system's password file /etc/passwd for authenticating peers with PAP. This option would be used only if you were invoking pppd to act as a PPP server to other machines that were dialing into your Linux workstation.

- ◆ `name` – Set the name with which this instance of `pppd` identifies itself. If `pppd` is running as a client, it will pass to a PPP server for authentication. If, however, `pppd` is running as a server, it returns this name to clients that are dialing into it, and uses this name to help look up authentication information. For example, suppose that your Linux machine's name is `loki.myexample.com`, but the ISP identifies you as `joe`. You can use the `name` option to override the default PPP behavior of setting my name to `loki.myexample.com` and have it use `joe` instead. CHAP and PAP use this option to help from their respective secrets files, `chap-secrets` and `pap-secrets`, the right secret to forward to the server. We discuss these secrets files at length later in the chapter.

- ◆ `+pap` – If authentication is requested, require authentication by PAP. This option helps to control the type of authentication used for the connection. If you strongly prefer one method of authentication over the other, then using the option `auth` and either the option `+pap` or `+chap` will give you what you want.

- ◆ `-pap` – Forbid authentication by PAP. This option helps to control the type of authentication used for the connection. If you will be authenticating yourself to a server, using this option can force CHAP authentication.

- ◆ `remotename` – Set the name of the server for CHAP and PAP authentication. CHAP and PAP use this option to help find the appropriate secret in their respective secrets files, `chap-secrets` and `pap-secrets`. We discuss these files later in the chapter.

Options for the Serial Port, Modem, and Flow Control

The following options help you to manipulate the modem or serial port, or manage flow control:

- ◆ `crtscts` – Use hardware flow control on the serial port, rather than software flow control. Always use this option, unless your serial port does *not* use a National Semiconductor 16550 UART. This option will be set by the `diald` daemon, which we introduce later in this chapter.

- ◆ `-crtscts` – Do not use hardware flow control.

- ◆ `local` – Use this option if you are connecting two workstations directly through their serial ports via a null-modem cable. This option does not use Carrier Detect (CD) on the serial port to determine when the connection is up. Do not drop Data Terminal Ready (DTR) to reset the modem before terminating the connection.

◆ lock – Use UUCP-style locking. With this option, pppd creates a lock file when it takes control of the serial port. This lets multiple applications – such as minicom – use the port. You should always use this option, unless you are certain that no other program will use this port.

◆ modem – Use this option if you are connecting to another system via a modem. This option uses Carrier Detect (CD) on the serial line before establishing the connection, and drops Data Terminal Ready (DTR) momentarily to reset the modem when the connection is closed. This option implies that option crtscts has also been used. It is controlled by diald daemon, which we discuss later in this chapter.

◆ xonxoff – Use software flow control (XON/XOFF characters). The use of this option on Linux systems is deprecated, and may require setting the ASYNC map to escape these characters.

Network-Configuration Options
The following options help pppd to configure your network on the fly:

◆ defaultroute – pppd activates a PPP interface to the ISP, usually named ppp0. Option defaultroute tells pppd to insert into the kernel's routing table an instruction that makes this newly created interface the default for this host. Please note that if the routing table already contains a default route, your system will become confused. (We discussed the concept of *default routes* earlier in this chapter, when we introduced the command route.)

◆ -defaultroute – Forbid making the interface that pppd creates into the default interface.

◆ -ip – Some ISPs permanently assign an IP address to each of their dial-up customers; this is called a *static IP address*. More commonly, an ISP assigns an IP address to a dial-up customer when that customer dials into ISP and establishes a connection. When an IP address is assigned on the fly in this way, it is called a *dynamic IP address*. The default is for pppd to negotiate an IP address with the PPP server with which it is making contact; option -ip disables this behavior. If option -ip is set, you must specify a pair of IP addresses, either on the command line or in one of the options files, using the syntax *localIP:remoteIP*, where *localIP* is the IP address that the ISP assigned to your host, and *remoteIP* is the IP address of the ISP's machine. The connection will fail either if the other side cannot use the addresses specified, or if no addresses are specified.

- ◆ +ip-protocol – Negotiate the parameters of an Internet-protocol connection. This option enables the use of IP over the PPP link, and is the default.

- ◆ -ip-protocol – Do not negotiate the parameters of an Internet-protocol connection. When set, this option disables the use of IP over the PPP link. This would use this option only if you wished to use PPP to establish a link with a Novell (IPX) network.

- ◆ ipcp-accept-local – Accept the peer's idea of what your local address is, even if you have specified an address to use. Normally, you will not use this option; if you did, you would use it on the client side – that is, when you use pppd to dial into an ISP.

- ◆ ipcp-accept-remote – Accept the peer's idea of what her address is, even if you have specified an address to use for the remote host. Normally, you will not use this option; if you did, you would use it on the client side – that is, when you use pppd to dial into an ISP.

- ◆ ipx-protocol – Negotiate the parameters of a Novell (IPX) connection with the peer. You would use this option only if you were using pppd to connect to a Novell network.

- ◆ -ipx-protocol – Do not negotiate parameters of an IPX connection with the peer. This is the default.

- ◆ noipdefault – The default behavior of pppd is to attempt to deduce your host's IP address from its host name. If your ISP assigns an IP address to your system dynamically, then you must use option noipdefault to suppress this behavior; otherwise, the connection will fail.

- ◆ proxyarp – Establish an ARP-table entry for the remote host (and network) through this interface. We discuss what the ARP table is later in this chapter, when we introduce the command arp.

- ◆ -proxyarp – Do not establish an ARP-table entry for the remote host (and network) through this interface. Setting the ARP-table entry through the PPP interface can be dangerous; therefore, when you set this option in file options, PPP will not let it be overridden in another configuration file (e.g., .ppprc). We discuss what the ARP table is later in this chapter, when we introduce the command arp.

FILES chap-secrets AND pap-secrets   Files chap-secrets and pap-secrets contain the secrets (or passwords, if you will) for authenticating a PPP connection via the CHAP and PAP protocols, respectively.

These protocols work quite differently internally; however, their secrets files are structured identically and are used in the same way, so we discuss them together.

pppd parses files chap-secrets and pap-secrets into white-space separated fields, as follows:

◆ The client identifier

◆ The server identifier

◆ The secret

◆ One or more optional IP addresses

The *client identifier* identifies the host that must authenticate itself. This is always the host that is acting as the PPP client: your Linux host, if it dials into another host (such as your ISP), or it will be one of the machines dialing into your Linux workstation if you are setting up a dial-in PPP server. Please note that this identifier is arbitrary: it can be the name of the client system, or it can be an account name that the server has assigned to the client system – or it can be an arbitrarily assigned name. All that matters is that the server and the client agree that the client will use this name to identify itself.

The *server identifier* identifies the host that requests authentication. This is always the host that provides PPP service: your ISP, if you are dialing to it; or your Linux workstation, if you are setting up a dial-in PPP server. This too can be an arbitrary identifier, although in practice it almost always gives the name of the system that is providing PPP services.

The *secret* is the password with which the client identifies itself to the server.

Finally, the fourth and subsequent fields hold IP addresses that the server can assign to the client once the client has succeeded in authenticating itself to the server.

The wildcard character '*' can be used in a client or a server identifier. This expands the range of names that can be matched. For example, a large ISP may have many modems that are served by a pool of terminal-server machines; which means that a client that dials into this ISP will have no way of knowing which machine it's trying to connect to. In this case, a single asterisk '*' can be used as the server identifier, which will match the name of any server.

When CHAP or PAP performs authentication, it looks up a secret by the combination of client name and server name. Thus, the combination of client identifier and server identifier must be unique within the secrets file, or authentication will not work. If an asterisk is used in the client or server identifier, CHAP or PAP use the combination of server identifier and client identifier that has fewest wildcard characters.

Because the names of client and server do not have to be the names of systems, but in fact are arbitrary strings, a server can grant different passwords not only to each *system* that dials in, but to each *user* who dials in – and thus grant connect privileges to some users and deny them to others. As you can see, PAP and CHAP give an enormous amount of flexibility to the sometimes vexing task of authenticating a connection.

An important point to remember is that a system uses the same secrets file both to authenticate itself to other systems, and to have other systems authenticate themselves to it. This will be shown in the example that follows.

An Example of Authentication

Authentication may be a little confusing at first; therefore, let's walk through an example.

In this example, we describe authentication for a host named loki. loki acts as a PPP server to a machine named heimdall that dials into it; it also dials into two different ISPs as a PPP client — the ISP "Little ISP", which consists of a single machine, and the ISP "Big ISP", which services many customers and has a pool of machines into which its customers dial.

The following gives the contents of file /etc/ppp/pap-secrets on loki:

```
heimdall loki        heimdall-loki-secret    192.168.3.4
loki      little-isp  littleisp-secret
joe       *           joe-bigisp-secret
sally     *           sally-bigisp-secret
```

The first entry is used by loki when machine heimdall dials into it. heimdall uses the string "heimdall" to identify itself to loki. loki uses this identifier and the server identifier "loki" to look up the appropriate secret — which in this case is the string "heimdall-loki-secret". When the connection is established, loki assigns heimdall the IP address 192.168.1.100.

The second entry is used by loki when it dials into "Little ISP". Here, loki uses the client string "loki" and the server string "little-isp" to find the appropriate secret — which in this case is the the string "littleisp-secret".

The third and fourth entries are used by loki's users Joe and Sally, respectively, when they use PPP to dial into Big ISP. Because Big ISP uses a pool of terminal servers, there is no easy way to know the identity of the host at Big ISP into which loki is dialing, so a single asterisk '*' is used to identify all of Big ISP's machines. When user Joe dials from loki into Big ISP, the combination of Joe's login identifier and an asterisk are used to look up his password — in this case, the string "joe-bigisp-secret". Likewise, when user Sally dials into Big ISP, PAP uses the combination of her login identifier and the asterisk to look up her secret — in this case, the string "sally-bigisp-secret".

So, you may ask, how does PAP know which identifiers to use? After all, in one example, we're using loki's name as the client identifier; in another instance, we're using users' login identifiers as the client identifier. The answer is that these identifiers are set by the PPP daemon pppd. How they are set depends upon the mode in which pppd is running: as a server, or as a client.

When pppd is running as a server, it uses as the client name the name that is passed to it by the client that is attempting to connect to it; and it uses as the server name either the name of the machine on which it is running (the default), or the name set by the pppd command-line option name. (By explicitly setting the name of a pppd server, you could have a number of pppd daemons running on your system, each listening to a different serial interface and each identifying itself differently to clients that dial in on that device's telephone line. This would let you tune authentication very precisely.)

When pppd is running as a client, it uses as the server name the name that is passed to it by the PPP server to which it is connecting, and it uses as the client name either the name of the machine on which it is running (the default), or the name set by the pppd command-line option name.

We discuss this at greater length later in the chapter, when we describe the script ppp-on.

FILES ppp-on, ip-up, ppp-on-dialer, ppp-off, AND ip-down   These files contain scripts that are executed at selected points as pppd is connecting to and disconnecting from a remote PPP server:

- ◆ /etc/ppp/ip-up — pppd executes this script automatically once the link-level protocol negotiation is complete and it has established its link with the PPP server. In this script, you can perform some routine tasks whenever the PPP link comes up, such as upload mail or download batches of news.

- ◆ /usr/sbin/ppp-off — This script turns off the PPP link to your provider. When you have set up an automatic dialer, like diald, this script is unnecessary.

- ◆ /usr/sbin/ppp-on — This script manually establishes a PPP connection. You will want to change the telephone number and login information in this script to customize it for your own use. You will use this script to make a PPP connection explicitly. Later in this chapter, we show you how to use the daemon diald to dial a PPP server automatically, so you will seldom if ever need to use this script.

- ◆ /etc/ppp/ppp-on-dialer — This script actually dials the telephone and logs your system into the remote system. This information is placed into a separate script because you will want to use it with other applications — in particular, the daemon diald. Unfortunately, writing a script to dial and log into another system is by no means an easy task, and much of it depends upon details of how your ISP has configured her system, so you will have to tinker extensively with this script. We discuss it in some detail later in this chapter.

- ◆ /etc/ppp/ip-down — pppd executes this script automatically when the PPP link goes down. You can use this script to perform some housekeeping tasks, such as cleaning up your routing table if you are not using pppd's option defaultroute.

The final step is to write scripts ppp-on and ppp-on-dialer. Before we get into that, however, we must discuss the subject of PPP authentication, because the method of authentication will greatly influence the contents of your scripts.

METHODS OF AUTHENTICATION   As we mentioned earlier, there are two methods by which your system can create a PPP connection with an ISP's machine:

◆ Using standard Linux-style logins and passwords

◆ Using CHAP or PAP for authentication

The method of using Linux-style logins and passwords is *much* more difficult to set up, because you must write a script that mimicks every keystroke you make when you login by hand into your ISP's system.

With CHAP and PAP authentication, pppd itself handles these details: your dialer script merely has to dial the telephone, and pppd itself takes care of handshaking and authentication with the ISP's machine.

The lesson is clear: *if your ISP offers CHAP or PAP authentication, use it!* Most ISPs do offer CHAP or PAP authentication, principally because it is required by the Windows 95 implemenation of PPP. Be sure to discuss this matter with a technician at your ISP before you start to write your PPP scripts.

That being said, we now describe how to write ppp-on and ppp-on-dialer. We first discuss how to write these scripts to use Linux-style login-and-password authentication; then we discuss how to write these scripts to use CHAP or PAP authentication.

PPP SCRIPTS USING LOGIN-AND-PASSWORD AUTHENTICATION   In this section, we describe how to write versions of ppp-on and ppp-on-dialer to use Linux-style login-and-password authentication.

ppp-on
The following gives an example version of ppp-on that uses login-and-password authentication to connect with a PPP server:

```
#!/bin/sh
#
DIALER_SCRIPT=/etc/ppp/ppp-on-dialer
#
exec /usr/sbin/pppd lock modem crtscts /dev/ttyS0 38400 \
        noipdefault defaultroute connect $DIALER_SCRIPT
```

As you can see, this script consists of only two commands.

The first command initializes environmental variable DIALER_SCRIPT to the name of the script that you will use to dial the telephone and log into the remote machine. We discuss that script in a moment.

The second command invokes `pppd`. As you can see, we use the absolute path name of `pppd` to avoid a security hole. We also prefix the command with the command `exec`: this command, as a security measure, executes `pppd` as a process in its own right, rather than as a child process of the script's process.

- `lock` — Write a lock file when it opens the modem's serial port.

- `modem` — Use modem-connect interaction with the serial port.

- `crtscts` — Use hardware flow-control on the modem.

- `/dev/ttyS0` — Use the modem plugged into device `ttyS0`. You should change this device to the serial port into which your modem is plugged, from `ttyS0` through `ttyS3`.

- `38400` — The speed at which the serial port is to be opened. This is adequate for a standard 28.8-baud modem.

- `noipdefault` — There is no default IP address; the IP address will be assigned dynamically by the ISP.

- `defaultroute` — When `pppd` creates the interface to the ISP, this option tells it to insert into the Linux kernel's routing table an instruction that makes this interface the default interface.

- `connect $DIALER_SCRIPT` — Execute the script named in environmental variable `$DIALER_SCRIPT` to establish the connection with the ISP's machine.

ppp-on-dialer
Now, we discuss how to write a version of `ppp-on-dialer` that uses login-and-password authentication to connect with the remote system.

This script is difficult to write and debug, principally because the task of logging into a system is not controlled by a protocol: rather, you must mimic what you would do were you logging into the system by hand, keystroke by keystroke. This task is not "rocket science," but it does require close attention to detail — and a lot of patience.

The easiest way to show you how to write such a script is to walk you through an example. The following example version of the script `ppp-on-dialer` does the following:

- Handshakes with your modem

- Dials the telephone

- Logs your system into the ISP's machine

The bulk of it builds a set of arguments to the Linux command chat, which is a command designed to conduct a dialogue with another system.

To begin, here is the entire script:

```
#!/bin/sh
#
TELEPHONE=phonenumber      # The telephone number for the connection
LOGIN=login                # The login identifier used with the ISP
PASSWORD=password          # The password for loki's account on its
  ISP

DIALSCRIPT=/tmp/dialscript.$$

trap "rm -f ${DIALSCRIPT}" exit INT HUP QUIT

umask 066
cat <<EOF > ${DIALSCRIPT}
TIMEOUT 3
ABORT '\nBUSY\r'
ABORT '\nNO CARRIER\r'
ABORT '\nNO ANSWER\r'
'' '\nAT\r'
OK ATDT$TELEPHONE
TIMEOUT 30
'ion.' '\r\d\r\d\r'
ogin:—ogin: $LOGIN
assword: $PASSWORD
EOF
/usr/sbin/chat -v -f ${DIALSCRIPT}
```

We now discuss each line in turn.

- TELEPHONE=*phonenumber* — Set the telephone number to dial. *phonenumber* is the number of your ISP's modem.

- LOGIN=*login* — Set the login identifier with which you will log into your ISP's system. *login* is the login identifier that your ISP assigned to you. This is not necessary with CHAP and or PAP, so do not set it if you have confirmed that you can use one of those protocols for authentication.

- PASSWORD=*password* — Set the password with which you will log into your ISP's system. *password* is the password that your ISP assigned to you. This is not necessary with CHAP and or PAP, so do not set it if you have confirmed that you can use one of those protocols for authentication.

◆ `DIALSCRIPT=/tmp/dialscript.$$` — This script writes the *dial script* — that is, the script that command `chat` executes to dial your modem and then log `pppd` into your ISP's machine. We generate a dial script, instead of passing the options as command-line parameters, as a security precaution: if we were to pass these arguments to `chat` as command-line parameters, the arguments (including your login identifier and password) would be visible to any user who can use the command `ps`. The shell `sh` replaces the suffix `$$` with the number of the process under which the Linux kernel is running the script. For example, if the Linux kernel executes this script as process number 757, then the dialing script will be written into file `/tmp/dialscript.757`.

◆ `trap "rm -f ${DIALSCRIPT}" exit INT HUP QUIT` — Here, we use the command `trap` to trap the signals `INT` (interrupt), `HUP` (hangup), and `QUIT` (process ends normally). If the process that is executing this script receives any of those three signals — each of which indicates that the process is terminating — then two commands are invoked: `rm`, to remove the dialscript file; and `exit`, to exit from the script. This ensures that the dialscript — with its login and password information — is deleted when the script concludes or is aborted.

◆ `umask 066` — The command `umask` sets the permissions given by default to any file created by this script. In this case, permissions 066 removes read, write, and execute permission from the owner of the file. This is a security measure, which helps to ensure that the dialscript file written by this script can be read only by the users who have reason to do so.

◆ `cat <<EOF > ${DIALSCRIPT}` — This command writes into the file defined by environmental variable `DIALSCRIPT` all of the following lines in the script, up to the line that contains the token `EOF`. By the way, the phrase `<<EOF` is an example of what is called a *here document* in shell nomenclature. The command `chat` will then execute the lines of the script in the order in which they appear here.

◆ `TIMEOUT 3` — This instruction tells `chat` to exit if your modem cannot dial and connect with the ISP's modem within three seconds. This prevents `chat` from hanging should the modem be unavailable — say, because someone kicked out its plug. You may wish to lengthen this time by a few seconds should it take your modem more than three seconds to establish a connection with the ISP's modem — say, because the telephone must ring several times before the ISP's modem answers, or because the modems must go through a lengthy negotiation sequence as they are connecting with each other (the whistling and bellowing you hear when the modems are first connecting).

◆ ABORT '\nBUSY\r' — This and the following two instructions tell chat what strings your modem returns to indicate that it cannot connect with the ISP machine's modem. The escape sequence \r indicates a carriage-return character; the escape sequence \n indicates a newline character. Most modems return the string BUSY when the telephone line to the ISP's modem is busy.

◆ ABORT '\nNO CARRIER\r' — Most modems return this string when it makes connection with the ISP's modem but does not receive a carrier signal. This will occur when, for example, you accidentally dial a voice telephone and a human being answers the telephone.

◆ ABORT '\nNO ANSWER\r' — Most modems return this string when there is no answer — that is, when the telephone has rung more than a pre-arranged number of times (usually ten) without being answered.

◆ '' '\nAT\r' — This and most of the following lines in the script comprise a *chat dialogue* between chat and the modem. The first element in the dialogue gives a string received from the modem; the second element gives what the script says in response to that. In this line, the modem says nothing (as indicated by the pair of apostrophes — also called single-quotation marks — with nothing between them); the script initiates the dialogue by sending the string AT to the modem, which is the standard "attention" instruction for most modems.

◆ OK ATDT$TELEPHONE — This line continues the dialogue with the modem. In this part of the dialogue, the modem sends the string OK (in response to the AT instruction sent in the previous line). In response, the script sends the string ATDT (which is the standard modem instruction for "attention, dial touch-tone") followed by the telephone number to dial as set by the environmental variable TELEPHONE, which we set earlier in the script. When this instruction is executed, your modem will dial the ISP's modem and make connection with it.

◆ TIMEOUT 30 — At this point, chat has dialed the ISP's modem and made connection with it. (If your modem could not make connection with the ISP's modem, either the connection would time out, or your modem would have returned one of the ABORT strings defined earlier, thus aborting the chat command.) At this point, we change the timeout from three to 30 seconds. This gives the script time to execute the dialogue with the ISP's modem, and log in. Note well that if you are able to CHAP or PAP, you will not need to execute the rest of the chat script as CHAP or PAP will handle the rest of the login automatically.

◆ `'ion.' '\r\d\r\d\r'` — This line continues the dialogue, except that at this point the dialogue is with the ISP's machine rather than with your modem. Here, the ISP displays some text (called a *banner*) that ends with the string `ion`. In response to the ISP machine's response, the script sends three carriage-returns (indicated by the `\r` escape sequence), separated by two brief delays (indicated by the `\d` escape sequence). In effect, the script taps the Enter key three times to get past the ISP's banner and get to the login prompt. Please note that this instruction is very specific to your ISP's machine: your ISP may not use a banner, or it may use a banner whose wording ends in something other than the string `ion`. This part of the dialogue you must fill in on your own, depending upon how your ISP has configured her system. Getting this part of the script right will require some trial-and-error on your part. Later in this chapter, we walk through the logging messages returned by `chat`, so you can follow exactly the prompts that the ISP's machine sends to you.

◆ `ogin:-ogin: $LOGIN` — This line continues the dialogue with the ISP's system. The script waits for a prompt that ends in the string `ogin:` (for `login`). The string `ogin:-ogin:` has a special meaning:

- `chat` is to wait a predetermined period of time for a string that ends in `ogin:`.

- If the string does not arrive, `chat` is to send a `break` signal (to jostle the ISP's system a little), then wait again for a string that ends in `ogin:`.

- If the string then does not come within the predetermined period of time, `chat` exits.

- If, however, `chat` does receive a string that ends in `ogin:`, then in response `chat` is to send the string defined by the variable `LOGIN`, which we defined earlier in this script.

- This part of the dialogue also depends upon what the ISP chooses to send as its login prompt. For example, if its login prompt does end in a colon ':', then this portion of the dialogue will fail. You must check how your ISP has configured its login procedure to ensure that this portion of the dialogue is letter-perfect. (As you can see, we were not kidding when we said that writing a dialer script is a vexing task!)

◆ `assword: $PASSWORD` — This line concludes our dialogue with the ISP's system. Here, the script waits for a string that ends with `assword:` — presumably indicating `Password:` or `password:`. In response to this prompt, the dialogue sends the string defined by the environmental variable `PASSWORD`, which we set a little earlier in this script. Again, you must make sure that the prompt is letter-perfect. However, once this is done correctly, you are finished — you've made connection with your ISP's machine.

◆ `EOF` — This line marks the end of the here document defined earlier in this script — and thus, the end of the lines that are echoed into the `DIALSCRIPT` file.

◆ `/usr/sbin/chat -v -f ${DIALSCRIPT}` — Now that we've built the dial-script, this command executes. The command `chat` will execute the instructions.

 ■ Argument `-f ${DIALSCRIPT}` tells `chat` to get its chat script from the file named in environmental variable `DIALSCRIPT` instead of from command-line arguments.

 ■ Option `-v` tells `chat` to log each step of the login process. The logging messages are captured by the daemon `syslogd` and by default are written into file `/usr/adm/messages` — although this may be different on your release of Linux. (We discuss `syslogd` at greater length later in this chapter.) This feature is invaluable when you are debugging the chat script, as we describe later in the chapter.

That's it — we're done. When this script executes, it builds the `DIALSCRIPT`, then calls `chat` to execute the script. When the script executes, `chat` uses the dialscript to connect with your modem, initialize it, dial your ISP's computer, walks through the login procedure, then removes the file that holds the chat script and exits.

Once this command has logged your system into your ISP's machine, it exits and returns control to `pppd` (remember, this script is invoked as an argument on `pppd`'s command line). `pppd` then negotiates with the ISP's PPP server, establishes the PPP link. Then and only then can your system start to exchange datagrams with the Internet.

Debugging the Scripts
Now the moment of truth has arrived: let's try it out. To do so, `su` to the superuser `root`, then type the command:

```
ppp-on
```

In a moment, this script will invoke the daemon `/usr/sbin/pppd`, build a chat script, then invoke command `chat` to execute the script. You should hear or see the modem dialing, then negotiating and making connection with the ISP's machine.

As we mentioned earlier, option -v to the command chat tells it to log all of its activity. The system log daemon syslogd then captures these messages and stores them — by default into file /usr/adm/messages, although your system may be configured to use another file. The following extract shows the logging messages that are generated when the example script given above is used to make a PPP connection successfully. We comment where necessary.

The first logging message shows the command chat being invoked, and the default timeout being set:

```
Dec 28 09:42:57 mysystem chat[5384]: timeout set to 10 seconds
```

The next three logging messages show chat executing instructions in our chat dialogue:

```
ABORT '\nBUSY\r'
ABORT '\nNO CARRIER\r'
ABORT '\nNO ANSWER\r'
```

The next logging messages show chat executing instruction '' '\nAT\r' in our chat dialogue:

```
Dec 28 09:42:57 mysystem chat[5384]: send (^JAT^M^M)
```

The next logging messages show chat executing instruction OK ATDT$TELE-PHONE in our chat dialogue:

```
Dec 28 09:42:57 mysystem chat[5384]: expect (OK)
Dec 28 09:42:57 mysystem chat[5384]: ^M
Dec 28 09:42:57 mysystem chat[5384]: OK—got it
Dec 28 09:42:57 mysystem chat[5384]: send (ATDT5554321^M)
```

That is, after we sent your modem AT, the script expects to hear OK from the modem. This string was received, as indicated by the message got it; and in response to this prompt, the script sends the modem the instruction to dial the ISP's telephone number. (Here we have set the ISP's telephone number to "5554321".)

The next logging message shows chat executing instruction TIMEOUT 30 in our chat dialogue:

```
Dec 28 09:42:58 mysystem chat[5384]: timeout set to 30 seconds
```

Now things get a little complicated. At this point, the script dials the ISP's modem and has made connection with it. The rest of the chat dialogue is talking not with your modem, but with the ISP's machine. The next logging messages show chat executing instruction 'ion.' '\r\d\r\d\r' in our chat dialogue — that is, the dialogue waits for a string from the ISP's machine that ends in the string ion., and in response sends a series of carriage-return characters, to skip past any miscellaneous junk that the ISP's displays before its login prompt:

```
Dec 28 09:42:58 mysystem chat[5384]: expect (ion.)
Dec 28 09:42:58 mysystem chat[5384]: ^M
Dec 28 09:43:16 mysystem chat[5384]: ^M
Dec 28 09:43:16 mysystem chat[5384]: CONNECT
 31200/ARQ/V34/LAPM/V42BIS^M
Dec 28 09:43:17 mysystem chat[5384]: ^M
Dec 28 09:43:17 mysystem chat[5384]: Welcome to Internet Service
 Provider^M
Dec 28 09:43:17 mysystem chat[5384]: Chicago, Illinois^M
Dec 28 09:43:17 mysystem chat[5384]: ^M
Dec 28 09:43:17 mysystem chat[5384]: enter 'guest' at login and
 password prompts^M
Dec 28 09:43:17 mysystem chat[5384]: for more information.-got it
Dec 28 09:43:17 mysystem chat[5384]: send (^M\d^M\d^M^M)
```

Our script waits for the Internet service provider's machine to send us a prompt that ends in the string ion. The Internet service provider displays a lot of information meant for human consumption, ending in the word information.—which is what the script wants. The phrase got it shows that the expected string was received. The script in response sends three carriage-return characters, with slight delays between them, to skip past this stuff—just as if you were interacting yourself with the ISP's machine, and pressed the Enter key several times.

The next logging messages show chat executing instruction ogin:-ogin: $LOGIN in our chat dialogue:

```
Dec 28 09:43:19 mysystem chat[5384]: expect (ogin:)
Dec 28 09:43:19 mysystem chat[5384]: ^M
Dec 28 09:43:19 mysystem chat[5384]: ^M
Dec 28 09:43:19 mysystem chat[5384]: User Access Verification^M
Dec 28 09:43:19 mysystem chat[5384]: ^M
Dec 28 09:43:19 mysystem chat[5384]: ISP1 login:-got it
Dec 28 09:43:19 mysystem chat[5384]: send (mylogin^M)
```

The ISP sends us some more stuff in response to the carriage-return characters. The script is awaiting a prompt that ends with the string ogin:; finally, it arrives and in response chat sends our host's login identifier.

The next logging message shows chat executing instruction assword: $PASS-WORD, which is the final instruction in our chat dialogue:

```
Dec 28 09:43:19 mysystem chat[5384]: Password:-got it
Dec 28 09:43:19 mysystem chat[5384]: send (mypassword^M)
```

The chat dialogue awaited a prompt that ends in the string assword:; when it was received, the script sent the password mypassword in response. The password was accepted — or the ISP's machine would have returned an error message.

At this point, our chat dialogue has successfully logged us into the ISP's machine. With the conclusion of the chat dialogue, the command `chat` exits and returns control to the command `pppd`. The following messages show the dialogue that `pppd` has with the ISP's PPP server:

```
Dec 28 09:43:20 mysystem kernel: PPP: version 2.2.0 (dynamic channel
  allocation)
Dec 28 09:43:20 mysystem kernel: PPP Dynamic channel allocation code
  copyright 1995 Caldera, Inc.
Dec 28 09:43:20 mysystem kernel: PPP line discipline registered.
Dec 28 09:43:20 mysystem kernel: registered device ppp0
Dec 28 09:43:20 mysystem pppd[5386]: pppd 2.2.0 started by dialout,
  uid 0
Dec 28 09:43:20 mysystem pppd[5386]: Using interface ppp0
Dec 28 09:43:20 mysystem pppd[5386]: Connect: ppp0 @@@-> /dev/ttyS3
Dec 28 09:43:23 mysystem pppd[5386]: local  IP address 207.241.63.61
Dec 28 09:43:23 mysystem pppd[5386]: remote IP address 207.241.63.62
```

And that's it – we have successfully set up your modem, dialed the ISP's modem, logged into the ISP's machine, and set up a PPP connection with the ISP.

There can be an error at any point in this process. The logging messages will show you the point at which it fails. For example, if the ISP's banner does not end in the string `ion.`, the script will fail at that point: it will halt, then just sit there and wait until the connection times out, then it will exit. To get around that problem, check carefully what the ISP has sent you, then modify the script to match what the ISP does send you. For example, your ISP may not send a banner, but immediately displays the login prompt; in this case, you can remove this line from the chat dialogue altogether.

You may have to run the script many times, correcting problems one at a time, until the script works correctly. In particular, the number of carriage returns you must send to get past a banner will be a matter of guesswork. Be patient, and remember that once you have the script working, you will not have to change it again.

If you are having a problem with the PPP portion of the dialogue – that is, your system can connect with the ISP and log in, but for some reason PPP negotiation fails – we suggest that you call your ISP and talk the problem over with a technical support person there. The error message returned by PPP will help. The ISP will be best able to advise you how you can configure command `pppd` so that your system can make a PPP connection with the ISP's PPP server.

PPP SCRIPTS USING CHAP OR PAP AUTHENTICATION   Now that we have shown you how to write scripts that use login-and-password authentication to connect with a remote PPP server, we now discuss how to do the same task using CHAP and PAP. As you will see, this approach eliminates much of the complexity of the chat script, and so is both easier to write and easier to debug.

ppp-on

The following gives an example of ppp-on that includes the options needed for authentication. In this example, our Linux workstation named myexample is dialing an ISP machine named myisp. We assume that you have already set up files chap-secrets and pap-secrets as we described above:

```
#!/bin/sh
#
MYNAME=myexample
ISPNAME=myisp
DIALER_SCRIPT=/etc/ppp/ppp-on-dialer
#
exec /usr/sbin/pppd name ${MYNAME} remotename ${ISPNAME} lock modem
  crtscts \
          /dev/ttyS0 38400 noipdefault defaultroute connect
  $DIALER_SCRIPT
```

The first three instructions in this script define three variables:

- ◆ MYNAME — This variable gives the name with which your site will identify itself to the remote PPP server. If you do not set this identifier, pppd by default will pass the name of your system.

- ◆ ISPNAME — This variable names the remote host into which you will be dialing. Often, this remote host is that of an Internet service provider, hence the variable's name.

- ◆ DIALER_SCRIPT — This variable names the script that dials the telephone and makes connection with the remote host's modem. We discuss this script later in the chapter.

The second command invokes pppd. As you can see, we use the absolute path name of pppd to avoid a security hole. We also prefix the command with the command exec: this command, as a security measure, executes pppd as a process in its own right, rather than as a child process of the script's process.

When we invoke pppd, we pass it the following command-line arguments:

- ◆ name ${MYNAME} — This argument sets the name with which pppd identifies itself. It will pass this name to the remote host's PPP server, and it will use this name to help find the correct secret (as stored in files pap-secrets and chap-secrets) to pass to the PPP server. If you do not set this argument, pppd by default uses the name of your host to identify itself.

◆ `remotename ${ISPNAME}` — This argument sets the name of the remote host to which `pppd` will be connecting. `pppd` will use this option to help find the correct secret to pass to the PPP server. Please note that this argument is optional. If you will be dialing into a pool of machines at the remote site (as is often the case with a large commercial ISP), you probably will not know the identity of the host with which you will be connecting; in this case, you should not use this option; rather, you should set the name of the server in the secrets file to a single wildcard '*', and use the local name (as set with the argument *name*) alone to look up the secret.

◆ `lock` — Write a lock file when `pppd` opens the modem's serial port.

◆ `modem` — Use modem-connect interaction with the serial port.

◆ `crtscts` — Use hardware flow-control on the modem.

◆ `/dev/ttyS0` — Use the modem plugged into device `ttyS0`. You should change this device to the serial port into which your modem is plugged, from `ttyS0` through `ttyS3`.

◆ `38400` — The speed at which the serial port is to be opened. This is adequate for a standard 28.8-baud modem.

◆ `noipdefault` — There is no default IP address: the IP address will be assigned dynamically by the ISP.

◆ `defaultroute` — When `pppd` creates the interface to the ISP, this option tells it to insert into the Linux kernel's routing table an instruction that makes this interface the default interface.

◆ `connect $DIALER_SCRIPT` — Execute the script named in environmental variable `$DIALER_SCRIPT` to establish the connection with the ISP's machine.

AN EXAMPLE DIALER SCRIPT   Earlier in this chapter, we presented a dialer script with which `pppd` could use login-and-password authentication when connecting to the remote host. As you probably noticed, such a script can be difficult to write, because it must recreate all of the keystrokes a human user would perform when she logs into the remote system by hand.

Now, we present a dialer script with which we will connect to a PPP server that uses PAP or CHAP authentication:

```
#!/bin/sh
#
TELEPHONE=phonenumber        # The telephone number for the connection
DIALSCRIPT=/tmp/dialscript.$$

trap "rm -f ${DIALSCRIPT}" exit INT HUP QUIT

umask 066
cat <<EOF > ${DIALSCRIPT}
TIMEOUT 30
ABORT '\nBUSY\r'
ABORT '\nNO CARRIER\r'
ABORT '\nNO ANSWER\r'
'' '\nAT\r'
OK ATDT$TELEPHONE
CONNECT ''
EOF

/usr/sbin/chat -v -f ${DIALSCRIPT}
```

We now discuss each line in turn.

◆ TELEPHONE=*phonenumber* — Set the telephone number to dial.
phonenumber is the number of your ISP's modem.

◆ LOGIN=*login* — Set the login identifier with which you will log into your
ISP's system. *login* is the login identifier that your ISP assigned to you.

◆ PASSWORD=*password* — Set the password with which you will log into your
ISP's system. *password* is the password that your ISP assigned to you.

◆ DIALSCRIPT=/tmp/dialscript.$$ — This script writes the *dial script* —
that is, the script that command chat executes to dial your modem and
then log pppd into your ISP's machine. We generate a dial script, instead
of passing the options as command-line parameters, as a security
precaution: if we were to pass these arguments to chat as command-line
parameters, the arguments (including your login identifier and password)
would be visible to any user who can use the command ps. The shell sh
replaces the suffix $$ with the number of the process under which the
Linux kernel is running the script. For example, if the Linux kernel
executes this script as process number 757, then the dialing script will be
written into file /tmp/dialscript.757.

◆ `trap "rm -f ${DIALSCRIPT}" exit INT HUP QUIT` — Here, we use the command `trap` to trap the signals `INT` (interrupt), `HUP` (hangup), and `QUIT` (process ends normally). If the process that is executing this script receives any of those three signals — each of which indicates that the process is terminating — then two commands are invoked: `rm`, to remove the dialscript file; and `exit`, to exit from the script. This ensures that the dialscript — with its login and password information — is deleted when the script concludes or is aborted.

◆ `umask 066` — The command `umask` sets the permissions given by default to any file created by this script. In this case, permissions `066` removes read, write, and execute permission from the owner of the file. This is a security measure, which helps to ensure that the dialscript file written by this script can be read only by the users who have reason to do so.

◆ `cat <<EOF > ${DIALSCRIPT}` — This command writes into the file defined by environmental variable `DIALSCRIPT` all of the following lines in the script, up to the line that contains the token `EOF`. By the way, the phrase `<<EOF` is an example of what is called a *here document* in shell nomenclature. The command `chat` will then execute the lines of the script in the order in which they appear here.

◆ `TIMEOUT 30` — This instruction tells `chat` to exit if your modem cannot dial and connect with the ISP's modem within 30 seconds. This prevents `chat` from hanging should the modem be unavailable, say, because someone kicked out its plug. You may wish to lengthen this time by a few seconds should it take your modem more than three seconds to establish a connection with the ISP's modem — say, because the telephone must ring several times before the ISP's modem answers, or because the modems must go through a lengthy negotiation sequence as they are connecting with each other — the whistling and bellowing you hear when the modems are first connecting.

◆ `ABORT '\nBUSY\r'` — This and the following two instructions tell `chat` what strings your modem returns to indicate that it cannot connect with the ISP machine's modem. The escape sequence `\r` indicates a carriage-return character; the escape sequence `\n` indicates a newline character. Most modems return the string `BUSY` when the telephone line to the ISP's modem is busy.

◆ `ABORT '\nNO CARRIER\r'` — Most modems return this string when it makes connection with the ISP's modem but does not receive a carrier signal. This will occur when, for example, you accidentally dial a voice telephone and a human being answers the telephone.

◆ ABORT '\nNO ANSWER\r' — Most modems return this string when there is no answer — that is, when the telephone has rung more than a pre-arranged number of times (usually ten) without being answered.

◆ '' '\nAT\r' — This and most of the following lines in the script comprise a *chat dialogue* between chat and the modem. The first element in the dialogue gives a string received from the modem; the second element gives what the script says in response to that. In this line, the modem says nothing (as indicated by the pair of apostrophes — also called single-quotation marks — with nothing between them); the script initiates the dialogue by sending the string AT to the modem, which is the standard "attention" instruction for most modems.

◆ OK ATDT$TELEPHONE — This line continues the dialogue with the modem. In this part of the dialogue, the modem sends the string OK (in response to the AT instruction sent in the previous line). In response, the script sends the string ATDT (which is the standard modem instruction for "attention, dial touch-tone") followed by the telephone number to dial as set by the environmental variable TELEPHONE, which we set earlier in the script. When this instruction is executed, your modem will dial the ISP's modem and make connection with it.

◆ CONNECT '' — At this point, chat has dialed the telephone and has made connection with the remote system's modem. When the connection is successfully made, we expect the modem to return the string CONNECT, which is the standard response returned by a modem when it has successfully connected with another modem. The script sends nothing in return — nor should it, because it is finished.

That's it — we're done. When this script executes, it builds the DIALSCRIPT, then calls chat to execute the script. When the script executes, chat uses the dialscript to connect with your modem, initialize it, and dials your ISP's modem. However, unlike the dialscript used with login-and-password authentication, there is no dialogue to log your server to the ISP, or to pass it the login or password strings: this interaction with the remote host is now handled by pppd itself, using CHAP or PAP (whichever the remote host's PPP server prefers). Given that the login-and-password portion of the dialogue is by far the most difficult portion to write and debug, this script is much easier to write than was our earlier script that used login-and-password authentication.

Once chat has made connection with the remote host's modem, it exits and returns control to pppd (remember, this script is invoked as an argument on pppd's command line). pppd then negotiates with the ISP's PPP server, authenticates itself to the server, and established the PPP connection. Then and only then can your system start to exchange datagrams with the Internet.

DEBUGGING THE SCRIPTS   Now the moment of truth has arrived: let's try it out. To do so, `su` to the superuser `root`, then type the command:

```
ppp-on
```

In a moment, this script will invoke the daemon `/usr/sbin/pppd`, build a chat script, then invoke command `chat` to execute the script. You should hear or see the modem dialing, then negotiating and making connection with the ISP's machine.

As before, option `-v` to the command `chat` tells it to log all of its activity. The system log daemon `syslogd` then captures these messages and stores them—by default into `file /usr/adm/messages`, although your system may be configured to use another file. The following extract shows the logging messages that are generated when the example script given above is used to make a PPP connection successfully. We comment where necessary.

The first logging message shows the default timeout being set:

```
Jan 28 06:30:45 myexample chat[6065]: timeout set to 30 secondsc
```

The next messages show `chat` setting the strings with which it will recognize that the modem has aborted dialing:

```
Jan 28 06:30:45 myexample chat[6065]: abort on (\nBUSY\r)
Jan 28 06:30:45 myexample chat[6065]: abort on (\nNO CARRIER\r)
Jan 28 06:30:45 myexample chat[6065]: abort on (\nNO ANSWER\r)
```

The next messages show the dialogue initialing the modem:

```
Jan 28 06:30:45 myexample chat[6065]: send (^JAT^M^M)
Jan 28 06:30:46 myexample chat[6065]: expect (OK)
Jan 28 06:30:46 myexample chat[6065]: ^M
Jan 28 06:30:46 myexample chat[6065]: OK—got it
```

The next logging messages show `chat` executing instruction `OK ATDT$TELE-PHONE` in our chat dialogue, and connecting with the remote host's modem:

```
Jan 28 06:30:46 myexample chat[6065]: send (ATDT18475563278^M)
Jan 28 06:30:46 myexample chat[6065]: expect (CONNECT)
Jan 28 06:30:46 myexample chat[6065]: ^M
Jan 28 06:31:03 myexample chat[6065]: ^M
Jan 28 06:31:03 myexample chat[6065]: CONNECT—got it
Jan 28 06:31:03 myexample chat[6065]: send (^M)
```

At this point, our chat dialogue has connected us to the ISP's modem. With the conclusion of the chat dialogue, the command `chat` exits and returns control to the command pppd. The following messages show the dialogue that pppd has with the ISP's PPP server:

```
Jan 28 06:31:04 myexample kernel: PPP: version 2.2.0 (dynamic
  channel allocation)
Jan 28 06:31:04 myexample kernel: PPP Dynamic channel allocation
  code copyright 1995 Caldera, Inc.
Jan 28 06:31:04 myexample kernel: PPP line discipline registered.
Jan 28 06:31:04 myexample kernel: registered device ppp0
Jan 28 06:31:04 myexample pppd[6067]: pppd 2.2.0 started by dialout,
  uid 0
Jan 28 06:31:04 myexample pppd[6067]: Using interface ppp0
Jan 28 06:31:04 myexample pppd[6067]: Connect: ppp0 @@@-> /dev/ttyS3
Jan 28 06:31:13 myexample pppd[6067]: Remote message:
Jan 28 06:31:14 myexample pppd[6067]: local  IP address
  207.241.63.111
Jan 28 06:31:14 myexample pppd[6067]: remote IP address
  207.241.63.126
```

And that's it – we have successfully set up your modem and dialed the ISP's modem, and set up a PPP connection with the ISP.

As with our earlier script that used login-and-password authentication, there can be an error at any point in this process. The logging messages will show you the point at which it fails. However, we must emphasize again that because this script lets pppd authenticate itself with the PPP server, instead of using a script to mimic the login-and-password procedure, this script is much simpler, and so has fewer points at which it can fail.

If you are having a problem with the PPP portion of the dialogue – that is, your system can connect with the ISP, but for some reason PPP negotiation fails – we suggest that you call your ISP and talk the problem over with a technical support person there. The error message returned by PPP will help. The ISP will be best able to advise you how you can configure command pppd so that your system can make a PPP connection with the ISP's PPP server.

And with this, we let out a sigh of relief, because we are now finished with PPP scripts – arguably the most vexing part of setting up networking. We now move on to the final stage of PPP configuration, where we start to enjoy the fruits of our labors.

TRYING IT OUT

If, after tinkering with scripts ppp-on and ppp-on-dialer, you think you've got it – the message log shows that a good PPP connection has been made – you can now try it out. Type the command:

```
ping whitehouse.gov
```

In a moment, you should see something like the following on your screen:

```
PING whitehouse.gov (198.137.241.30): 56 data bytes
64 bytes from 198.137.241.30: icmp_seq=0 ttl=243 time=236.8 ms
64 bytes from 198.137.241.30: icmp_seq=1 ttl=243 time=262.0 ms
64 bytes from 198.137.241.30: icmp_seq=2 ttl=243 time=192.0 ms
64 bytes from 198.137.241.30: icmp_seq=3 ttl=243 time=192.0 ms
```

Congratulations! Your Linux workstation is now plugged into the Internet.

Conclusion

This concludes our introduction to configuring networking on your Linux workstation. At this point, your Linux workstation should be talking with the outside world, either through an Ethernet connection to a local network or a PPP connection to an Internet service provider.

This system of using dialing scripts to establish a PPP link with an ISP is complicated, and we must admit that it has some Rube–Goldberg elements in it – in particular, the portions of the script that walk you through the login dialogue with the ISP's machine. For these portions of the script, you will have to review your logging file to see exactly what prompts your ISP is sending you at every step of the login process. However, once the script is debugged, you can depend upon its running dependably with no maintenance at all (assuming, of course, that your ISP doesn't do something stupid, like change its login prompt). Also, the scripts execute relatively briskly, so you will not notice its complexity.

Most important, you now have what you have been working toward for the last three chapters: you will have grafted your Linux machine onto the Internet. All of Cyberspace is now open to you – so, go play!

Elementary Troubleshooting

Now that you have set up your connection and have started to work with it, you will probably start to encounter problems. Your ISP may be difficult to connect to; some hosts may not be reachable; some commands may not work as you expect. These problems will become more frequent as you begin to set up an intranet, as we describe in Part III of this book. So, it's important to learn how to use monitoring tools to diagnose problems and fix them.

Philosophy of Debugging

Debugging problems with your network setup is simple in principle, but sometimes difficult to master in practice. To successfully debug a problem, you must first isolate it, then change whatever is broken.

Isolating problems is the difficult part. For this, we have monitoring tools. Because every problem is different, we cannot describe them all here; however, we can show you how to use the basic monitoring tools that you have at your disposal.

Most problems will fall into either of two catagories: *hardware faults* and *configuration errors*.

If you suspect a hardware fault is the cause of your problem, replacing the suspect hardware with "known-good" hardware is your best option. To isolate which item of hardware is in error, you may have to divide the hardware into modules. For example, in a twisted-pair Ethernet network, the hardware falls into three parts: the port on the hub, the media cables running to the card, and the network card itself. Any one part of the hardware could be bad, so each must be tested separately.

Because of the complexity of configuration, configuration errors are usually more difficult to diagnose than hardware faults. Unfortunately, they are also more common.

Configuration is performed through two types of files:

♦ *Shell scripts*, or small programs that configure your Linux workstation.

♦ *Configuration files*, with a custom syntax designed for the program that they configure. Although these are usually simple methods for specifying options they can also be as rich as shell scripts.

The only advice we can offer here with regard to debugging configuration problems is that you must attempt to understand the file — its format and content.

SHELL SCRIPTS
A shell script is really just a bundle of commands that are executed when the Linux kernel starts up. For example, the following section of script /etc/rc.d/rc.inet2 starts the inetd super server:

```
# Start the INET SuperServer
if [ -f ${NET}/inetd ]; then
   echo -n " inetd"
   ${NET}/inetd
else
   echo "no INETD found.  INET cancelled!"
   exit 1
fi
```

The line starting with a pound sign '#' is a comment. It's meant to tell you what the script intends to do. These will be your clue to where to start looking. Every other line is a command, which either is built into the shell that executes the script or is an executable program in its own right. In either case, there probably is a man page for it that gives you more information.

We cannot provide a tutorial on shell scripts, but the man page for Gnu's Bourne Again Shell (bash) – available by the command man bash – should give you enough information to understand and troubleshoot the scripts distributed with Linux.

CONFIGURATION FILES

In the case of custom configuration files, the man page for the program in question is the best starting point. If the configuration file is complex, it may have a man page of its own. Most configuration files are also well commented, to help guide you when modifying them.

Understanding how the configuration works will be your best weapon for diagnosing and fixing configuration programs.

Monitoring Tools

Linux comes with a variety of tools that you can use to monitor your TCP/IP network. These tools are invaluable when you are attempting to isolate a problem.

In this section, we introduce the most commonly used monitoring tools:

◆ arp – Print the kernel's address resolution table.

◆ ping – Check the connectivity path to a machine.

◆ netstat – Show active sockets, interfaces, or routing information from the current state of the kernel's networking and interprocess communications data structures.

◆ traceroute – Show the gateways you must pass through to get to a particular host.

◆ syslogd – Capture and save error and diagnostic messages.

There are other programs that we describe later in the book that are useful for debugging specific pieces of the network. The most common of these are commands nslookup and host, which automate the process of converting names into IP addresses and back (that is, DNS).

We discuss these in Chapter 8, when we describe how you can set up domain-name service on an intranet.

ARP

As we described in Chapter 1, Ethernet is a broadcast medium. Each Ethernet card has a unique address that is burned into it. The Ethernet address for the source machine and the destination machine are written onto the beginning of each Ethernet frame; every Ethernet card on the local Ethernet network examines the destination address of each frame broadcast across the network, but reads only the frames addressed to itself. These addresses let Ethernet emulate a point-to-point link on the broadcast medium.

The Linux kernel keeps a table that links IP addresses with Ethernet addresses. This table uses the Address Resolution Protocol (ARP) to encode information, and so is called the ARP table.

The command `arp` lets you examine and manipulate the contents of your system's ARP table.

`arp` is a powerful command that gives you full control over your system's ARP table. You will rarely, if ever, need to modify the ARP table. However, from time to time a problem will arise that will require that you examine the contents of the ARP table. In particular, you will need to examine your system's ARP table to determine if the two workstations are attempting to use the same IP address. To view the ARP table, type the command:

```
arp -vn -a
```

Option `-vn` tells `arp` to print verbose output in numeric format (that is, display IP addresses rather than host names). Option `-a` tells it to print a summary of every Ethernet device with which it interacts. If you are running Ethernet on your system, this command will print something like the following:

```
Address                  HWtype   HWaddress          Flags Mask
 Iface
192.168.39.2             ether    00:40:05:26:2F:E8  C     *
 eth0
192.168.39.3             ether    00:00:C0:E2:81:30  C     *
 eth0
```

- ◆ Column `Address` gives the IP address of the host.

- ◆ Column `HWtype` gives the hardware type – in this case, Ethernet.

- ◆ Column `HWaddress` gives the hardware address at which this IP address is found – in this case, the address burned into the host's Ethernet card.

- ◆ Column `Iface` gives the kernel interface through which the host is accessed.

As you can see, each IP address has its own hardware address. If, however, more than one IP address were found at a given physical address, you would know which host or hosts needed to be reconfigured so your network could operate correctly.

There are other options to `arp` that you will need if you feel you must modify the ARP table by hand. For further information, see the manual page for `arp`.

PING

As we described in Chapter 1, command `ping` sends the ICMP message `ECHO_REQUEST` to another machine. On receipt, the distal machine returns ICMP message `ECHO_REPLY` to the sender.

When two machines can "ping" each other, it proves that they can communicate across the network.

As we described earlier in this chapter, IP address `127.0.0.1` is the loopback address — that is, the address at which a host can address itself. When we type command `ping 120.0.0.1`, with no other options, we see the following:

```
PING 127.0.0.1 (127.0.0.1): 56 data bytes
64 bytes from 127.0.0.1: icmp_seq=0 ttl=255 time=0.500 ms
64 bytes from 127.0.0.1: icmp_seq=1 ttl=255 time=0.518 ms
64 bytes from 127.0.0.1: icmp_seq=2 ttl=255 time=0.553 ms
64 bytes from 127.0.0.1: icmp_seq=3 ttl=255 time=0.520 ms
64 bytes from 127.0.0.1: icmp_seq=4 ttl=255 time=0.519 ms
```

The output of this command shows the following:

◆ The size of the datagram that was received.

◆ The ICMP sequence number (`icmp_seq`) that was assigned to this `ping` program. This is one of the most important fields, as we see later in the chapter.

◆ The time-to-live (`ttl`) of the datagram.

◆ The calculated round-trip time for delivery.

The pinged host reflects the data that `ping` transmitted. This lets `ping` calculate the round-trip time, and other statistics.

Under Linux, `ping` by default sends a continuous stream of datagrams to the recipient host. This continues until you interrupt `ping` by pressing `control-C`. When you type `control-C` to halt `ping`, it prints a summary of its activity, as follows:

```
-- 127.0.0.1 ping statistics --
10 packets transmitted, 10 packets received, 0% packet loss
round-trip min/avg/max = 0.500/0.527/0.554 ms
```

When you interrupt `ping`, it prints summary information about the pinging, including the total number of datagrams sent and received, and some statistics about the round-trip time.

Analyzing Output

ping usually is used to test connectivity between two hosts: whether the link between two hosts is up or down. One of three outcomes is possible: the connection is up, the connection is down, or the connection is intermittent. We discuss each in turn.

Connection Is Up

When the connection is up, we see 0% packet loss — or 0% plus the last packet, depending on our timing when we pressed control-C to interrupt the program. This indicates good connectivity.

Connection Is Down

When the connection is down, we get 100% loss of datagrams. In this case, you should check whether something is physically wrong with the network — for example, whether the cable is disconnected or one of the interfaces has not been configured.

You should note that the debugging process includes checking the work of the network software. One of us once worked with a technician who could not be bothered to remember IP addresses. When using ping, he insisted on using the name of the host rather than the IP number and when he could not get through, he assumed a connectivity problem. Of course there was not a connectivity problem to the host we were trying to diagnose; rather, there was a connectivity problem to the DNS server that translated that host's address. Because he didn't simplify debugging by eliminating DNS as the source of the problem at the start, we ended up tracing a non-problem for an hour before we found the real culprit. The lesson here is simplify the system as much as possible when you are debugging.

Connection Is Intermittent

A third situation is one of intermittent connectivity from one host to another. This situation is characterized by missing datagrams.

You can detect this by inspecting the icmp_seq numbers: if there are some missing then you have intermittent connectivity between the hosts you are trying to debug.

Intermittent connectivity is a minor problem when datagrams between the two hosts are routed via the Internet. Indeed, much of the TCP protocol is built to recover from the situation where a few datagrams are lost on the Internet in routing.

This situation should never or almost never happen on an intranet. If it does, it indicates that you have a faulty connection somewhere perhaps due to improper or failing cabling, or you have an overloaded Ethernet segment that is taking so long to get a datagram onto the intranet that ping has already sent the next datagram.

Another situation that causes loss of datagrams is when you use ping to interact with a remote site, and the outgoing datagrams invoke diald to dial the telephone and connect with your ISP. The datagrams generated while the connection has not yet come up will disappear into the "twilight zone"; however, once the PPP link has been made, the datagrams should be returned properly. You can check this situation by examining the `icmp_seq` number: the first ICMP sequence number will be a value larger than one, but once the connection has been made with the ISP, there should be few or no gaps in the ICMP sequence numbers.

OPTIONS   `ping` has a number of command-line options that you will encounter as you use it for diagnoses. The following gives those most commonly used:

- `-c` *count* – Send *count* datagrams. This is useful if you do not wish to have to press `control-C` to end the flow of `ECHO_RESPONSE` messages.

- `-f` – "Flood" `ping`: that is, send datagrams one after the other, or one every hundredth of a second. For each datagram sent, print a ".", and for each datagram received, print a backspace character (which erases a period). With this option, you can monitor how many datagrams are being lost by looking at the number of periods that are accumulating on your display.

- `-i` *interval* – Change the interval between the transmission of datagrams to *interval* seconds. By default, `ping` sends one datagram every second. This option is incompatible with the option `-f`.

- `-s` *size* – Change the size of each datagram to `size` bytes. By default, the datagram is 64 bytes long (56 bytes data plus eight bytes of headers). This option is useful if you believe that the size of the datagram has something to do with a problem you are trying to diagnose.

- `-p` *pattern* – Set to *pattern* the 16-byte data pattern sent in each datagram. This option is useful if you are debugging a problem that you believe is related to the data that you are sending over the network.

There are other options to `ping` that you may find useful when you're trying to debug a particularly difficult problem. For further information, see the manual page for `ping`.

NETSTAT

Command `netstat`, as its name implies, gives you information about network status. Actually, it has three functions:

- Displays the current state of the kernel's routing table

- Displays statistics about each of the active network interfaces configured on your Linux system

♦ Displays a list of active network connections and the state that each is in

The third display is useful if you are trying to debug a particular program; but here, we are concerned principally with the first two displays. We examine them in detail.

REVIEWING THE ROUTING TABLE   To see the current state of the kernel's routing table you can use the command:

```
netstat -r -n
```

Option -r tells netstat to print information about the routing table.

Option -n tells netstat to print IP addresses rather than host names. If you do not use this option, netstat will use DNS to resolve host names into IP addresses, and it may time out repeatedly when DNS is not available.

When you type this command, you see something like the following:

```
Kernel IP routing table
Destination     Gateway         Genmask         Flags   MSS Window
  irtt Iface
192.168.1.0     0.0.0.0         255.255.255.0   U       1500 0
  0 eth0
127.0.0.0       0.0.0.0         255.0.0.0       U       3584 0
  0 lo
0.0.0.0         192.168.1.100   0.0.0.0         UG      1500 0
  0 eth0
```

The following describes the columns in this output:

♦ Destination — The destination or destinations you can reach on the interface. Address 0.0.0.0 indicates the default destination. This destination is very important: as we described earlier in this chapter, when we introduced the command route, this is the destination that receives all of the datagrams that are not explicitly routed by other entries in the routing table.

♦ Gateway — The address of the machine that routes datagrams to this address, if your machine cannot transmit datagrams directly to that destination.

♦ Genmask — The netmask of the address associated with this interface.

♦ Flags — Flags describe the interface: most commonly, you will see U, which means that the interface is up or usable; G, which means that the route uses a gateway; and H, which means that the target of the route is a host.

◆ MSS – The maximum segment size – that is, the size in bytes of the largest datagram that your machine can send on this interface.

◆ Window – This column is unused in an intranet. Ignore it.

◆ irtt – This column is unused in an intranet. Ignore it.

◆ Iface – The name of the interface by which this host is accessed.

The most important entry comes last in the display – the default destination. In this example, all datagrams that cannot be routed to the network with address 192.168.1.0 will be sent to the host at address 192.168.1.100.

REVIEWING INTERFACES   netstat's option -i tells it to display information about interfaces. When you type the command

```
netstat -I
```

you see something like this:

```
Kernel Interface table
Iface   MTU Met  RX-OK RX-ERR RX-DRP RX-OVR  TX-OK TX-ERR TX-DRP TX-
OVR Flags
lo      3584  0   5987      0      0      0   5987      0      0
0 BLRU
eth0    1500  0  43046      0      0      0  25488      0      0
0 BRU
```

The most important columns in this display are as follows:

◆ Iface – The name of the interface. lo is the "loopback" interface, and eth0 the Ethernet interface.

◆ MTU – The interface's maximum transmission unit in bytes.

◆ RX-OK – The number of datagrams received correctly.

◆ RX-ERR – The number of datagrams received with errors.

◆ TX-OK – The number of datagrams transmitted correctly.

◆ TX-ERR – The number of datagrams transmitted with errors.

As we write this, command netstat -i is in a state of flux. If you find this display useful, we suggest keeping an eye on this source.

TRACEROUTE

Command traceroute is a tool with which we can follow the approximate route that an IP datagram takes as it wanders around the Internet in search of its destination. We say *approximate* because on the Internet, routing is dynamic and changes almost kaleidoscopically: one datagram may take one route to a destination, whereas a second datagram sent only moments later may take an entirely different route to the destination.

In Chapter 1, we gave an example of this command in use; here, we introduce it in more detail.

HOW TRACEROUTE WORKS   traceroute works by sending a stream of UDP datagrams to the destination host. The first group of three UDP datagrams has a time-to-live of one, the second has a time-to-live of two, and so on. This continues either until traceroute receives an ICMP PORT_UNREACHABLE message (because nothing is listening on the port that traceroute has chosen), or the time-to-live exceeds a configurable maximum (default, 30).

When the first router receives the first UDP datagram (the one whose time-to-live is one), that datagram's time-to-live will be exhausted. The first router returns an ICMP TIME_EXCEEDED message to the originating host and discards the datagram. The datagram with the time-to-live of two will fail similarly at the second host along the route; the datagram with the time-to-live of three will fail similarly at the third host along the route, and so on.

traceroute reads the source address of each TIME EXCEEDED message it receives, to discover the gateways along the path between the transmitting host and its destination. It then prints information about each gateway.

INTERPRETING THE OUTPUT   The commonest use of traceroute is simply to invoke it with the name of host whose route you wish to trace. For example, to trace the route to system whitehouse.gov, we would type the following:

```
traceroute whitehouse.gov
```

The following of this command will resemble the following:

```
traceroute to whitehouse.gov (198.137.241.30), 30 hops max, 40 byte
packets
1  poolf6-061.wwa.com (207.241.62.126)  134.387 ms  128.189 ms
139.468 ms
2  hq1-e0/4.wwa.net (207.152.107.1)  129.491 ms  139.345 ms
249.575 ms
3  dchi0-hssi8-0.wwa.net (206.158.151.33)  439.375 ms  129.438 ms
139.546 ms
4  core0.chi1.nap.net (207.112.248.65)  219.346 ms  129.4 ms
129.555 ms
5  aads.sprint.net (198.32.130.13)  219.466 ms  329.392 ms  219.477
ms
6  144.232.0.145 (144.232.0.145)  179.456 ms  179.402 ms *
7  * sl-bb2-chi-0-0-0-155M.sprintlink.net (144.232.0.130)  172.083
ms *
8  144.232.8.41 (144.232.8.41)  182.238 ms  169.397 ms  169.502 ms
```

```
9   144.232.2.194 (144.232.2.194)   369.383 ms   559.58 ms   209.261 ms
10  sl-bb6-dc-6-1-0.sprintlink.net (144.232.8.46)   199.436 ms
209.399 ms   209.449 ms
11  208.28.7.17 (208.28.7.17)   289.478 ms   499.473 ms   269.43 ms
12  sl-eop-1-0-T1.sprintlink.net (144.228.72.66)   209.514 ms
209.497 ms   199.478 ms
13  * whitehouse.gov (198.137.241.30)   202.097 ms   219.157 ms
```

The leftmost column gives the number of the gateway along the route: 1 indicates the first gateway, 2 indicates the second, and so on.

After that comes the name of the gateway host, followed by its IP address in parentheses.

Then comes three round-trip times for accessing that gateway host – traceroute in fact sends three UDP datagrams with a given time-to-live, to give you a better idea of how long the trip to each host along the route actually takes.

For example, entry

```
4   core0.chil.nap.net (207.112.248.65)   219.346 ms   129.4 ms
129.555 ms
```

indicates that host core0.chil.nap.net is the fourth gateway along our host's route to whitehouse.gov. Accessing it took 219 milliseconds in one instance, and 129 milliseconds in the other two.

When traceroute receives an ICMP TIME_EXCEEDED datagram with a time-to-live less than or equal to one, it prints an exclamation point !. Certain ICMP packets generate messages in the traceroute report, as follows:

- ◆ Host unreachable: !H

- ◆ Network unreachable: !N

- ◆ Protocol unreachable: !P

The traceroute manual page describes other messages in this way.

USES OF TRACEROUTE   traceroute's best use is to determine if a gateway along the path is overloaded and so is delaying the transfer of datagrams. You can see this as an exaggerated round-trip time for datagrams going to a particular gateway.

Later in this book, we describe the mysteries of routing datagrams on an intranet (or local-area network) and get into some the complexities of routing.

As an aside, do you remember what we said in Chapter 1 about the Internet being decentralized, to help it survive an atomic war? This design also helps the Internet to survive natural disasters. For example, when Los Angeles was most recently hit with a severe earthquake, a hacker determined that his house had not been heavily damaged by using the ping and traceroute programs to determine that the workstation in his house was up.

SYSLOGD

The last of the diagnostic programs we introduce here is, arguably, not a diagnostic program at all — yet it may be the most useful of the lot. This is the daemon `syslogd`, which is a clearinghouse for all system messages from the kernel, system daemons, and any other program that generates log or error messages. `syslogd` collates these messages and appends them into log files, or displays them on the system's console. Knowing where to look for a particular message can help you to save hours of time debugging a problem.

`syslogd` listens on three channels for messages: a special kernel device, which is the source of kernel messages; a UNIX domain socket, which is the source for all messages generated on this machine; and a UDP socket, which is the source for messages from remote machines. It uses the settings in its configuration file `/etc/syslog.conf` to figure out what it should do with each *class* of message.

CLASSES OF MESSAGES   Messages are classified by two factors: facility and level. We describe each in detail.

Facility

The *facility* describes the part of the system where the message was generated. There is no hard-and-fast rule that says which facility an application must use; however, some uses are obvious. The following gives the facilities that `syslogd` recognizes, and what each usually is used for:

- `auth` and `authpriv` — The facilities used by the user-authentication (login) system.

- `cron` — The facility used by the `cron` daemon.

- `daemon` — The facility used by miscellaneous daemons.

- `kern` — The facility used by the Linux kernel itself.

- `lpr` — The facility used by the `lpr` (printer) daemon.

- `mail` — The facility used by the mail daemon.

- `news` — The facility used by the news daemon.

- `syslog` — The facility used by `syslogd` itself.

- `user` — The facility reserved for user-specific applications.

- `uucp` — The facility used by the UUCP daemon.

- `local0` through `local7` — The facilities available for use by miscellaneous daemons and applications. For example, the application `chat` (which we discussed at length earlier) writes its messages to facility `local2`.

The `security` facility is a deprecated synonym for the `auth` facility. It's best to avoid using this facility, as it will probably be removed from future versions of `syslogd`.

Please note that some applications used under Linux were in fact developed on operating systems that do not have a well-developed `syslogd` system. These applications may well not use `syslog`, and instead rely on an application-specific logging system. The is true for many popular applications used for managing news, so don't be surprised should you find that there are no messages from these systems in your logs.

Level

The *level* describes the severity of the condition that generated the log message. The level can be one of the following values, ordered from lowest priority to highest:

◆ `debug` — Debugging messages.

◆ `info` — Miscellaneous information messages.

◆ `notice` — Something may be wrong, but not necessarily so.

◆ `warning` — A condition has been seen that may cause trouble if not checked. `warn` is a deprecated synonym for this level.

◆ `err` — An error condition. `error` is a deprecated synonym for this level.

◆ `crit` — A critical error.

◆ `alert` — A severe error.

◆ `emerg` — An irrecoverable error has occurred within the kernel. `panic` is a deprecated synonym for this level.

As with facility, there is no hard-and-fast rule for determining the level of a message — the application itself must decide this. Still, the system of levels used by `syslogd` have proven itself over time.

syslog.conf   `syslogd` configures itself by reading file `/etc/syslog.conf`. This file instructs `syslogd` how to dispose of messages, based on their facility and level. As it comes out of the box, Linux has a version of `syslog.conf` that disposes of messages in a reasonable way. We saw this in action earlier, when we discussed how to read the messages output by the command `chat`. However, you can modify this file to have `syslogd` behave as is most useful to you and the users of your system.

`syslog.conf` consists of a series of entries, each of which has the following syntax:

```
selector action
```

Please note that *selector* and *action* must be separated by one or more tab characters — space characters will not work.

Selectors

A *selector* consists of a facility and a level separated by a period. It matches all messages with a matching facility and a level higher than or equal to the specified level. For example, the selector

```
mail.info
```

matches all messages from the mail facility and that have a level of info or higher.
    You may use a single level and a set of facilities. For example, the selector

```
auth,authpriv.info
```

selects all messages from either the auth or the authpriv facilities, at a level info or higher.
    You can also use some wildcard notation:

- The character "*" matches all facilities (when it appears to the left of the period) or all levels (when it appears to the right of the period).

- The word none matches no level for a particular facility.

You can also combine selectors with a semicolon ';'.
With these rules in mind, let's look at a fairly complex example selector:

```
*.notice;kern.debug;lpr.info;mail.crit;news.err;auth,authpriv.none
```

This selector matches the following types of messages:

- *.notice – All messages at or above level notice

- kern.debug – All kernel messages at level debug or higher (i.e., all kernel messages, as debug is the lowest level)

- lpr.info – All lpr messages at or above level info

- mail.crit – All mail messages at or above level crit

- news.err – All news messages at or above level err

- auth,authpriv.none – No messages from facilities auth or authpriv

So far, we have described the basic syntax for selectors, as defined by Berkeley UNIX. Linux adds the following enhancements to this syntax:

- You can prefix the level with an '=' to mean only messages at this level.

- You can prefix the level with a '!' to reverse the sense of the match.

- You can combine the '=' and '!' operators.

For example:

◆ mail.=crit – Match mail facility messages at level crit alone

◆ mail.!err – Match mail messages at any level less than that of err

◆ mail.!=err – Match mail messages at any level except err

Actions

syslogd's matching facility would be useless if syslogd could not do anything with the messages it received. Therefore, the right side of each line gives the *action* to take when a message has matched a particular selector.

The following actions are possible.

◆ *Log to a regular file or to a terminal* – If the action field contains the full path name of a file, the log message is appended onto that file. If syslogd must create the file, it does so with "wide-open" permissions – that is, anyone will be able to read the contents of the file. This may not be appropriate (as we saw earlier in this chapter, when command chat wrote your ISP's login and password into file /usr/adm/messages), so you may wish to create the file by hand and reset its permissions more restrictively before you start up syslogd. If you prefix a '-' to the name of the file, syslogd will sync the file on the disk after it has written a message into that file. This will help prevent losing a message if the system crashes before the file system is updated. This feature is particularly important when you want to capture messages of facility emerg, which the kernel generates just before it goes down. You may also specify the name of a terminal device; for example, /dev/console tells syslogd to write the message onto the console device.

◆ *Log to a named pipe* – If the action field begins with a '|', syslogd sends the message to the specified named pipe. You must first have used command mkfifo to create the named pipe. If the command is to be useful, you must also define a program to read the pipe and take an appropriate action on the messages that it receives.

◆ *Log to a syslogd on another machine* – If the actions field begins with an '@', the message is sent to the syslogd of another machine. If you have several Linux machines to administer, this simplifies matters: you can use one machine as the master logging machine for all Linux machines, and therefore have to look in only one set of files for all error messages. You can also use this facility to log critical messages on another, functioning machine in the case that the system generating the messages is about to crash.

♦ *Send to the terminals of logged on users* – If the action field contains a
user, a comma-separated list of users, or the '*' character, syslogd writes
the message onto every terminal device on which that particular user is
logged in.

Default syslog.conf
The following gives the default syslog.conf file that comes with Slackware Linux:

```
*.=info;*.=notice          /usr/adm/messages
*.=debug                   /usr/adm/debug
*.warn                     /usr/adm/syslog
```

The first line directs all messages with any facility and a level of either info or
notice into the file /usr/adm/messages.

The second line directs all messages with a level of debug into the file /usr/
adm/debug.

The third line directs all messages with a level between warn and emerg into file
/usr/adm/syslog.

This is a good, workable configuration of syslogd. However, you may wish to
modify it so that it better serves your purposes.

LOGGING FILES   In this sub-section, we suggest some changes you may wish to
make to how messages are stored in logging files. These are just suggestions: syslogd will work quite well if you accept none of these ideas. However, we hope that
this discussion widens your grasp of what syslogd can do for you.

To begin, we prefer for security reasons to log all messages from facilities auth
and authpriv into a separate file that is not readable by all users. To accomplish
this under the standard setup, we do the following:

1. As the superuser root, create file /usr/adm/auth.log, as follows:

```
touch /usr/adm/auth.log
chmod 600 /usr/adm/auth.log
chown root:sys /usr/adm/auth.log
```

2. Then, we use a text editor to change the default /etc/syslog.conf so
that it reads as follows:

```
*.=info;*.=notice;auth.none;authpriv.none      /usr/adm/messages
*.=debug;auth.none;authpriv.none               /usr/adm/debug
*.warn;auth.none;authpriv.none                 /usr/adm/syslog
auth.*;authpriv.*                              /usr/adm/auth.log
```

3. Finally, we tell syslogd to re-read its configuration, by sending it the
HUP signal, as follows:

```
kill -HUP $(cat /var/run/syslogd.pid)
```

After these modifications, all unauthorized attacks against the login facility are logged in file `auth.log`, which only `root` can modify.

This is a *small* security step, which means that if someone attempts to break into your system and they wish to hide their tracks by modifying your log files, they must have root privileges to do it.

Summary

This section gives a glimpse of some of the diagnostic tools that we will be using to test the networking setups that we do later in this book.

The examples given here are not exhaustive, but are designed to give you a preview of the tools that you will be using later, as well as to give you ideas for what tools are needed to design solutions to networking problems.

Autodialing

Earlier in this chapter, we discussed how to write script `ppp-on`, which dials your Internet service provider, makes connection, and plugs your system into the Internet via PPP.

This is a marvelous thing – to graft your local Linux host onto the global network of computers! Yet, there are problems, the principal one being that for bits to flow between your machine and the Internet, you must sit at your machine and issue a command to make the connection with your ISP. You can use the `cron` daemon to dial your ISP regularly, in order to perform such tasks as exchanging mail with the Internet (which we discuss in Chapter 5). However, it is still rather a bother to have to execute a script before you can start surfing the Web.

Fortunately – now that you have `ppp-on` debugged and running correctly – there is a way to tell your Linux machine to dial your ISP automatically, whenever a datagram is addressed to a machine outside of your intranet. This magic is performed via a daemon called `diald`. This section will show you how to compile and set up `diald`.

How diald Works

`diald` is a package written by the Swedish programmer Eric Schenk. It works as follows:

 ◆ `diald` creates a *proxy* IP site (that is, an internal ersatz IP site) for your true default-destination site – usually that of your ISP.

 ◆ `diald` then creates a SLIP connection to that proxy site. Thus, the kernel will "think" that the connection to the default site is up, and will route datagrams to it.

◆ diald monitors the proxy site. When it detects datagrams being routed to the proxy, it dials the telephone and makes connection to the real default site, then redirects the datagrams to it.

◆ diald then monitors the connection. When no datagram has passed over the connection for a predetermined period of time, diald breaks the PPP connection with your ISP and hangs up the telephone. It then resumes waiting for another datagram to be addressed to your ISP.

Compiling diald

If your system does not have diald already installed on it, you must do the following to compile and install it.

To begin, diald requires that your Linux kernel have support for transparent proxying (CONFIG_IP_TRANSPARENT_PROXY) and SLIP (CONFIG_SLIP) compiled into it. We did so in the kernel we built at the beginning of this chapter.

Next, you must obtain a copy of the diald package and compile it. diald is included with the Slackware release included with this book. If you are using another release of Linux and your release does not include diald, you can use lynx or Netscape to download the sources from Web site:

```
http://www.dna.lth.se/~erics/diald.html
```

(If you are unfamiliar with the Web or with Web browsers, we introduce them in Chapter 4.) At the time of this writing, the most recent release was diald-0.16. tar.gz.

When you have found the diald release, su to the superuser root; then copy the release into directory /usr/src. To explode the archive, type command:

```
tar xvzf diald-0.16.tar.gz
```

This command opens the archive, uncompresses it, creates directory dial-0.16, and copies all of the archive's files into it. Please note that the name of the diald directory reflects the number of its release; thus, if you are using a release of diald other release 0.16, the name of the directory will have been changed to reflect the release that you are using.

REVIEW THE MAKEFILE
Before you compile diald, you must review its Makefile — the file that controls the building of diald.

Makefile contains four paths that you can change if you wish:

```
# dctrl goes here
BINDIR=/usr/bin
# diald goes here
```

```
SBINDIR=/usr/sbin
# the manual page goes here
MANDIR=/usr/man
# the configuration files go here
LIBDIR=/usr/lib/diald
```

The defaults are all set to reasonable values. You should change them only if you are certain that using these values would do something untoward on your Linux system. There is no need to create directory /usr/lib/diald — this is created for you, with proper permissions, when you install diald.

EDIT CONFIG.H

Before you compile diald, you must edit file config.h. This file sets the paths for some directories and executables that diald uses.

The file contains a number of paths and file names that you can configure, if necessary:

The two most important are:

```
#define DIALD_CONFIG_FILE "/etc/diald.conf"
#define DIALD_DEFS_FILE "/usr/lib/diald/diald.defs"
```

Change DIALD_DEFS_FILE to the value of the Makefile's variable LIBDIR — and only if you changed the value of LIBDIR from its default.

The next variable sets the locking files used by diald:

```
#define LOCK_PREFIX "/var/spool/locks/LCK.."
```

As we noted in Chapter 2, all programs on your system that work with the modem — including minicom (which you can use to dial directly to other systems) and mgetty (which you can use to manage incoming calls) — must use the same locking strategy: that is, they must write their lock files into the same directory, and name their lock files in the same way. config.h gives a reasonable default value, but you must make sure that it conforms to the strategy used by the other programs on your system that work with your modem. If you do not, more than one program will attempt to seize control of the modem at the same time, which will create all manner of difficulty.

The next variable indicates whether the lock file should use text or binary format: 1 indicates text, 0 indicates binary:

```
#define PIDSTRING 1
```

The default is text, which is reasonable.

The next variable sets the directory where diald writes its file diald.pid:

```
#define RUN_PREFIX      "/var/run"
```

This variable is set to the Linux default. Do not change it unless you are certain it is wrong.

The next variables set the paths for the programs `route` and `ifconfig`:

```
#define PATH_ROUTE "/sbin/route"
#define PATH_IFCONFIG "/sbin/ifconfig"
```

These variables are set to the Linux default. You can use the command `ls` to confirm whether they are correct. Do not change them unless you know they are wrong.

The next variable sets the path for the program `bootpc`:

```
#define PATH_BOOTPC        "/usr/sbin/bootpc"
```

This variable is set to the Linux default. Do not change it unless you know it is wrong.

Finally, the last user-configurable variable sets the path for the program `pppd`:

```
#define PATH_PPPD        "/usr/sbin/pppd"
```

Again, this is set to the Linux default. Use `ls` to confirm that is correct. Do not change this variable unless you know that it is wrong.

If you made any changes to this file, save it. Now, you are ready to compile.

COMPILATION

To compile, type the following commands:

```
make depend
make
```

Compilation should sail through without any problems at all. If compilation aborts with an error, check whether the changes you entered into `Makefile` and `config.h` (if any) did not introduce errors, such as stray characters that might confuse the compiler.

If problems persist, ask your local C guru to help you.

Installation and Configuration

Once `diald` is compiled, type the following command to install it:

```
make install
```

This installs the `diald` binaries and its internal configuration files.

One task that the automatic installation does not do, however, is write the run-time configuration file `/etc/diald.conf`. This you must prepare and install by hand.

PREPARE DIALD.CONF

File /etc/diald.conf configures diald for your system. Its options must be selected specifically for your system.

The following gives an example, bare-bones version of diald.conf that has been configured for PPP that uses dynamic IP addresses:

```
mode ppp
connect /etc/ppp/diald-dialer
device /dev/ttySport
speed 38400
modem
lock
crtscts
pppd-options name myexample remotename myisp
local 192.168.0.1
remote 192.168.0.2
dynamic
defaultroute
include /usr/lib/diald/standard.filter
```

Let's review these instructions one at a time:

- ◆ mode ppp — Tell diald to connect to your ISP through PPP.

- ◆ connect /etc/ppp/ppp-on-dialer — This names the dialscript that diald will use to connect to your ISP. We use the dialer script ppp-on-dialer, which we prepared for use with ppp-on.

- ◆ device /dev/ttySport — The device through which the connection is to be made. This is usually (although not always) a serial port. port gives the number of the port itself, from 1 through 4.

- ◆ speed 38400 — The speed of the device named in the previous option. In this instance, since we're using a modem, this gives the speed of the modem.

- ◆ modem — This tells diald that connection will be made via modem.

- ◆ lock — This tells diald to write a lock file when it opens the device named above. This is necessary to prevent other programs that work with serial ports, such as minicom or mgetty, from attempting to seize the port while diald is using it.

- ◆ crtscts — This option tells diald to use hardware flow-control to manage the device named above. This is necessary for a high-speed modem connection.

◆ pppd-options name myexample remotename myisp — Option pppd-options passes additional options directly to the PPP daemon pppd. This lets you pass to pppd options that diald itself does not handle; these include PPP options, such as those that relate to authentication. In this example, we use pppd-options to pass two arguments to pppd: name, which sets the name with which pppd identifies itself to the PPP server; and remotename, with which we set the name of the PPP server, for purposes of looking up the appropriate secret. In this example, we have set name to myexample and remotename to myisp. Please note that you should include this line in diald.conf *only* if you are using PAP or CHAP authentication (in which case you must set the name and remotename arguments appropriately, as you did in script ppp-on). If you are using login-and-password authentication, do not include this line in diald-conf.

◆ local 192.168.0.1 — This option sets the IP address for your local machine. The actual address given here does not matter, as long as it is one of the "hobbyist" addresses, as we described in Chapter 1; and it does not match any other IP address you are using on your intranet.

◆ remote 192.168.0.2 — This option sets the IP address for the proxy remote system with which diald is connecting via SLIP. Again, the actual address given here does not matter, as long as it is one of the "hobbyist" addresses, as we described in Chapter 1; and it does not match any IP address you are using on your intranet.

◆ dynamic — This tells diald that the Internet service provider assigns the IP address dynamically.

◆ defaultroute — This tells diald to place an entry in your host's routing table that makes the route it establishes to the proxy server the default route for datagrams. This will ensure that it sees all of the datagrams that your system is attempting to send to the Internet.

◆ include /usr/lib/diald/standard.filter — standard.filter is the file that diald reads to determine when to dial your ISP, how long to keep the connection alive, and when to drop the connection.

As you probably have noticed, most of the options given here are identical to those used on the pppd command line in our script ppp-on.

diald.conf can also hold a number of rules that you can use to set what sorts of datagrams diald will handle, and how long it will keep a connection alive. The default settings work pretty well, but once you gain some experience with diald, you may wish to tinker with these rules. For details, use the man command to view the manual page for diald.

The copy of dial.conf given above is for modem-based PPP connections that use a dynamic IP address. If your system does not fit this profile, use the command man to read the manual page diald-examples. This manual page gives example diald.conf scripts for other commonly seen configurations; and it also gives examples of setting rules to manage how long a connection is kept alive.

Start diald

To fire up diald, su to the superuser root; then type the command:

```
diald
```

Note that you do not need to add an ampersand '&' after this command. The diald daemon will start up on its own, read its configuration files, and set itself in memory.

If there is an error in a configuration file, diald will print a diagnostic message, then exit. In most instances, there was a typographical error in file /etc/diald.conf. Use the diagnostic message to find what the problem is; if necessary, check file diald.conf and make sure that all is well. Then, try again.

Once the diald daemon comes up without error, try it out. Type the command:

```
ping whitehouse.gov
```

In a moment, diald will detect the outgoing datagrams that the command ping has generated, then dial the telephone and make the connection automatically. Congratulations! You now have autodialing set up on your machine.

diald will keep the connection alive until you kill the ping command. Shortly after it detects the last ICMP datagram passing over the connection (by default, 30 seconds), diald will break the connection with the ISP, hang up the telephone, and wait for another outgoing datagram to appear.

Automatically Start diald

Once you are sure that diald is working correctly, su to the superuser root; then add the following lines to the end of file /etc/rc.d/rc.inet2:

```
# Turn on the diald daemon.
echo "Starting up the diald daemon ..."
diald
```

This ensures that diald is invoked whenever you boot your Linux system.

Summary

In this chapter, we described the following processes to set up networking software on your Linux system:

◆ Compiling a Linux kernel that supports networking

◆ Performing elementary configuration, including editing files `hosts`, `services`, and `inetd.conf`

◆ Using networking commands to bring up networking on your system, and inserting those commands into the appropriate `rc` files so that networking is turned on automatically when you boot your Linux system

◆ Troubleshooting some elementary problems with networking and how to use monitoring tools

◆ Writing a script to bring up a PPP connection to an Internet service provider to connect your machine to the Internet

◆ Setting up autodialing on your machine to dial your ISP automatically

Chapter 4

Commands That
Use Networking

IN THIS CHAPTER

- ◆ ftp: transfer files
- ◆ telnet
- ◆ Usenet news
- ◆ Browsers

AT THIS POINT in your exploration of Linux networking, your Linux machine is talking with other hosts on the Internet. The work of compiling software and altering configuration scripts is done: now it's time to have some fun exploring the Internet.

And to help you explore the Internet, Linux offers numerous useful applications. Many of these applications are classics, tools that you may have encountered in other times and places. Other tools may be new to you.

In this section, we introduce four commonly used networking applications:

- ◆ `ftp`, which lets you transfer files to and from a remote host

- ◆ `telnet`, which emulates a terminal plugged into a remote host

- ◆ `trn`, which lets you read and post Usenet news

- ◆ `lynx` and Netscape Navigator, which let you browse the World Wide Web

These certainly are not the only applications that can be run over the Internet, but they are some of the more common and more useful ones.

Please note that another set of commands exists, called the r* commands (because each begins with the letter r) that we introduce in Chapter 6. These commands are used almost always on intranets rather than on the Internet: they are useful, but present a security risk, and so they are made available only to local users (who, presumably, are trustworthy). If you are plugging your Linux system into an intranet via Ethernet rather than into the Internet via a modem, after you read this chapter, you may want to skip ahead to Chapter 6 and also read the section on the r* commands.

ftp: Transfer Files

`ftp` is an application that uses the TCP/IP File Transfer Protocol (FTP) to help you transfer files from one host to another. `ftp` uses the Transmission Control Protocol (TCP) to transfer data reliably.

`ftp` is one of the oldest TCP/IP applications, and for that reason, its text-oriented interface is rather clumsy. However, it remains one of the most useful tools for doing the unspectacular but necessary job of copying a file from one host to another.

In this section, we show you how to invoke `ftp` and use it to log into another system; and we show you its most commonly used commands.

The FTP Protocol

`ftp` implements the File Transfer Protocol (FTP) described in RFC 959, dated October 1985. A copy of this RFC can be downloaded from the InterNIC Web site (www.internic.net)

In brief, FTP describes a suite of instructions that an FTP client can send to an FTP server, and the messages that the server sends in reply. FTP also describes the channels that the client and server establish between them, to allow the client to send commands to the server even while a file is being uploaded to the server or downloaded from it.

No need exists to go into the details of this protocol, but if you are interested, we urge you to read it. Like most Internet RFCs, RFC 959 is clearly written and is accessible even to persons not deeply versed in Internet lore.

Using ftp: An Example

`ftp` is a command that has a large number of subcommands and options. However, in most instances, you use only a handful of its available commands and options; for this reason, the easiest and best way to learn how to use `ftp` is to walk through an example `ftp` session.

In this section, we walk through a simple task: downloading a file from a publicly available archive at the University of Kansas. The following subsection gives you a synopsis of `ftp`'s commands and options.

Invoking ftp, and Logging In

To invoke command `ftp`, type

```
ftp hostname
```

where *hostname* is the host with which you want to exchange files; or type

```
ftp ipaddress
```

where *ipaddress* gives the IP address of the host with which you want to exchange files.

For example, the University of Kansas has available online numerous translations of Norse sagas. If you want to browse the available texts, you type:

```
ftp ukanaix.cc.ukans.edu
```

Once the connection is made, you see:

```
Connected to raven.cc.ukans.edu.
220-
220-
220-  You have connected from: fred@myipprovider.com
220-
220-  For assistance call 864-0110 or to report network problems
 call 864-0200
220-
220-  Login as 'kufacts' for access to the Campus Wide Information
 System.
220-           'lynx' for access to the World Wide Web using Lynx.
220-           'www' for access to the World Wide Web using Lynx.
220-           'linemode' for access to the World Wide Web using
 Line Mode.
220-           'history' for history network resources.
220-           'ex-ussr' for former Soviet Union info.
220-
220-  At password prompt hit enter.
220-
220-
220-
220-
220-
220 raven.cc.ukans.edu FTP server (Digital UNIX Version 5.60) ready.
Name (ukanaix.cc.ukans.edu:fred):
```

Each message returned by the FTP server is prefixed with a number that gives the message's type, as described in the FTP protocol. For example, the 220 that prefixes each line of text in the previous example means that that line of text is an instance of message 220 (as described in RFC 959), which indicates that the FTP service is now ready for a new user.

Before you exchange files with the remote host, ftp requires that you log into that host. The ftp client, by default, sends the remote host the login with which you logged into your Linux system. In this example, the user was logged into his Linux host as fred; thus, ftp selected that name as his default login identifier for the remote host's ftp server.

The login identifiers that the remote host recognizes vary from one host to another. As you can see from the message returned by the University of Kansas's FTP server, this site recognizes numerous logins for people who want to look at specialized groups of files. However, practically every host that makes files available to the public via FTP recognizes one special login identifier: anonymous. A host is not required to recognize anonymous as a login identifier, but most do, because that is standard Internet practice. Thus, because we do not have a login identifier on the University of Kansas's host, and we do want to download a file, we will log in as anonymous, as the following shows:

```
Name (ukanaix.cc.ukans.edu:fred): anonymous
331 Guest login ok, send ident as password.
Password:
230 Guest login ok, access restrictions apply.
Remote system type is UNIX.
Using binary mode to transfer files.
ftp>
```

◆ Message 331 indicates that the login identifier you typed is recognized, and a password is needed. Most systems ask user anonymous to enter his e-mail address as a password. Obviously, the host has no way to check whether the address you type is bogus or not; but as a courtesy, you should enter your correct e-mail address.

◆ Message 230 indicates that the login identifier and password are correct, and that the user should proceed.

◆ Please note the warning message that binary mode is being used to transfer files. The FTP protocol recognizes two types of transfer modes: text and binary. Text mode is 7-bit, and is useful only for text files. Binary mode is 8-bit and is used to transfer binary files, including executables and compressed or encrypted text files. Text mode is largely obsolete, but you must be sure that you are in binary mode if you are downloading a binary file; otherwise, you will download a fileful of junk.

At this point, ftp displays its ftp> prompt. You can now begin to enter commands.

BROWSING THE REMOTE SITE

When you use ftp to log into a remote host, the remote host sets you in a "home" directory. This directory can contain files and other directories; its contents and your permissions depends entirely on what the remote host has chosen to make available to you.

The ftp command dir displays the contents of the directory that you are in. For example, when you first log into host ukanaix, command dir shows the following directories available to you:

```
ftp> dir
200 PORT command successful.
150 Opening ASCII mode data connection for /bin/ls
  (207.241.63.17,1072).
```

```
total 5
drwxr-sr-x    2 13       32           512 Apr 29  1993 bin
drwxr-sr-x    2 13       32           512 Apr 29  1993 etc
drwxr-sr-x    2 13       32           512 Apr 29  1993 lib
drwxr-sr-x   14 13       32           512 Jul 17  1995 pub
drwxr-sr-x    3 13       32           512 Apr 29  1993 usr
226 Transfer complete.
ftp>
```

The output of this command resembles that of the Linux command ls -l. dir can take arguments; and its arguments can, in turn, take the wildcard characters * and ?.

The directories you see here are those usually made available to an anonymous user. Directories bin, etc, lib, and usr hold files that are "visible" to the anony- mous user. This is done to help encapsulate the anonymous user within his own environment, so a malicious user cannot wreak havoc on the host system. Directory pub usually holds files that are available to the public, and this is the directory whose contents we want to explore.

To change directories, use the command cd. For example, to change into direc- tory pub, use the command cd pub, as follows:

```
ftp> cd pub
250 CWD command successful.
ftp> dir
200 PORT command successful.
150 Opening ASCII mode data connection for /bin/ls
  (207.241.62.119,1118).
total 12
lrwxrwxrwx    1 13       32            11 Sep  1 19:14 DosLynx ->
  WWW/DosLynx
drwxr-sr-x    6 13       32           512 Jan 10  1995 WWW
drwxr-sr-x    2 13       32           512 Jul 14  1995 arch
drwxrwxr-x    4 13      203           512 Dec  3  1995 business
drwxrwxr-x    2 13      204           512 May  3  1994 caveat
drwxr-sr-x    3 13       32           512 Apr 12  1994 chemistry
drwxr-sr-x    3 13       32           512 Feb 24  1995 dos
drwxr-sr-x    9 20553  20312          512 May 19  1997 history
drwxrwsr-x    2 13     20242          512 Apr  9  1995 hmatrix
drwxrwsr-x    6 20135    202          512 Feb 15  1997 ippbr
drwxrwsr-x   11 20170  20313          512 Nov 19  1996 libraries
lrwxrwxrwx    1 13       32             8 Sep  1 19:14 lynx ->
  WWW/lynx
drwxr-sr-x    2 13       32           512 Mar  1  1995 mac
drwxrwsr-x    2 13      204           512 Mar 16  1995 windows
226 Transfer complete.
ftp>
```

The ftp command cd also recognizes the shorthand '..' for the parent directory of the directory you are now in. So, to take a step back up the directory tree, use the command cd ...

To see which directory you are in, use another familiar command: pwd. For example:

```
ftp> pwd
257 "/pub" is current directory.
ftp>
```

DOWNLOADING A FILE

In this example, we want to download a file from ukanaix that holds a translation of the Icelandic Laxdaela saga. So, we use the dir command to explore the directory tree, until we find the directory that holds the file that we want:

```
ftp> dir l*
200 PORT command successful.
150 Opening ASCII mode data connection for /bin/ls
 (207.241.63.17,1077)
-rwxr-xr-x   1 20553     20312      95662 Dec 24  1996 lancelot.zip
-rwxr-xr-x   1 20553     20312     141053 Nov  8 01:05 laxdaela.zip
226 Transfer complete.
```

Command dir l* helps us find the file we're looking for, without cluttering the screen with extraneous files. This is important because ftp, unfortunately, has no analogue for the command more – no way exists to display the contents of a directory one screenful at a time.

Now that we have located the file that interests us, we have to download it. Our first step is to issue command binary to ensure that we're in binary mode:

```
ftp> binary
200 Type set to I.
```

Type I stands for "image," which is the term that the FTP protocol uses for binary.

Now, we will issue the command hash. This tells ftp to display a hash mark after it has downloaded a portion of the file (usually one kilobyte). This command is strictly for the ftp client; it does not cause an interaction with the server, so the acknowledgment message is not prefixed with a message number:

```
ftp> hash
Hash mark printing on (1024 bytes/hash mark).
```

This being done, we use the command get to retrieve the file laxdaela.zip:

```
ftp> get laxdaela.zip
local: laxdaela.zip remote: laxdaela.zip
200 PORT command successful.
```

```
150 Opening BINARY mode data connection for laxdaela.zip
  (207.241.63.17,1078)
(141053 bytes).
######################################################################
######################################################################
226 Transfer complete.
141053 bytes received in 42.8 secs (3.2 Kbytes/sec)
ftp>
```

The file-transfer session is largely self-explanatory:

1. The client requested file laxdaela.zip. We could have set the name of the file into which this file was copied; because we did not, it is written into a file of the same name on the client's host.

2. The server opened a TCP connection with the server's host, and opened it in binary mode.

3. As the client receives data and stores it, it writes hash characters # onto the screen, to show you that it is at work.

4. When the file is entirely downloaded, ftp tells you how much data it downloaded and how quickly the data moved across the Internet.

Now that we have downloaded the file we want, we will use the command quit to terminate the connection and exit from ftp:

```
ftp> quit
221 Goodbye.
```

And that, in brief, is how you use ftp to download a file.

ftp Commands

ftp offers a rich set of commands. As we previously noted, you will seldom use these commands; however, being acquainted with them is useful, if only because these or similar commands are used by other networking commands – in particular, the command smbclient, which we introduce in Chapter 9.

The following list summarizes the most commonly used ftp commands:

♦ ! *command* – Invokes the shell on your local host to execute *command*.

♦ ? [*command*] – Prints a summary of how to use *command*. When used without a *command*, list all recognized commands.

♦ append *localfile* [*remotefile*] – Appends the contents of *localfile*, which is on the local host, onto the end of *remote*, which is on the remote host.

- `ascii` — Shifts to text (ASCII) mode.

- `binary` — Shifts to binary ("image") mode.

- `cd` *directory* — Changes directory on the remote host. The symbol '`..`' represents the parent directory of the current directory.

- `chmod` *mode remotefile* — Changes the permissions of a file on the remote system to *mode*. The FTP server on the remote host ignores this command if you lack appropriate permission.

- `close` — Closes the connection with the remote system. You can then use the command `open` to open a connection with another remote system, without exiting from `ftp`.

- `delete` *remotefile* — Deletes file *remotefile* from the remote host. The FTP server on the remote host ignores this command if you lack appropriate permission on the remote host.

- `dir` [*remotedirectory*|*remotefile*] [*localfile*] — Lists the contents of a directory. If used with no arguments, this command lists the contents of the current directory. If invoked with argument *remotefile*, then show information about that file. Note that *remotefile* can include the wildcard characters * and ?, so this command can list multiple files. If invoked with argument *remotedirectory*, the command lists the contents of that directory. Finally, if invoked with argument *localfile*, this command writes its output into file *localfile* on the local host.

- `exit` — Closes the connection with the remote host and exits from `ftp`.

- `get` *remotefile* [*localfile*] — Retrieves *remotefile* from the remote host. If optional argument *localfile* is used, this command gives *remotefile* the name *localfile* when it copies the file onto your local host.

- `glob` — Toggles whether `ftp` recognizes the wildcards * and ? as wildcard characters, and expands them accordingly. If "globbing" is turned off, `ftp` treats * and ? as literal characters within file names. This command helps you retrieve a very oddly named file.

- `hash` — Prints a hash symbol # after transferring a block of data, usually one kilobyte. This command is meant to give you some visual feedback about how file downloading or uploading is going.

- `lcd` *localdirectory* — Changes to directory *localdirectory* on your local host.

- `mdelete` *files* — Deletes the multiple *files* from the remote host. *files* can include the wildcard characters * and ?, so you can name multiple files at once.

◆ mget *files* – Downloads multiple *files* from the remote host. *files* can include the wildcard characters * and ?, so you can name multiple files at once.

◆ mkdir *remotedirectory* – Creates directory *remotedirectory* on the remote host. The remote host will ignore this command if you lack appropriate permissions.

◆ mput *files* – Uploads multiple *files* to the remote host. *files* can include the wildcard characters * and ?, so you can name multiple files at once.

◆ newer *file* – Downloads *file* from the remote host if and only if it is newer than the identically named file on your local host. This command is useful when you need to periodically download an updated copy of a given file.

◆ open *remotehost* – Opens a connection with remote host *remotehost*. *remotehost* can be either a host name, or an IP address.

◆ prompt – Toggles prompting. By default, ftp prompts you for confirmation before it processes a file through the commands mget, mput, or mdel. You can use this command to turn off prompting, or restore it again.

◆ put *localfile* – Uploads *loadfile* to the remote host.

◆ pwd – Displays the name of the working directory on the remote host.

◆ quit – Closes the connection with the remote host, and exits ftp.

◆ reget *remotefile* [*localfile*] – Continues getting a file. If *localfile* is smaller than *remotefile*, then ftp assumes that *localfile* is a partially downloaded copy of *remotefile*, and it downloads the rest of *remotefile*, beginning at the point where it assumes the break occurred. This command is useful when the download of a huge file is interrupted for whatever reason.

◆ rename *oldfilename newfilename* – Changes the name of a file on the remote host, from *oldfilename* to *newfilename*.

◆ reset – Resets the queue of commands that the client is exchanging with the server. This may be necessary if the server becomes confused.

◆ rmdir *remotedirectory* – Removes directory *remotedirectory* from the remote host. The FTP server on the remote host will ignore this command if the remote host does not grant you permission to remove directories.

◆ size *remotefile* – Asks the remote host to tell you the size of *remotefile*.

◆ system — Asks the remote host to tell you what operating system it is running.

◆ umask *newmask* — Sets to *newmask* the default permissions given to files you create on the remote server.

◆ user *login* [*password*] — Logs into the remote machine with which ftp has established a connection. *login* gives your login identifier on the remote machine; *password* gives your password.

◆ verbose — Toggles running ftp in verbose mode. In verbose mode, ftp displays all messages it receives from the server. This is the default.

We have not discussed the less-used of ftp's commands. These include synonyms for the commands given in the preceding list, and commands to invoke some of ftp's lesser-used features, such as setting and executing macros. To see a summary of all of ftp's commands, go to its manual page by typing the command **man ftp**.

ncftp

Command ncftp is a more sophisticated version of ftp. It uses the curses library to paint some text windows on the screen, and lets you work through them. We have found it to be cleaner and simpler to use than the default ftp client that comes with Linux.

Although ncftp is a not the standard version of ftp, it recognizes all standard ftp commands, and fully implements the FTP protocol. If you plan to use ftp more than sporadically, learning ncftp is worth your time. For details on how to use it, type the command **man ncftp** to read its manual page, or just start it up and use it — if you are at all familiar with ftp's commands, you will find ncftp easy to learn.

This concludes our introduction to the command ftp.

In Chapter 7, we describe how to set up an FTP server for an intranet.

telnet

We now move on to a much simpler network application, but one equally as useful as ftp: telnet.

telnet is a terminal-emulation program that works over a TCP/IP network. When you invoke telnet and connect with a remote system, you can log into that remote system, give it text commands, and receive text output — just as if you were sitting at a terminal that was plugged directly into that host.

You may have noticed our emphasis on the word "text." That is because telnet works only in text mode — you cannot exchange graphic information (that is, mouse clicks or mouse-pointer movements) via the TELNET protocol.

telnet implements the TCP/IP TELNET protocol, as defined in RFC 854. A copy of this RFC can be downloaded from the InterNIC Web site.

Invoking telnet

It is easy to invoke telnet: simply type its name, followed by the name of the host to which you want to connect. For example, to open a telnet to connect to host myexample, type the command:

```
telnet myexample
```

Figure 4-1 shows an xterm window in which you have done just that.

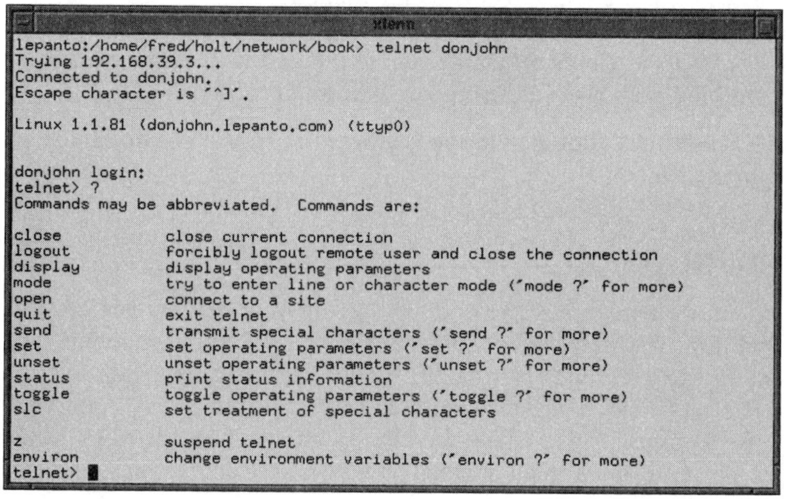

```
lepanto:/home/fred/holt/network/book> telnet donjohn
Trying 192.168.39.3...
Connected to donjohn.
Escape character is '^]'.

Linux 1.1.81 (donjohn.lepanto.com) (ttyp0)


donjohn login:
telnet> ?
Commands may be abbreviated.  Commands are:

close           close current connection
logout          forcibly logout remote user and close the connection
display         display operating parameters
mode            try to enter line or character mode ('mode ?' for more)
open            connect to a site
quit            exit telnet
send            transmit special characters ('send ?' for more)
set             set operating parameters ('set ?' for more)
unset           unset operating parameters ('unset ?' for more)
status          print status information
toggle          toggle operating parameters ('toggle ?' for more)
slc             set treatment of special characters

z               suspend telnet
environ         change environment variables ('environ ?' for more)
telnet>
```

Figure 4–1: telnet session

As you can see, telnet connects to the remote host. The TELNET server on the remote host gives you a login prompt; you can then log in (assuming you have an account on the remote host) and begin to give it commands.

Giving Commands to telnet

Occasionally, you will need to give commands directly to `telnet`. To enter `telnet`'s command mode, type its escape character. By default, this is `control-]`; however, the default escape character will vary from one host to another, depending upon what it was set to when `telnet` was compiled. `telnet` always tells you what the escape character is when you invoke it; and if you want, you can use a command-line argument to reset the escape character to one that you prefer.

In Figure 4-1, we typed the `telnet` escape character instead of logging in. `telnet` responded by showing us its prompt:

```
telnet>
```

As you can see in Figure 4-1, we then gave `telnet` the command ?, which asks `telnet` to print a summary of its commands.

To see a detailed a description of a `telnet` command, type its name plus a ? at the `telnet` prompt.

To exit from `telnet`'s command mode and return to working with the remote host, simply type **Enter** at the `telnet` prompt.

You will seldom, if ever, need to invoke any of `telnet`'s commands; however, two commands you will use fairly frequently are the following:

◆ `open` *hostname* – Closes the connection to the host with which you are now working, and opens a connection to host *hostname*.

◆ `quit` – Closes the connection to the host with which you are working, and exits from `telnet`.

Environment

When you log into a remote host, `telnet` will set up your environment as it is defined on that host. This may create some problems for you if the environmental variable `TERM` is set to a terminal device other than the one you are using.

`telnet` offers numerous command-line arguments and interactive commands that you can use to tune `telnet`'s operation. You will rarely, if ever, need to invoke these options; however, for a good summary of them; see the manual page for `telnet`. To view it, simply type the command **man telnet**.

This concludes our brief introduction to `telnet`.

We give a longer example of `telnet` in Chapter 5, when we show you how to use `telnet` to build a mail message by hand.

Usenet News

The next networking application we introduce helps you to read and post news. Through the early 1990s, Usenet news was a major generator of traffic on the Internet, and although it has been displaced by the World Wide Web as the bandwidth king, it still generates an enormous amount of traffic on the Internet.

If you are new to the Internet, you may not be familiar with news. Therefore, in this section, we briefly introduce news – what it is and how it works – and then introduce `trn`, which is the newsreader that we recommend.

What Is News?

Usenet news is a worldwide discussion group in which anyone who has access to the Internet can participate. Unlike mail, which usually is a correspondence between two people, news is like posting your thoughts onto a giant bulletin-board that can be read by anyone who has access to Usenet news.

So, you ask, just what is Usenet? Briefly defined, *Usenet* is a group of persons who share information through the medium of news.

Usenet news can be tremendously useful. For example, suppose that you are having a problem configuring a Linux box and *The Linux Network* did not tell how to perform a particular task (however unlikely that may be). You could post a question to the appropriate newsgroup. Your message would be distributed around the world in a few hours, and in such a way that most of the other people who read it would be Linux network administrators like yourself. If one of them had already solved your problem, he could then send you his solution to the problem.

GROUPS AND THREADS

A global bulletin-board would not be very useful if it did not organize its messages in some way; Usenet news uses two methods to organize its traffic: by *groups* and by *threads*.

NEWSGROUPS   A group, as its name implies, is a group of people who discuss a specific topic. Groups are organized hierarchically, beginning with a broad topic, and narrowing down to a more specific topic. A group's name shows its place within the news hierarchy: topics are separated by periods, with the most general newsgroup appearing at the beginning (left) of the name, and the most particular at its end (right). For example, `comp` (for "computer") is one of the general subjects, and `os` (for "operating systems") is one of the many subjects under computers. Thus, if you're interested in news about the Linux operating system, you look in group `comp.os.linux`. Linux, in turn, is a pretty broad topic all by itself, and is divided into numerous subtopics. For example, `comp.os.linux.networking` discusses matters relating to Linux networking, and `comp.os.linux.setup` discusses matters relating to setting up Linux and its many packages.

Some groups are moderated, others are not. A moderated group, as its name implies, is moderated by a volunteer whose job it is to filter out postings that are not related to the group's topic or otherwise not worthy of reproduction. An unmoderated group, on the other hand, has no moderator. The discussion tends to be more freewheeling.

The signal-to-noise ratio varies wildly from one group to another. As a rule of thumb, the more technical a group is, the better the discussion.

Heading 5High-level groups

The high-level groups are well-defined:

- `comp` — Topics that relate to computers.

- `news` — Topics that relate to the Usenet itself.

- `sci` — Scientific topics.

- `rec` — Recreational topics.

- `soc` — Social issues.

- `talk` — Political, religious, and issue-related discussions.

- `misc` — Everything else.

- `alt` — "Alternate." Everything not covered under one of the other major topics, including `misc`. This is *Weekly World News* of Usenet news, where people chat about kinky sex, alien abductions, Elvis sightings, their detestation of Barney the Dinosaur, and other such pastimes. By definition, the alternate newsgroups are freewheeling and unmoderated. If you enjoy ranting or have voyeuristic tastes, this is for you.

THREADS   A thread is a conversation within a group. Each thread has a subject, which is given in its title. However, like human conversations, the discussion within a thread can drift far from its original subject.

Anyone who participates in a newsgroup can start a new thread. However, no guarantee exists that anyone else will join in. For example, if you were participating in group `comp.os.linux.networking` and posted your networking question to the group, your posting and all replies to it would comprise a thread within the group.

ORGANIZATION OF POSTINGS   News postings (also called *articles*) are organized and archived first by group and then by thread.

As we will see shortly, when you read news, your reader lets you browse the available newsgroups, and then helps you select the thread or threads that interest you. Only when you have selected a group and a thread will it start to display postings. Any other approach would be too chaotic to be useful.

News Architecture

Like most TCP/IP-based applications, Usenet news is a client-server system. Although it was invented before high-speed networking was available, it fits the client-server model well.

NNTP

Before the advent of high-speed networking, the news reader had to read its articles from a local file system. Though it was possible to share the news spool via the network file system (NFS), the architecture of the news-server software caused large problems with sharing news this way.

To solve this problem, the Network News Transfer Protocol (NNTP) was created to allow server-to-server and server-to-client distribution of news. This solution remains in use to this day.

The NNTP, like the mail protocol (SMTP), defines headers that are embedded in a news message, to help with the organization and distribution of news. The following are some of the important messages:

- `From` — The e-mail address of the person who posted this article (also called the *poster*)

- `Newsgroups` — The groups in which this article appears

- `Date` — The date this article was posted

- `Message-ID` — An identifier unique to each article

- `References` — A list of message identifiers to which this article is relevant

In the rest of this section, we discuss how news software uses the information in these headers to help keep chaos at bay.

THE NEWS SERVER

The server side of the equation is called *news server*. This is basically a host that holds a repository of news articles, called a *news spool*, and that is equipped with software that distributes articles to other servers and to clients.

Although it is an interesting network project, setting up a news server is beyond the scope of this book.

NEWS CLIENT

A *news reader* is the client program that retrieves articles from a news server and displays them on the screen for your perusal. Most news readers also help the user to post articles.

At first glance, the job of the news reader appears to be simple:

◆ Display the available articles.

◆ Skip the articles the user has already read.

In fact, the job is a little more difficult than that. As we described earlier, Usenet news is a fluid series of discussions, grouped on common subjects. If, for example, you have a question on Linux networking, a newsgroup exists whose subject matter is Linux networking. Thus, a newsreader must group postings both by group and by thread.

Most newsreaders let the user select a group, and then the newsreader displays the threads for that group in a menu format, enabling the user to choose the threads he wants to read. Articles arranged like this are said to be *threaded*. The news reader connects articles into a thread by reading the contents of the headers `Message-ID` and `References` in each message. This enables news readers to make sense of the ever-shifting environment of Usenet news.

This concludes our brief introduction to Usenet news. This introduction is by no means exhaustive; however, you now know enough to begin to use news. Next, we discuss how to invoke a news reader and begin to skein the threads of Usenet news.

The trn Newsreader

Countless newsreaders are available for Linux. We have chosen to introduce one, called `trn`, because in our opinion, it is robust yet easy to use.

`trn` is a text-based news reader with some advanced features that make scanning or reading numerous newsgroups quickly an easy task. `trn` may seem terse to you at first, but as you come to realize how much time you could spend separating the Usenet's wheat from its chaff, you'll appreciate how economical it is to use.

INSTALLING TRN

`trn` is installed as part of the standard Slackware release. If you are using this release, it should already be installed on your Linux system.

If, for some reason, `trn` is not part of your Linux release, you can download a copy from the Internet and install it yourself by following these steps:

1. Download the source file for the latest version, which is release 3.6. The source files are located at URL
   `ftp://ftp.uu.net/networking/news/readers/trn/trn-3.6.tar.gz`, if you can use a Web browser. If you're using `ftp`, log anonymously into site `ftp.uu.net`; then, use the `cd` and `dir` commands to find and download file `networking/news/readers/trn/trn-3.6.tar.gz`.

2. Once you have downloaded the source file, move it into directory /usr/src (or whichever directory you use to store your sources). Then, de-archive it by typing the command **tar xvzf trn-3.6.tar.gz.**

Next, compile the sources, as follows:

1. cd into directory trn-3.6.

2. Type the command **./Configure.** This invokes a script that walks you through configuring trn to run on your system. Read each prompt carefully. You should accept the default at each prompt, except for the following:

   ■ At the prompt Do you want to access news via NNTP? [n] type **y,** for yes.

   ■ At the prompt Berkeley/V7 format for full name in /etc/passwd? [n] type **y,** for yes.

   ■ At the prompt What hostname appears in the From line of this machine's postings? type **/etc/HOSTNAME.** This file holds your machine's host name, and is built when you installed networking onto Linux.

   ■ At the prompt What is the default editor on your system? [/usr/bin/vi] type the name of your favorite text editor, if you prefer another editor to vi.

3. When the configuration script is finished, it writes file config.h. If you are an experienced C programmer, it is a good idea to read this file over to make sure that it is correct. If everything looks good, then type the command **make** to compile the sources.

4. Compilation takes some time, depending upon the speed of your machine. When compilation is finished, type the command **make install** to install trn.

If you run into a problem, check the FAQ for trn. See the end of this chapter for directions on how to obtain a copy.

And that's it. Now you can start to work with trn.

CONFIGURING trn

Before you begin to use trn, you must configure it for your network.

Reading news in a networked environment is simple when your Linux box has access to an established NNTP server. In all probability, your Internet service provider has a news server that you can use, but be sure to check first. A little inquiry will get you the address of a host that will make news available to you. In this example, the news server is `news.mydomain.com` and our news clients are `trn` and `netscape`.

If you choose to use the copy of `trn` that ships on the disks that come with this book, you must tell it the name of the host that has made its NNTP available to you. You can do this in either of two ways:

◆ Edit file `/etc/nntpserver` and insert the name of the host. For example:

`news.myexample.com`

◆ Set environmental variable `NNTPSERVER` to the name of the host, as in the following command:

`export NNTPSERVER=news.myexample.com`

INVOKING trn

Invoking `trn` is easy — just type

`trn`

`trn` **replies as follows:**

```
Trying to set up a .newsrc file—running newsetup...
Welcome to trn.  Here's some important things to remember:
o Trn is an extension of rn and has a similar command syntax.
o To access all the new features, specify the options -x and -X.
  These
  options MAY be on by default, but it won't hurt to be redundant.
o Single-character commands don't require a carriage return—only
  commands that let you type in an argument.
o At ANY prompt, you may type 'h' for help.  There are different
  help
  menus, depending on the context. Also, typing <esc>h in middle of
  a
  multi-character command will list escape substitutions.
o Typing a space to any prompt means to do the normal thing.  You
  could
  spend all day reading news and never hit anything but the space
  bar.
o If you have never used the news system before, you may find
  articles
  in news.announce.newusers to be helpful.
o Please consult the man page for complete information.
Creating /home/chris/.newsrc to be used by news programs.
Done.
To add new group use "a pattern" or "g newsgroup.name".  To get rid
  of
newsgroups you aren't interested in, use the 'u' command.
[Type space to continue]=
```

This is the screen you see when you first start trn. To continue, press the space-bar. trn then says:

```
No unread news in subscribed-to newsgroups.  To subscribe to a new
newsgroup use the g<newsgroup> command.

****** End of newsgroups—what next? [qnp]
```

Here you seem to be stuck. trn is saying that no news remains to read and is asking you whether you want to subscribe to new newsgroups, but it doesn't list any newsgroups to which you can subscribe. You can get help at most trn prompts by pressing the letter **h**. When you do so, trn replies:

```
Newsgroup Selection commands:
t          Toggle the newsgroup between threaded and unthreaded
  reading.
c          Catch up (mark all articles as read).
A          Abandon read/unread changes to newsgroup since you started
  trn.
n          Go to the next newsgroup with unread news.
N          Go to the next newsgroup.
p          Go to the previous newsgroup with unread news.
P          Go to the previous newsgroup.
-          Go to the previously displayed newsgroup.
1          Go to the first newsgroup.
^          Go to the first newsgroup with unread news.
$          Go to the end of newsgroups.
g name     Go to the named newsgroup. Subscribe to new newsgroups this
  way.
/pat       Search forward for newsgroup matching pattern.
?pat       Search backward for newsgroup matching pattern.
           (Use * and ? style patterns.
l pat      List unsubscribed newsgroups containing pattern.
m name     Move named newsgroup elsewhere
o pat      Only display newsgroups matching pattern.
O pat      Like o, but skip empty groups.
a pat      Like o, but also scans for unsubscribed newsgroups
L          List current .newsrc.
&          Print current command-line switch settings.
&switch {switch}
           Set (or unset) more command-line switches.
&&         Print current macro definitions.
&&def      Define a new macro.
!cmd       Shell escape.
q          Quit trn.
x          Quit, restoring .newsrc to its state at startup of trn.
^K         Edit the global KILL file
           pattern in every newsgroup.
v          Print version and the address for reporting bugs.
[Type space to continue]
```

Like most text-mode programs, trn uses your pager (for example, more or less) to help display text in screenfuls. This may cause your display to be a little different than we have shown here.

In our case, we're looking at a list of newsgroups that we can read, and a perusal of the help list shows that l is the choice we need.

As we're interested in Linux, we will search for newsgroups whose names contain the word "linux," as the following shows:

```
No unread news in subscribed-to newsgroups.  To subscribe to a new
 newsgroup use the g newsgroup command.
****** End of newsgroups—what next? [qnp] l cycle
Completely unsubscribed newsgroups:
comp.os.linux.networking
comp.os.linux.setup

****** End of newsgroups—what next? [qnp] g
 comp.os.linux.networking
Newsgroup comp.os.linux.networking not in .newsrc—subscribe? [ynYN]
```

As you can see, two newsgroups include the word "linux" in their titles. trn then asks whether we want to *subscribe* to these groups. Subscribing does not require the payment of a fee; it simply means that trn will record the fact that these groups interest you, and will automatically scan these groups for articles you have not yet read whenever you invoke it. To select the default option – which is the first one given in brackets after the prompt – simply press the spacebar. When you press the spacebar at this prompt, trn then asks:

```
Put newsgroup where? [$^Lq]
```

trn is asking where to put the newsgroup. Again, press the spacebar to select the default option. When you do so, trn then prompts:

```
1621 unread articles in comp.os.linux.networking—read now? [+ynq]
```

If you press y at this prompt, trn displays all the articles in the newsgroup. trn groups individual articles by thread (by subject). trn doesn't possess any artificial intelligence: it simply groups articles by matching the text in the article's Subject header. However, if you press + or the spacebar, trn threads the articles together. This is a more useful option, so we will select it. trn replies as follows:

```
comp.os.linux.networking—1618 articles

a John von Neumann       1  >2 NIC and Routing
b Isaac Newton           1  >ncpfs - ncp_free_all_inodes: INODES
LEFT!!!
d Wilhelm Leibnitz       2  >Telneting as root....
  George Berkeley
```

```
e Jean Bernoulli        4  >"Sorry - PPP not available..."
  Colin Maclaurin
  George Boole
  Brook Taylor
+f Gabriel Cramer        2  >ISDN recommendations
  Leonhard Euler
g Hipparchus            1  China
i Alan Turing           3  nfs,nis and nis+
  Alan Turing
  Alan Turing
j Alan Turing           2  NIS +
  Renee Descartes
l David Hilbert         1  >Networking through a SOCKS server
o Gregor Reisch         3  >News-reading OFFLINE
  Immanuel Kant
  George Hegel
- Select threads (date order)-Top 2% [>Z] -
```

Each thread is identified by a letter in the first (leftmost) column. Not every letter is listed: trn skips the letters that it uses for commands. For example, c is not listed because it's trn's "catch up" command, which marks every unread article in this newsgroup as read.

If you are looking for information about ISDN, the thread named ISDN Recommendations may be worth reading. To mark it for reading, press the letter for that thread – in this case, f. This tags the thread for reading, as indicated by the plus sign + that appears next to the f. To untag this thread, press f a second time: trn responds by removing the +.

Usually, you mark and read the threads that interest you, and then use the c command to throw away the rest. To see another screenful of threads, press the spacebar.

After you tag all the threads that interest you, you can read their articles by pressing the Enter key. In this case, we see the articles on ISDN:

```
comp.os.linux.networking #5846 (1 + 1619 more)    ( )+-( )-[1]
From: "Gabriel Cramer" <cramer@pearlygates.org>-[1]
Newsgroups: comp.os.linux.networking,comp.os.linux.hardware,comp.os.
+           linux.help
[1] Re: ISDN recommendations
Date: Fri Oct 31 18:15:11 EST 1997
Organization: Telecom Finland News Service
Lines: 68
Mime-Version: 1.0
Content-Type: text/plain; charset=3Dus-ascii
Content-Transfer-Encoding: 7bit
X-Mailer: Mozilla 4.03 [en] (X11; I; Linux 2.0.31 i586)
Hi
> Pierre de Fermat wrote:
>
> Hi all,
>
```

```
> I have devised a proof that for any integer n > 2 there exists
> no a, b, and c such that a^n + b^n = c^n.  Unfortunately, this
> news article is too small to contain it.
>
Clearly, you need a connection with a wider bandwidth.   ISDN
 probably
is the answer—but look out for NT, it's got some problems.
[snip]
>
—MORE—(48%)
```

As you can see, the article display is simple. At the top left are the headers. After that, the text of the article is displayed. The symbols at the top right are called the *article tree*. This is a crude graphical representation of the thread: you can use the arrow keys to move through the tree and view the articles, if you want to get a better handle on the discussion.

While you're reading an article, you may choose to contribute to the discussion. You can post a reply to the message you are reading in either of two ways:

◆ Press f to invoke trn's *follow-up* command. This command generates a new, blank message and opens your favorite text editor (as set by the environmental variable EDITOR), so that you can type in your words of wisdom. When you have finished typing and exit from the editor, trn gives you the option of either posting your article or dumping it into the bit bucket. If you choose to post it, trn automatically posts your article to the thread, where it will be read by persons around the world.

◆ Press F to invoke trn's *Follow-up* command. This command also generates a message, but this message holds the text of the message that you are reading. This is useful if you want to comment on a specific point in the message you are reading. trn prefixes each line in the quoted message with a > symbol. Again, trn invokes your favorite text editor, so that you can edit this message and add your comment. When you exit from the editor, trn again gives you the option of throwing the message away or posting it; if you choose to post it, trn automatically posts it to the thread you were reading.

This concludes our brief introduction to trn. trn has many features that we have not explored, but you now know enough to install and configure trn, invoke it, select newsgroups and threads, read news, and post replies – which are, after all, the essential tasks of any news reader.

Netiquette

Much has been written about *netiquette* — the proper manner of behaving on the Internet. This may sound like a topic more suited to Miss Manners than to a book entitled *The Linux Network*, but a network actually is about people interacting with each other, and interactions generally go more smoothly if the people follow a few simple principles. We suggest the following:

- When posting a question, look before you ask. Most technical groups have a file of FAQs; check it before you post a question. Also, the question may have been answered in a recent thread; check that group's archive (at site `http://www.dejanews.com`) before you post your question. This is not just polite, it is practical, because re-asking a recently answered question will not get you the answer you need, and may get you flamed by some short-tempered participant.

- When posting a question, stick to the topic: Don't post a question about mountain biking in a group devoted to compilers or medieval music.

- When posting a question, don't post an article and request that the answer be e-mailed back to you, because you are too busy to read the group. If you really cannot read the group, add the word "poster" to the `Follow-ups:` header. This causes answers to be mailed to you automatically. If you do this, be sure to note it in your article, and promise (and follow through) with a summary of the answer to your question, so the group will benefit.

- Don't post an article unless you have something substantial to say.

- In follow-up postings, be careful with the attribution of text. Most people don't like others putting words into their mouths.

- Be rational in your replies, even if the person to whom you're replying has angered you: the quickest way to be ignored is to lose your temper.

We can sum up netiquette as a corollary to the Golden Rule: if you don't like people flaming you, insulting you, quoting you out of context, wasting your time with witless comments, or filling your system's disk with *non sequiturs* and pointless articles, then don't do it to other people.

Browsers

If you have recently returned from a sojourn on Mars, you may not have heard of the World Wide Web or Web browsers.

So, to summarize:

◆ The *World Wide Web* (WWW) consists of thousands of machines around the world from which you can use the Hypertext Transfer Protocol (HTTP) to download files written in Hypertext Markup Language (HTML), as defined in RFCs 1945 and 2068. A *markup language* is a language that "marks up" a document – that is, that marks how each element of a document is to be laid out on a physical page.

◆ The WWW is *worldwide*, because the machines that offer this service are physically located around the world. The WWW is a *web*, because HTML (being a form of hypertext) can address other HTML documents anywhere on any other machine that has an HTTP, FTP, or Gopher server – thus interconnecting all of these machines into a formation that resembles a web – a rather snarled and tattered web, if truth be told, but a web nonetheless.

◆ A *browser* is an interactive program that interacts with an HTTP server to download and display documents written in HTML. The browser interprets markup instructions in the document to assemble the physical page on your screen. Practically all browsers also can work with FTP and Gopher servers to retrieve documents.

The WWW is attractive both because of its interconnected nature, and because it supports graphics as well as text. The WWW and browsers are two of the principal reasons why the Internet has gone from a playground for hackers and "propeller-heads" to a worldwide commercial resource.

Various browsers are available for Linux. In this section, we introduce two of them:

◆ lynx, a text-based browser that comes from the University of Kansas

◆ Netscape Navigator, the most popular commercial browser

In Chapter 7, we discuss how to set up a Web server for your local intranet.

lynx

lynx is a free browser that is maintained and supported by a group based at the University of Kansas. Unlike other browsers, lynx is text-based.

lynx enables you to view Web pages (or their text portions, at least), click *anchors* to jump from one Web site to another, fill out interactive forms, invoke common gateway interface (CGI) scripts, download files, and most other basic HTTP tasks. However, lynx cannot display graphics, play streaming video or sound, or execute Java applets.

lynx does not support the Web's glitzier features. However, it is easily run from your Linux console or from within an xterm or telnet window, and it runs much faster than any graphically oriented browser. For the many instances when the content of a Web site interests you more than how prettily it is laid out – in particular, if you want to view some Linux documentation that is in HTML format – you will find lynx to be most useful.

INSTALLING lynx

lynx requires no installation: it is included as a standard part of practically every Linux release. So, once you have your network up, you can start browsing immediately.

INVOKING lynx

Invoking lynx is easy: log into your Linux system, either at the console or through a telnet or xterm window, and then type

lynx *startup.site*

where *startup.site* names the Web site you want to view. For example, the command

lynx www.linux.org

invokes lynx. Once connection is established with your Internet provider, lynx then downloads and displays the home page for linux.org.

If you want, you can invoke lynx without naming a *startup.site* – just type

lynx

lynx then uses its own home site of lynx.browser.org as its start-up site, and downloads and displays the home page from that site.

If, for some reason, lynx cannot make contact with the start-up site – either its default site or the one you named on the command line – lynx displays an error message and exits. If you want, you can select another start-up site and try again; once you have made contact with a start-up site, lynx will then let you jump to any other site on the Internet.

You can also use lynx to display a local file written in HTML. To do so, just type

lynx *file.path*

where *file.path* is the path name of the file you want to display.

AN EXAMPLE SESSION

The following example gives a brief session with lynx: we use lynx to search the Library of Congress's Thomas Project for information about legislation concerning the Internet that is pending in the 105th Congress. So that you can see what we're doing, we will be running lynx from within an xterm window.

To begin, we invoke lynx to download the Library of Congress's home page:

lynx www.loc.gov

Once our Linux system establishes a connection with our Internet provider, lynx requests the home HTML page from the Library of Congress, and displays it, as shown in Figure 4-2.

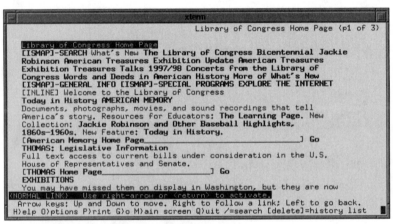

Figure 4-2: Home Page for the Library of Congress

Let's take a careful look at this screen, so that you can see how lynx handles complex pages:

♦ To begin, the top line is highlighted. This is to show where the cursor is positioned on the page. You can use the up-arrow and down-arrow keys to move the cursor among the interactive elements on the page. An *interactive element* is, as you can imagine, an element on the page that enables you to do something. This usually is an *anchor* that enables you to jump to another Web page, but it can also be an interactive form, or a field into which you can type information.

♦ At the third line from the bottom is another highlighted line. This is lynx's information line: it gives information about how you can enter information into the interactive element that is highlighted on the screen. In this instance, the element that is highlighted is a normal link, and lynx notes that, to *invoke* this link (to jump to the Web site that it names), you press either the right-arrow key or the Return key (also called the Enter key).

♦ The bottom two lines give a brief synopsis of lynx's most commonly used commands, which are the following:

■ Up arrow – Moves the cursor up to the next interactive link on the page.

■ Down arrow – Moves the cursor down to the next interactive link on the page.

■ Right arrow – Follows a link.

■ Left arrow – Returns to the page you were viewing before this one.

■ H – Invokes lynx's interactive help screens. These give, among many other things, a summary of lynx's keystroke commands; a lynx tutorial; synopses and tutorials on HTML; and links to various Internet search services, including Yahoo!, Alta Vista, and Lycos.

■ O – Views and modifies the options set for lynx. Among the options you can set are the character set that lynx uses, the default editor, and whether lynx can recognize EMACS-style or vi-style cursor-movement commands. When you invoke this option and modify your options, lynx writes your preferences into file .lynxrc in your home directory.

■ P – Prints the current page. This name is a little misleading: when you invoke this command, lynx displays a screen that enables you to save the page to a file, mail it, or print it to the screen – lynx does not let you spool a file directly to the printer.

- G – Goes to another Web site. When you invoke this command, lynx enables you to type in the full URL of the site to which you want to go. lynx can handle URLs for the protocols http, ftp, and nntp, among others. For example, to read news from the news server at foobar.com, type the command G, and then at the prompt, type the URL **nntp://nntp.foobar.com.**

- M – Returns to the main screen – that is, the top of the principal frame of the current page.

- Q – Quits lynx.

- / – Searches for a string within the current page.

- Del key – History list: by repeatedly pressing this key, move the cursor to interactive elements on which it had been positioned previously.

Several other useful commands not mentioned in Figure 4-2 include the following:

- Ctrl-G – Cancels the current action. This is most useful when lynx is hung while trying to download a page from a site that is inaccessible.

- a – Adds a link or document to your file of bookmarks.

- d – Downloads the current document into a file. lynx prompts you for the name of the file into which you want to save the document.

- l – Lists the links in the current document.

- v – Views your bookmark file. (The *bookmark* file is a file on your local host in which you can store the URLs of sites that interest you, so that you can visit them later.) If you want, you can then select a link from the bookmark file and invoke it.

Lines that are prefixed with [ISMAP] show the contents of an image map. An *image map* is a picture, each part of which is mapped to a particular link. lynx cannot show the image map's picture, but it does display the links to which the image map is linked. A well-written Web page includes a text description of each link in an image map, for use by lynx and other text-based browsers. However, not all Web pages are well written, so in some instances, you just see the entry [LINK]; you just have to guess what that link means.

Lines that are prefixed with [INLINE] give ordinary text and links that are part of the page itself.

Two lines in this figure are enclosed in brackets and followed by the word [GO]. These lines give links to interactive forms. You can enter information into a form in a variety of ways: through check boxes, from pick lists, or by typing information into a template.

One of the interactive forms interests us in particular: the one labeled THOMAS Home Page. Figure 4-3 shows what we see when we use the down-arrow key to move the cursor to this field.

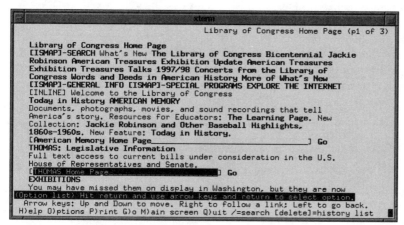

Figure 4-3: THOMAS interactive form

Note lynx's information line (the third line from the bottom of the screen). It now tells us that this is an interactive pick list, and tells us how to pick an entry from the list. Figure 4-4 shows us what we see when we press the Return key to invoke the form.

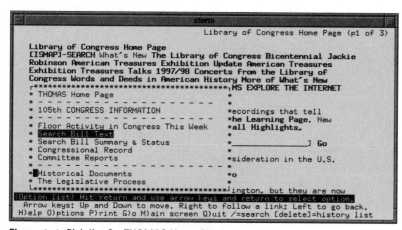

Figure 4-4: Pick list for THOMAS Home Page

As you can see, a small text window has popped up on the lynx screen. You can use the up-arrow and down-arrow keys to move the cursor to the entry in the pick list that you want; in this instance, we have moved it to the entry Search Bill Text, because we want to search for the word Internet in the text of pending bills. To select the entry that the cursor is on, we then press the Return key.

When we have made our selection, the phrase Search Bill Text appears in the form's text field. We then press the down-arrow key to move the cursor to the interactive element that is labeled [GO] and press the Return key. This dispatches the form to the Library of Congress site for executing, and the Library of Congress site, in this instance, responds by moving us into the Search Bill Text Web page. Figure 4-5 shows this page.

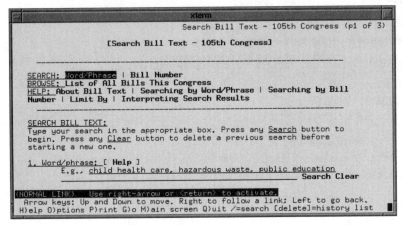

Figure 4-5: Search Bill Text screen

As you can see, the cursor is fixed at the first interactive element on the screen, which lets us search the text of bills for a particular word or phrase. Figure 4-6 shows what we see when we press the Return key to select this option.

The Library of Congress site has forwarded us to the field into which we can type the word or phrase that describes our interest. As you can see, we have typed the word "Internet." To execute the search, we press the down-arrow key to move the cursor to the interactive element marked Search, and then press the Return key to invoke that element. The Library of Congress site responds by searching its database for legislation that includes the word "Internet"; Figure 4-7 shows the result of the search.

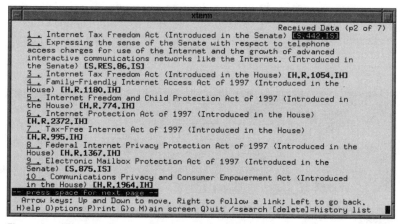

Figure 4-6: Enter a word for a search

```
                                                              xterm
                                           Received Data (p2 of 7)
 1 . Internet Tax Freedom Act (Introduced in the Senate) [S.442.IS]
 2 . Expressing the sense of the Senate with respect to telephone
access charges for use of the Internet and the growth of advanced
interactive communications networks like the Internet. (Introduced in
the Senate) [S.RES.86.IS]
 3 . Internet Tax Freedom Act (Introduced in the House) [H.R.1054.IH]
 4 . Family-Friendly Internet Access Act of 1997 (Introduced in the
House) [H.R.1180.IH]
 5 . Internet Freedom and Child Protection Act of 1997 (Introduced in
the House) [H.R.774.IH]
 6 . Internet Protection Act of 1997 (Introduced in the House)
[H.R.2372.IH]
 7 . Tax-Free Internet Act of 1997 (Introduced in the House)
[H.R.995.IH]
 8 . Federal Internet Privacy Protection Act of 1997 (Introduced in the
House) [H.R.1367.IH]
 9 . Electronic Mailbox Protection Act of 1997 (Introduced in the
Senate) [S.875.IS]
 10 . Communications Privacy and Consumer Empowerment Act (Introduced
in the House) [H.R.1964.IH]
-- press space for next page --
  Arrow keys: Up and Down to move. Right to follow a link; Left to go back.
 H)elp O)ptions P)rint G)o M)ain screen Q)uit /=search [delete]=history list
```

Figure 4-7: Results of the search of THOMAS Project

To view the text of a particular bill, we simply press the down-arrow key to the line for that bill, and then press the Return key.

When we finish working with lynx, we press the **Q** key to invoke lynx's Quit command.

REVIEWING lynx

This concludes our brief introduction to using lynx. This example shows only a few of lynx's features; however, even an elementary knowledge of how to use lynx enables you to perform some fairly useful and interesting tasks.

When you invoke lynx, it looks for file .lynxrc in your home directory. This file contains instructions with which you can tune lynx as you prefer. To view a copy of this file, use lynx's **o** (options) command, and instruct lynx to save the file. You can then edit this file as you prefer; comments in the file will be sufficient to guide you.

For a complete summary of lynx's commands, type **h** (for help) at lynx's command prompt. The **h** command also enables you to invoke the lynx tutorial, which explains lynx thoroughly.

For a complete summary of lynx's many command-line options, see the manual page for lynx; to view this page, type **man lynx**.

Netscape Navigator

Netscape Navigator is the most popular browser in use on the Internet today. It is a fully featured browser that supports frames, graphics, and Java applets; it also has plug-ins available for such features as streaming audio.

Describing Netscape Navigator in detail is beyond the scope of this book – the program is too large and is evolving too rapidly for us to summarize. Fortunately, Netscape Navigator's visual interface is well laid out and is largely self-explanatory. Figure 4-8 shows the release 3.1 of Netscape Navigator being run on Linux.

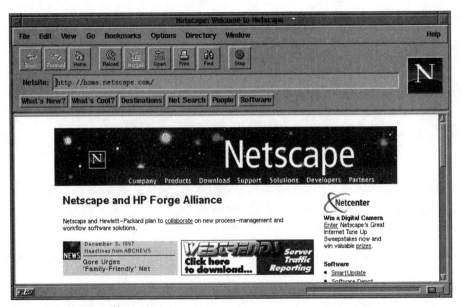

Figure 4-8: Netscape Navigator

To go to a URL, just type it into the text field at the top of the Netscape Navigator window, and then press the Enter key.

To download an evaluation copy of Netscape Navigator, use the program `ftp` or `ncftp` to access site `ftp.netscape.com`. Look in directory `/pub` for the software you want to download; fortunately, the directory tree at this site is largely self-explanatory. Please note that Netscape Navigator is the browser itself; Netscape Communicator is a package that includes Netscape Navigator plus various other tools. Netscape's Professional Edition includes user tools plus tools that developers can use to construct Web pages.

To install Netscape Navigator, use command `tar` with its `-z` option to uncompress and de-archive the files. The executable `netscape` should go into a directory that is available to all users (usually either `/usr/X11/bin` or `/usr/local/bin`). See the `READ.ME` file included in the archive for information on how to install the other parts of the release, in particular the file of Java classes.

Summary

In this chapter, we introduced some of the more common applications you use to explore the Internet. These include:

♦ `ftp`, for downing files from other Internet sites

♦ `telnet`, which implements a virtual terminal with which you can work with other systems on the Internet

♦ `trn`, a reader for network news

♦ `lynx`, a text-based Web browser

Chapter 5

Configuring Mail to Use Networking

IN THIS CHAPTER

- ◆ Privacy and security
- ◆ Mail protocols
- ◆ Implementing mail
- ◆ Designing a mail configuration
- ◆ Configuring mail

AT THIS POINT in our exploration of Linux networking, your Linux system is hooked into the outside world: either into the Internet via an Internet service provider (ISP) or into an intranet via Ethernet. You can use networking clients, such as FTP and Web browsers, to explore Cyberspace.

One task remains, however, before you can say that your Linux is fully hooked into the world network: you have to configure your Linux system so that you can send and receive electronic mail.

E-mail is one of the oldest applications to be implemented on the Internet; for years, it was *the* reason for getting hooked up to the Internet.

In the nascent years of the Internet, numerous mutually exclusive protocols for exchanging e-mail were developed. Matters are simpler now, because the more-obtuse methods of handling mail have fallen by the wayside. However, configuration of electronic mail still presents some challenges:

- ◆ You must select from among numerous methods for moving mail to and from your Linux workstation. The right method for your situation may not be obvious.

- ◆ The configuration of electronic mail programs can be daunting at times. This is due partially because mail is inherently a complex task, and partially because most commonly used mail programs (which come from the early days of the Internet) use a terse and complex configuration language that, at first glance, appears impenetrable to nonhackers.

In this chapter, we walk you through setting up e-mail on your system:

◆ First we discuss mail in the abstract, by introducing the most commonly used mail transportation protocols, and how mail is implemented under UNIX and Linux.

◆ Next we discuss practical configuration: designing a mail configuration that best suits your needs, and then configuring some of the most important mail tools.

Before we begin with these items, however, we discuss briefly the vital topic of the security and privacy of electronic mail.

Privacy and Security

Talking up front about privacy as it relates to e-mail is important. Privacy in e-mail communication is especially important today, because e-mail is now used as a general tool for distributing information – a purpose for which it was never designed.

We must be blunt: because the protocols for transmitting mail were written in the early, innocent days of the Internet, they are *open*. This means that anyone who has access to any of the equipment between your e-mail's source and its destination can read your mail in its entirety. Furthermore, as system administrator, you must warn your users that while their e-mail resides on your Linux workstation's file system (before the users have read it), you and anyone else with the root password on the mail machine can read their mail.

To summarize: if you do not encrypt your e-mail, anything you write into an e-mail message can be read by the entire world. You should not write anything into an e-mail message that you would not write on a postcard.

Further, as we show later in this chapter, forging an e-mail message that appears to be quite authentic is trivially easy, at least to a nonexpert. Your users should be cautious before they act on anything they learn via e-mail.

That being said, let's get to work.

Mail Protocols

Numerous protocols define how to transport mail from one host to another. In this section, we describe two of the most important protocols – SMTP and POP3. We also discuss UUCP, an antique but still useful protocol.

SMTP

Simple Mail Transfer Protocol (SMTP) is the protocol used to exchange mail between hosts on the Internet. It's described by RFC 822.

Chapter 1 gave an example of using the SMTP protocol to transport an electronic mail message. In this section, we discuss SMTP in more detail. We also give a detailed example of how a cracker can interact with an SMTP server by hand to forge a mail message.

HOW SMTP WORKS

SMTP is described by Internet RFC 821. It is a classic client-server system:

◆ On the server machine, an SMTP server "listens" to port 25.

◆ An SMTP client that connects to that port passes a series of commands to the server, with which it identifies itself to the server, and then uploads a mail message.

◆ In response to each command, the server sends a response that indicates success or failure.

SMTP COMMANDS

The following list gives some of the commands defined by the SMTP protocol:

◆ HELO *sitename* — Client machine *sitename*, which has connected to port 25 on the server machine, introduces itself to the server machine's SMTP server. If the server replies OK (message number 250), the client machine can proceed.

◆ MAIL FROM: <*user@sitename*> — Client machine initiates a mail message from user at *sitename*. Again, the server sends message 250 (OK) if all is well and the client can proceed.

◆ RCPT TO: <*user@sitename*> — The client machine identifies the *user* to whom the mail message is addressed.

◆ DATA — The client transmits the body of the message. The server replies with message 354, which indicates that it will passively receive and store what the client transmits until the client sends a line that consists of a single period "." character. The body of the message includes most of the common mail headers, including the lines From:, To:, Subject:, and Reply-To:.

◆ QUIT — The client is finished, and closes the connection with the server.

Clearly, SMTP is fairly straightforward. In the next subsection, we see SMTP in action.

AN EXAMPLE SMTP SESSION

To illustrate the SMTP protocol, we will demonstrate how to forge an e-mail message.

In this example, we demonstrate a trick that crackers use to fool naive users into sending them their passwords. Needless to say, no user should ever tell anyone her password, not even the system administrator.

Please note that this example is meant to illustrate how SMTP works. Actually forging mail is, at best, discourteous, and it could land you in serious trouble.

To forge a mail message, we give a series of commands directly to our Linux workstation's SMTP server. We use the command `telnet` to talk directly to the SMTP server. As Chapter 4 describes, command `telnet` can take an optional argument that gives the number of the port to which you want to connect. By giving a port other than 23 (the port to which the TELNET server listens), you can use `telnet` to talk directly to other TCP/IP servers. This is a useful method for checking, connecting to, and ensuring that a given server is alive and operating correctly.

The following code gives the text of our conversation with the SMTP server on a Linux workstation named `heimdall.myexample.com`. The lines in italic type indicate what we type, and the lines in plain type indicate the SMTP server's replies:

```
telnet localhost 25
Trying 127.0.0.1...
Connected to localhost.
Escape character is '^]'.
220 heimdall ESMTP Sendmail 8.8.5/8.8.5;
HELO heimdall.myexample.com
250 heimdall  Hello heimdall.myexample.com [192.168.1.100]
MAIL FROM: <root@heimdall.myexample.com>
250 <root@heimdall.myexample.com>... Sender ok
RCPT TO: <naiveuser@heimdall.myexample.com>
250 <naiveuser@heimdall.myexample.com>... Recipient ok
DATA
354 Enter mail, end with "." on a line by itself
From: System Administrator <root@myexample.com>
To: Naive User <naiveuser@myexample.com>
Subject: Barbarians at the Gates!!!!!
Reply-To: evil@crackers.org
It has come to our attention that crackers may have broken into
our system. We need all users to reply to this message with their
network login and password so we can re-encrypt them on the
server to close the security hole. Simply reply to this message
and add your login name and password here:
   Login Name:
   Password:
And we will re-encrypt the passwords this evening after 5 PM to
restore the system.
Thanks
```

```
.
250 WAA21757 Message accepted for delivery
QUIT
221 heimdall closing connection
Connection closed by foreign host.
```

Let's look at this conversation in detail.

The first step in this forgery is to connect the SMTP server daemon. This program runs on the Linux machine and awaits incoming connections:

```
telnet localhost 25
```

We use `telnet`'s port option to connect to port 25, which is the well-known port for the SMTP server (as set in file `/etc/services`).

The mail server is active and so responds with its banner line:

```
220 heimdall.myexample.com ESMTP Sendmail 8.8.5/8.8.5
```

This banner line tells you the name of the server you're connected to, what protocol it supports, and the version of the mailer and the configuration files, as well as the server's idea of the local time.

Next you have to tell the server who you are:

```
HELO heimdall.myexample.com
250 heimdall Hello heimdall.myexample.com [192.168.1.1]
```

Some implementations of SMTP require this instruction; and it never hurts to send it. Please note that although the server can use DNS to verify that the system is who it claims to be, in the default configuration, the SMTP server will trust a client delivering the mail, and will relay it without change. If, for example, you say that the message is coming from system `whitehouse.gov`, the SMTP server may well accept it as coming from there.

The server returns a response consisting of a code (in this case, 250) and a detailed message (in this case, `WAA21757 Message accepted for delivery`). RFC 821 defines the codes of the messages that the server will return; the server itself determines the text, which can be as terse or as detailed as the server's implementor chooses to make it.

We then use the command `MAIL FROM:` to tell the SMTP server who is transmitting the mail message:

```
MAIL FROM: <root@myexample.com>
250 <root@myexample.com>... Sender ok
```

In most cases, the SMTP server has no way to tell whether the user named in this command really sent the message. For example, if we say the user is `president@whitehouse.gov`, the SMTP server will naively accept it.

Next, we use the command `RCPT TO:` to tell the SMTP server who the user is that is to be the recipient of the message:

```
RCPT TO: <naiveuser@myexample.com>
250 <naiveuser@myexample.com>... Recipient ok
```

Next, we use command `DATA` to transmit the message. The SMTP server reads as data everything you transmit; to end the transmission, we send a line that consists of a single "." character. Please note that the mail message has two sections: a *headers* section (also called the *envelope* section), and the *body* of the message. A blank line must separate the headers from the body:

```
DATA
354 Enter mail, end with "." on a line by itself
From: System Administrator <root@myexample.com>
To: Naive User <naiveuser@myexample.com>
Subject: Barbarians at the Gates!!!!!
Reply-To: evil@crackers.org
It has come to our attention that crackers may have broken into
our system. We need all users to reply to this message with their
network login and password so we can re-encrypt them on the
server to close the security hole. Simply reply to this message
and add your login name and password here:
   Login Name:
   Password:
And we will re-encrypt the passwords this evening after 5 PM to
restore the system.
Thanks
.
250 WAA21757 Message accepted for delivery
```

Finally, the command

```
QUIT
```

closes the connection with the SMTP server.

We have now transmitted our message to "Naive User." Hopefully, she is not as naive as `evil@crackers.org` thinks she is, and turns this message over to her system's administrator rather than answering it.

An SMTP server, by design, is pretty much open to all comers. Some people take advantage of this fact to latch onto an Internet provider's machine and send hundreds or thousands of mail messages around the Internet. These parasitic bulk mailings, called *spam*, have grown from a nuisance on the Internet to a serious problem.

This concludes our discussion of SMTP. At the end of this chapter, we give sources where you can find more information on this protocol.

POP3

The Post Office Protocol (POP) describes how a user can download a batch of mail from one machine to another. The third version of this protocol is described in RFC 1939, and usually is called POP3 by Internet *cognoscenti*.

WHY ANOTHER MAIL TRANSPORT PROTOCOL?

At this point, you may be asking why the Internet defines multiple mail transport protocols. SMTP is a workable, useful protocol; why do we need another protocol?

The answer to this question lies not in SMTP itself, but in the practical details of how SMTP works to handle mail:

◆ In brief, when a user uses a mail program to write a mail message, the mail program writes a file of instructions and data in a spool directory.

◆ An SMTP daemon that periodically examines the spool directory discovers the new file in the directory, and attempts to upload it to the appropriate system. (We will discuss later in this chapter just how the daemon determines what the appropriate system is.)

◆ If the daemon cannot upload the message to the system to which the message is addressed, the daemon leaves the message in the spool directory. If it cannot upload the message after a set period of time (usually one to three days), the daemon returns the message to its sender as undeliverable (in other words, *bounces* it), and removes it from the spool directory.

If the hosts on a network are continually connected to the network, this scheme works well: a message arrives in the spooler, the daemon finds it and delivers it, and that is that.

However, if a host is connected to the network intermittently, a message may linger in the mail server's spool directory for days, as it waits for the host to which it is addressed to plug itself into the network. During that time, the SMTP daemon continually checks the message: examining its status, trying to connect to the host to which the message is addressed, checking dates to see whether it should be bounced, and so on. The cost of delivering one message via SMTP to a host that is not continually connected to the network can be quite high. And if the network has many hosts that are connected only intermittently — which is the case with an ISP, most of whose hosts are connected intermittently via dial-up connections — then the SMTP daemon is continually working with hundreds or thousands of spooled messages at any given time, which is a severe drain on its computing resources.

Clearly, SMTP is impractical for networks that have hosts connected intermittently, and in fact, most ISPs do not use SMTP to deliver mail to their customers. What an ISP needs is not an active, "push" protocol for delivering mail, but a passive, "pull" protocol, in which the mail server simply leaves the mail addressed to a given host in a file or directory set aside for that host, and forgets about it. When a host connects to the network, it requests its mail, and the mail server transmits that host's mail to it – a much simpler operation than trying to push the mail out to a host.

Most ISPs use a batch, pull-oriented protocol to deliver mail to their customers. Numerous such protocols are in use. In this chapter, we discuss two of the most useful of these protocols: POP3 and UUCP.

HOW POP3 WORKS

As we noted earlier, POP3 is a protocol that delivers a batch of mail to a host upon request.

Please note that the Post Office Protocol (POP) is not the same thing as an Internet service provider's Point of Presence (POP) – yet another example of "acronym overload" in the terminology of networking.

POP3 is a fairly simple client-server protocol:

◆ The server listens to port 110, which is the well-known port for POP3, as set in file /etc/services.

◆ When the client connects to the server, it passes the server the name of the user who wants to download her mail, and her password.

◆ The server checks the user's name and password; if they check out, the server then downloads to the client the contents of the user's mailbox. The client can then request that the server delete the contents of the user's mailbox, or leave it intact.

Clearly, POP3 is designed for distributing mail to individual users. It's particularly useful for distributing mail to single-user machines, such as a Windows 95 machine.

POP COMMANDS

Like an SMTP session, a POP3 session is a conversation carried out between a client and server: the POP3 client sends commands to the POP3 server, and the server replies with messages and data.

RFC 1939, which defines the POP3 protocol, defines the messages and commands that POP3 clients and servers use to converse with each other. The POP3 commands include the following:

◆ USER *userid* – Give the *userid* whose mailbox will be manipulated. *userid* must identify a user who is recognized by the system on which the POP3 server is running. The server indicates whether *userid* is recognized.

◆ PASS *password* — Give the user's password. The server indicates whether *password* is recognized.

◆ LIST — List the messages in the user's mailbox. The server gives a summary of the message in the user's mailbox, and then gives the number and length of each message.

◆ RETR *messagenumber* — Retrieve message number *messagenumber*. The server writes the message to the client. The server transmits a line that consists of a single ".' to indicate that the transmission is finished.

◆ DELE *messagenumber* — Delete message number *messagenumber* from the user's mailbox. The server indicates whether it could delete the message.

◆ QUIT — Close the POP3 session and break the connection with the POP3 server.

In the next subsection, we show these commands in action.

AN EXAMPLE POP3 SESSION
The following code gives an example POP3 session. We performed this session by hand, by using command telnet to connect to port 110 on our local host.

The following gives the test of our session. What we type appears in italics; the server's replies appear in Roman:

```
telnet localhost 110
Trying 127.0.0.1...
Connected to localhost.
Escape character is '^]'.
+OK heimdall POP3 Server (Version 1.004) ready.
USER naiveuser
+OK please send PASS command
PASS mypassword
+OK 2 messages ready for naiveuser in /usr/spool/mail/naiveuser
LIST
+OK 2 messages; msg# and size (in octets) for undeleted messages:
1 1821
2 751
RETR 2
+OK message 2 (751 octets):
X-POP3-Rcpt: naiveuser@heimdall.myexample.com
Return-Path: <evil@crackers.org>
Received: by heimdall.myexample.com
        id m0y6MbR-0000ikC; Sat, 21 Feb 98 15:36 CST
Message-Id: <m0y6MbR-0000ikC@heimdall.myexample.com>
From: System Administrator <root@myexample.com>
To: Naive User <naiveuser@myexample.com>
Subject: Barbarians at the Gates!!!!!
Reply-To: evil@crackers.org
It has come to our attention that crackers may have broken into
```

our system. We need all users to reply to this message with their
network login and password so we can re-encrypt them on the
server to close the security hole. Simply reply to this message
and add your login name and password here:
   Login Name:
   Password:
And we will re-encrypt the passwords this evening after 5 PM to
restore the system.
Thanks
.
DELE 2
+OK message 2 marked for deletion
QUIT
+OK heimdall POP3 Server (Version 1.004) shutdown.
Connection closed by foreign host.

Let's look at this session in detail.

First, we use command telnet to connect to port 110 on our local host:

telnet localhost 110
Trying 127.0.0.1...
Connected to localhost.
Escape character is '^]'.
+OK heimdall POP3 Server (Version 1.004) ready.

When we connect with port 110, the POP3 server announces that it's ready.

Next, we use POP3 commands USER and PASS to tell the server whose mailbox
we want to read:

USER naiveuser
+OK please send PASS command
PASS mypassword
+OK 2 messages ready for naiveuser in /usr/spool/mail/naiveuser

Next, we use the command LIST to get a detailed listing of the messages in the
mailbox:

LIST
+OK 2 messages; msg# and size (in octets) for undeleted messages:
1 1821
2 751

Then, we use command RETR to retrieve the second message in the mailbox:

RETR 2
+OK message 2 (751 octets):

The POP3 server sends the message, and concludes the message with a single '.'
character.

Finally, we use command DELE to delete the second message from the mailbox:

```
DELE 2
+OK message 2 marked for deletion
```

Now, we are finished — and we quit:

```
QUIT
+OK heimdall POP3 Server (Version 1.004) shutdown.
Connection closed by foreign host.
```

LIMITATIONS OF POP3

POP3 assumes that it is downloading an individual user's mailbox. Because a user's mailbox is a mail message's final destination — it has no place further to go — POP3 throws away all information about to whom the mail was addressed. Clearly, POP3 is suitable only for downloading mail to an individual user — not to a host or intranet that may have many users.

For downloading batches of mail for an entire domain, not just an individual user, we recommend using the UUCP protocol. We describe this protocol a little later in this chapter.

Note that using POP3 as a crude means of downloading batches of mail addressed to the multiple users of a given domain is possible. For example, an ISP may write all the mail going to a domain into a single mailbox. Practical reasons exist for doing this — principally because most ISPs charge a great deal more for UUCP service than they do for POP3.

However, a domain that uses POP3 to download its mail is faced with the problem of forwarding the mail to the correct user or users on the intranet. This can be done by writing a custom application that can do the following:

◆ Read the archive of mail.

◆ Break the archive into individual messages.

◆ Read the header on each message.

◆ Figure out the user to whom the message is addressed.

◆ Forward the message to that user.

Later in this chapter, we give an example of such an application.

If you decide to build your own intranet, you probably will want to set up your own POP3 server. This is particularly useful in delivering mail to any Windows 95 machines that are connected to your intranet. We describe in Chapter 9 how to set up and configure a POP3 server under Linux, if you are interested.

A related protocol, IMAP4, is described by RFC 1730. This protocol is more sophisticated than POP3; however, it is not yet as widely used as POP3.

This concludes our discussion of POP3. We now move on to discuss the UUCP protocol.

UUCP

The *UNIX-to-UNIX Communication Protocol* (UUCP) is one of the most venerable of the protocols used on the Internet.

As we mentioned in Chapter 4, when we introduced the UUNET, UNIX machines used UUCP to network machines before the Internet became widely available: UNIX machines dialed into each other, and then used UUCP to exchange mail and execute commands.

At the risk of oversimplification, a UUCP session uses command uucico to copy a set of *command files* and *data files* from the sending machine to the recipient machine. Either machine can dial the other. After files have been uploaded, the UUCP program uuxqt on the recipient machine reads command files one by one, and executes them. Some of the command files may use the data in one or more of the uploaded data files. The commands that the sender machine can execute on the recipient machine depend upon the permissions that the recipient machine has granted to the sender; this permission varies from one sender to another, and from one recipient to another.

To send a mail message via UUCP, the sender machine creates a data file that holds the body of the message, and a command file that invokes the mail-handling program on the recipient machine to read the data file and process it appropriately. When the sender machine and the recipient machine connect to each other – either can dial the other – the sender uses command uucico to copy the message's command file and data file to the recipient; the receiver then invokes uuxqt to execute the command file; and uuxqt, in turn, invokes the mail-handling program to process the mail message in the data file, and insert it into the appropriate user's mailbox.

UUCP is superior to POP3 for handling batches of mail addressed to a domain. Unlike POP3, which stores all mail in a single file and throws away addressing information, UUCP stores each mail message in its own file and uses the message's envelope to build the command file with which it delivers the message. Thus, no need exists to use a filter or a special program to pick apart the mail archive and re-mail the messages.

Unfortunately, this flexibility comes at a price: Internet service providers are phasing out support for UUCP, or are making it prohibitively expensive, in part because of the difficulties in configuring UUCP correctly. UUCP may be superior, but you may also find it to be too expensive to be practical.

Later in this chapter, we show you how to configure UUCP on your system to receive and process incoming mail messages (no need exists to use it to process outgoing messages), on the off chance that you find an ISP that offers UUCP service at a reasonable price.

And with this lament, we conclude our discussion of Internet mail protocols. In our next session, we take up just how these protocols are implemented under Linux.

Implementation of Mail

Under Linux and other flavors of UNIX, mail is implemented not as a single tool, but as a set of interchangeable tools. These tools fall into two categories:

◆ *Mail User Agents* (MUAs) – These programs help users to write and read mail messages.

◆ *Mail Transport Agents* (MTAs) – These programs transport the mail from the MUA to the mailbox (or mailboxes) of its recipients.

These tools are interchangeable: that is, any MUA should work with any MTA, and vice versa. You will configure one MTA for your Linux system. However, you probably have to support a variety of MUAs to suit your users' tastes and needs.

We discuss each class of tools in turn.

Common MUAs

Mail user agents fall into two major categories: text-based and GUI-based:

◆ Among the most popular of the text-based MUAs are elm and pine. Both are extensively documented, in manual pages and in tutorial documents, and both run under Linux.

◆ Among the most popular of the GUI-based MUAs are Eudora, Microsoft Exchange, and Netscape Messenger. The first two run only on Windows 95; however, Netscape Messenger runs on both Windows 95 and Linux. In Chapter 9, when we discuss how to connect Windows 95 to a Linux-based intranet, we show you how to configure Linux and Windows 95 so that Windows 95 users can read mail received by your Linux system. You should note that we have excluded the Macintosh platform. Both Eudora and Netscape Messenger are available for the Macintosh. Because this book focuses on Windows 95 and Linux, you will not find a discussion of how to configure these clients on the Macintosh platform. You can be sure, however, that the configuration is similar.

Regarding which MUAs you should support, in our experience, both text-based and GUI-based MUAs present some difficulties to persons who are unfamiliar with them. A GUI-based system may be a better choice if you want to limit the time you spend holding users' hands.

Each MUA has its strengths and weaknesses. Selecting an MUA is as much a matter of taste as the choice of paper, pen, and ink is for a person who still writes letters by hand. Therefore, you should be prepared to offer your users a variety of MUAs, and to support each in its peculiarities.

Common MTAs

Under Linux, the most commonly used mail transport agents are sendmail, smail, and qmail.

Although a given system can support many different MUAs, it will use only one MTA. Therefore, the choice of MTA is a key decision you will make in setting up networking on your Linux workstation.

In this chapter, we show you how to configure sendmail as your system's MTA. Given the importance of the choice of MTA – and given that sendmail is controversial in certain circles – we discuss our decision in some detail.

SENDMAIL

sendmail is the workhorse MTA of the Internet. When sendmail was designed, the Internet was called *ARPANet* and it connected numerous different computer architectures, including Berkeley UNIX (which we describe in Chapter 1), DEC 20-Twenex, and VAX VMS. Each architecture had its own methods for delivering e-mail (which was the "killer application" of the nascent Internet), and naturally, these methods were mutually incompatible.

To help bring order out of this chaos, programmer Eric Allman took upon himself the job of tying all of these e-mail systems together. The result is sendmail.

sendmail really encompasses three functions in one:

♦ *A computer language* interpreter for a computer language, which allows the complete manipulation of the envelope section of an e-mail message.

♦ *A highly configurable mail routing agent* that can read a mail message's address, determine where the message is to be delivered, and determine how it should be handled.

♦ *An implementation of the SMTP protocol,* both as a client, for transmitting mail messages to another system's SMTP server, and as a server, for receiving mail messages from any MTA that complies with RFC 821.

As you can imagine, sendmail is a very complicated program. sendmail also must be *privileged* to do its job – that is, it must have the same permission to modify the contents of your system as does the superuser root.

sendmail's complexity and the fact that it is privileged combine to make it a major security problem on many UNIX workstations, for the following reasons:

- ◆ Because `sendmail`'s configuration is complex, botching configuration occurs easily, in ways that make your system easier to break into.

- ◆ Because `sendmail` is privileged, a cracker who uses `sendmail` to break into a system assumes `root` privileges on that system – and can therefore totally trash the system.

The most notorious incident of a cracker exploiting this situation occurred in November 1988, when Robert T. Morris, Jr., unleashed his "worm" program, which brought the Internet to its knees. Since then, `sendmail` has lived under the security microscope of thousands of security experts, who have combed it for flaws. Many of the problems with `sendmail` have been fixed over the years, but we advise any security-conscious administrator to keep a weather eye on `sendmail` configuration for any machines that she runs.

Given that `sendmail` is difficult and possibly dangerous to use, you may well ask why we still recommend using it as your mail transport agent. We do so for the following reasons:

- ◆ `sendmail` has been probed, tested, and improved for 20 years – practically since the advent of the Internet. Newer MTAs are less battle-scarred because they are less battle-tested.

- ◆ `sendmail` does the best job of envelope configuration of any of the MTAs that we have seen.

One way to ensure `sendmail` is secure on your system is to run the latest version. Currently, the latest version of `sendmail` is version 8.8.8. Most releases of Linux ship with release 8.8.5; while this isn't the latest version, 8.8.5 has fixed all the latest security bugs.

This concludes our brief introduction to `sendmail`. We again visit `sendmail` later in this chapter, when we discuss how to configure it.

This concludes our discussion of mail in the abstract. We now discuss just how to set up mail on your Linux workstation – beginning with a discussion of how to translate the theory of mail into a practical design for your system.

Designing a Mail Configuration

Now that we have discussed mail in the abstract, the time has come to discuss just how you should handle mail on your Linux system.

The two primary aspects to designing a mail system are the following:

- ◆ How to handle outgoing mail
- ◆ How to handle incoming mail

As is our custom, we discuss each in turn.

Outgoing Mail

Your Linux system ships with a stock configuration file designed to work on an Internet-connected machine. Because this is what you have, the configuration requires that you make only one decision: how to deliver mail to the recipient's machine via SMTP:

◆ *Deliver every mail message directly to the machine to which it is addressed* — This is fast, but you will see problems with mail delivery when the recipient's machine is down or otherwise unavailable.

◆ *Relay all mail through your ISP's SMTP server* — Also called a *smart host*. This is the mail equivalent of the `default` instruction that you have inserted into your Linux kernel's routing table. This alternative is slightly slower and is very sensitive to problems with your ISP's mail server; however, you will not encounter situations where some mail messages get through and others do not.

A *smart host* is called "smart" because it knows how to forward mail that your local mail server does not know how to forward correctly. Also, the smart host probably is continually connected to the Internet, and therefore has a better chance of delivering mail to a host that is connected to the Internet only intermittently.

Unless you have a compelling reason not to do so, we suggest that you forward outgoing mail to a smart host, and let that host's administrator grapple with problems of configuration and delivery for you.

Be sure to speak with the administrator of the network to which you will be uploading mail, and get both the name and IP address of the machine that will act as your smart host. Insert this information into file `/etc/hosts`, as we described in Chapter 3. You also need to give the name of the smart host to `sendmail`; we discuss how to do this later in this chapter.

Incoming Mail

Clearly, choosing how to transmit outgoing mail is straightforward. Configuring incoming mail is harder, principally because of the variety of methods available to you for downloading mail.

To choose the method with which you will download incoming mail, you must consider the following:

◆ *Will your system be connected to the network continually or intermittently?* If your system is connected continually to the network, then you can use SMTP to receive messages as they arrive at the network into which your Linux workstation is connected. However, if your workstation is connected only intermittently (as is the case in which you are dialing into an ISP), then you have to receive mail in batches, using POP3, UUCP, or some other batched protocol.

◆ *Does your system have one user or multiple users?* If your workstation is receiving mail in batches and it has only one user, then POP3 makes the most sense. If your system has multiple users – or if your Linux system eventually will become a gateway for your own intranet – then using UUCP for batch downloads is preferable. Please note that your choice may be limited by your budget, as many ISPs now charge a premium for UUCP service.

For both incoming and outgoing mail, be sure to discuss with the administrator of the network to which you are connected just what mail options are available to you, and what makes sense for you.

Mail-Configuration Scenarios

Now that we have discussed the principles of how to configure mail, let's walk through a few scenarios, and see these principles in action.

CATHERINE: A SINGLE-USER HOME SYSTEM

In this scenario, Catherine has a Linux system in her home. She is the only person who uses her Linux system.

To save money, Catherine purchased a standard PPP connectivity package from a local ISP, which includes:

◆ Outgoing mail: SMTP (relayed)

◆ Incoming mail: POP3

The ISP will give Catherine a login account on its machine. She has adjusted her Linux system's mail such that outgoing mail appears to have been transmitted from the ISP, and so that replies are sent to her account at the ISP.

Every time Catherine writes a mail message, `diald` automatically dials the ISP and uploads the message to the ISP's SMTP server.

All incoming mail will be funneled into her mailbox at the ISP; she will use a POP3 client to download it and read it at her leisure.

RICHARD: IN THE MESH, OPTIMAL SCENARIO

The *mesh* refers to those Internet domains that have only an MX record and no A records. (We describe what MX and A records are in Chapter 8, when we describe how to set up Domain-Name Service.) A system that is in the mesh has a registered domain, but is connected to the Internet only intermittently; usually, it connects to the Internet through a dial-up account at an ISP.

A domain in the mesh may have one user or multiple users. With regard to mail, domain in the mesh uses SMTP to transmit mail; however, it must receive mail via some other mechanism than direct SMTP: ISP funnels mail directed to domain into a batch file or directory, from which the domain's mail-server machine can download it periodically.

Richard's Linux system is in the mesh: he has registered it with the NIC, but accesses the Internet via a dial-up account with an ISP. Richard's wife and children use his Linux system to send and receive electronic mail.

Richard's ISP is enlightened enough to offer UUCP service at a reasonable price, so his mail is configured as follows:

◆ Outgoing mail: SMTP (relayed)

◆ Incoming mail: UUCP

The ISP funnels into a UUCP directory all mail messages addressed to anyone at Richard's domain.

Every time a user on Richard's system writes a mail message, diald automatically dials the ISP and uploads the message to the ISP's SMTP server.

Richard's machine dials into the ISP several times every day and uses UUCP to download his and his users' mail. Each user's messages are routed directly into the correct mailbox.

GEORGE: IN THE MESH, NEARLY OPTIMAL SCENARIO

George's Linux workstation system has multiple users and is also in the mesh. His local ISP offers UUCP service at a reasonable price. However, George's ISP is not near him, which means that telephone charges are a major consideration. For this reason, George wants to both send and receive his mail in batches; this enables him to limit his connectivity to late at night, when telephone charges are lower. For this scenario, UUCP is a more than reasonable solution:

◆ Outgoing mail: UUCP

◆ Incoming mail: UUCP

IVAN: IN THE MESH, LESS-THAN-OPTIMAL SCENARIO

Ivan's Linux system has multiple users and is also in the mesh. Unfortunately, no ISP in his locale offers UUCP service at a reasonable price. All he can afford is the less-than-optimal solution offered by the ISP, in which the ISP offers him a login and mailbox (as with Catherine's scenario), but routes into that mailbox all mail addressed to any user in Ivan's domain. Therefore, his mail is configured like Catherine's:

◆ Outgoing mail: SMTP (relayed)

◆ Incoming mail: POP3

As with Richard's system, every time a user on Ivan's system writes a mail message, `diald` automatically dials the ISP and uploads the message to the ISP's SMTP server.

Incoming mail is more of a problem. Ivan's machine dials into the ISP several times every day and uses a POP3 client to download the file of mail addressed to users at his domain. However, this scenario is complicated by the fact that Ivan had to program a way to read the downloaded mailbox of incoming mail and insert each message into the correct mailbox. A little later in this chapter, we describe a utility, `fetchmail`, that does this job for you.

MARIAN: FULLY CONNECTED

Marian is a programmer who specializes in Linux-based solutions. She has her own Internet domain, and has purchased a dedicated connection from an ISP, so her Linux system is fully connected to the Internet 24 hours a day, 7 days a week.

Marian's system uses a dial-up connection via ISDN, into a telephone number that the ISP dedicated to her account. The ISP also provided domain-name mapping for her domain, and helped her to program her Linux system's firewall, to help keep crackers and other such low-lifes out of her system.

To handle mail, Marian's system uses the following:

◆ Outgoing mail: SMTP (direct)

◆ Incoming mail: SMTP

Marian and her employees use her domain to send and receive all mail directly.

This scenario concludes our discussion of how mail works. We now discuss how to configure mail on your Linux system so that you can bring the configuration of choice into reality.

Configuring Mail

Now that we've discussed the wherefore and the why of mail, let's get down to work. In this section, we discuss how to configure mail on your Linux workstation.

Please note that that you do not have to install any of the programs that we describe in this section. All of these programs are part of standard Linux releases, and should already be installed on your Linux system.

Configuring Sendmail

To configure `sendmail` to upload mail, you must modify `sendmail`'s configuration file `/etc/sendmail.cf`.

`sendmail.cf` is a large file, written in a style that brings new meaning to the word "terse." For that reason, we do not describe its contents in detail. Rather, we include several example versions of `sendmail.cf`; one of which is used by each of the mail scenarios that we just described. You can pick the scenario that best suits how you will be using mail in your situation; we also show you how to modify the appropriate configuration file so that it works with your Linux workstation.

FORMAT OF SENDMAIL.CF

Most instructions in `sendmail.cf` consist of a two-character code, followed immediately by the value to which that code is set. No white space or punctuation separates the code from the value to which it is set. For example, if we were setting code XX to value `foobar`, we would type:

```
Xxfoobar
```

See the end of this chapter for sources of information on `sendmail`'s configuration language.

CHANGES NEEDED TO SENDMAIL.CF

To configure `sendmail`, you must modify `sendmail.cf` to name the following:

♦ The smart host

♦ The host that you are — that you are masquerading as

We discuss each in turn.

NAMING THE SMART HOST   At the beginning of this chapter, we discussed what a *smart host* is. If you decide to use a smart host, then you must set code DS in `sendmail.cf` to name the smart-relay host, as follows:

```
# "Smart" relay host (may be null)
DShostname
```

where *hostname* gives the full name of the host that will be handling your mail.

For example, to name host `smtp-server` at domain `myisp.com` as your smart host, set `DS` as follows:

```
DSsmtp-server.myisp.com
```

This will force `sendmail` to send to `smtp-server.myisp.com` all mail that is not addressed to users on your local system.

NAMING YOUR HOST   At the beginning of this chapter, we discussed some of the decisions that you must make to manage incoming mail properly. In brief:

◆ If your system is going to be plugged into the Internet 24 hours a day, 7 days a week, then outside systems can transmit mail directly to your host's SMTP server.

◆ However, if your Linux workstation is plugged into the Internet only intermittently, any attempt to transmit a message to your system while it is off the air will fail, and the message will be bounced back to the sender. In this case, you must enlist the service of a *mail spooler* — a system that is always on the air, and will receive your mail for you and store it, so that your Linux system can retrieve it when you are ready for it.

If you will be using a mail spooler, you must set code `DM` in `sendmail.cf` to the name of the machine that will be spooling mail for you:

```
# who I masquerade as (null for no masquerading) (see also $=M)
Dmspoolermachine
```

This tells `sendmail` to rewrite your mail messages' headers so that they appear to come from the mail-spooler system rather than from your home system. This method of replacing one system's name with another is called *masquerading*, because one system is passing itself off as another. (We encounter masquerading again in Chapter 8, when we discuss how to use IP masquerading to let all hosts on an intranet use a single IP address to interact with the Internet.)

For example, if your ISP's mail-server host is named `smtp-server.myisp.com`, then to masquerade as that host, set `DM` as follows:

```
# who I masquerade as (null for no masquerading) (see also $=M)
Dmsmtp-server.myisp.com
```

If you are an individual, you can put in the name of your provider's SMTP server here and mail will be returned to it. You also have to reconfigure your MUA to place the name of the mail-spooler into the `Reply-To:` portion of each outgoing mail message's header, so that replies to your mail are sent to the correct system.

CONFIGURING THE SCENARIOS

In the previous section, we described five scenarios, each of which used a different configuration of mail to meet a different set of needs. In this section, we describe how to configure sendmail to fulfill each scenario.

On the CD-ROM included with this book are five example sendmail configuration files:

- ◆ sendmail.cf — The "vanilla" sendmail configuration file

- ◆ smtp-direct.cf — Configure sendmail to transmit mail directly to the host to which it is addressed

- ◆ smtp-relay.cf — Configure sendmail to use a smart host to relay mail

- ◆ smtp.cf — Configure sendmail to download mail via SMTP

- ◆ uucp.cf — Configure sendmail to use UUCP

For each scenario, we describe the example configuration file you should use, as well as how to modify it to work with your host and your ISP.

CATHERINE: A SINGLE-USER HOME SYSTEM   In this scenario, Catherine has a Linux system in her home. She is the only person who uses her Linux system. She does not have a domain registered with the NIC. Her setup includes:

- ◆ Outgoing mail: SMTP (relayed)

- ◆ Incoming mail: POP3

If your setup resembles Catherine's, you should use configuration file smtp-relay.cf:

1. Back up the file /etc/sendmail.cf.

2. Copy smtp-relay.cf into /etc/sendmail.cf.

3. Edit /etc/sendmail.cf and make the following changes:

4. Change the line beginning

   DMmyexample.com

   to the login identifier that your ISP has assigned to you as in the following example:

   DMcatherine@myisp.com

We strongly recommend that your login identifier on your local machine be the same as that at your ISP. Otherwise, when `sendmail` posts an outgoing message from your machine, it will look like it came from a nonexistent user on the ISP's machine.

5. Change the line beginning

`DSesmtp:mailrelay`

to read

`DSesmtp:myisp.com`

or whatever your ISP's mail-relay machine happens to be.

Later in this chapter, we show you how to use POP3 to download mail into your mailbox.

RICHARD: IN THE MESH, OPTIMAL SCENARIO   Richard's Linux system is in the mesh: he has registered it with the NIC, but accesses the Internet via a dial-up account with an ISP. Richard's wife and children use his Linux system to send and receive electronic mail. His setup includes:

◆ Outgoing mail: SMTP (relayed)

◆ Incoming mail: UUCP

If your setup resembles Richard's, you should use configuration file `smtp-relay.cf`:

1. Back up the file `/etc/sendmail.cf`.

2. Copy the file of your choice into `/etc/sendmail.cf`.

3. Edit `/etc/sendmail.cf` and make the following changes:

4. Change the line beginning

`DMmyexample.com`

to the login identifier that your ISP has assigned to you as in the following example:

`DMcatherine@myisp.com`

We strongly recommend that your login identifier on your local machine be the same as that at your ISP. Otherwise, when `sendmail` posts an outgoing message from your machine, it will look like it came from a nonexistent user on the ISP's machine.

5. Change the line beginning

   DSesmtp:mailrelay

   to read

   DSesmtp:myisp.com

   or whatever your ISP's mail-relay machine happens to be.

You do not have to configure sendmail to handle mail received via UUCP, because UUCP downloads mail, and then remails it locally – all mail received by sendmail via UUCP looks to sendmail like a message mailed by someone who is logged into your system; and sendmail is already configured to do that.

Later in this chapter, we show you how to configure UUCP to download your mail.

GEORGE: IN THE MESH, NEARLY OPTIMAL SCENARIO   George's Linux worksta-tion system has multiple users and is also in the mesh. His local ISP offers UUCP service at a reasonable price. George wants to both send and receive his mail in batches; this enables him to limit his connectivity to late at night, when telephone charges are lower. His setup includes:

- ◆ Outgoing mail: UUCP

- ◆ Incoming mail: UUCP

If your setup resembles George's, you should use configuration file uucp.cf:

1. Back up the file /etc/sendmail.cf.

2. Copy uucp.cf into /etc/sendmail.cf.

3. Edit /etc/sendmail.cf and make the following changes:

4. Change the line beginning

   DMmyexample.com

   to the name of your domain. Your domain must be registered before this will work.

5. Change the line beginning

   DSuucp-dom:gail

   to read

   DSuucp-dom:*myisp.com*

   where *myisp.com* names the host from which you will be downloading your UUCP mail.

Later in this chapter, we show you how to configure UUCP to exchange mail with your UUCP provider.

IVAN: IN THE MESH, LESS-THAN-OPTIMAL SCENARIO Ivan's Linux system has multiple users and is also in the mesh. Unfortunately, no ISP in his locale offers UUCP service at a reasonable price. All he can afford is the less-than-optimal solution offered by the ISP, in which the ISP offers him a login and mailbox (as with Catherine's scenario), but routes into that mailbox all mail addressed to any user in Ivan's domain. Therefore, his mail is configured like Catherine's:

- Outgoing mail: SMTP (relayed)

- Incoming mail: POP3

If your setup resembles Ivan's, you should use configuration file `smtp-relay.cf`:

1. Back up the file `/etc/sendmail.cf`.

2. Copy the file of your choice into `/etc/sendmail.cf`.

3. Edit `/etc/sendmail.cf` and make the following changes:

4. Change the line beginning

   `DMmyexample.com`

   to the name of your domain. Your domain must be registered before this will work. Your ISP will be responsible for funneling into your mailbox all mail addressed into your domain.

5. Change the line beginning

   `DSesmtp:mailrelay`

   to read

   `DSesmtp:myisp.com`

   or whatever your ISP's mail-relay machine happens to be.

Later in this chapter, we show you how to use POP3 to download your mail, and distribute it to your users.

MARIAN: FULLY CONNECTED Marian is a programmer who specializes in Linux-based solutions. She has her own Internet domain, and has purchased a dedicated connection from an ISP, so her Linux system is fully connected to the Internet 24 hours a day, 7 days a week.

To handle mail, Marian's system uses the following:

◆ Outgoing mail: SMTP (direct)

◆ Incoming mail: SMTP

If your setup resembles Catherine's, you should use configuration file `smtp-relay.cf`:

1. Back up the file `/etc/sendmail.cf`.

2. Copy the file of your choice into `/etc/sendmail.cf`.

3. Edit `/etc/sendmail.cf` and make the following changes:

4. Change the line beginning

   `DMmyexample.com`

   to the name of your domain. Your domain must be registered before this will work.

5. Change the line beginning

   `DSesmtp:mailrelay`

   to read

   `DSesmtp:myisp.com`

   where `myisp.com` is the name of your ISP machine to which you will be uploading mail.

In the next sub-section, we describe how to "turn on" `sendmail` so that it can receive incoming mail via SMTP. Otherwise, no further configuration is needed: `sendmail` itself handles all the details.

This concludes our discussion of configuring `sendmail`. Clearly, we are just scratching the surface of what `sendmail` can do; but this is enough to get you and your users "on the air" and exchanging mail with other persons through the Internet.

INVOKING SENDMAIL

`sendmail` can be invoked in either of two ways:

◆ By an MUA, to handle a message that a user has created with the MUA

◆ By the `inetd` daemon, to receive an incoming mail message via SMTP

We discuss each in turn.

HANDLING A MESSAGE FROM AN MUA   Actually, this situation is quite easy: practically all MUAs under Linux are preconfigured to invoke `sendmail` to process a user's message.

You do not have to do anything for an MUA to invoke `sendmail` and hand it a user's message for processing.

If you are interested in how MUA is configured to interact with `sendmail`, see the documentation that comes with that MUA.

HANDLING A MESSAGE FROM SMTP   As we mentioned earlier, one of `sendmail`'s many jobs is to act as the SMTP daemon for receiving incoming mail. You need to turn on sendmail to receive incoming mail in any of the following three scenarios:

♦ If your machine will be receiving Internet mail directly via SMTP (as does Marian's machine, previously described).

♦ If your machine will be using `fetchmail` to download mail, either for a single-user system (as does Catherine's system) or for a multiple-user system (as does Ivan's system).

♦ If you will be setting up an intranet, and your machine will be acting as the mail router for the other machines on your intranet. (We describe how to set up an intranet in Part III of this book.)

In fact, the only time you do not want to set up `sendmail` to act as an SMTP server is when your system will be receiving incoming mail via UUCP *and* is the only machine on your intranet.

In this subsection, we describe how to configure `sendmail` so that it can handle incoming mail via SMTP. Actually, this job is quite easy, because no configuration is needed for `sendmail` itself, apart from what we already described.

`sendmail` normally is invoked by the daemon `inetd`. We introduce `inetd` in Chapter 3, but to review briefly:

♦ `inetd` is a master daemon that listens to ports of all the servers described in its configuration file /etc/inetd.conf.

♦ When `inetd` hears a datagram arriving on one of those ports, it invokes the appropriate application to process the incoming data.

`inetd` spares you from having to clutter memory with multiple daemons, each listening to its own port.

To configure `inetd` so that it invokes `sendmail` to process mail arriving via SMTP, insert the following line into file /etc/inetd.conf:

```
smtp   stream   tcp      nowait   root      /usr/sbin/tcpd      sendmail -v
```

This line may already be in your system's copy of /etc/inetd.conf, but commented out. If this is the case, uncomment the line by removing the pound sign # from the beginning of the line.

After you make this change to /etc/inetd.conf, you must restart inetd to force it to re-read its configuration file, as follows:

- ◆ Type command

  ```
  ps -ax | grep inetd
  ```

  This will show you information about the inetd process.

- ◆ The first (leftmost) number in the line returned by the previous command shows you inetd's process identifier. Type command

  ```
  kill processid
  ```

  where *processid* is inetd's process identifier.

- ◆ Type command

  ```
  /usr/sbin/inetd
  ```

  Note that & doesn't appear at the end of this command.

That's all there is to it. inetd will now invoke sendmail to handle messages arriving via SMTP.

Configuring fetchmail

If you have decided to use POP3 to move mail from an external mail server to your system, then you need to implement a POP3 client. This client connects to the POP3 server on your mail server's machine, identifies you to the server, and then copies your mail onto your local system – either into your mailbox or into the SMTP daemon for remailing.

Most Linux releases come with a standard POP3 client named fetchmail. This client is quite complex, and can be used to download mail by using numerous different protocols, not just POP3; however, in this section, we concentrate on using it with POP3.

fetchmail works in a fairly sophisticated way:

1. First, fetchmail reads a set of configuration rules that tells it how it should dispose of incoming mail.

2. Then, fetchmail reads your mailbox on the machine that is handling your mail. You can tell it to use any one of numerous protocols to read your mail; these protocols include POP3.

3. `fetchmail` breaks the contents of the mailbox into individual messages, and then feeds each message into your system via your system's SMTP server. To your system, this process looks like an SMTP client on your mail server is transmitting messages to you.

`fetchmail` recognizes a large number of command-line switches – far more than we can describe here. However, most information is passed to `fetchmail` through its configuration file, `.fetchmailrc`.

In this section, we describe how to configure `fetchmail` for two different situations:

◆ *To download mail for a single user* – This would be used by Catherine's system, where she is the only person using her Linux workstation, and she does not have a domain registered.

◆ *To download mail for multiple users* – This would be used by Ivan's system, where he has multiple users and a registered domain, and his ISP funnels all mail addressed to his domain into a single mailbox.

We discuss each situation in turn.

CONFIGURING FETCHMAIL FOR A SINGLE-USER MAILBOX

In this configuration, `fetchmail` downloads mail from a *single-user mailbox* – a mailbox that holds mail addressed to one user. In this description, we assume that you are the single user who is downloading mail.

To download mail from a single-user mailbox, do the following:

1. Using your favorite text editor, edit file `.fetchmailrc` in your home directory. Insert into this file the following text:

```
poll myisp.com protocol POP3 user myisploginid with password
myisppassword
```

where *myisp.com* is the name of the system at your ISP from which you will be downloading mail, *myisploginid* is the identifier with which you log into the ISP's mail system, and *myisppassword* is the password with which you log into the ISP's mail system. This tells `fetchmail` to read the contents of *myisploginid*'s mailbox on system *myisp.com*, and load its contents into your mailbox. By default, `fetchmail` will empty your mailbox on *myisp.com* as it loads its contents into your mailbox on your Linux workstation.

2. After you finish editing .fetchmailrc, save it and exit from your text editor. Then, use the command chmod to change permissions on .fetchmailrc, as follows:

```
chmod 600 .fetchmailrc
```

This command means that only you and the superuser root can read the contents of .fetchmailrc. This is important, to keep busybodies from reading .fetchmailrc and learning your password on your mail server machine.

3. After you make these changes, type command:

```
fetchmail
```

By this point in your work with this book, your system should be able to dial out automatically. fetchmail will poll your mail provider and download all mail into your mailbox.

CONFIGURING FETCHMAIL FOR A MULTIUSER MAILBOX

A *multiuser mailbox* holds mail that is addressed to numerous different users. As we described with Ivan's system, often a customer will ask an ISP to funnel into a single mailbox all of the mail addressed to a given customer's domain, as an inexpensive alternative to UUCP or SMTP service for incoming mail.

You can configure fetchmail to read your incoming mail and remail each message to the appropriate user on your system. This is by no means a full substitution for UUCP service, because by funneling mail into a mailbox, the ISP has to throw away the message's envelope — which, among other things, explicitly names the user to whom the message is addressed — but if you want to have your own domain and are on a tight budget, this method is workable.

As you can imagine, configuring fetchmail to handle a multiuser mailbox is much more complicated than configuring it to handle a single-user mailbox. In this subsection, we walk you through the configuration, and then we show the result of a mail run using fetchmail. We assume that you have configured inetd so that it will invoke sendmail to handle mail arriving via SMTP, as we described earlier.

PREPARING .FETCHMAILRC   To begin, you need to prepare a version of .fetch-mailrc that has the following structure:

```
poll isp_mail_machine
  protocol POP3
  localdomains localdomain
  no dns
  no envelope
  user myisploginid with password myisppassword to
        localuser
        localuser
```

```
     . . .
     localuser
here
```

Please note that the indentation is simply to make this file more legible; it has no significance *per se*.

Let's examine this one clause at a time.

- ◆ As with the example in the previous subsection, the `poll` instruction tells `fetchmail` to poll system *isp_mail_machine*.

- ◆ The `protocol` clause tells `fetchmail` to use the POP3 protocol to retrieve mail.

- ◆ The `localdomains` clause names the local domain or domains whose mail is being funneled into the mailbox that will be downloaded to your system. `fetchmail` will use this information to identify the user in your local domain to whom a mail message is addressed, and then route the message to her.

- ◆ Optional clause `no dsp` tells `fetchmail` not to use DSP to confirm the identity of the system from which mail was received. For a multiuser mailbox, DSP confirmation often creates more problems than it solves.

- ◆ Optional clause `no envelope` tells `fetchmail` not to attempt to identify the person to whom mail is routed from the entries `Received` and `X-Envelope-To` in the mail message's header. We discuss this at greater length later in this chapter.

- ◆ The `user` clause names the user and password to be used to retrieve mail from the mail server. The keyword `to` at the end of this clause indicates that the mail can be addressed to one of the following *localusers*. The keyword `here` that follows the user names indicates that these users belong to your local system rather than to the remote system from which mail is being downloaded.

When `fetchmail` reads a mail message, it tries to figure out to whom it should go; in this instance, it will look for addresses that contain one of the local domains. `fetchmail` then matches the user in the address with one of the local users named in the list of *localusers*. When it finds a match, `fetchmail` instructs the SMTP daemon on the local system to route that message into the local user's mailbox. If, however, `fetchmail` cannot find a match between a user to whom a mail message is addressed and the list of *localusers*, it instructs the SMTP daemon to route the message into the mailbox of the user who invoked `fetchmail` — usually the super-user `root`, although it could be almost any user.

Clearly, `fetchmail`'s ability to handle multiuser mailboxes enables you to use it to route mail to the users at a local domain – provided the domain has a relatively small number of users, and those users do not have any unusual addressing requirements. However, flaws exist in this approach, because reverse-engineering a mail message's envelope from the contents of its header isn't always possible.

ENVELOPE OR NO ENVELOPE   As we mentioned earlier, lines `Received:` and `X-Envelope-To:` in the mail message's header give information about the mail message's envelope:

◆ Line `X-Envelope-To:` gives a copy of the envelope itself. However, this is not a standard feature of a mail message: not every MTU is configured to insert this line into a message's header, or an MTU may be configured to give this line a different name.

◆ Line `Received:` names the user that received a mail message. The user named in this line usually is the one to whom the message was addressed – but not always. In cases where an ISP funnels into a single mailbox all mail for the multiple users of a given domain, the `Received:` line is misleading, because it names the user who owns the mailbox rather than the user to whom the message is intended.

The question is whether you should let `fetchmail` read lines `X-Envelope-To:` and `Received:` when it is processing a message, or whether you should use the instruction `no envelope` to tell `fetchmail` to ignore the envelope lines. This is an issue because of the way `fetchmail` processes a mail message:

1. When `fetchmail` tries to figure out the user who should receive a mail message, it first reads the line `X-Envelope-To:`.

2. If no user is listed, `fetchmail` then reads line `Received:`.

3. If no user is listed, `fetchmail` then reads lines `To:`, `Cc:`, and `Bcc:`.

Given what we said about how the `Received:` line can be misleading, you should use the following rules of thumb:

◆ If the mail messages you receive from your ISP contain the line `X-Envelope-To:`, then you should let `fetchmail` interpret the envelope instructions: do *not* use instruction `no envelope`.

◆ If, however, the messages you receive from your ISP do not contain the line `X-Envelope-To:`, then you should tell `fetchmail` not to interpret the envelope instructions: do use instruction `no envelope` in your `.fetchmailrc`.

AN EXAMPLE .FETCHMAILRC   Now that we've discussed how to write a .fetch-mailrc in the abstract, let's see it in practice. Consider the following situation:

◆ A Linux workstation owns domain myexample.com.

◆ This workstation has two users, fred and chris.

◆ The users' mail is funneled into the mailbox of user pseudouser on the machine of their ISP, myisp.com.

The following .fetchmailrc tells fetchmail how to retrieve mail from myisp.com and distribute it to fred and chris:

```
poll myisp.com
  protocol POP3
  localdomains myexample.com
  no dns
  no envelope
  user pseudouser with password pseudouserspassword to
        fred
        chris
  here
```

When fetchmail is invoked, it uses protocol POP3 to poll system myisp.com, and then downloads the contents of the mailbox owned by user pseudouser. As it reads each message in pseudouser's mailbox, fetchmail looks for addresses that contain the name of the local domain, myexample.com. When it finds such a message, fetchmail checks whether the user to whom the message is addressed is either fred or chris. If the message is addressed to either of those users, fetchmail tells the SMTP server at myexample.com to route the message into that user's mailbox; if it is not addressed to either of those users, then fetchmail tells the SMTP server at myexample.com to route the message into the mailbox of the user who has invoked fetchmail.

AN EXAMPLE RUN   Now that we have configured fetchmail, let's take a look at it in action. The following shows the output of fetchmail when user fred on myexample.com runs fetchmail with its -v flag set, which tells fetchmail to write a verbose description of its actions.

To begin, we see fetchmail logging into the POP3 server at myisp.com:

```
fetchmail: 4.3.8 querying myisp.com (protocol POP3) at Sun Mar  8
  10:07:24 1998
fetchmail: POP3< +OK QUALCOMM Pop server at myisp.com starting.
fetchmail: POP3> USER pseudouser
fetchmail: POP3< +OK Password required for pseudouser.
fetchmail: POP3> PASS *
fetchmail: POP3< +OK pseudouser has 2 message(s) (6486 octets).
```

Clearly, fetchmail has used the POP3 instructions we described earlier to log into the POP3 server. The server, in turn, informs fetchmail that pseudouser's mailbox has two messages in it.

fetchmail next interrogates the POP3 server for detailed information about the contents of pseudouser's mailbox:

```
fetchmail: selecting or re-polling default folder
fetchmail: POP3> STAT
fetchmail: POP3< +OK 2 6486
fetchmail: POP3> LAST
fetchmail: POP3< +OK 0 is the last read message.
fetchmail: 2 messages for pseudouser at myisp.com.
fetchmail: POP3> LIST
fetchmail: POP3< +OK 2 messages (6486 octets)
fetchmail: POP3< 1 1639
fetchmail: POP3< 2 4947
fetchmail: POP3< .
```

The POP3 server tells fetchmail that two messages are in the mailbox, neither of which has been read. fetchmail now retrieves the first message from the mailbox:

```
fetchmail: POP3> RETR 1
fetchmail: POP3< +OK 1639 octets
reading message 1 of 2 (1639 bytes)
fetchmail: passed through fred@myexample.com matching myexample.com
fetchmail: SMTP< 220 myexample sendmail ready at Sun, 8 Mar 98 10:07
 CST
fetchmail: SMTP> EHLO myexample.com
fetchmail: SMTP< 500 Command unrecognized
fetchmail: SMTP< 220 myexample #1 ready at Sun, 8 Mar 98 10:07 CST
fetchmail: SMTP> HELO myexample.com
fetchmail: SMTP< 250 myexample Hello myexample.com
fetchmail: forwarding to myexample.com
fetchmail: SMTP> MAIL FROM:<nobody@myisp.com>
fetchmail: SMTP< 250 <nobody@myisp.com> ... Sender Okay
fetchmail: SMTP> RCPT TO:<fred@myexample.com>
fetchmail: SMTP< 250 <fred@myexample.com> ... Recipient Okay
fetchmail: SMTP> DATA
fetchmail: SMTP< 354 Enter mail, end with "." on a line by itself
fetchmail: SMTP>. (EOM)
fetchmail: SMTP< 250 Mail accepted
 flushed
fetchmail: POP3> DELE 1
fetchmail: POP3< +OK Message 1 has been deleted.
```

fetchmail read the first message from the POP3 server at myisp.com. It examined the message for addresses that named domain myexample.com; when it found one, it examined the address to see whether it mentioned either of the users named in fetchmail's configuration – that is, users chris or fred. In this instance, the message was addressed to fred@myexample.com, so fetchmail succeeded in figuring out who should receive the message. fetchmail then opened a connection to the SMTP server at myexample.com and used the SMTP instructions we described earlier to pass the message to myexample.com's SMTP server. The SMTP server then managed the gritty details of delivering the message into fred's mailbox. Finally, after the SMTP server acknowledged that it had accepted the message from fetchmail, then – and only then – did fetchmail tell the POP3 server to delete the message from pseudouser's mailbox.

fetchmail then processes the second message in pseudouser's mailbox:

```
fetchmail: POP3> RETR 2
fetchmail: POP3< +OK 4947 octets
reading message 2 of 2 (4947 bytes)
fetchmail: passed through chris@myexample.com matching myexample.com
fetchmail: forwarding to myexample.com
fetchmail: SMTP> MAIL FROM:<nobody@myisp.com>
fetchmail: SMTP< 250 <nobody@myisp.com> ... Sender Okay
fetchmail: SMTP> RCPT TO:<chris@myexample.com>
fetchmail: SMTP< 250 <chris@myexample.com> ... Recipient Okay
fetchmail: SMTP> DATA
fetchmail: SMTP< 354 Enter mail, end with "." on a line by itself
#********************** .********************** .********************
 ******* .*******************fetchmail: message 2 was not the
 expected length (5032 != 4947)
fetchmail: SMTP>. (EOM)
fetchmail: SMTP< 250 Mail accepted
 flushed
fetchmail: POP3> DELE 2
fetchmail: POP3< +OK Message 2 has been deleted.
```

This reiterates what fetchmail did to process the first mail message, with the exception that the message is addressed to user chris rather than user fred.

Now that both messages have been processed, fetchmail logs out of the POP3 server on myisp.com and the SMTP server on myexample.com, and exits:

```
fetchmail: POP3> QUIT
fetchmail: POP3< +OK Pop server at myisp.com signing off.
fetchmail: SMTP> QUIT
fetchmail: SMTP< 221 myexample closing connection
fetchmail: normal termination, status 0
```

INVOKING FETCHMAIL   After you prepare your configuration file for `fetchmail`, the next step is to write a script that will invoke `fetchmail` to download your mail. We suggest that you do the following:

1. Move the `.fetchmailrc` file into a place that is publicly owned and easily accessed by the superuser `root`. We suggest moving it into file `/usr/local/etc/fetchmail.rc`, but you may prefer to keep it elsewhere.

2. After you copy the configuration file, make sure that it is owned by the user who is going to run it (probably `root`), and then use command `chmod` to set its permissions to 600 (as we described earlier).

3. Prepare a script to invoke `fetchmail`. We suggest that it read as follows:

   `fetchmail -f /usr/local/etc/fetchmail.rc —syslog`

   - Option `-f` names `fetchmail`'s configuration file – in this case, `/usr/local/etc/fetchmail.rc`.

   - Option `—syslog` tells `fetchmail` to use the log daemon `syslogd` to handle error messages and status messages. We describe `syslogd` in Chapter 3.

   This script should be owned by `root`, and have permissions 700 – that is, readable, writable, and executable only by its owner.

You may want to insert a call to your script into `root`'s `crontab` file. This ensures that `fetchmail` is invoked regularly to download your mail.

This concludes our introduction to `fetchmail`. The description given here will get you up and running with `fetchmail`. If you need more information to tune `fetchmail` to meet some special problems, or if you simply are curious about it, the manual page for `fetchmail` will tell you what you need to know.

Configuring a POP3 Server

As we described earlier, if you build an intranet, you may want to use a POP3 server to distribute mail to the single-user systems on your intranet – particularly to systems that are running Windows 95.

For a description of how to install and configure a POP3 server under Linux, see Chapter 9.

Configuring UUCP

Earlier, we discussed UUCP and how it compares with POP3. In this section, we describe how to configure UUCP on your Linux workstation to download a batch of mail.

UUCP exists in numerous implementations. Although the implementations of UUCP all behave basically the same, they vary widely in how their configuration files are organized. The UUCP implementation used, by default, under Linux is called Taylor UUCP, after its creator, Ian Taylor. The following description works only with Taylor UUCP; using it with, say, HoneyDanBer UUCP, will lead to results that are at best disappointing.

Taylor UUCP uses numerous configuration files. All are kept, by default, in directory /var/lib/uucp/taylor_config, although under your release of Linux, they may be kept elsewhere. Our work involves three configuration files: call, port, and sys. In the rest of this section, we describe how to configure these files on system heimdall so that it can use UUCP to download mail from system uucp_server.myisp.com.

FILE CALL

The first step in configuring UUCP to receive a download of mail is to insert an entry into file /var/lib/uucp/taylor_config/call. This file names the hosts that we can contact via UUCP; it is roughly equivalent to networking file /etc/hosts. The name call reflects the fact that when UUCP was designed, systems telephoned each other directly, rather than communicated via a network.

Each entry in call has the format *system_name login password*.

Each entry has three tokens. The tokens must be separated by one or more white-space characters.

In our example, to call system uucp_server and log in as heimdall, using mypassword as our password, we would place the following entry into call:

```
uucp_server login_id mypassword
```

FILE PORT

The next step is to insert an entry into file /var/lib/uucp/taylor_config/port. Each entry in this file defines a *port* – a physical means by which one or more remote systems can be contacted via UUCP. In networking terms, a port is roughly equivalent to an interface. Just as a networking interface can be used to communicate with multiple systems, a port can be used to contact more than one remote system.

The definition of a port has the following format:

```
port portname
instruction
instruction
   . . .
instruction
[blank line]
```

The first line in the definition of a port names the port being defined. The name of the port is followed by one or more UUCP instructions. The instructions that are used vary from one type of port to another. A blank line marks the end of this port's definition.

A port can use a physical port on your system – usually a serial port that has a modem plugged into it. In this case, the description of a port would refer to an entry in configuration file `/var/lib/uucp/taylor_config/dial`, which defines types of dial-out devices and how they talk with each. Our example does not require this, as we are piggybacking our connection through the networking command `telnet`, which we introduce in Chapter 4.

The following defines port `uucp_server`. This port is used to contact host `uucp_server.myisp.com`:

```
port uucp_server
type pipe
command /usr/local/bin/telnet -8 -E uucp_server.myisp.com
```

The first line names the port as `uucp_server`. This is followed by two instructions: a `type` instruction, and a command instruction.

Instruction `type` gives the type of port this is. It can be one of the following:

◆ `direct` – A direct connection, usually via a serial port.

◆ `modem` – The port access is a modem. This is the default.

◆ `pipe` – The port is a pipe that runs through another program.

◆ `stdin` – The port runs through the standard input and standard output.

◆ `tcp` – The port is a TCP port.

If the port is type `pipe`, which is the case in this example, the port's definition must include a `command` instruction that names the program through which the UUCP connection will be piped. In this example, we will use `telnet` to connect to the other host, as follows:

```
command /usr/local/bin/telnet -8 -E uucp_server.myisp.com
```

Please note that in this example, we are using command `/usr/local/bin/telnet` rather than the default `telnet` program `/bin/telnet`. This version uses the SOCKS library – or rather, will use the SOCKS library when we prepare this command when we describe the SOCKS library in Chapter 8.

◆ Option -8 tells `telnet` to use 8-bit encoding – in other words, enable `telnet` to transmit binary data.

◆ Option -E turns off the use of the escape character. This prevents the TELNET session from aborting if the binary data being transmitted across the TELNET link accidentally contains the escape character.

The final option names the host to be contacted via telnet – in this case, uucp_server.myisp.com.

The definition of a port that connects via a program such as telnet is much simpler than the definition of a port that connects via a modem or other physical device. You likely will never need to use UUCP to connect via a physical device, but if you are interested in how to do so, we give some sources of information at the end of this chapter.

FILE SYS

The last configuration file that you need to modify is /var /lib/uucp/taylor_ config/sys. This file holds definitions of systems – that is, how to contact and work with a remote system.

The following code gives the definition for remote system uucp_server:

```
system uucp_server
myname heimdall
call-login *
call-password *
time any
local-send /var/spool/uucppublic /tmp
local-receive /var/spool/uucppublic /tmp
remote-send /var/spool/uucppublic /tmp
remote-receive /var/spool/uucppublic /tmp
protocol iag
protocol-parameter g timeout 20
protocol-parameter g retries 10
protocol-parameter i window 8
protocol-parameter i packet-size 1024
chat ogin:-\n-ogin: \L\n ssword:-\n-ssword:\P\n
chat-timeout 60
port uucp_server
```

The definition of a system begins with a system instruction, which names the system being described. This is followed by one or more lines of instructions. A blank line terminates the description. The following describes the instructions that comprise the body of this definition.

To begin, instruction

```
myname heimdall
```

gives the name by which your system will identify itself to system uucp_server – in this example, heimdall.

The next instructions

```
call-login *
call-password *
```

set the login string and password that will be used to log into the remote system. UUCP will use the `call-login` string to expand escape sequence \L in the `chat` instruction, described later, and it will use the `call-password` string to expand escape sequence \P in the `chat` instruction. An asterisk indicates that the string will be taken from the configuration file `call`, which was previously described.

The instruction

```
time any
```

sets the time at which it is "legal" to contact the remote system. The argument `any` means that the remote system can be contacted at any time. This instruction was used back in the days when systems running UUCP dialed each other directly; often, `any` was used to limit calls to the evening hours, when telephone rates were cheaper.

The instructions

```
local-send /var/spool/uucppublic /tmp
local-receive /var/spool/uucppublic /tmp
remote-send /var/spool/uucppublic /tmp
remote-receive /var/spool/uucppublic /tmp
```

name directories from which files can be sent to the remote system, and into which files can be written from the remote system:

- ◆ `local-send` names the directories whose files the local system can send to the remote system.

- ◆ `local-receive` names the directories into which the local system can write files that it requests from the remote system.

- ◆ `remote-send` names the directories whose files the remote system can request from the local system.

- ◆ `remote-receive` names the directories into which the remote system can write files that it wants to send to the local system. This instruction is the one that truly matters with regard to downloading mail via UUCP.

Instructions

```
protocol iag
protocol-parameter g timeout 20
protocol-parameter g retries 10
protocol-parameter i window 8
protocol-parameter i packet-size 1024
```

set the communications protocols that the local system and the remote system use to communicate with each other, and some of the parameters used by those protocols. Discussing UUCP communication protocols in any detail is beyond the scope of this book; however, the instructions given here are typical for a UUCP installation, and should work for you without modification.

Instruction

```
chat ogin:-\n-ogin:\L\n ssword:-\n-ssword:\P\n
```

gives the "chat script" that defines how the local system logs into the remote system. The syntax of the UUCP chat script is nearly identical to that of the PPP chat script that we described in Chapter 3 – in fact, the syntax of the PPP chat script is largely a copy of the syntax devised for UUCP.

In brief, a chat script consists of a series of pairs of prompts and replies – the prompt coming from the remote system, and the reply being sent by the local system in reply to the prompt. The escape sequence \n sends a newline character – much like pressing the Return key on your keyboard.

This example consists of two prompt-reply pairs:

◆ In the first pair, a prompt that ends in the string ogin: receives the escape sequence \L in reply. This escape sequence sends the login identifier with which the local system logs into the remote system. The string that this escape sequence represents is set by the instruction call-login, previously described.

◆ In the second pair, a prompt that ends in the string ssword: receives the escape sequence \P. This escape sequence sends the passwords with which the local system logs into the remote system. The string that this escape sequence represents is set by the instruction call-password, previously described.

Tinkering with the chat instruction is, by far, the hardest part of preparing a UUCP interface to a remote system. For most installations, however, the preceding example works quite well.

The next instruction

```
chat-timeout 60
```

sets how long the timeout is for the connection – that is, if the local host cannot log into the remote host within 60 seconds, UUCP aborts the session.

Finally, command

```
port uucp_server
```

defines the port, as defined in file /var/lib/uucp/taylor_config/port, that UUCP will use to connect to this system. We discussed file port earlier in this section.

This concludes our discussion of how to configure UUCP to download a batch of mail from an ISP. The ISP, of course, has to configure its system to spool your mail into a UUCP-accessible directory and initiate the downloading of files when the local host connects to it.

INVOKING UUCP

Finally, to use UUCP to connect to the remote host and download mail, use the following command:

```
/usr/lib/uucp/uucico -s uucp_server
```

Command `uucico` manages the task of making the connection with the remote system, and also manages the uploading and downloading of files. Option `-s` names the system with which `uucico` should connect. After it downloads the command files from the remote system, `uucico` invokes command `uuxqt` to read the command files and execute them.

You should embed this command within file `/usr/spool/cron/crontabs/uucp`, and set it for the times when you want to download mail.

This concludes our discussion of how to use UUCP to download and distribute mail on your system. If you find an ISP that offers this service at a reasonable price, consider yourself fortunate — UUCP is old technology, but it remains the best technology for distributing batches of mail.

Summary

In this chapter, we discussed Internet mail, and how to configure your Linux system to manage it.

We first discussed the most commonly used mail protocols: SMTP, POP, and UUCP.

We then discussed how mail is implemented under Linux: through mail transport agents (MTAs), of which the most commonly used is `sendmail`, and mail user agents (MUAs), of which a great variety is used under Linux.

After laying the groundwork of theory, we introduced the nuts and bolts of configuring mail. We first discussed five commonly encountered mail setup scenarios, each of which described the needs of a particular type of user. Then, we went into the details of configuring software to run mail: `sendmail`, `fetchmail`, POP3, and UUCP.

Part III

Creating an Intranet

Chapter 6

Wiring Multiple Machines via Ethernet into an Intranet

IN THIS CHAPTER

- ◆ Assigning IP addresses
- ◆ Wiring the machines together
- ◆ Configuring the network
- ◆ Testing and debugging the network

AT THIS POINT in your reading, you have learned how to add networking hardware and software to your Linux machine, and how to configure your machine so that it can communicate with an existing network – either via modem or via Ethernet.

Now, we discuss how to build an intranet of your own. This intranet will connect two or more computers via Ethernet.

Please note two caveats about the descriptions in this chapter:

- ◆ The descriptions in this chapter, and in Chapters 7 and 8, assume that the machines on your intranet run Linux. Further, we assume that each machine has had an Ethernet card installed in it, as described in Chapter 2, and has the Linux networking software installed and configured on it, as described in Chapter 3. (If you have already connected a machine to an intranet via Ethernet, you have to install a second Ethernet card into it. We discuss this specialized topic later in this chapter.) In Chapter 9, we tackle the special topic of how to add to your intranet machines that are running Windows 95.

- ◆ The descriptions in this chapter describe how to perform elementary configuration of your intranet, so that the machines on it can communicate with each other. However, this chapter does not go into the configuration required to let the hosts on your intranet exchange datagrams with machines on other networks. We assume that you should learn to walk before you learn to run, so we defer that advanced topic until Chapter 8.

273

That said, let's get started.

Assigning IP Addresses

The first step to configuring your intranet is to assign an IP address to your intranet. So, which address should you use?

Well, you could request a class-C network address from the InterNIC. However, this could cost you some money. Fortunately, a much simpler option is available: use one of the "hobbyist" IP network addresses.

As we mentioned in Chapter 1, Internet RFC 1597 reserves the following network addresses for TCP/IP-based networks that are not connected to the Internet:

◆ Class-A network 10.0.0.0

◆ Class-B networks 172.16.0.0 through 172.31.0.0

◆ Class-C networks 192.168.1.0 through 192.168.255.0

No host on the Internet can use any of these addresses: they are reserved strictly for internal use by intranets. These addresses are guaranteed not to collide with any IP address on the Internet — in fact, any datagram that has a "hobbyist" address will not be recognized by any gateway or router on the Internet.

We suggest that you pick for your network one of the class-C networks in the preceding list. When assigning IP addresses to individual hosts, the convention is to begin with host address 1, and then dole out the remaining IP addresses in order. We have found it helpful to give "special" machines (for example, gateways or routers) IP addresses beginning with 100, so that the addresses of these machines are easier to remember.

Our example intranet, called myexample.com, will use hobbyist address 192.168.1. It consists of the five machines listed in Table 6-1.

TABLE 6-1 MYEXAMPLE.COM

Name	IP Address	Host's Type
thor	192.168.1.1	Ordinary host
odin	192.168.1.2	Ordinary host
baldur	192.168.1.3	Ordinary host
heimdall	192.168.1.100	Gateway
loki	192.168.1.101	PPP dial-in server

◆ An *ordinary host* is connected to your intranet alone.

◆ A *gateway* is connected to both your intranet and another network. This other network can be either another intranet via a second Ethernet card or the Internet itself via a dial-up connection to an Internet service provider. As the word *gateway* suggests, this host will be responsible both for forwarding datagrams from the ordinary hosts to hosts on the outside network and for forwarding to the ordinary hosts on your intranet all datagrams received from the outside network.

◆ A *PPP server* is an ordinary host that has a dial-in modem attached to it, and that is running the PPP daemon pppd in server mode. Outsiders can dial into this host and connect to your intranet via PPP.

Although we do not discuss gateways in this chapter, you should remember that your intranet will have a gateway to the outside world. In all likelihood, this gateway will be the machine that you configured in Part II to communicate with another network via Ethernet or modem.

The advantage to using a hobbyist address is that it gives you a large set of IP addresses that you can use on your intranet, without having to ask anyone's permission of the InterNIC, and without worrying that somehow you'll collide with a real Internet address.

The disadvantage, however, is that the machines to which you assign these addresses will not be able to exchange data directly with hosts on the Internet: your hosts will not have legitimate Internet-usable IP addresses that hosts on the Internet can use to send them datagrams. Your gateway machine will have a second, legitimate IP address that is assigned to it by the network to which it is connected.

Fortunately, work-arounds for this problem exist: *IP masquerading* and *SOCKS*. In Chapter 8, we show you how to use these methods so that the hosts on your intranet will be able to exchange datagrams with hosts on the Internet.

Wiring the Machines Together

If you've gotten this far, we assume that the following has already occurred:

◆ You have installed an Ethernet card into each of your machines, as we described in Chapter 2.

◆ You have chosen an IP network address for your network, and have assigned an address to each machine in the network.

You are now ready to wire the machines together to form an intranet. In this section, we discuss the tools and materials you need, and how to perform the wiring.

Adding a Second Ethernet Card

As noted earlier, we assume in this chapter that you have already installed an Ethernet card into each of your machines, as we described in Chapter 2.

However, if the *gateway* machine – the machine through which the other machines on your intranet will communicate with the outside world – is already linked into an intranet via Ethernet, then you will have to add a second Ethernet card to the machine.

The rule of thumb is one Ethernet card for each Ethernet network to which a machine is linked.

Installing a second Ethernet card has the same difficulties as installing the first Ethernet card, particularly when allocating system resources. In addition, a second Ethernet card has the special problem of creating the interface to it.

Recall from our discussions in Chapters 1 and 3 that a physical device is accessed through a kernel interface to that device. When your system has one Ethernet card in it, the Ethernet driver probes for the card when you boot your Linux system, and automatically creates kernel interface eth0 to that card.

For example, if you have installed a Novell NE2000 Ethernet card (or a clone thereof), you will see the following messages on your screen when you boot your Linux system:

```
Dec 28 16:58:42 myexample kernel: ne.c:v1.10 9/23/94 Donald Becker
(becker@cesdis.gsfc.nasa.gov)
Dec 28 16:58:42 myexample kernel: NE*000 ethercard probe at 0x340:
00 40 05 22 bf 0f
Dec 28 16:58:42 myexample kernel: eth0: NE2000 found at 0x340, using
IRQ 5.
```

The driver probes for the card automatically. When the driver finds the card, it reads the card's IRQ, base address, and Ethernet address (in this case, 00 40 05 22 bf 0f). Then, the driver creates interface eth0 to this card.

However, this process has some problems when your machine has two Ethernet card in it:

♦ Autoprobing can create only interface eth0. You must create interface eth1 by hand.

♦ Worse, autoprobing may "find" the wrong Ethernet card – it may assign interface eth0 to the card that you want to have interface eth1. Because you will be adding information to your kernel's routing table by interface (as we described in Chapter 3), assigning the interfaces correctly is very important – otherwise, the datagrams that want to be routed to your internal intranet will be routed to the "outside" Ethernet network, and vice versa.

Thus, you must somehow tell the kernel which interface to assign to each Ethernet card, and you must stop the Ethernet drivers' autoprobing from interfering with your assignments.

You do this by passing arguments to the Linux kernel when you boot it. Argument ether lets you specifically create an interface to a specific Ethernet card. Argument reserve lets you protect a portion of memory from autoprobing.

We discuss each argument in turn.

ether

Kernel argument ether enables you to create an interface to an Ethernet card. It takes three clauses:

♦ The IRQ by which the card is accessed

♦ The card's port address

♦ The name of the interface

For example, suppose that you have two Ethernet cards: one that has IRQ 5 and port address 0x340, that you want to access through interface eth0; and a second that has IRQ 10 and port address 0x300, that you want to access through interface eth1. To assign these interfaces, you would give your kernel the follow arguments when you boot it:

```
ether=5,0x340,eth0 ether=10,0x300,eth1
```

Note that no white space separates any clause within either ether argument.

The kernel creates these interfaces for you, subject to the usual caveats – that the hardware is installed and configured correctly, and does not interfere with other hardware in your Linux workstation.

Please note that which interface you assign to which card doesn't matter. What does matter is that the interfaces be assigned consistently, so that you can add the correct information to the kernel's routing table.

By the way, the 0x that prefixes the port address indicates that it is a hexadecimal (base-16) address. Hexadecimal notation is the standard way to give addresses in computer memory. If you are unfamiliar with hexadecimal notation, we suggest that you consult any primer on computer programming.

reserve

Argument `reserve` tells the kernel to reserve a chunk of memory. In effect, it turns off autoprobing for any devices whose port addresses lie within that chunk of memory.

`reserve` takes two clauses:

◆ The address at which the kernel begins reserving

◆ The number of bytes of memory to reserve

For example, to protect our two Ethernet cards from being autoprobed, we would use the following form of the `reserve` argument:

```
reserve=0x300,128
```

This reserves 128 bytes beginning at address 0x300. In effect, this argument sets aside the chunk of memory from 0x300 through 0x37F, and protects from autoprobing every physical device whose port address lies within that chunk of memory.

Please note that you should use this clause carefully. Otherwise, you might accidentally stop the kernel from autoprobing a device that should be autoprobed.

MODIFYING lilo.conf

To pass arguments to the kernel when you boot your system, you need to modify file `/etc/lilo.conf`. The `append` clause lets you pass arguments to a kernel automatically when you boot it.

For example, to pass the `ether` and `reserve` arguments to kernel `netkernel` when you boot it, you would add the following clause to the entry for `netkernel` in file `lilo.conf`:

```
append = "reserve=0x340,32 ether=5,0x340,eth0"
```

After making this change, the entire entry for `netkernel` should appear as follows:

```
image = /netkernel
  root = /dev/device
  label = netkernel
  append = "reserve=0x340,32 ether=5,0x340,eth0"
```

device names the device that holds your machine's root file system; for example, `hda1` (the first partition of your system's IDE drive A).

After you make this change, run command `lilo`. This ensures that the changes you make to `lilo.conf` are "visible" when you reboot your Linux system.

This concludes our discussion of adding a second Ethernet card to your Linux workstation. For more information on Ethernet, see the references given at the end of this chapter.

Create a Twisted-Pair Ethernet Network

Now that all Ethernet cards have been installed into your Linux workstations, the next step is to physically string wire to connect the machines together. A big wiring job involves a lot of grunt work, particularly if you are running twisted-pair cable to connect machines that are far apart. However, some planning helps to make this job manageable.

In this section, we discuss how to physically install twisted-pair Ethernet in your home or office. We also discuss the simpler job of installing thin-coax Ethernet. For your own sanity, we strongly suggest that you read this section *before* you run to the store or begin work.

PLAN YOUR NETWORK

The first step in building your network is to plan carefully just what you intend to do.

As we describe in Chapter 1, a *twisted-pair Ethernet network* consists of individual cables that run from each workstation to a central device, or *hub*.

At the computer's end, the cable is terminated at a *wall jack* (also called a *surface-mount jack*). This jack closely resembles the wall jack into which you plug a telephone. A *patch cable* is used to plug the computer's Ethernet card into the wall jack.

At the hub's end, the cable is terminated at a *terminating block*. (A terminating block is sometimes called a *harmonica*, because its row of RJ-45 sockets resembles the row of holes in that musical instrument.) A patch cable plugs a port on the terminating block into a port on the hub.

You should first decide where to place the terminating block and the hub. This location should be as central to your network as possible and have an electrical outlet nearby, yet be easily protected from busy fingers. A storage room or telephone closet are good places to set up your terminating block and hub. Pick carefully, because moving this equipment is extremely difficult after your network has been wired.

You should next figure out which rooms will have computers in them. This is relatively easy in an office. However, these decisions are harder in a home – for example, does your husband want his computer in the bedroom or the basement? Once you know which rooms will have computers in them, you must carefully select where you want to position the wall jack. The wall jack should be positioned both to make the computer easiest to use (for example, it should not be positioned next to the door), and to make running cable from the terminating block easy.

Sketch a diagram that shows the location of each computer, and of your terminating block and hub.

Next, sketch exactly how you intend to run cable from the terminating block to each wall jack. Decide whether you want to run cable through walls, or staple it along baseboards. Your diagram should note all twists and turns through walls and along baseboards.

Then, use a tape measure to measure exactly how long the path is from the terminating block to each wall jack. Remember that a given twisted-pair cable cannot be longer than 300 feet (including the patch cable at each end of the connection). To meet this requirement, you may have to reposition the terminating block or one or more of the computers; otherwise, you will have to buy repeaters, which greatly increases the cost of setting up your network.

SUPPLIES FOR WIRING TWISTED-PAIR ETHERNET

To install twisted-pair Ethernet, you must have the following supplies:

- ◆ One or more Ethernet hubs – The hubs with one port for each of the machines you will be wiring together. If you are daisy-chaining hubs together, each hub must also have two ports for connecting to other hubs.

- ◆ A terminating block.

- ◆ A wall jack for each Ethernet connection – If possible, use wall jacks that have screw terminals in them, for easier installation.

- ◆ Either enough CAT 5 cable to reach from your hubs to every workstation, or enough premade CAT 5 patch cables to do the same – Your diagram will tell you how much cable you need. Buy some extra, to take care of some wastage. Try to get cable that meets the specifications for TIA/EIA 568A CAT 5. This cable is tested to carry signals up to 100MB and will save you the hassle of rerunning your network cables when you switch to 100MB Ethernet. Please note that each type of cable uses its own set of colors for the insulator of each wire. When we describe later in this section how to terminate a cable, we assume that the colors of the strands are those of 568A CAT 5 cable.

If you are installing the cabling yourself instead of having a contractor do it, then you also need:

- ◆ Cabling staples, and a staple gun that can fire them.

- ◆ A bag of male terminators for the cable.

- ◆ An RJ-45 crimping tool.

- ◆ 10- to 20-foot Cat 5 patch cables. You need two for each computer: one to go from the wall jack to the computer, and one to go from the terminating block to the hub. These should be 24- or 26-gauge stranded CAT 5. Avoid solid CAT 5, because it doesn't hold up as well to being moved.

RUNNING TWISTED-PAIR CABLE

At this point, you have drawn your diagram, made your measurements, and purchased your equipment. You're now ready to start stringing cable.

ETHERNET CABLE   As we noted earlier, our examples assume that you are using cable and terminators that meet the TIA/EIA specification 568A. If you strip one of these cables, you will find that it contains four bundles of two wires (or strands) twisted together — hence, the name *twisted pair*. The twist of the strand within a pair, as well as the overall twist of the pairs, among themselves and within the cable, is designed to reduce the effect of external electrical devices on the signals within the cables.

The pairs of strands are designated by color, as shown in Table 6-2.

TABLE 6-2 COLORS OF CABLE STRANDS

Signal	Ground Pair	Strand
1	Solid blue	Blue stripe
2	Solid orange	Orange stripe
3	Solid green	Green stripe
4	Solid brown	Brown stripe

Each pair is designated by color. The signal is transmitted on the wire that has the solid color, and the ground is sent on the wire that has the same color in stripes.

THE RJ-45 TERMINATOR   Looking at a male RJ-45 terminator shows that it has eight metal slides embedded in a plastic plug. The exposed edge of each slide is a flat strip of copper, which is designed to touch the corresponding spring connector within the female jack. The interior edge of each slide is sharpened, so that it can cut through the insulation in a strand and touch the metal wire within it. Channels in the connector guide each strand to the area under its slide's knife.

Each of the contacts has a number, from 1 to 8. When you hold an RJ-45 male connector with the clip side away from you and the contacts facing you, the contacts are numbered, as shown in Figure 6-1.

Ethernet uses contacts 1 and 2 to receive, and contacts 3 and 6 to transmit. TIA/EIA 568A specifies which strand in the CAT cable should be connected to a given contact. This specification, also called the *connection sequence*, is given in Table 6-3.

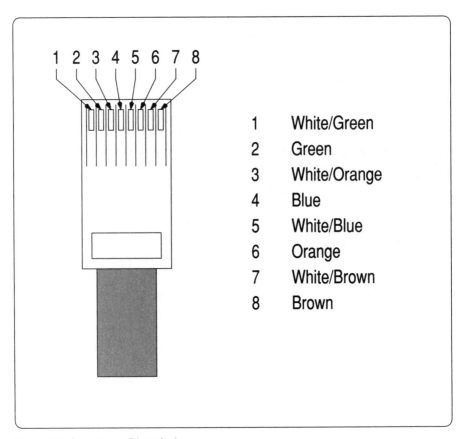

Figure 6-1: Contacts on RJ-45 jack

TABLE 6-3 RJ-45 CONNECTION SEQUENCE

Contact	Strand	Color
1	Pair 3 ground	Green stripe
2	Pair 3 signal	Solid green
3	Pair 2 ground	Orange stripe
4	Pair 1 signal	Solid blue
5	Pair 1 ground	Blue stripe

Continued

Contact	Strand	Color
6	Pair 2 signal	Solid orange
7	Pair 4 ground	Brown stripe
8	Pair 4 signal	Solid brown

Ethernet receive is carried on pair 3 (green strands) and Ethernet transmit is carried on pair 2 (orange strands). Pairs 1 and 4 are dead. This wiring scheme enables the twist in the wire to cancel noise, as it is designed to do.

THE CROSSOVER CABLE   In normal Ethernet cable, the connection sequence at each end of the cable is the same as given in Table 6-3. This is called a *straight-through connection*. The Ethernet equipment itself handles the connection of transmit to receive. For example, an Ethernet hub transmits on contacts 1 and 2 and receives on contacts 3 and 6, whereas an Ethernet card receives on contacts 1 and 2 and transmits on contacts 3 and 6.

However, if you want to use twisted-pair Ethernet to connect exactly two machines, you can dispense with the need for an Ethernet hub by making a cable that swaps the send-and-receive pairs. Such a cable is sometimes called a *crossover cable*.

To wire a crossover cable, terminate one end, as shown in Table 6-2, and then terminate the other end, as shown in Table 6-4.

TABLE 6-4 CROSSOVER CABLE

Contact	Conductor	Color
1	Pair 2 ground	Orange stripe
2	Pair 2 signal	Solid orange
3	Pair 3 ground	Green stripe
4	Pair 1 signal	Solid blue
5	Pair 1 ground	Blue stripe
6	Pair 3 signal	Solid green
7	Pair 4 ground	Brown stripe
8	Pair 4 signal	Solid brown

A crossover cable swaps the send-and-receive pairs in the Ethernet cable, much as a null modem swaps the send-and-receive strands in a serial cable. This enables you to connect two computers through their Ethernet ports.

Please note that some hubs have a special *uplink* port that is wired this way for connection to another hub with a normal cable. If your configuration requires a crossover, you are better served by making a short crossover cable and labeling it as such. Then, wire the rest of your circuit straight through, so the you can use it later when the configuration no longer requires the crossover.

TERMINATING A CABLE WITH AN RJ-45 PLUG   To terminate a cable with a male RJ-45 connector, do the following:

1. Strip about half an inch (1.25 centimeters) of outer insulator from the cable.

2. Untwist the strands and lay them flat in the pattern that you want them to terminate in – either the pattern given in Table 6-3 or, if you are wiring one end of a crossover cable, the pattern given in Table 6-4. As we noted earlier, the twist is designed to prevent the cable from picking up electrical noise. *We cannot stress enough that you must undo as little of this twist as possible when you terminate a cable.*

3. Use a wiring sequence that does not split the transmit and receive signals across pairs.

4. After you set the sequence, press all eight strands into the connector as far as they go. Ideally, you should be able to press in all eight strands until each touches the plastic at the end of the connector.

5. Put the male connector into the socket on the crimping tool.

6. Press the handle of the tool to crimp the slides onto the strands. The knife edges in the plug will pierce the insulation on each strand, and make the connection.

You probably will have to take a couple of tries to get this right, at least until you become skilled with using the crimping tool. Thus, we recommend that you leave a little extra cable at the end where you will terminate with a male RJ-45 plug. If you make a mistake, just snip off the spoiled end and try again.

TERMINATING THE WALL JACKS   To terminate a cable wall jack, do the following:

1. Cut the cable close to the place where you want to mount the jack. If your wall jacks have screw terminals (which are easy to use), or if you have become skilled with the crimping tool, then cut the cable to within 6 inches (9 centimeters) of the jack. Otherwise, leave a little extra cable, in case you make a mistake.

2. Strip the outer sheath from an inch to an inch and a half (2.5 to 4 centimeters) of the end of the cable, to expose the four twisted pairs of strands. Again, undo as little of the twist as possible.

If you are crimping the wires onto an RJ-45 plug, follow the directions given above. However, if you are attaching the strands to a screw jack, do the following:

1. Strip $^3/_8$-inch of insulation (1 centimeter) from each of the strands.

2. Bend the end of each strand over the end of a screwdriver to form a hook.

3. Place the hook over the screw, with the tail running clockwise. This way, the conductor is drawn in towards the screw as you tighten it, making a better connection.

4. Screw down each strand onto the jack in the sequence you use when terminating an RJ-45 plug.

To screw down the wires in the proper order, you must identify which screw terminal is connected to contact 1 on your wall jack. In most jacks, the clip faces up, away from the wall to which the jack has been attached. Figure 6-2 shows a mounted jack and the screw on the baseplate that corresponds with each contact.

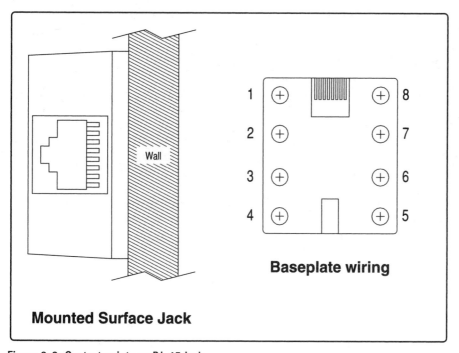

Baseplate wiring

Mounted Surface Jack

Figure 6-2: Contact points on RJ-45 jack

If your screw jacks differ from the norm, you have to figure out which screw terminals correspond to the eight contacts, and then screw down the wires accordingly.

TESTING TWISTED-PAIR CONNECTIONS   Testing the connectivity of cables that you make or install can be difficult, principally because a network can fail at many points: an Ethernet card, the card's configuration, the physical cable, or the hub. As we describe in Chapter 3, the key to debugging is to isolate each element and test it separately.

If you want, you can buy any one of the variety of cable testers. These cost about $40 and up.

If you do not want to spend money on a dedicated cable tester, you can test with two workstations. Most of the network card setup programs include a diagnostic program for testing the link to another card of the same manufacturer and type. You can connect both workstations to the hub via a cable that you know is good (for example, a pre-made cable) and run the program.

After the program exchanges frames with the other side, you know that all your equipment is good. If you then use a suspect cable and the programs no longer can exchange frames, you know that the cable is the problem.

As you add each computer to your network, test it in the same way. Once you know that the machines are working correctly, your network should work without trouble.

Thin-Coax Ethernet

As we note in Chapter 1, thin-coax Ethernet connects all machines through a single coaxial cable. The machines dangle off the cable, much like the charms on a charm bracelet. No hub is required.

This configuration means that thin-coax Ethernet is much easier to wire than wiring twisted-pair Ethernet. However, it also means that thin-coax Ethernet is limited to connecting together machines that are near each other – usually within the same room.

To use thin-coaxial cable, you must have the following:

◆ Enough thin-coax cables to connect your machines – You need one cable for each of the machines that you are connecting, minus one. For example, if you are connecting three machines, you need two cables; if you are connecting five machines, you need four cables. We strongly suggest that you buy preterminated 20- or 30-foot cables. You can buy thin-coaxial cable in bulk and terminate it yourself, but doing this is quite difficult.

◆ One BNC T connector for each machine you are attaching to the network.

◆ Two BNC 50-ohm terminating resistors – one for each end of the network.

The female thin-coax connector has a collar on it. The collar has a diagonal slit in it. Female connectors are on the terminator and on the short end of the T connector.

The male thin-coax connector is round and has no collar. A short stem projects from the side of the connector. This stem slips into the slit in the female connector's collar, and is used to secure the male connector within the female. Male connectors are on the Ethernet card itself and on the long stems of the T connector.

To join two Ethernet connectors, slip the female connector onto the male. Align the slit in the female connector's collar with the stem on the male connector; then, twist the collar until the stem slides to the far end of the slit.

To connect the machines, first plug the T connector onto each Ethernet card. Drape a cable between each computer; be careful not to kink the cable in any way. Plug the cable into each computer's T connector.

Most computers in the network will have two cables attached to their T connectors. The computer at each end of the network will have only one cable attached to its T connector: attach a 50-ohm terminator onto each of those T connectors.

Configuring the Network

We discuss in Chapter 3 how to configure the machines on your network to communicate with each other. This section largely is a review of the material presented in Chapter 3, but the material is reorganized somewhat here so that understanding it in your new, intranet-ready environment is easier.

Compile a Kernel

To begin, each ordinary host should have a Linux kernel that is configured as described in Chapter 3.

If the machine is an *ordinary host* – a host that is connected to your intranet alone – then you may want to configure the kernel as we describe in the section "Configuring an Ordinary Host" in Chapter 3.

Edit /etc/HOSTNAME

Use a text editor to edit file /etc/HOSTNAME. Write into this file the name you have given this host.

You probably did this when you installed Linux onto your machine, but making sure never hurts.

Edit /etc/rc.d/rc.inet1

Next, use a text editor to edit file /etc/rd.c/rc.inet1, as follows:

1. Set variable IPADDR to the IP address that you are assigning to this host.

2. Set variable NETMASK to the value appropriate for the class you've given your network. For example, if you're giving your intranet a class-C address, then set NETMASK to 255.255.255.0.

3. Set variable NETWORK to the IP address you've chosen for your intranet. This should be the same as the value to which you set IPADDR, but with the last number set to 0. For example, if you assigned this host IP address 192.168.1.3, then the value of NETWORK should be set to 192.39.1.0.

4. Set variable BROADCAST to the IP address that is used for broadcasting on your intranet. This should be the same as the value to which you set variable NETWORK, except that the final 0 should be replaced with the number 255.

5. Next, uncomment (remove the # from the beginning) the following line that reads:

   ```
   # /sbin/ifconfig eth0 ${IPADDR} netmask ${NETMASK}
   ```

6. Uncomment the following line that reads:

   ```
   # /sbin/route add -net ${NETWORK} netmask ${NETMASK}
   ```

After you make these changes, save the file and exit from your editor.

EDIT /etc/hosts

Finally, you must edit file /etc/hosts to give the name and IP address of each machine on your intranet. For example:

```
192.168.1.1    thor thor.myexample.com
192.168.1.2    odin odin.myexample.com
192.168.1.3    baldur baldur.myexample.com
192.168.1.100  heimdall heimdall.myexample.com
192.168.1.101  loki loki.myexample.com
```

Please note that we use /etc/hosts just to get your intranet up and running. In Chapter 8, we discuss how to set up domain-name service on your intranet.

/etc/host.conf

File /etc/host.conf configures various aspects of a host. order is the directive that presently interests us, because it sets the order in which the host interrogates sources of domain-name information.

Edit file /etc/host.conf so that directive order reads as follows:

```
order hosts, bind
```

This tells the host first to read file /etc/hosts for domain-name information, and then to use the bind package to retrieve domain-name information from domain-name service.

We assume that you are not yet running DNS, so the order of lookup must be hosts first, and then bind. If you do not use this order, any traffic with one of the hosts on your local intranet will trigger a DNS lookup to your ISP's server, and thus dial a connection with your ISP.

In Chapter 8, we show you how to set up DNS on your intranet and how to modify /etc/host.conf to use the DNS service you set up.

EDIT /etc/resolv.conf

Your next task is to modify file /etc/resolv.conf. This file configures name resolution, which we discuss at length in Chapter 8; for now, however, you need to add an entry to this file that will identify the system from which your intranet receives domain-name service.

Edit the file and insert the following entry:

```
nameserver ip.address
```

where ip.address gives the IP address of the machine that will be providing domain-name service to your intranet. If your intranet will be connected to an external network via Ethernet, get this address from the person who administers the external network; if, however, your intranet will be connected to the Internet via a PPP link to an Internet service provider (ISP), get this address from technical support at the ISP.

Presently, we assume that you have *not* set up DNS on your intranet, and therefore are looking up addresses from file /etc/hosts; in this case, ip-address should be the address of your local machine. In Chapter 9, when we discuss how to set up DNS, we show you how to modify this file to use the DNS you have set up on your intranet.

This concludes our discussion of how to configure the hosts on your intranet. Now we turn on the network and set the hosts to talk with each other.

Testing and Debugging the Network

At this point you've done the following for each host on your intranet:

◆ Installed an Ethernet card

◆ Compiled a kernel and installed it

◆ Configured networking software

◆ Strung wire or cable between the machines and plugged them into
   each other

Now comes the moment of truth: Can your machines talk with each other? In
this section, we discuss testing your intranet, and some debugging steps you can
take if it doesn't work as you expect.

Testing

As we said earlier, most Ethernet cards come with a diagnostic program that
enables you to test the installation of the network card and the connectivity to
another machine running the same card and the same diagnostic program. If you
have set up two machines that can talk to each other via this hardware and software, you are ready.

When we debug in this way, we are building on what we already know: in this
case, that the two machines can talk to each other by using the simple diagnostic
tool that was provided with the network cards.

Now, you want to know whether the Linux kernel can use the hardware you
installed. To find out, try the following:

1. Start at the first machine. If you've properly configured the kernel to
   know the resources that the network card is using, no error messages
   should display when the kernel comes up. If you modified
   /etc/rc.d/rc.inet1 as we described above, the network card should be
   configured properly.

2. Run the following command.

   `netstat -nr`

3. This command shows the kernel's routing table. Is the Ethernet interface
   shown with the proper Ethernet and IP addresses? If not, then something
   went wrong with activation of the interface to the Ethernet card. Make
   sure that rc.inet1 is configured properly. Also, make sure that rc.inet1
   is executable – some text editors silently delete execute permission when
   you use them to edit a script.

4. Try having the host ping itself. For example:

```
ping myexample
```

5. If this results in a string of responses with very short times (less than 2 ms), then this machine is probably working correctly.

6. Now move to the second machine and repeat tests 1 through 4. After the second machine can ping itself by IP address, you can be reasonably assured that it also is working correctly.

Now for the big test:

1. Start *Also Sprach Zarathustra* by Richard Strauss on your CD player.

2. At the climax of the "Sunrise" section – just before cymbal crash on the climatic C-major chord – try to ping the first machine by IP address.

3. If it works, you should see a stream of responses from the first machine. Congratulations! Your intranet is now up and running.

If this didn't work, it's time to start debugging.

1. Turn off the CD player.

2. Go back to the beginning with the first machine. Confirm that it can still ping itself and that command `netstat -nr` still shows the Ethernet card in the routing table.

3. Return to the second machine and retest it as you tested the first machine.

If both hosts pass these tests, try the command:

```
ifconfig -a
```

This shows you all interfaces on the machine. You should see the Ethernet interface configured to use the IP address that you have chosen. If both machines are set up correctly, confirm that the machines are configured to use different IP addresses.

◆ Make sure that the hosts have different names. Giving two hosts the same name means that they read the same IP address out of file `/etc/hosts`.

◆ Check whether your Ethernet cards have light-emitting diodes (LEDs) on them. Twisted-pair Ethernet cards should have, at a minimum, a link LED, which indicates that the link to the hub is established properly. Furthermore, twisted-pair Ethernet cards should have an activity LED. If you are attempting to ping another machine on the network, the activity LED should flash once each second as the machine transmits packets. If this fails, then something is wrong with either the card, the cable, or the hub.

As a last resort, follow the instructions given in Chapter 3 for setting up your network manually. Seeing things step by step helps to unveil any problems in your network's hardware or configuration.

Summary

This chapter discusses how to wire multiple Linux workstations together to form an intranet.

First, physically wiring workstations together is described. Two different wiring schemes are described: one for thin-coaxial Ethernet, and the other for twisted-pair Ethernet. The tools, supplies, and wiring techniques needed for each are described in detail.

Next, configuring networking on each workstation is described. This involves adding entries to a number of configuration files.

Finally, techniques for testing and debugging your intranet are presented. The "philosophy" of debugging is described, and then the steps you can take to isolate a problem, diagnose it, and fix it.

Chapter 7

Providing Services to the Machines on Your Intranet

IN THIS CHAPTER

- ◆ What is a daemon?
- ◆ Sharing file systems
- ◆ Remote printing
- ◆ The X Window system

IN THE PREVIOUS chapter, you set up an intranet by wiring two or more machines together, assigned each machine its own IP address, and configured networking software on the machines so that they can communicate with each other.

So far, so good. However, you want to do a lot more with your network than simply have the machines ping each other. So, in this chapter, we discuss how to set up *networking services* on your intranet: that is, how each machine can supply services to all other machines on your intranet.

In this chapter, we cover the following topics:

- ◆ What a *daemon* is
- ◆ How to configure some of the most popular and useful daemons to provide services on your intranet, including:
  - ■ The inetd server
  - ■ The Apache Web server
  - ■ The ftpd server, to provide FTP and anonymous FTP service
  - ■ The telnetd server, to provide TELNET service
- ◆ Discussions of software that lets you share system resources, including NFS and Samba

- ◆ Using the Berkeley r* commands

- ◆ How to share a printer over the network

- ◆ How to set up and use xdm, the X display manager

Please note that one important daemon — named, which provides domain-name service — is discussed in Chapter 8.

We have our work cut out for us in this chapter – so let's get started.

What Is a Daemon?

A *daemon* is a program that is in continuous execution on your Linux system. It waits for an event that it is monitoring to occur – say, for a file to appear in a particular directory, or a datagram to appear on a network port – and then it takes an appropriate action. Linux and other UNIX systems use daemons to perform a variety of tasks, from printing files to downloading Web pages.

The word "daemon" is taken from the Greek word for an *intermediary*, and has no supernatural or religious significance. (Stan Kelly-Bootle defines "daemon" as "One of the many puckish processes raising merry hell in the bowels of UNIX.")

In this chapter, we introduce some of the daemons that you can run on a Linux workstation to provide networking service to other Linux workstations on your intranet. Each daemon watches one or more well-known ports, and provides a well-defined service.

inetd

The first daemon we look at is inetd, the "supervisor" daemon. We work with inetd in Chapter 3, but it is worth a further look here.

inetd is the Internet superserver. It listens to a set of ports; when a datagram arrives on a port to which inetd is listening, inetd "awakens" the program that handles input from that port, and then hands off control of the port to that program. After the program finishes its work and exits, inetd resumes listening to the port.

This method means that instead of cluttering memory with dozens of daemons, each listening to a single port and consuming precious memory, a single daemon can handle this task, and awaken the programs that are needed at a given time. This method means that response to an incoming datagram is a little slower than it would be if the program that controls a given port is already loaded into memory; but in most instances, the delay is barely noticeable, and is well worth the improved efficiency that inetd offers.

File /etc/inetd.conf describes the ports to which inetd listens, and the program it should awaken to handle input on each port.

Please note that using inetd is not an either/or proposition: you can run inetd to handle input on ports that receive input infrequently, and let a standalone daemon handle traffic on a heavily trafficked port. Most popular servers can be run either as standalone programs or through inetd. The configuration that best meets the needs of your system is not always obvious, and may well change over time.

For more information on inetd, see the description in Chapter 3. Its manual page also contains helpful information.

Apache

inetd, as useful as it is, simply performs housekeeping. In the next few sections, we look at the daemons that actually provide services to the machines on your intranet. Appropriately, the first of these daemons is the Apache HTTP server.

In case you've just returned from a sojourn on Mars, a Web server services requests using the Hypertext Transfer Protocol (HTTP). It returns files – usually documents written in the Hypertext Markup Language (HTML).

The name *Apache* has nothing to do with the native people who live in the Southwest U. S. Rather, the name is a play on the phrase "a patchy server," because Apache began life as a series of patches to the NCSA Web server – one of the first Web servers, which came from the National Center for Supercomputer Applications at the University of Illinois.

Apache is one of the best arguments we've seen for free software. It is the most widely used Web server on the Internet today, and is regarded by many *cognoscenti* as being the equal of, or superior to, costly Web servers from well-known corporations.

Proper management of a Web server is a complex subject, much of which is beyond the scope of our discussion. In this section, we discuss how to install Apache and perform simple configuration so that you can supply static Web pages to the users on your intranet.

INSTALLING APACHE

On most releases of Linux, Apache comes preinstalled and preconfigured. If you are using Slackware, you can skip this section. However, if you are using an older release of Linux, we describe how to find out whether Apache is installed on your Linux system, and if it is not, how to install a binary copy onto your system.

FINDING APACHE ON YOUR SYSTEM   The first step is to determine whether
Apache is already running on your Linux system. To check this out, type command
ps -ax. This shows you the daemons that are running on your system. If you see
one or more entries for the command `httpd`, then you are already running Apache
(or some other HTTP daemon).

If command `ps -ax` does not show you a process named `httpd`, another way to
check whether Apache is installed is to type command

```
telnet localhost 80
```

This uses `telnet` to connect to port 80 on your local host; port 80 is the well-
known port for an HTTP server. When you type this command, you should see
something like the following:

```
Trying 127.0.0.1...
Connected to localhost.
Escape character is '^]'.
```

If you then type a random string, such as `foo`, you should see something like the
following:

```
<HEAD><TITLE>Bad Request</TITLE></HEAD>
<BODY><H1>Bad Request</H1>
Your browser sent a query that
this server could not understand.<P>
</BODY>
Connection closed by foreign host.
```

If you see output like this, then your system clearly is running an HTTP server —
even if you could not communicate with it.

If you do not see output like this, then your system is not running an HTTP
server; however, your system may have an HTTP server installed that is not turned
on. In either case, you need to locate where the server is stored on your system,
because this tells you the location of the server's configuration files. To find the
server, type the command:

```
find / -name httpd -print
```

This uses the command `find` to comb your entire system to find files with the
name `httpd`. This file could be stored almost anywhere, but two likely places are
`/usr/local/etc/httpd/bin` and `/usr/sbin`.

Apache's configuration files are kept in a directory named `httpd/conf`; usual
locations for this directory include `/var/lib` and `/usr/local/etc`. For example,
on Slackware, the Apache executable is kept in file `/usr/sbin/httpd`, and the configuration files in directory `/var/lib/httpd/conf`.

If you cannot find Apache on your system, then you have to install it; we describe how to do this in the next section. If you do find Apache, then skip ahead a page or so to the subsection "Configuring Apache."

INSTALLING APACHE ONTO YOUR SYSTEM   To install Apache, follow these steps:

1. Find a binary archive of Apache for Linux. You can compile Apache yourself if you want, but using a precompiled version is much easier. Check the notes that came with your copy of Linux and see whether the release comes with a copy of Apache. If it does, then you should use that copy. If, however, your release of Linux does not come with a precompiled copy of Apache, you can download one from Web site `http://www.apache.org`. Just follow the directions to download the correct release (1.2.4 or later) and the correct operating system (Linux, in case you were wondering).

2. Copy the contents of the archive into a convenient directory. You need to use the following command `tar` to de-archive the files

   `tar xvzf archivename`

3. If the archive has the suffix `.gz` or `.tgz`; however, use command

   `tar xvZf archivename`

   if the archive has the suffix `.Z`.

4. Extracting the contents of the archive should create a directory with the name

   `Apache_version`

   where `version` gives the version of Apache you have, such as

   `Apache_1.3`

   Within the Apache directory should be a directory named `src`. In the `src` directory should be a file named `httpd`. `su` to the superuser `root`, and then copy file `httpd` into an appropriate directory; we suggest `/usr/sbin`, although `httpd` works equally well if placed into another directory.

With that, the Apache binary is installed onto your machine. A few steps remain to perform before you can launch Apache, however; the following subsections walk you through those steps.

CONFIGURING APACHE
The configuration of the Apache server is managed by three configuration files: `httpd.conf`, `srm.conf`, and `access.conf`.

Example versions of these files are located in directory `conf` within the Apache release's directory. They are named, respectively, `httpd.conf-dist`, `srm.conf-dist`, and `access.conf-dist`. Copy each to its namesake; for example, `cp file httpd.conf-dist` to `httpd.conf`.

Next, you should edit these files, to configure Apache to suit your preferences.

Each configuration file is discussed in detail in the Apache documentation, which is in directory `htdocs` in the Apache archive. If you do not have the Apache source archive, you can download a copy from Web site `http://www.Apache.org/docs`, or retrieve a copy from the Slackware release included on the CD-ROM that accompanies this book

We next discuss each configuration file in turn.

EDIT httpd.conf   The first file you should edit is `httpd.conf`. This file performs the most basic configuration of Apache.

The file contains a series of keys, each of which controls some behavior of Apache. Each key is followed by the value to which the keyword controls that aspect of the server's behavior.

In practically every instance, a keyword is set to a reasonable default value. We discuss the few keywords whose values you may want to set:

- ◆ `CacheNegotiatedDocs` — By default, Apache asks Web proxy servers not to cache the documents they download. Uncommenting this option turns off this feature, thus enabling proxy servers to cache documents downloaded from your site. If you do not know what a *proxy server* is, then you probably do not need to set this option.

- ◆ `ErrorLog` — The name of the file into which Apache logs errors. The default is `logs/error_log`; the fact that this name does not begin with a backslash, /,indicates that it is contained within the directory named by option `ServerRoot`.

- ◆ `Group` — The user group under which Apache runs. The default is group -1 — again, a group with minimal permission. This option applies only if Apache is run in standalone mode.

- ◆ `HostnameLookups` — If set to on, this option tells Apache that when it receives a request for a Web page, it should look up the name of the host and log that name, rather than simply logging the IP address of the requester. This feature adds some overhead to Apache, but it makes the log file much more legible. This option applies only if Apache is run in standalone mode.

◆ `KeepAlive` — The number of keep-alive requests that Apache will accept during any given connection with a client. A *keep-alive* request is sent by a client to the server when the client wants to download multiple documents within a single TCP connection. This spares the client the overhead of creating a TCP connection with the server for each and every little image within a Web page.

◆ `KeepAliveTimeout` — A Web page can consist of many documents, each of which holds HTML, an image, ordinary text, or some other element in the Web page. The Web client will send a stream of requests for documents as it reads and interprets the Web page. This option sets the number of seconds to wait for the next request for a document during a given TCP connection. If no request occurs during this period of time, Apache concludes that the client is finished, and closes down the TCP connection with the client. This option is set to a reasonable default, although you may eventually want to tune it.

◆ `MaxClient` — The maximum number of clients that can be connected to your server at any given time. Again, this helps to prevent your system from being "brought to its knees" by Web traffic.

◆ `MaxRequestsPerChild` — The maximum number of requests that a child process can make before it dies.

◆ `MaxSpareServers` — This option sets the maximum number of Apache processes that will be running at any given time. This option helps to prevent Apache from spawning new processes uncontrollably when your site receives a heavy load of Web traffic, thus bringing your system "to its knees."

◆ `MinSpareServers` — The minimum number of server processes that are running at any given time. If Apache is already running on your system, you probably noticed that more than one instance of the `httpd` processing is running; Apache spawns more Web server processes, based on the number of requests your system is receiving. You should tune this option, based on the amount of traffic you expect to handle; one or two processes probably is sufficient if you will be handling only the occasional request for a Web page; however, if your site will receive many requests, you may want to increase the number of processes. Experience will enable you to determine the optimal number of processes.

◆ `PidFile` — The name of the file into which Apache writes its process identifier (PID) when it comes up.

◆ Port – The port to which Apache listens. By default, Apache watches port 80, which is the well-known port for HTTP transactions. However, you can tell Apache to watch a different port, if you use Apache to perform an out-of-the-ordinary task, such as executing a custom demonstration or developing a Web site that you do not want to be publicly accessible yet. This applies only if Apache is run in standalone mode.

◆ ProxyRequests – Set this to on if you want to enable the proxy server. If you don't know what a proxy server is, you probably don't need it.

◆ ScoreBoardFile – The name of the file within which Apache stores information about its internal operation.

◆ ServerAdmin – You should set this to the e-mail address of the person who administers Apache on your system. Apache will send mail to the administrator if something goes wrong. You must set this option.

◆ ServerName – The name of your system, if you want to set it to something other than the name of your Linux workstation. You may want to set this option if you plan to supply documents to the Internet at large. Please note that the name to which you set this option must be a real name – that is, one that can be resolved by Internet DNS.

◆ ServerRoot – This names the directory that holds Apache configuration files and log files. The default is /usr/local/etc, although the person who compiled Apache for you may have changed this. Later in this section, you set up this directory and move the configuration files into it. You may want to change this option, although you should only do so for a good reason.

◆ ServerType – This sets how Apache runs: either standalone, or invoked through inetd. The default is standalone – that is, Apache runs as a daemon on its own, instead of being invoked through inetd.

◆ StartServers – The number of server processes to start when Apache first comes up.

◆ Timeout – The number of seconds before a request to send or receive a document times out. You may want to increase or decrease this value, to help ensure that Apache operates most efficiently.

◆ TransferLog – The name of the file into which Apache logs transactions – that is, requests for HTML files and CGI programs.

◆ User – The user as whom Apache runs. The default is to run as user
nobody; the point is to have Apache run as a user who has no permission
to change anything on your system, to minimize the damage Apache can
do to your system should a cracker attack it. Again, this applies only if
you run Apache in standalone mode.

The only option you must set is ServerAdmin. The others should be set to reasonable defaults, although you may want to modify them over time, as you gain
experience using Apache.

EDIT srm.conf   File srm.conf sets what can be seen by persons who use your
Apache server. As with file httpd.conf, this file consists of a series of keywords, to
each of which a value is given. Practically all the keywords come preset to a reasonable default value, so you probably never have to edit this file; however, if you
intend to work with Apache, knowing what is in this file is a good idea.
The following list discusses the more important keywords:

◆ AccessFileName – Name the file that holds access-control information in
a given directory. This usually is named .htaccess.

◆ AddDescription – Insert a brief description after a file named in a server-
generated index. For example, instruction

AddDescription "Fred's resume" resume.html

links a brief description to file resume.html.

◆ AddEncoding – Tell Apache the type of compression to use for
compression on the fly, should the browser support it. For example,
instruction

AddEncoding x-compress Z

tells Apache that a file with suffix .Z should be compressed or
decompressed using compress.

◆ AddLanguage – Specify a document's language. Apache can negotiate
with a browser to set the language in which information should appear.
Language is set by a two-character code, and by a suffix appended onto
the file; please note that the two codes are usually – but not always – the
same. For example, instruction

AddLanguage fr .fr

adds French (code fr) to Apache's repertoire of languages, and tells it to
use files with suffix .fr

◆ Alias — Set an *alias* and the value the alias represents. When Apache finds the alias in one of its configuration files, it substitutes the string for it. For example, instruction

```
Alias /icons/ /var/lib/httpd/icons/
```

tells Apache to substitute /var/lib/httpd/icons/ whenever it reads string /icons/. An alias is rather like a word processor's search-and-replace feature, and has the same problems.

◆ DefaultIcon — Name the icon to use for files that do not otherwise have an icon set for them.

◆ DirectoryIndex — This keyword names the file or files to use as a directory index. It almost always is set to index.html.

◆ DocumentRoot — This keyword gives the full path name of the directory that holds the system-wide documents that Apache can distribute. This usually is directory htdocs under the Apache file, as set by keyword ServerRoot in file httpd.conf.

◆ HeaderName — Name the file to be prefixed to directory indexes.

◆ IndexIgnore — Name the directories and files that Apache should ignore when it prepares its indexes. Filenames can include wildcard characters.

◆ LanguagePriority — Set the priority languages to use. For example, instruction

```
LanguagePriority en fr de
```

sets the linguistic priority to English, and then French, and then German.

◆ ReadmeName — Name the README file that Apache displays by default. For example, instruction

```
ReadmeName README
```

sets the name of the README file to README.

◆ Redirect — Redirect a browser to a URL that has been renamed or moved from your system. For example, the instruction

```
Redirect resume.html
http://www.myexample.com/~fred/newresume.html
```

redirects queries for resume.html to newresume.html, which presumably holds an updated version of this file.

♦ `UserDir` — This keyword names the directory into which a user can put personal Web files. For example, if this keyword is set to `public_html` (as it almost always is), then when the Apache server at `myexample.com` receives a request for the document with URL `http://myexample.com/~fred/resume.html`, Apache looks for file `public_html/resume.html` under `fred`'s home directory.

EDIT access.conf   File `access.conf` sets permission for how files can be accessed. You should review this file to ensure that permissions are set to suit your preferences.

The structure of this file is as follows:

```
<Directory directory-path-name>
instruction
instruction
instruction
</Directory>
```

`directory-path-name` gives the full path name of the directory whose permissions you are setting. Each `instruction` sets an option that controls some aspect of how the directory's contents can be accessed.

The following describes some of the instructions that can be used to set permissions.

Instruction `Options` enables you to set some options on how this directory is accessed. It can be set to `All`, `None`, or to any combination of the following:

♦ ExecCGI

♦ FollowSymLinks

♦ Includes

♦ MultiViews

For example, instruction

```
Options Indexes FollowSymLinks
```

tells Apache to build and use indexes within this directory, and to follow symbolic links set within this directory. (As a security measure, Apache will not follow symbolic links unless you explicitly tell it to do so.)

Instruction `AllowOverride` sets the options that a directory's `.htaccess` can override. It can be set to `All`, or any combination of the following:

- All
- AuthConfig
- FileInfo
- Limit
- Options

Instructions `order`, `allow`, and `deny` let you set who can and cannot retrieve files from this directory.

Instruction `order` sets the order in which the `allow` and `deny` instructions are read and interpreted. Reading an instruction first enables it to set the base permissions; the other instruction then sets exceptions.

Instruction `allow` names the sites whose requests will be fulfilled. This can be set to `all`, `none`, or an indefinite number of host names.

Instruction `deny` names the sites whose requests will not be fulfilled. This can be set to `all`, `none`, or an indefinite number of host names.

For example, instructions

```
order allow,deny
allow all
deny sleezykidporn.com
```

tell your server to fulfill requests from all hosts except `sleezykidieporn.com` — you want nothing to do with that site, so requests from it will be rejected.

Example entry

The following code gives example instructions for directory `htdocs`, which file `srm.conf` named as the directory that holds your system's hypertext documents:

```
<Directory /usr/local/etc/httpd/htdocs>
Options FollowSymLinks
AllowOverride None
order allow,deny
allow all
deny sleezykiddieporn.com
</Directory>
```

You can name any number of directories in this file. You should, at least, configure permissions for directories `htdocs` and `cgi-bin`.

COPYING CONFIGURATION FILES   After you finish modifying your configuration files, copy them into directory `conf` under Apache's root directory, as set by keyword `ServerRoot` in file `httpd.conf`.

TURNING ON APACHE

To turn on Apache, `su` to the superuser `root`, and then invoke Apache (or rather its executable, which is named `httpd`) with option `-f` set to the full path name of configuration file `httpd.conf`. For example:

```
/usr/sbin/httpd -f /var/lib/httpd/conf/httpd.conf
```

As this example demonstrates, the executable file `httpd` does not need to be stored in Apache's root directory.

Note, too, that you do not need to follow this with an ampersand (&). This also assumes that you are running Apache as a standalone daemon, which is the way it usually is used.

If a problem occurs – for example, you make a typographical error when modifying a configuration file – Apache prints an error message and exits. Otherwise, you simply see the shell prompt return.

To test Apache, try connecting to it via `telnet`, as we described earlier in this section. If the test passes, the users on your intranet can now download Web pages from your Linux workstation.

REINVOKING APACHE WHEN REBOOTING   Now that you have configured Apache and know how to bring it up, the next step is to modify your system's configuration so that Apache is launched automatically whenever your system reboots.

Two ways to do this are available, one for each of the two different ways that Apache can be run:

◆ If you will be running Apache as a standalone daemon, which is the usual method of running it, you will modify one of the scripts in directory `/etc/rc.d` to launch Apache when you reboot your system.

◆ However, if you want to run Apache through `inetd`, you must revise file `/etc/inetd.conf`.

We discuss each method in turn.

Edit the rc file

To launch Apache as a standalone daemon, do the following:

1. `su` to the superuser `root`, and then `cd` to directory `/etc/rc.d`.

2. Execute command:

   ```
   grep httpd rc*
   ```

This tells you whether a command to launch an HTTP daemon is already in one of the `rc` files.

3. If the command is present in one of the `rc` files, check the following:

   ■ That the code that invokes the HTTP daemon is not commented out

   ■ That the code invokes `httpd` from the directory in which it resides

   ■ That the code uses the `-f` command to give the full path name of file `httpd.conf`

4. If the `httpd` command is commented out, or if it is incorrect in some way, fix it. Once this is done, you are finished. However, if the command is not present, then insert the following into file `rc.local`:

```
echo Launching Apache ...
/binpath/httpd -f /confpath/httpd.conf
```

where `binpath` is the path of the directory that holds `httpd`, and `confpath` is the path of the directory that holds `httpd.conf`.

To check whether this works, simply reboot your system. Apache should be launched without any difficulty.

Edit /etc/inetd.conf

If you intend to launch Apache through `inetd` (which is *not* the recommended way to run Apache), insert the following into file `/etc/inetd.conf`:

```
www stream tcp nowait root /binpath/httpd /binpath/httpd -f
/confpath/httpd.conf
```

Where in the file you place this line doesn't matter; however, it probably should go immediately after `finger`, which immediately precedes `www` in file `/etc/services`.

After you make this change, kill the `inetd` daemon and then restart it, as we described earlier.

This concludes our description of how to set up Apache. In the next section, we discuss how to work with Apache.

WORKING WITH APACHE

Now that you have Apache up and running, give it a try.

To begin, log in as the superuser `root`; then, `cu` to directory `htdocs` under Apache's root directory.

Next, type the following (if you don't want to type this, it's on the CD-ROM included with this book, in file `test.html`):

```
<HTML>
<HEAD>
<TITLE>Test Web Page</TITLE>
</HEAD>
<BODY BGCOLOR="#FFFFFF" VLINK="#CD5C5C">
<H1><CENTER>Test Web Page</CENTER></H1>
<P>
This is a test Web page. If you put this into directory
 &quot;htdocs&quot;, you will be able to use the <B>Apache</B> Web
 server to download it to a browser.
<P>
If you can read this, then <I>congratulations!</I> You now have
 <B>Apache</B> working on your Linux system!
</BODY>
</HTML>
```

Save the text into file `test.html`.

Now, type the command **lynx localhost/test.html** to view this test page. You should see the congratulatory Web page appear on your screen.

If the page does not appear, make sure that you installed it into the correct directory, and that you typed the right URL.

Now, you can start to install Web pages into directory `htdocs`; they will be available to any user on your intranet.

APACHE AND WINDOWS 95   Linux and Windows 95 working together on the same intranet is a powerful combination for building Web pages. Consider the following scenario, which is possible with the Linux/Windows 95 combination:

◆ Use Samba to export to Windows 95 the directory in which you have your Web pages stored.

◆ Use a Web-page builder, such as Netscape Composer, to build a Web page. (Hint — be sure to turn off caching on the browser, or you may not see the updates to the Web page.)

◆ Use Apache on your Linux system to immediately download the Web page you're building onto a browser running Windows 95.

In this way, you can work on a Web page, while viewing how the page will appear to users on the Web. And because processing is distributed over two machines, the system works quite efficiently.

For detailed information on how to hook a machine that is running Windows 95 into your intranet, see Chapter 9. This chapter also discusses Samba, a package that uses Windows-style networking to let you mount Linux directories as network drives on a Windows 95 system.

This concludes our discussion of Apache. This only scratches the surface of what you can do with Apache, but it should be sufficient to get Apache up and running on your intranet. For information on advanced Web tasks, such as running CGI scripts and Java applets, see the references at the end of this chapter.

ftpd

The next daemon to come under our microscope is `ftpd`.

`ftpd` is the daemon that services requests that use the File Transfer Protocol (FTP). `ftpd`'s job is to log in the user and provide access to the appropriate file space.

`inetd` invokes `ftpd` whenever a datagram arrives on FTP's well-known port, which is port 21.

FLAVORS OF FTP

FTP accepts two kinds of authentication:

◆ The user already has an account on the machine that is providing FTP service. A user has to provide his login identifier and password to log into his account.

◆ The user does not have an account on the machine that is providing FTP service. He is allowed to use *anonymous login* (the user enters `anonymous` as his login identifier, and his e-mail address as a password); the FTP daemon then places the user into a special area of the FTP server's machine that is allocated for anonymous users.

Within your intranet, FTP is useful for moving files between MS-DOS or Windows and Linux, but `rcp` is much better at moving a file between two UNIX machines. In Chapter 9, we discuss using FTP to download files from a Linux workstation to a Windows 95 machine.

FIREWALLS AND SECURITY

The FTP client sends commands to the `ftpd` via port 21, which is the well-known port for FTP. This port is used to control the connection. Whenever the server begins to download a file to the client (or vice versa), the FTP client and `ftpd` negotiate to use a port for the data connection. Thus, FTP can be using two ports at once: one through which the client and server exchange commands and status information, and another through which the data flows.

The dual-port design of FTP enables you to implement control easily – commands pass on the command channel, data on the data channel, and that's that. Unfortunately, this dual-channel design makes passing data through a firewall difficult. Thankfully, you won't have to worry about this, as the problem has been solved by both the designers of SOCKS and of IP masquerading.

One other note about FTP: it doesn't encrypt any information that it sends. This is very important to security-conscious system administrators, because anyone who is sitting on a machine that is forwarding datagrams between the FTP client and the FTP server is able to read the datagrams as they fly past – including the datagram that contains the password with which you logged into the FTP server. So, as a rule of thumb, you should question the wisdom of using FTP, outside of point-to-point connections or within an intranet, for anything other than an anonymous connection.

INSTALLATION AND CONFIGURATION

`ftpd` comes preinstalled and configured on every version of Linux that we have seen. You do not have to do anything to start it up or configure it.

telnetd

`telnetd` is the daemon that handles TELNET connections. Like `ftpd`, this daemon comes with every release of Linux; you do not have to install or configure it in any way.

LOGGING IN

`inetd` invokes `telnetd` whenever a datagram arrives on its well-known port – in this case, port 23. `telnetd` then negotiates with the client to determine the parameters of the connection, including the values of certain environmental variables.

Two important environmental variables for `telnetd` are TERM and DISPLAY:

◆ TERM describes the type of terminal to which you are connected.

◆ DISPLAY points to your X Window display. (We discuss X Window later in this chapter.)

Please note that while `telnet` handles these variables, the command `rlogin` does not!

After the negotiation phase, `telnet` hands the connection to the `login` program, which authenticates the user and generates a login session.

On the remote machine, the `login` program is connected to a *pseudo-terminal*. You should note that pseudo-terminals are a limited resource in UNIX, so this puts an effective limitation on the number of `telnet` (or `rlogin` or `slogin`) connections that you can have. If you need to, you can increase the number of pseudo-terminals in Linux by recompiling the kernel.

SECURITY

From a security standpoint, `telnet` is now frowned upon, because, like `ftp`, it passes the authentication information (your login identifier and password) in plain text over the network. Programming a machine to capture the start of a `telnet` session is a simple task, enabling someone to grab your login identifier and password literally "from the ether" of the network.

Although they have problems of their own, the `r*` commands definitely are better in this regard than `telnet`.

INSTALLATION AND CONFIGURATION

`telnetd` comes preinstalled and configured on every version of Linux that we have seen. You do not have to do anything to start it up or configure it.

This concludes our discussion of commonly used daemons. We now move on to more advanced – and more complex – services that your intranet's machines can provide to each other.

Sharing File Systems

By now, you probably have worked with your Linux system long enough to be familiar with the concept of *mounting* a file system. Each physical device holds a file system, and mounting enables you to graft a physical device's file system onto the file system with which you are already working.

The physical devices whose file systems you use are usually inside your Linux workstation – on its hard disk or CD-ROM drive. However, Linux and other UNIX systems enable you to share physical devices over a network: you can mount all or part of another machine's file system onto your file system, just as if it were on a physical device within your Linux workstation.

In years past, when disk space was expensive, machines with a large disk commonly loaned chunks of that disk to other workstations on the network, for purposes of simple storage. Now that disk storage costs a few cents a megabyte, machines don't usually give each other raw disk space. However, networks still loan each other disk space, as a simple way to distribute files to those systems.

Two popular packages exist for distributing file resources:

◆ The network file system (NFS)

◆ Samba

NFS is used principally to distribute disk resources among workstations that are running Linux or other flavors of UNIX. Samba is used principally to distribute disk resources to machines that are running Windows 95 or Windows NT.

In this section, we show you how to use NFS to distribute disk resources among the Linux workstations on your intranet. We also discuss Samba briefly; for a detailed discussion of Samba, see Chapter 9, where we discuss how to integrate Linux with Windows 95 on the same network.

Network file system

The *network file system* (NFS) is used to share files and directory hierarchies among Linux systems, or Linux and other UNIX systems. Although NFS client/server systems are available for Windows 95 and Windows NT, we believe that Samba is better suited to the task of sharing files between Linux and Windows 95/NT.

Two operations that you need to worry about with NFS are accessing file systems on other machines (also called *mounting remote file systems*) and granting to remote systems access to local file systems (or *exporting file systems*). We discuss each in turn.

EXPORTING FILE SYSTEMS

Exporting file resources is handled by a daemon named `rcp.nfsd`. To start up this daemon, just `su` to the superuser `root`, and then type the following command:

```
/usr/sbin/rpc.nfsd
```

To start this daemon when you boot your Linux system, insert this command into one of your system's `rc` files. Under Slackware, this command is in file `/etc/rc.inet2`, although it may be commented out; if it is commented out, you can just uncomment it by removing the `#` at the beginning of the command line.

`rcp.nfsd` takes numerous options, some of which are clever hacks, but most of which you'll never use. For details, see the manual page for `nfsd`.

CONFIGURATION FILE /ETC/EXPORTS File `/etc/exports` names the file systems that can be mounted by other workstations on your intranet. Each line in `/etc/exports` references one exported file system, using the following format:

```
file-system [remote-machines]["("access-flags")"]
```

For example, if you want to export directory `/usr/local` (and all of its subdirectories) on `thor` to all hosts on domain `myexample.com`, add the following line to `/etc/exports`:

```
/usr/local *.myexample.com
```

When specifying the host to mount, you can use the characters * and ? as wild-cards, as you would in MS-DOS.

After you have modified etc/exports, you must tell the rcp.nfsd to reread it. You can do this by sending it the hangup (or HUP) signal. First, use the command ps -x to determine which process ID it's running under. You will see something like the following:

```
PID TTY STAT   TIME COMMAND
  ? S     0:10 init [4]
  ? SW    0:00 (kflushd)
  3 ?  SW<  0:00 (kswapd)
  4 ?  SW   0:00 (nfsiod)
  5 ?  SW   0:00 (nfsiod)
  6 ?  SW   0:00 (nfsiod)
  7 ?  SW   0:00 (nfsiod)
 13 ?  S    0:00 /sbin/update
 14 ?  S    0:00 /sbin/kerneld
 51 ?  S    0:00 /usr/sbin/crond -110
 70 ?  S    0:01 /usr/sbin/klogd
 74 ?  S    0:00 /usr/sbin/inetd
 78 ?  S    0:00 /usr/sbin/rpc.mountd
 80 ?  S    0:00 /usr/sbin/rpc.nfsd
```

and so on.

The output of ps will be long on a busy machine, so we use grep to do some of the dirty work of choosing the right line for us. For example, the command

```
ps -x | grep "rpc.nfsd"
```

returns

```
80 ?  S     0:00 /usr/sbin/rpc.nfsd
```

The first token in the line is the process ID (or PID); you can verify this in the long display in the preceding code. So, to have the daemon reread the exports file, you send the HUP signal to the daemon by its PID, in this case 80:

```
kill -HUP 80
```

No response is received, but the rpc.nfsd has reread the /etc/exports file, so now you should be able to mount the file system from a remote host.

In general, a mount like this should be done read-only — you want the remote system to be able to read the files in the exported directory, but not be able to write into the directory or modify the files within the directory. To make the exported directory read-only, add the modifier (ro) to the entry within /etc/exports, as follows:

```
/usr/local *.myexample.com(ro)
```

Machines that are running other versions of UNIX, such as Solaris, may run into a problem if they try to mount a file system exported from a Linux system. For security reasons, Linux, by default, refuses file system mounts from nonprivileged ports. Because anyone can build a Linux system and thus have a root account from which to do mounts, we feel that this precaution does not enhance security much. We mention this only because other operating systems have dropped this requirement; so to mount a Linux file system on some other versions of UNIX, you may have to specify the insecure flag in the /etc/exports file, like this:

```
/usr/local sunos.myexample.com(insecure)
```

For other options, read the manual page exports, which describes /etc/exports and the options you can use in it.

MOUNTING REMOTE FILE SYSTEMS

To mount a remote file system, simply use the mount command with the following format:

```
mount options remote-system:exported-file-system local-file-system
```

For example, to mount a file system exported from thor onto system heimdall, the superuser on heimdall should execute the command:

```
mount thor:/usr/local /usr/local
```

This is useful if you want to make packages that you port on thor available to heimdall without having to recompile them. Also, you probably should use the mount command's flag -ro, to make this newly mounted file system read-only, as follows:

```
mount -ro thor:/usr/local /usr/local
```

This concludes our brief introduction to NFS, which gives you enough information to get NFS up and running for practically all normal uses. For more information, see the manual pages for nfsd, exports, and mount.

Samba and smbfs

Samba is a package that implements Windows-style resource sharing. With Samba, a machine that is running a variant of UNIX (including Linux) can export its resources – including files and printers – and make them available to users who are running Windows 95, Windows NT, or OS/2. The Samba package enables you to tie into your intranet machines that are running Windows 95 or Windows NT quite easily.

smbfs is an extension to the Linux file system. It enables you to mount Windows 95 file resources onto your Linux file system. You can then use your standard Linux commands – cp, mv, tar, and the like – to work with the files in the mounted file resource, just as if they were directly on your Linux system's hard disk.

 For information on Samba and smbfs, see Chapter 9.

The Berkeley "Remote" Commands

As we noted in Chapter 1, the TCP/IP protocols were originally implemented by the University of California, Berkeley, under the UNIX operating system. The Berkeley UNIX implementation of TCP/IP networking, through its socket library, remains the basis of networking throughout the Internet.

Berkeley UNIX also left its mark on TCP/IP networking through a set of commonly used commands: the Berkeley remote-processing commands – also called the Berkeley r* commands, because each begins with the letter *r* (for *remote*). These commands are called *remote* because each modifies a commonly used UNIX command so that it works *remotely* on another system.

The need for some means of remote access for networked hosts became clear early in the design and implementation of TCP/IP. While the group working on this problem was busy designing telnet, the Berkeley group designed and built an "interim" solution, the r* commands. Unfortunately the r* commands have some features built in for convenience that telnet does not have, and thus the "interim" solution lives on to this day.

The most commonly used r* commands include the following:

- ♦ rlogin – Log into a remote host.

- ♦ rcp – Copy a file to or from a remote host.

- ♦ rsh – Execute a shell command on a remote host.

The twist that the r* commands bring to these tasks is that a host can declare that another host is equivalent to itself – and so bypass password security. When a host declares another host to be *equivalent*, it is declaring that identically named accounts on both systems refer to the same user. For example, if host baldur declares that host odin is an equivalent host, baldur is declaring that account fred on odin is owned by the same person that owns account fred on itself, and therefore, it (baldur) will grant to anyone who is logged in as fred on odin access to all of fred's files on baldur, without asking that user for a password.

Further, an individual user (including root) can declare that a user with the same name on another host is equivalent to herself, and so bypass password security.

Please note that we say the r* commands bring a "twist" to these tasks rather than an "enhancement," because this method of granting equivalency is a two-edged sword. Although enabling users to access systems throughout the network without having to retype their passwords is very useful, when an intranet is connected to the Internet, deliberately turning off password security for individual users or for entire systems punches a huge, gaping hole into your system's security.

With that caveat, we show you how to set up and configure the r* commands on your intranet.

Security and the r* commands

Much of the security of the r* commands (rlogin, rsh, rcp) is based on the assumptions that the hosts on a network can communicate with each other, and that the network cannot be accessed by the world at large. These assumptions were somewhat reasonable in the early days of the Internet, when root access was limited to few people and TCP/IP stacks were rare on operating systems that had little access control to the reserved ports.

Today, neither assumption is true. Any cracker or vandal can install Linux or FreeBSD and have access to privileged ports, or they can use an operating system such as MS-DOS, which has no access control. This change is a serious enough blow to the security of the r* commands that completely disallowing use of these services on any network directly connected to the Internet is probably a good idea.

So, to summarize:

♦ If your network intranet is not connected to the Internet – or is connected to the Internet only briefly and intermittently – the r* commands are a useful convenience to yourself and your users.

♦ When your network becomes connected to the Internet for lengthy periods of time, you should think seriously about turning off the r* commands altogether.

That being said, let's get to work.

Turning on the r* servers

Support for the r* commands is built into every release of Linux. You simply have to ensure that this support is turned on. In this section , we walk you through the process of ensuring that the r* services are turned on.

/etc/services

The r* commands use three network services:

- ◆ exec, which uses the well-known port 512
- ◆ login, which uses the well-known port 513
- ◆ shell, which uses the well-known port 514

Make sure that the following lines appear in your system's copy of file /etc/services, and are not commented out:

```
exec            512/tcp
login           513/tcp
shell           514/tcp            cmd
```

If an entry begins with a # character, then it is commented out. To uncomment it, remove the # character.

/etc/inetd.conf

Because the r* commands are used only intermittently, their servers are usually accessed through inetd (which we introduced earlier in this chapter).

To turn on the r* servers, check file /etc/inetd.conf; make sure that the following entries are present and not commented out:

```
shell    stream  tcp     nowait  root    /usr/sbin/tcpd  in.rshd -L
login    stream  tcp     nowait  root    /usr/sbin/tcpd  in.rlogind
exec     stream  tcp     nowait  root    /usr/sbin/tcpd  in.rexecd
```

If you must add or uncomment one or more of these entries, be sure to restart the inetd daemon (as described earlier in this chapter) so that it will reread its configuration file.

Repeat these steps for each Linux system on your intranet.

TESTING

To test whether the r* service has been turned on, type the following command:

```
rlogin localhost
```

This command uses the login to log you into your local host.

Because we have not yet configured the r* servers, you should see a login prompt. When you type your password, you will be logged into your Linux system via the login server.

Now, type the command **who**. This command will show that you are logged in twice; one login session will be marked (localhost), to show that the login session originated from host localhost (which is, of course, a synonym for the host you are now using).

To exit, just log out as you usually do. You will be returned to your original login session.

Configuring the r* commands

Now that the r* servers are turned on, we come to the more complex task of configuring these commands.

Configuration means granting or refusing permission to bypass password security to hosts or individuals. This involves two files:

- ◆ /etc/hosts.equiv, which grants permission on a host-by-host basis

- ◆ ~/.rhosts, in which a user can declare a user account on another machine to be equivalent to her account on this machine

We discuss each in turn.

/etc/hosts.equiv
This file names one or more equivalent hosts. An *equivalent host* is a host whose users are equivalent to the users of the same name on the current system.

In its simplest form, this file just names hosts. For example, file /etc/hosts.equiv on our example system thor would grant equivalent status to the other hosts on our example intranet, as follows:

```
odin
baldur
heimdall
loki
```

This means, in effect, that user chris on odin, baldur, heimdall, or loki can log into chris's account on thor without entering a password. The only exception is the superuser root — a person logged in as root on one of these systems cannot use rlogin to log into thor. (We discuss in a moment how you can grant superuser privileges via rlogin.)

DENYING EQUIVALENCY   You can also explicitly deny equivalency to the users of a host. To do so, simply prefix the host's name with a hyphen (-). For example, if thor wants to deny equivalency to any user on system loki, it prefixes loki with -, as follows:

```
odin
baldur
heimdall
-loki
```

This overrides anything that any user may place into her copy of file .rhosts. (We discuss this file soon.)

GRANTING EQUIVALENCY TO INDIVIDUAL USERS You can modify a host's entries so that equivalency is granted only to selected users on a given host, or is denied to selected users on that host. To modify a host's entries, simply name the user on the same line as the host, prefixed with + or -, to grant or deny permission, respectively. For example, consider the following:

```
odin          marian -ivan
baldur        +chris
heimdall
-loki
```

We have modified the entry for host odin to deny equivalency to users marian and ivan. If either of these users tries to rlogin from host odin, he or she will have to enter a password. All other users on odin are granted equivalency; so if user chris tries to rlogin from odin, he will be admitted without having to enter a password — assuming that account chris exists on thor (the system in this example).

Here, too, we have modified the entry for host baldur so that it extends equivalency to user chris. This implies that no other user on baldur has equivalency — if any user other than chris tries to rlogin from baldur, she will have to enter a password.

One additional point should be made: granting equivalency is not reciprocal. That is, if system baldur names system loki as an equivalent system, that does not imply that loki recognizes baldur as an equivalent system — nor is loki under any obligation to do so.

GLOBAL EQUIVALENCY Granting equivalency to all hosts is possible, but doing so is a very bad idea. However, we mention it here so that you understand what is happening if you encounter this configuration.

To grant equivalency to all users on all hosts, simply set hosts.equiv to read as follows:

```
+
```

Of course, if your intranet is connected to the Internet, then this extends equivalency to every user on every host on the Internet.

You can limit this to selected users. For example setting hosts.equiv to

```
+ +chris +fred
```

grants equivalency to users chris and fred on any host on your network. Again, if your intranet is connected to the Internet, then any chris or any fred will be able to rlogin to this host without entering a password.

 Just to be clear: Using + in place of a host's name is a very bad idea. You should *never* do this.

.rhosts

Individual users can also grant equivalency to their analogues on other hosts. To do so, a user edits file .rhosts in her home directory.

For example, if user marian on host baldur puts the entry

```
loki
```

into file .rhosts in her home directory, then user marian on loki will be able to log into baldur without having to enter a password. The point is that if a user has accounts on many machines, and each account uses the same login identifier, entering the appropriate entries into file .rhosts will let that user jump from one system to another without having to continually reenter a password.

If a user's account on another machine uses a different login identifier, the user can enter into .rhosts her login identifier on that system. For example, if marian's account on system loki has the login identifier janim, then she can identify janim as being equivalent to marian, as follows:

```
loki janim
```

Hereafter, whenever the user is logged into system loki as janim, she will be able to log in to marian's account on baldur without having to enter a password.

THE SUPERUSER'S .rhosts   As we noted earlier, naming a host in file hosts.equiv grants across-the-board equivalency to all users on that host – or rather, to all users *except* the superuser root. So, does a way exist for the superuser to log into another system or execute a command on it?

The answer is yes, and the way to do it is for the superuser to grant equivalency in her .rhosts file.

For example, if the superuser on host baldur wants to grant equivalency to her sister superusers on hosts loki and odin, she would place the following entries into file .rhosts in her home directory:

```
loki
odin
```

Thereafter, the superusers on those systems can assume `root` privileges on `bal-dur` without having to enter a password.

PRECEDENCE BETWEEN hosts.equiv AND .rhosts   Clearly, equivalencies can be granted in two ways: through the systemwide `file   /etc/hosts.equiv` and through individual users' `.rhosts` files.

So far, so good. However, what happens if an entry in an `.rhosts` file contradicts an entry in `hosts.equiv`? Which then takes precedence?

The answer is simple: `hosts.equiv` takes precedence. No entry in a `.rhosts` file can overrule what is set in `/etc/hosts.equiv`.

For example, if the `baldur` version of `hosts.equiv` contains the entry

```
-loki
```

and user `marian` then puts the entry

```
loki janim
```

into her `.rhosts` file, the `r*` server will ignore `marian`'s entry, and user `janim` will have to enter a password when she tries to log into `baldur`.

There is one very important exception to this rule: if the superuser `root` grants equivalency to the superuser `root` on another host, that takes precedence over anything that is entered in her system's `hosts.equiv` file.

Clearly, `root`'s ability to grant equivalency is very powerful — and very dangerous. As a rule, `root`-level equivalency should not be granted unless there is an overwhelming need to do so.

r* Commands

Now that we have discussed how to turn on and configure the `r*` services on your intranet, we briefly discuss how to use the commands themselves.

rcp

`rcp` enables a user to copy a file from a remote host to his local host, or from his local host to the remote host. He must have appropriate permissions on both hosts: read permission for the file he wants to copy, and write permission for the directory into which he wants to copy the file.

The syntax of `rcp` is simple, and closely resembles that of the copy command `cp`. To copy a file to a remote host, use the syntax:

```
rcp filename remotehost:remotedirectory
```

where *filename* names the file on the local system that you want to copy onto the remote host, *remotehost* names the machine to which you want to copy the file, and *remotedirectory* names the directory on the remote host into which you want to copy the file.

To copy a file from a remote host onto your local system, simply turn the arguments around:

```
rcp remotehost:filename [localdirectory]
```

filename gives the full path name of the file you want to copy to your local system, and *localdirectory* gives the directory into which you want to copy *remotefile*. If you do not name a *localdirectory*, rcp copies the file into the directory you are now in.

For example, to copy file foo into directory /tmp on remote host baldur, use the following command:

```
rcp foo baldur:/tmp
```

To copy file /etc/passwd from remote host baldur into your local directory and rename it baldur.passwd, use the following command:

```
rcp baldur:/etc/passwd baldur.passwd
```

Like the command cp, rcp recognizes the flags -r and -p:

◆ Flag -r performs a *recursive copy*: if you name a directory instead of a file to copy, rcp will recursively copy that directory, and then copy all of its files and directories, and then copy all the directories' files and directories, and so on until it reaches the end of the directory tree. This is a simple way to copy many files at once.

◆ Flag -p is the "preservation" flag: it tells rcp to set the creation and modification times of the copied files it creates to the creation and modification times of the original files. By default, rcp sets the creation date of the file it writes to the time that it creates the copy rather than to the date that the original file was created.

At this point, you have a good working knowledge of how to use rcp. You will seldom, if ever, need to use rcp's more esoteric features, but for a full description of rcp, see its manual page.

rlogin

Command `rlogin` enables you to log into a remote host, just as if you were sitting down at that machine's keyboard. This command assumes that you have a login account on *remotehost*. As a convenience, `rlogin` automatically uses the login identifier and password you entered on your local host to log you into the remote host.

This command is quite simple:

```
rlogin remotehost
```

where *remotehost* names the host that you want to log into. For example, to log into remote host `baldur`, type:

```
rlogin baldur
```

By default, `rlogin` tries to log you into *remotehost* under the login identifier with which you logged into your local host. To log in under another identity, use the option `-l`. For example, to log into host `baldur` as user `joe`, type:

```
rlogin -l joe baldur
```

If all goes as planned, `rlogin` will log you into the remote host automatically, and you will see that host's login prompt. However, in the following situations, `rlogin` will ask you to enter a password for the remote system:

- ◆ *remotehost* does not name the host at which you are working as an equivalent host.

- ◆ You use the `-l` option to use a different login identifier to log into the remote host than you used to log into the local host.

- ◆ The remote host does not recognize your login identifier.

- ◆ Your password on your local host does not match your password on the remote host.

If logging in fails, `rlogin` shows you a login prompt for the remote system. You can then enter your login identifier and password, just as if you were sitting at the remote host's keyboard.

rsh

Command rsh enables you to execute a command through the shell on a remote host. You will use this command less frequently than rsh or rcp, but it is quite useful nonetheless.

The syntax of this command is simple:

```
rsh remotehost command
```

where *remotehost* is the remote host on which you want to execute the command, and *command* is the command you want to execute. This assumes that you have a login account on the remote host, and thus have permission to execute commands on that machine.

For example, if you want to use the command who to see who is logged into remote host heimdall, use the command:

```
rsh heimdall who
```

rsh executes command who on remote host baldur, and then displays the output of the command on your screen.

If you lack permission to execute a command on the remote host, rsh displays the message

```
Permission denied.
```

As we noted, rsh redirects onto your screen the output of the command it executes on the remote host. rsh can also pass input you generate on your local machine into the command it executes remotely. You can use these features to build some fairly complex interactions between your local host and the remote host. For example, the following command uses rsh to redirect the output of the command tar to a tape device that is plugged into remote host baldur:

```
tar cvzf - /home/fred | rsh baldur 'cat - > /dev/tape'
```

This command is worth a little further explanation:

◆ The left-hand clause, tar cvzf - /home/fred, copies the contents of directory /home/fred (and its subdirectories) into a tape archive, and then writes the archive to the standard output (as indicated by the hyphen, -).

◆ The output of tar is piped (|) to rsh.

◆ Then, the right-hand clause, rsh baldur 'cat - > /dev/tape', reads the standard input and passes it to the command cat on host baldur. cat, in turn, reads its standard input (thus reading the output of tar), and redirects it to file /dev/tape, which is the block-special device for the tape drive.

Thus, the output of tar on one machine is written onto a tape on another machine. This is a good example not only of the rsh command, but also of the general UNIX design of performing a complex task by joining together a number of small, well-defined, well-designed utilities.

One last note: the command 'cat - > /dev/tape' is enclosed within apostrophes (also called single-quote marks), which is to keep the shell on your local machine from interpreting the redirection command rather than passing it as part of the rsh command. (Protecting commands from such premature interpretation by the shell is called *quoting*.) rsh occasionally presents some interesting problems in quoting, depending upon how sophisticated the work is that you want to do.

This concludes our introduction to the r* commands. Next, we move on to another, related problem: printing on a remote machine.

Remote Printing

So far in this chapter, when we have talked about sharing resources, we have meant software resources. For example, when we set up an FTP server on one of the machines in our intranet, we can make files of text or data (such as our hosts file) easily accessible to all the machines on the intranet.

However, the benefits of networking go beyond sharing software resources. With a properly configured network, you can share physical resources as well: instead of plugging a printer or a CD-ROM device into every machine, you can simply plug the device into one machine and make it accessible to all machines on the intranet. This benefit of networking goes beyond a convenience: it can save you some serious money as well.

In this section, we discuss how you can plug a printer into one of the Linux systems on your intranet, and configure your intranet so that every machine on your intranet can print on that printer.

Printing in a Nutshell

The configuration of printers under Linux is beyond the scope of this book. However, to help you understand the discussion that follows, let's briefly review how printing works under Linux.

Printing under Linux involves three elements: a printing command, called lpr; a daemon, called lpd; and a configuration file, called /etc/printcap:

◆ The command lpr spools a file for printing: it copies the file into a spool directory, and prepares a set of instructions as to how that file should print. Among these instructions is the name of the printer on which the file should print. If you do not explicitly name the printer on which the job is to be printed, lpr uses the printer named lp (for "line printer") by default.

◆ The daemon lpd checks the spool directory approximately every 30 seconds to see whether any new files appear in it. If it finds a new file in the spool directory, lpd reads the instructions that lpr wrote for printing that file.

◆ When lpd finds the name of the printer on which the job should be printed, it retrieves the instructions that describe how to print a job on that printer. These instructions are kept in file /etc/printcap. lpd uses these instructions to configure the file for printing on that particular printer.

The instructions that you can place in /etc/printcap comprise a printer-control language that is both quite extensive and quite difficult to understand. Fortunately, printcap entries have been prepared for practically every popular make of printer; when you installed Linux onto the computer into which you have plugged your printer, chances are that the installation program copied the correct printcap description for your printer into file /etc/printcap, and made it the default.

A discussion of how to write or debug printcap entries is well beyond the scope of this book. However, we do discuss one special printcap instruction: rm, which tells the printer daemon lpd to dispatch a printing job to another host. By using this instruction, you can tell the printer daemon on a machine that doesn't have a printer plugged into it, to dispatch the print job to another machine that does have a printer, and let that machine's printer daemon manage the printing of the job.

Configuring Remote Printing

The description of configuring remote printing assumes the following:

◆ Your intranet has one Linux workstation that has a printer plugged into it, and that its printcap file and lpd daemon are correctly configured for printing to it. For the sake of convenience, we call this machine the *printer server.*

◆ Your intranet has one or more other Linux workstations that you want to configure so that they can print jobs on the printer that is plugged into the printer server. For the sake of convenience, we call these machines the *printer clients.*

You do not have to do anything to configure the printer server to receive jobs from the printer clients.

To configure a printer client to spool jobs to the printer server, su to the superuser root, and then edit file /etc/printcap as follows:

1. Comment out the entry for printer `lp`, which is the default printer. The entry starts with the unindented line that begins with the instruction `lp` and all lines that follow up to the next unindented line. To comment out a line, place a # at its beginning.

2. Add the following line to `/etc/printcap`:

   ```
   lp:rm=printer_server
   ```

   where *printer_server* is the name of the printer server.

3. Turn on the printer daemon by typing

   ```
   /usr/sbin/lpd
   ```

   No & is needed at the end of this line.

Repeat these steps on each of your printer-client machines.

REMOTE PRINTING: AN EXAMPLE

For an example, suppose that a printer is plugged into host `baldur` (address `192.168.1.3`) on our example intranet. For machine `odin` to be able to print jobs on `baldur`'s printer, `odin`'s file `/etc/printcap` should be edited so that the entry for the default printer `lp` reads as follows:

```
lp:rm=baldur
```

That's all there is to it. Thereafter, when you print a job on `odin`, its printer daemon will forward the print job to the printer daemon on `baldur`, which will print the job on `baldur`'s printer.

TESTING

To test whether printing is set up correctly, turn on the printer, and then type the following command:

```
lpr /etc/passwd
```

In a moment, the following steps will occur:

◆ Command `lpr` will copy file `/etc/printcap` into the print client's print-spool directory.

◆ The line-printer daemon `lpd` will find the file in the spool directory and read it.

◆ `lpd` reads the entry for the default printer `lp` from `/etc/printcap` and sees that the job should be forwarded to the print server.

- ◆ `lpd` copies the file into the spool directory on the print server over your Ethernet network.

- ◆ `lpd` on the print server discovers the file in its spool directory, reads information about the default printer from its copy of `/etc/printcap`, and dispatches the file to the printer.

- ◆ The job appears on the printer.

All this should take no more than a few seconds.

EDITING /etc/rc.d/rc.local

To ensure that printing is turned on when the printer-client workstations are booted, insert the following commands into file `/etc/rc.d/rc.local`:

```
# Start the various INET servers.
if [ -f /usr/sbin/lpd ]; then
    echo "Starting lpd ..."
    /usr/sbin/lpd
done
```

This concludes our discussion of printing remotely. For sources of more information on printing, see the references at the end of this chapter.

The X Window System

The X Window System (or X Window, for short) is a graphical interface that was created by the Project Athena group at the Massachusetts Institute of Technology (MIT). It is the graphical interface to various flavors of UNIX, including Linux.

Unlike most graphical interfaces, including those used by the Macintosh or the Windows family of operating systems, X Window was designed to be run over a network. Machines that use X Window can provide graphical services to each other across a network – a feature of X Window that is extremely powerful and, unfortunately, much underutilized.

In the rest of this section, we will refer to XFree86, which is a freely available version of X Window that is used in Slackware Linux (and many other Linux packages as well).

In this section, we describe XFree86 briefly, and then discuss the features of XFree86 that use networking:

- ◆ The X display manager

- ◆ Security and authorization

We assume that XFree86 has been installed onto your Linux workstation, is configured correctly, and is running more or less to your satisfaction.

What Is XFree86?

You can think of XFree86 as being the UNIX GUI; however, it really is much more than that. XFree86 is a client-server graphical system that is designed to work over a network:

- The server can process graphical instructions and draw pictures on the user's screen.
- The client tells the server what images to draw.

XFree86 inverts the traditional definition of client-server systems: the system that you normally consider the client (in other words, the workstation on your desk) is now the server, and the system that you normally consider the server (the UNIX machine in the air-conditioned room in the basement) now runs the clients. (Of course, with many Linux systems, both client and server are running on the same machine.) While this might seem strange, it can be summed up easily:

- An XFree86 program is an *X client* and is analogous to a Windows application.
- The display that an XFree86 program runs on is an *X Window server*.

An XFree86 server is analogous to a PC running Windows 95 or Windows NT, but a major difference exists: A PC that is running Windows 95 or Windows NT can run code only in its local memory and on its CPU, because the functions that a Windows application uses to manipulate the display can operate only local graphics hardware. However, XFree86 splits the client and server and uses the network to transport information between them. This design decision was a source of considerable criticism when XFree86 was first released and high-speed networking wasn't widely available; but now, when you can build an Ethernet-based intranet for your basement for less than $100, XFree86 makes much more sense.

Naming the Display

Graphical programming for any system is inherently difficult. The difficulty in creating applications for XFree86 or Microsoft Windows is enhanced by the event-based nature inherent in GUI-based applications, so most applications are based on toolkits that combine common operations into easy-to-use functions.

One thing that all XFree86 applications must do is initiate a connection to the X server. In XFree86 programming shorthand, this is called *opening the display*.

In nearly every case, the job of opening the display is handled by a canned XFree86 routine that uses the environment variable DISPLAY to determine the server to communicate with.

Forming the value of the display variable is easy: it's the name or IP address of the machine running the server, suffixed with a colon and a display number. So, the first display on thor.myexample.com is called either:

```
thor.myexample.com:0
```

or

```
thor.myexample.com/unix:0
```

 If you haven't seen it before, you should notice that the first object is numbered 0. This is common in UNIX and in many systems based on the C programming language, in which an array is numbered from 0 rather than 1.

The first form, thor.myexample.com:0, is suitable for use from any host on a network that can reach thor.myexample.com. It uses the TCP/IP network to communicate between client and server.

The second format, thor.myexample.com/unix:0, uses a different method of communications called a *UNIX domain socket*, which exists to allow faster communication, although it can be used only when the client and the server are on the same machine.

In most cases, the default script that manages an XFree86 login sets the DISPLAY variable properly and makes sure that its value is available to all of your XFree86 clients.

For future reference, you should note that the telnet command carries the value of the DISPLAY variable, if set, across a connection to another machine, but the rlogin command doesn't. Also, depending on what type of authentication you use with XFree86, you may need to make sure the other machine has the proper "keys" to access the display.

We must note that, in fact, the display on thor.myexample.com is referred to as

```
thor.mydomain.com:0.0
```

or

```
thor.mydomain.com/unix:0.0
```

The .0 part refers to screen number. Because only one monitor is usually plugged into a Linux workstation, you can leave off the screen specification.

xdm

xdm (X display manager) is the system in XFree86 that controls access to the display. xdm can broadcast either of the following:

- ◆ A login window that accepts a user name and password, and logs in the user.

- ◆ A list of possible hosts that are willing to support a graphic login. The user can choose one; that host then handles the login.

In the simplest case, you will want to provide an X display on your Linux workstation, (perhaps to arouse the envy in that guy with the Windows NT workstation down the hall), which is a matter of changing the run level in of the system to 4 where XFree86 runs:

```
# Default runlevel.
id:4:initdefault:
```

At run-level 4, your system runs an XFree86 display and a TTY shell that you can reach by pressing Ctrl-Alt-F6. If you have any other machines that can act as XFree86 servers and that are reachable by broadcast on your network, they should also respond to the presence of this server by updating their menus. (This will happen at the next logout if someone is logged in, or after the ping button has been pressed with the default X chooser application.)

If some X terminals on your intranet do not understand the *X Display Manager Control Protocol* (XDMCP), you can force a login on them by adding a line in file /usr/X11R6/lib/X11/xdm/Xservers. This file contains one line for each display; each line has the following format:

```
HostName:ScreenNumber foreign
```

In fact, you can combine two terminals to turn that spare 386 or 486 system into an X terminal and use it to run that application that accesses the company's current inventory of widgets from Netscape. To do this, insert into /etc/inittab an instruction like the following:

```
x1:4:respawn:/usr/X11R6/bin/X -indirect hostname
```

or

```
x1:4:respawn:/usr/X11R6/bin/X -broadcast
```

or

```
x1:4:respawn:/usr/X11R6/bin/X -query hostname
```

The first form of this instruction puts up a chooser menu from all X hosts available at your site that can be seen on the chosen host. This format is appropriate if you have multiple hosts running xdm, and your users have a strong reason to choose one host from the many, or if you currently have a single xdm host and plan to add more later.

The second form of this instruction configures the X server to broadcast a query and display a login from the first xdm host that replies. This is useful if you are running xdm on several hosts, and which one your users log into doesn't matter. The broadcast method offers a crude form of load balancing: in theory, a lightly loaded host will respond more quickly than a heavily loaded one (although we wouldn't depend upon this method alone).

The third form of this instruction sends the query directly to the host named on the command line. This is useful when you want to either load balance manually, or when you want to tie a particular X terminal to a particular host, for whatever reason.

After you insert the instruction, start XFree86 at run-level 4.

X Server Security: xhost and xauth

We have yet to mention security after the user authenticates himself. Some means of controlling access to the X server must be present after a user logs in. Having the capability to display images from any remote computer can be considered from a security standpoint anything from a mere nuisance to a major security problem. However, this threat pales in comparison to the possibility that someone could easily interject a program that reads and records all the keystrokes that you make until you log into another account on another computer or use the su command to assume root privileges to undertake some administrative duty.

Security under XFree86 comes in two flavors: *host-based* and *authentication-key-based*.

We discuss each in turn.

xhost

Host-based authentication is simple to maintain and use, but it doesn't offer much security. With host-based X security, you maintain a list of hosts that you allow to access your display. Unfortunately, any user logged into that host or who can rsh into that host can access your display. Further, you can allow any host on your network or the Internet to access your display.

Host-based authentication is maintained by the program xhost. This is simple to use. To allow a host to access your display, type the following command:

```
xhost +hostname
```

The *hostname* here is optional — but be careful, because if you do not specify *hostname*, you will give permission to access your display to all hosts on the Internet.

To restrict a host from accessing your display, use the following command:

```
xhost -hostname
```

Again, *hostname* is optional. In this case, access is restricted and authentication will fall back to xauth, which we discuss next.

Finally, you can use xhost with no arguments at all. This tells you whether access control is in place (command xhost + turns off access control completely) and, if it is in place, which hosts can connect without resorting to the xauth security model.

xauth

xauth maintains security based on authentication keys. The *authentication key* security model relies upon common access to a cryptographic key between the server and the client. With xdm, the default key is simply a random number generated by the X server at startup time. The server employs a cryptographically secure, random-number generator, which assumes that no way exists to determine what the next random number or key is based on, or what the current or last random number or key is. xdm makes sure to write this key into a file in the home directory for the user's clients. When authentication is required, clients access this file with the key. This is all handled by the X libraries.

This process works well if either the client is on the same machine as the xdm server or the file is on a shared directory, but some of the utility of X is lost if you cannot arbitrarily start clients on any machine and have them access your display. At the same time, you do not want to have any user on a machine access your display so you can simply start an xterm on it. The program xauth provides you with a way out.

xauth enables you to manipulate the authentication information in your X authentication key file. This file is usually called .Xauthority in your home directory. To list the contents of this file, you can use xauth's list subcommand, which works as follows:

```
xauth list
thor.mydomain.com:0  MIT-MAGIC-COOKIE-1
  602e0f530d1b382c2741571c102b410a
thor.mydomain.com/unix:0  MIT-MAGIC-COOKIE-1
  602e0f530d1b382c2741571c102b410a
```

A specific display can be listed as follows:

```
xauth list $DISPLAY
thor.mydomain.com/unix:0  MIT-MAGIC-COOKIE-1
  602e0f530d1b382c2741571c102b410a
```

Usually, you will not need to list the displays to which you have access, but you will need to grant access to a login that you have on another machine. xauth's sub-command extract extracts the key for a display to a file, as follows:

```
xauth extract filename $DISPLAY
```

The subcommand merge merges the contents of a file (presuming you wrote it with the using the subcommand extract) into your .Xauthority file. The format looks like this:

```
xauth merge filename
```

If you use a single dash as the filename, the subcommands extract and merge read from the standard input and write to the standard output. You can combine this command rsh to transfer the current authentication key between two machines on the network, as follows:

```
xauth extract - $DISPLAY | rsh remote-machine-options
 /usr/X11R6/bin/xauth merge -
```

Note that you may have to specify the full path to xauth on the remote machine, because the X binaries are usually not in the path that rsh uses on the remote machine.

After this, you should be able to run XFree86 clients on the remote machine with your display. Normally, we would rely on the DISPLAY environmental variable to identify the display to the client.

As we said before, in nearly all cases, an X library routine handles opening the display. Likewise, we normally would use the DISPLAY environmental variable to specify the correct X server; but we may also use the option -display, as follows:

```
rsh remote-machine-options /usr/X11R6/bin/xterm -display $DISPLAY
```

After you pass the xauth key to the remote machine, a command like the preceding will start an xterm from the remote machine.

Summary

In this chapter, we discussed the services that the workstations on your intranet can provide to each other.

First, we described what a *daemon* is, and introduced some of the most commonly invoked daemons: inetd, which is the master daemon for listing requests for services; telnetd, which fulfills requests for TELNET services; ftpd, which fulfills requests for FTP services; and the Apache Web server, which services requests for Web pages.

We then discussed how to use the network file system (NFS) to share disk resources over a network.

Next, the Berkeley "remote" (or r*) commands were discussed. These include rlogin, which permits users to log into other machines on the intranet without having to reenter a user identifier or password; rsh, which executes a program on another machine on the intranet; and rcp, which copies a file from one machine to another on the intranet. We discussed both how to set up the servers to service these commands, and how to use these commands' clients.

Next, we discussed how to use the Linux lp daemon to print a document on another machine on the intranet. This involves modifying a printcap description for a printer; in this way, permitting multiple machines on your intranet to redirect their print jobs to one machine is quite easy, thus letting one machine effectively act as your intranet's printer server.

Finally, we discussed how to configure the X Window System on your intranet's workstations so that the machines on your intranet could share X Windows resources. The key is to configure the X authentication systems properly, so that appropriate machines and users can share X resources, but outsiders are excluded.

Chapter 8

Setting Up a Gateway to the Internet

IN THIS CHAPTER

- ◆ Configuring hosts
- ◆ IP masquerading
- ◆ SOCKS
- ◆ Domain-name service

AT THIS POINT in our exploration of networking, we have shown you how to do the following:

- ◆ Configure your Linux machine so that it can talk with the Internet via an Internet service provider (ISP), or with another network via Ethernet.

- ◆ Build an intranet by using Ethernet to wire together multiple machines in your home or office, and configure those machines to provide services to each other.

In this chapter, we tie the two concepts together: we show you how to configure a Linux workstation as a *gateway*, so that the other machines on your intranet can use it to exchange data with hosts on the Internet.

This chapter covers the following topics:

- ◆ Configuring the machines on your intranet to forward datagrams to a gateway, and configuring the gateway to forward datagrams to the outside world.

- ◆ Setting up IP masquerading, which lets all machines on your intranet access the Internet directly by *piggybacking* onto the gateway machine's Internet-visible IP address.

- ◆ Setting up SOCKS, which is another way to let machines on your intranet exchange datagrams with machines on the Internet.

- ◆ Setting up domain-name service for the machines on your intranet.

335

With these few tools, you can give every host on your intranet full access to the outside world through your intranet's gateway host.

That said, let's begin.

Configuring Hosts

The first step is to configure the hosts on your intranet so that they can interact with hosts outside of your intranet.

The gateway host does not need any changes to its configuration – it can already interact with hosts outside of your intranet.

However, the "ordinary" hosts on your intranet – the hosts that are physically connected to your intranet alone – need to change their configuration slightly so that they can begin to converse with hosts outside of your intranet: you must add to each ordinary host's routing table an entry that makes the gateway machine the `default` host. When this is done, a host will forward to the gateway machine every datagram that it does not know how to route itself, anticipating that the gateway machine will know how to route it.

Before we plunge into modifying an ordinary host's routing table, let's review routing briefly:

◆ Chapter 1 introduces the concept of a *routing table*, a table within the Linux kernel that states which interface on the TCP/IP network-access tier should be used to physically reach a given host.

◆ Chapter 3 discusses how to modify the kernel's routing table. In brief, some programs modify the routing table on their own; for example, the PPP daemon `pppd` can insert a `default` entry into the kernel's routing table when it connects with the ISP's host. For our ordinary hosts, however, we will use the command `route`.

◆ Chapter 6 discusses how to add an ordinary host to your intranet. To connect an ordinary host via Ethernet to the intranet with IP address `192.168.1`, we first used the command `ifconfig` to connect the Ethernet card with network `192.168.1.0` via interface `eth0`, as follows:

```
/sbin/ifconfig eth0 192.168.1.0 netmask 255.255.255.0
```

◆ Then, we used command `route` to inform the routing table that datagrams for network `192.168.1.0` should be routed to the device accessed via interface `eth0`:

```
/sbin/route add -net 192.168.1.0 dev eth0
```

Now we must add one more entry to the routing table. This entry will tell the kernel to forward to our gateway machine all datagrams that it otherwise does not know how to route. In our example intranet, our gateway machine is named heim-dall (after the mythological god who guarded the rainbow bridge to Valhalla), and has the IP address 192.168.1.100; thus, we use the following form of the command route:

```
/sbin/route add default gw 192.168.1.100 metric 1
```

Argument add tells route to add this entry to the routing table. Argument default tells route that the host named in this entry is the default host to which should be forwarded all otherwise-unroutable datagrams; and gw indicates that the host is a gateway.

When this entry is inserted into an ordinary host's routing table, that host will forward to the gateway machine all datagrams it does not otherwise know how to route. In effect, this will be all datagrams that are addressed to hosts that lie outside your intranet – including every host on the Internet. The gateway host, in turn, will itself forward these datagrams to the host that is defined as its default, and that host will either route the datagrams correctly or forward them to *its* default host. And so, the datagrams will percolate through the Internet until they either arrive at their destination or reach a dead end.

You should add this command to file /etc/rc.d/rc.inet1, with the IP address set to that of your intranet's gateway host. A form of this command may already be in the file, but commented out:

```
# /sbin/route add default gw ${GATEWAY} metric 1
```

If you see this command, uncomment it. Earlier in the file, uncomment the line

```
#GATEWAY="192.168.39.1"
```

and set it to the IP address of your intranet's gateway host.

Now, reboot your system so that these changes will take effect.

That's all that needs to be done to reconfigure ordinary hosts.

However, some more work needs to be done before the ordinary hosts on your intranet can directly access the outside world like your gateway system can: you must install some software that lets datagrams be addressed from ordinary hosts to external hosts, and back again.

The next two sections describe the two methods for doing this: IP masquerading and SOCKS.

IP Masquerading

Let's assume for a moment that your intranet consists of two hosts. One is an ordinary host that is plugged into your intranet, and to which you have assigned IP address 192.168.1.2. The other host, which is the intranet's gateway to the Internet, has been assigned IP address 192.168.1.1 on your intranet, and has been assigned IP address 207.241.63.126 by the Internet service provider with which it establishes a PPP connection.

Clearly, when the gateway host has its PPP link to the Internet up and running, a user who is sitting at that gateway machine can exchange datagrams with a host on the Internet. However, when that PPP link is running, could a user who is sitting at the ordinary host also exchange datagrams with a host on the Internet?

At first glance, you would think that the answer to this question is "Yes." After all, the ordinary host can build a datagram with the IP address of an Internet host with which it wants to communicate, and route that datagram to the gateway host; and the gateway host can (or should) route the datagram automatically to the host to which it is addressed.

However, in reality, this "Yes" answer is only half-true: the ordinary host *can* address datagrams to a host on the Internet and the gateway host will forward them, but the remote host on the Internet has no way to send a datagram in reply. Figure 8-1 shows why this is so.

Host 192.168.1.2 builds a datagram that is addressed to the Library of Congress's host loc.gov, whose IP address is 140.147.2.12. However, the source-host address that the ordinary host put into the datagram is its IP address on the intranet, which is 192.168.1.2. As we explained in Chapter 1, the block of class-C IP addresses that begins with 192.168 is reserved for intranets, and, therefore, no Internet host will have any of these addresses. Thus, when host loc.gov receives the datagram from your ordinary host, it cannot reply, because the source address in the IP header is set to an unresolvable address.

So, you ask, why can the gateway host exchange datagrams with a host on the Internet? After all, it too has a intranet IP address (in this case, 192.168.1.1). The reason, simply, is that the gateway machine has two IP addresses, one for each network interface. One IP address (192.168.1.1) is assigned to its Ethernet interface, eth0, with which it communicates with the hosts on its intranet; and the other IP address (207.241.63.126) is assigned to the PPP interface, ppp0, with which it communicates with the ISP (and by extension, therefore, with all other hosts on the Internet). This second IP address is a legal Internet address, rather than one of the hobbyist IP addresses, and so it can be used by hosts throughout the Internet to send datagrams to the gateway host.

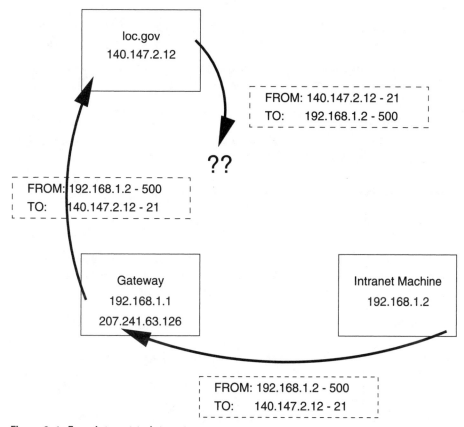

Figure 8-1: From intranet to Internet

Does a way to work around this problem exist, so that users on your ordinary hosts can interact directly with hosts on the Internet? The answer, fortunately, is "Yes" — through the use of *IP masquerading.*

How IP Masquerading Works

IP masquerading is software that is built into the Linux kernel's firewall software. A *firewall* enables you to control the flow of datagrams through a host: you can set explicitly the addresses to which a host can send datagrams, from which it can receive datagrams, and for which it can forward datagrams.

The IP masquerading software works as follows:

◆ The masquerading software examines each outward-bound datagram.

◆ When a datagram is being forwarded from an ordinary host on the intranet to another host on the Internet, the masquerading software edits that datagram:

■ The masquerading software changes the datagram's source-address field to the address assigned by the ISP – in other words, the address can be used throughout the Internet.

■ It changes the datagram's source-port field to a special value that it uses to identify the intranet host that dispatched the datagram.

■ It saves the original IP address and source-port number in an internal cache.

◆ When the gateway host receives a datagram from a host on the Internet, the masquerading software reads it. If the datagram is addressed to a source port that the masquerading software has used to identify a system on the intranet, the software edits the datagram to restore the original IP address and source port, and then routes the datagram to the machine on the intranet that should receive it.

Figure 8-2 illustrates this process.
Here, we have inserted IP masquerading into the situation shown in Figure 8-1:

◆ The masquerading software maps all datagrams from port 500 on local host 192.168.1.2 to port 722 (an unused port that it picked at random) on IP address 207.24.63.126 – and the software remembers that it made this mapping.

◆ The masquerading software then dispatches the datagram to port 21 at Internet address 140.147.2.12 (the FTP server on host loc.gov).

◆ When the FTP server at loc.gov receives this datagram, it thinks that it is talking to port 722 on host 207.24.63.126, which is a legal Internet address, and therefore sends its reply datagrams to that port on that host.

◆ When 207.241.63.126 (your gateway host) receives a packet for port 722, it recalls that that address actually indicates port 500 on host 192.168.1.2 on its intranet; the gateway host then edits the datagram appropriately, and dispatches it to that host in the usual fashion.

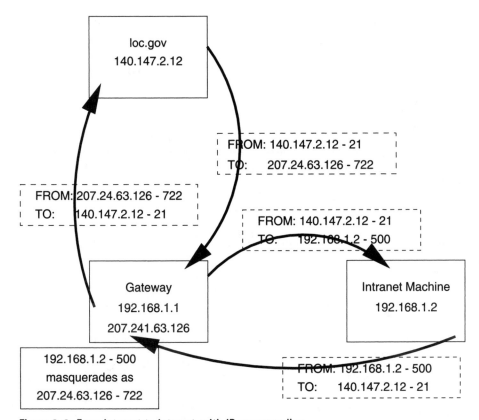

Figure 8-2: From intranet to Internet, with IP masquerading

To the user who is sitting at host 192.168.1.2, it appears that he is talking directly with the FTP server at loc.gov, although he actually is masquerading as a user on his intranet's gateway host 207.241.63.126.

If this description seems a little confusing, don't worry: You do not need to understand the ins and outs of IP masquerading to install it and have it do its work for you.

Installation of Masquerading

As we mentioned, IP masquerading is built into the Linux firewall software. This software is part of the Linux kernel; you do not have to download any additional code.

IP masquerading requires that you build a kernel that has the Linux firewall built into it. IP masquerading itself is implemented as part of the firewall software. Thus, implementing IP masquerading requires the following steps:

◆ Compile a new kernel that includes the firewall and IP masquerading.

◆ Install the new kernel.

◆ Use the command `ipfwadm` to turn on IP masquerading.

We now go through each step in turn.

COMPILE THE KERNEL AND THE KERNEL MODULES

We described how to recompile the kernel in Chapter 3. The kernel we compiled in that chapter contains all the code you need to run IP masquerading. However, just to make sure, when you type

```
make config
```

to configure the kernel, you should have answered y to the following questions:

◆ `Prompt for development and/or incomplete code/drivers (CONFIG_EXPERIMENTAL)` — This tells `make` to prompt you about experimental features of the kernel. IP masquerading is considered an experimental feature (although it appears to be solid); therefore, you must answer y to this prompt, or you will not see the prompt to include IP masquerading in your kernel.

◆ `Enable loadable module support (CONFIG_MODULES)` — This tells `make` that you want the kernel to be able to handle *loadable modules* — a module of code that it loads when needed, but that does not otherwise reside in memory. IP masquerading is implemented as a loadable module; thus, you must answer y to this prompt to be able to run IP masquerading.

◆ `Networking support (CONFIG_NET)` — This means that you want networking support within the kernel. Undoubtedly, this is already set to y — but it never hurts to make sure.

◆ `Network firewalls (CONFIG_FIREWALL)` — This means that you want your Linux kernel to include its firewall feature.

◆ `TCP/IP networking (CONFIG_INET)` — Answer y to this prompt to tell `make` that you want the kernel to support TCP/IP networking. Again, this switch probably already is set to y, but it never hurts to make sure.

◆ `IP: forwarding/gatewaying (CONFIG_IP_FORWARD)` — Include in the kernel support for IP forwarding/gatewaying.

◆ `IP: firewalling (CONFIG_IP_FIREWALL)` — Include support for IP firewalls. Please note that this is not the same as `CONFIG_FIREWALL`, asked earlier.

- ◆ IP: masquerading (EXPERIMENTAL) (CONFIG_IP_MASQUERADE) — At last: include IP masquerading in the kernel.

- ◆ IP: always defragment (CONFIG_IP_ALWAYS_DEFRAG) — Tell IP always to defragment datagrams. (We discussed IP fragmentation in Chapter 1.) This is not strictly necessary, but including it in your kernel is a good idea.

- ◆ Network device support (CONFIG_NETDEVICES) — Support network devices. This does not add any particular code to your kernel, but it will ask you about some network devices, only one of which (the DUMMY device) interests us.

- ◆ dummy net driver support (CONFIG_DUMMY) — Include support in the kernel for the dummy net driver. Again, this is not strictly necessary, but including it is a good idea.

Make sure that the configuration answers y to each of these prompts. If it does not, then answer y to the prompt where the default is not y, and then compile and install the kernel as we described in Chapter 3.

CONFIGURE MASQUERADING

In Chapter 3, we compiled masquerading directly into the kernel, rather than implementing it as a module. If you compiled masquerading into your Linux kernel, you do not have to do anything to configure it; skip to the next section.

If you chose to implement masquerading as a module rather than compile it into the kernel, you must add some code to a file in directory /etc/rc.d, described next, so that the IP masquerading modules are loaded when you boot your Linux kernel.

Slackware comes with a file called rc.modules; you should modify this by default. If you are using a release of Linux other than Slackware, directory /etc/rc.d may or may not contain this file; if it does not, modify file rc.local instead. First, make sure that command

```
/sbin/depmod -a
```

is present in the file, and is not commented out. rc.modules has this command in it, but it may be commented out; if it is, remove the # that precedes it.

Next, add the following commands to the script (or make sure that they are not commented out):

```
/sbin/modprobe ip_masq_ftp
/sbin/modprobe ip_masq_raudio
/sbin/modprobe ip_masq_irc
```

Save your changes, and be sure that this script is executable – some text editors will silently remove execute permission from a script when you edit it. Then reboot your Linux system, to ensure that these changes are operational on your system.

TURNING ON IP MASQUERADING   At this point, the IP masquerading bits are loaded into your Linux kernel. One step remains, however: to turn on IP masquerading. To do so, you must use the command `ipfwadm` (that is, "IP firewall administration").

As we mentioned earlier, a firewall examines datagrams as they enter and leave your Linux host. You can set a rule, or *policy*, that controls which datagrams the firewall will permit to pass through and which it will deny. You can set one or more policies for any or all of the following functions:

◆ *accounting* – What information the firewall records about each datagram as it passes through the firewall

◆ *input* – Which datagrams the firewall permits to enter from the Internet

◆ *output* – Which datagrams the firewall permits to leave your Linux host

◆ *forwarding* – Which datagrams the firewall permits your Linux host to forward from or forward to other hosts on your intranet

The command `ipfwadm` enables you to set a policy for one of these firewall functions; thereafter, the firewall will enforce the policy on all datagrams.

As we mentioned earlier, IP masquerading is implemented as part of the firewall software. To turn on IP masquerading, you must set a policy for the firewall's forwarding function. You can use `ipfwadm` either to turn on IP masquerading for all machines on your intranet, or to turn it on only for selected machines. If your intranet is small – say, five machines or fewer – then turning on IP masquerading for the entire intranet is a reasonable thing to do. However, if your intranet is large – say, more than five machines – you may want to restrict masquerading privileges to selected machines whose users really need it. When you make this decision, you should decide which users truly need direct access to the Internet (remember, machines that do not enjoy IP masquerading will still have indirect access to the Internet, through mail and news). You should consider just how much of a load your Internet access can bear – if you are accessing the Internet through a modem, one user on a browser can fill up the connection all by herself.

After you decide, you can modify script `/etc/rc.d/rc.inet2` to turn on IP masquerading. First, insert the following commands at the end of this script:

```
echo "Starting up IP masquerading ..."
ipfwadm -F -p deny
```

The option `-F` tells `ipfwadm` that you're setting a policy for the forwarding of datagrams. Option `-p deny` tells `ipfwadm` that you're setting the default policy, which is to deny – or turn off – the forwarding of any datagrams.

The next commands set some policies that create exceptions to the default policy of denying the forwarding of datagrams.

If you want to extend IP masquerading to every machine on your intranet, insert the following command into script `rc.inet2`:

```
ipfwadm -F -a m -S ip.address/24 -D 0.0.0.0/0
```

The following list describes the arguments to this command:

◆ `-F` — Set a forwarding policy.

◆ `-a m` — Append a policy to the policies already set. `m` indicates *masquerade*. Thus, we now have set two policies: the default policy of denying forwarding, plus the policy of masquerading datagrams from the hosts that the rest of this command will identify.

◆ `-S ip.address/24` — Masquerade datagrams from the named sources. `ip.address` gives the IP address that you have assigned to your intranet (for example, `192.168.1.0`). In other words, this policy tells the firewall to masquerade the datagrams from any host on this network. The `/24` gives a shorthand for the bit-mask for this network; `24` indicates that the mask is 24 bits (3 bytes) long — in other words, this is a class-C network.

◆ `-D 0.0.0.0/0` — Set the IP addresses of destination hosts to which the firewall software will forward datagrams. `0.0.0.0/0` tells the firewall to set no restrictions on the hosts to which masqueraded datagrams will be sent — in other words, this tells the firewall to forward masqueraded datagrams anywhere.

If you want to limit IP masquerading to a few selected machines, use the following form of the command:

```
ipfwadm -F -a m -S ip.address/32 -D 0.0.0.0/0
```

Here, `ip.address` gives the IP address of an individual host whose datagrams you want to masquerade, rather than the IP address of the entire intranet. For example, if you want to masquerade the datagrams from the host with IP address `192.168.1.3`, use its address in place of the network address `192.168.1.0`. Note, too, that the number of bits in the bitmask is 32, not 24 (or 8 or 16). You must insert into `/etc/rc.d/rc.net2` one such command for each machine whose datagrams you want to masquerade.

That's all there is to it.

A firewall can be finely tuned to manage traffic between your intranet and the Internet. You can set rules to control which hosts can transmit datagrams to the Internet, which Internet hosts they can (or cannot) communicate with, and which Internet hosts can interact with the hosts on the intranet. You can even control which ports (and therefore, which protocols) can be used to communicate among hosts.

Test and Troubleshoot

Now that IP masquerading has been installed on your Linux gateway and, we hope, configured correctly, the time has arrived to turn on and test IP masquerading.

To turn on IP masquerading, simply reboot your Linux gateway system.

To test it, do the following:

1. Log into a host on your intranet, other than the gateway machine. Do so either by walking over to it, or through `rlogin` or `telnet`.

2. From that nongateway host, type the following command.

```
ftp ftp.loc.gov
```

Your gateway host should dial your Internet provider's host, and connect you to the FTP server at the Library of Congress. (As we previously noted, you cannot use `ping` to test masquerading, because the ICMP host-to-host protocol doesn't have a source-port field, and therefore can't be masqueraded.) In a moment, you should see the response:

```
Connected to rs7.loc.gov.
```

Congratulations! You have IP masquerading running correctly. Now users can run TELNET sessions, FTP sessions, Web browsers, or other interactive software from any host on your intranet to which you have granted masquerading privileges, just as if their machines were plugged directly into the Internet.

If your test did not work, please review the directions given previously in this chapter, and make sure that you built and installed masquerading correctly. If you are certain that you built IP masquerading correctly and it still doesn't work, see the end of this chapter for sources of information to help you.

SOCKS

SOCKS (an abbreviation for "SOCKetS") is an alternative to IP masquerading. It differs from IP masquerading principally in that it works at the application level rather than at the network level: instead of having the gateway's network software examine and modify each datagram that it permits to pass through, you modify each application that uses networking so that it uses a special daemon that understands how to forward datagrams properly. This approach to forwarding datagrams is called *proxying*.

SOCKS appeals to people who prefer a solution that is "cleaner" than IP masquerading: some system administrators simply are not comfortable with a solution wherein the kernel rewrites the headers of datagrams before they are delivered.

Because SOCKS works at the application level, it can do some things that IP masquerading cannot. For example, masquerading stops outside clients from accessing services on the individual machines on your intranet: this makes sense, because masquerading is designed to make outside machines think they are talking to a single host – the gateway host. For example, if you have a TELNET service running on each of the machines on your intranet, a user who is outside your intranet cannot see the TELNET services on these machines, because your internal network is hidden by your masquerading. However, if you instead use SOCKS as a proxy server on your gateway, you can directly reach from the outside world the TELNET server on each of your intranet's machines.

Masquerading, however, does have the advantage of being easier to set up and maintain. By setting up masquerading on a single gateway machine, you can extend Internet services to all applications on all hosts on your intranet; whereas if you use SOCKS, you must individually modify each network application on each host on your intranet.

In brief, SOCKS proxying is more robust than IP masquerading, but this robustness is purchased at the price of being more difficult to set up.

How Does SOCKS Work?

SOCKS consists of a daemon server that runs on your intranet's gateway machine, and a library of networking functions that is linked into each application that you want to proxy.

The SOCKS server listens for connections on the well-known TCP port 1080. When a user invokes an application that has the SOCKS library linked into it, the application connects to the SOCKS server on the gateway machine; this application is, in effect, the SOCKS client.

When a SOCKS client connects to the SOCKS server, the first item of information that the client transmits is the IP address and port of the remote server that the client wants to talk to. The SOCKS server then acts as a "go-between": it connects to the remote server, and then forwards to the remote server all datagrams from the local client to the remote server, and forwards to the local client all datagrams received from the remote server.

As you can see, SOCKS proxying lets selected applications on your intranet access hosts on the Internet. This also works in the other direction: unlike IP masquerading, SOCKS proxying lets hosts on the Internet directly address hosts on your intranet, because the SOCKS proxying server has access to both address spaces – it knows about both the Internet address space and the clients that are on your intranet. Because routers on the Internet know how to send a datagram to the host that is running the SOCKS proxying server, the SOCKS server can forward datagrams to the correct host on your intranet.

Getting SOCKS

SOCKS is distributed by Nippon Electric Company (NEC). NEC asks you to fill out a questionnaire (name, e-mail address, and so forth) to obtain the current URL. The main page is

```
http://www.socks.nec.com
```

and the page for getting the source code is

```
http://www.socks.nec.com/socks5.html
```

After you fill out the questionnaire, the NEC Web site gives you the URL from which you can download the latest source code. Download it and unpack it where you normally store source code (by custom, directory /usr/src).

A beta version of SOCKS is available without filling out the questionnaire; to obtain this version, check URL:

```
ftp://ftp.nec.com/pub/socks/socks5/socks5-beta-0.17.2-
   exportable.tar.gz
```

We urge you to fill out the questionnaire and obtain the latest sources, if possible. However, the beta version helps you get SOCKS up and running if you aren't able to reach the Web from your host.

The latest version of SOCKS currently is V1.0R4. The complete build takes about 4.2MB, so make sure you have that much space before you start.

Building and Installing SOCKS

After you copy the SOCKS archive into directory /usr/src, su to the superuser root, and then use the following command to extract the tar archive:

```
tar xvzf socks5-v1.0r4.tar.gz
```

Enter the directory that was created when you unpacked the source code:

```
cd socks5-v1.0r4
```

Run the configure script and set a default SOCKS server:

```
./configure —with-default-server=socks.myexample.com \
    —with-srvpidfile=/var/run/socks5.pid
```

The configure process attempts to tailor the installation files to suit your system. Unfortunately, configure finds both the ping and traceroute programs in their current location, not the location that you move them to after you install their

"SOCKS-ified" replacements. This causes the `ping` command to silently fail for internal hosts. To fix this, edit the relevant sections of the file `include/config.h` to resemble the following:

```
/* define this to the path of your traceroute... */
#define TROUTEPROG "/usr/bin/traceroute.orig"
/* define this to the path of your ping */
#define PINGPROG "/bin/ping.orig"
```

Once configuration is finished, run `make` to build and install the software:

```
make ; make install
```

If everything goes without a hitch, you'll have the SOCKS daemon and a few SOCKS-ified clients installed into directory `/usr/local/bin`. If you type the command

```
ls -l /usr/local/bin
```

you should see the following files (among others already installed there):

```
--x-x-x  1 root   root   133305 Jan 10 16:52 rarchie*
--x-x-x  1 root   root    90458 Jan 10 16:52 rfinger*
--x-x-x  1 root   root   156086 Jan 10 16:52 rftp*
--x-x-x  1 root   root    90686 Jan 10 16:52 rping*
--x-x-x  1 root   root   161379 Jan 10 16:52 rtelnet*
--x-x-x  1 root   root    92079 Jan 10 16:52 rtraceroute*
-rwxr-xr-x  1 root   root     1212 Jan 10 16:52 runsocks*
--x-x-x  1 root   root    90473 Jan 10 16:52 rwhois*
-rwxr-xr-x  1 root   root   118604 Jan 10 16:52 socks5*
-rwxr-xr-x  1 root   root      670 Jan 10 16:52 stopsocks*
```

In addition, you'll have two versions of the SOCKS library in directory `/usr/local/lib` — `libsocks5.a` and `libsocks5_sh.so`.

Finally, installation copies the appropriate manual pages into the hierarchy under directory `/usr/local/man`.

Now that SOCKS is compiled and installed, you have to perform two levels of configuration: configuration of the SOCKS server and configuration of the SOCKS clients. We discuss each in turn.

Configuring a SOCKS Server

As we mentioned earlier, the gateway machine on your intranet must run a SOCKS daemon server. This section describes how to configure and invoke this server.

After you configure and build the software, three things remain for you to do to run a SOCKS server:

◆ Make sure that the name `socks` appears in file `/etc/services`.

◆ Prepare configuration file `/etc/socks5.conf`, so that the server knows which parameters to use when it starts up.

◆ Make sure that file `/etc/rc.d/rc.local` contains instructions to invoke and run the daemon.

We discuss each in turn.

MODIFYING /ETC/SERVICES The entries in `/etc/services` look like this:

```
socks           1080/tcp
socks           1080/udp
```

These entries can appear anywhere in the file, although the custom is to order the entries by port number, to make an entry easy to find.

PREPARE /etc/socks5.conf

Now that you have modified `/etc/services`, you must prepare the configuration file for the SOCKS server. This file, named `socks5.conf`, resides in directory `/etc`. In this section, we show you how to set up a simple configuration file for what is called a *dual-homed server*. This is a fancy term for saying that the server has two network interfaces: in your case, an Ethernet interface to your local intranet, and either a PPP interface to speak to the Internet via an ISP or an Ethernet connection to connect to an external network (that, presumably, leads eventually to the Internet).

When you installed SOCKS on your gateway system, the installation script wrote a copy of `socks5.conf` into directory `/etc`. You must now modify this file to suit your preferences.

In this example, we want to configure the SOCKS server to perform two tasks:

◆ Permit hosts in our intranet (`192.168.1.0`) to access hosts outside our intranet.

◆ Permit clients that are outside our intranet to access hosts within our intranet only through the `ssh` secure shell service.

To do these tasks, we use the SOCKS instructions `permit` and `deny`. Both use the same format:

```
[permit|deny] auth cmd src-host dest-host src-port dest-port [user-
  list]
```

Several ways are available with which you can specify the hosts that you want the SOCKS server to recognize. In most cases, you'll want to stick to network addresses that are specified as follows:

```
ip.address/[n|subnet mask]
```

Use n if you are using the default subnet mask for your network class, and use subnet mask if you are not.

Here is a typical socks5 configuration for the gateway at myexample.com:

```
# File: /etc/socks5.conf—A socks5 config file for a dual homed
  server
#
#                     Src              Dst              Src  Dst
#Action Auth   Cmd    addr             addr             Port Port
permit  -      -      192.168.1.0/n    -                -    -
permit  -      -      -                192.168.1.0/n    -    22
deny    -      -      -                -                -    -
# End of file: /etc/socks5.conf
```

This example has two permit instructions and one deny instruction:

◆ The first permit instruction tells the SOCKS server to let any host on network 192.168.1.0 access any destination host or port. (A hyphen, -, means *any*).

◆ The second permit instruction tells the SOCKS server to let any host that is outside our intranet (network 192.168.1.0) access any host that is within our intranet, but limit connections to port 22, which is the well-known port for the ssh secure shell. (For more information on ssh, see Chapter 10.)

◆ The deny instruction turns off all connections except those explicitly allowed by the two permit instructions.

You can place any number of configuration instructions into file /etc/sock5.conf. For details, see the manual page for socks5.

MODIFY /etc/rc.d/rc.local

Now that you have set up the configuration file for SOCKS, the last task is to add some commands to file /etc/rc.d/rc.local. These commands, which follow, start the SOCKS daemon when you boot Linux on the gateway machine:

```
if [ -x /usr/local/bin/socks5 && -f /etc/socks5.conf ]
then
        echo "Turning on the SOCKS server ..."
        socks5 -p -n 10 && echo -n ' socks5'
fi
```

These instructions first check that files /usr/local/bin/socks5 and /etc/socks5.conf exist, and then invoke the SOCKS server.

After you add these instructions to /etc/rc.d/rc.local, reboot your machine. After you reboot your machine and log in, type the command

```
ps -ax
```

to see which daemons are running on your machine. You should see several entries for socks5.

Configuring SOCKS Clients

Now that you have configured and turned on the SOCKS server, you must config- ure the SOCKS clients. Note that this is not done on the SOCKS server, but instead occurs on a Linux machine on your internal network that must use the SOCKS server to reach the Internet. A SOCKS client is like an ordinary networking client, but it has been modified to work through the SOCKS server rather than directly over the Internet.

To run a SOCKS-ified client, you must perform two tasks:

◆ Configure the SOCKS library on each ordinary host, to use SOCKS in the way that you prefer.

◆ Modify your networking applications so that they work through SOCKS rather than directly over the Internet.

We discuss each task in turn.

CONFIGURING THE SOCKS LIBRARY

Now that the SOCKS server is up and running on your intranet's gateway machine, you must perform one more configuration task: write a configuration file that the SOCKS library reads to learn how you want SOCKS-ified applications to behave. By default, this configuration file is /etc/libsocks5.conf (although you can change this default when you compile SOCKS on your system).

By embedding SOCKS options in this file, you can tell the SOCKS client library whether it should connect directly or through a SOCKS server, what kind of SOCKS server to use, and the port on the server through which it should connect.

Each entry in /etc/libsocks5.conf has the following syntax:

```
proxy cmd dest-host dest-port [userlist [proxylist]]
```

wherein the individual parts of this syntax mean the following:

- ◆ proxy identifies the type of proxy server. Valid values include socks5, which indicates a SOCKS server, version 5, and noproxy, which indicates that a connection should be made directly rather than through a SOCKS server.

- ◆ cmd names the command that this entry covers, if any. The recognized commands include b (for bind), c (for connect), p (for ping), t (for traceroute), and - (for any command).

- ◆ dest-host identifies the host to which the commands affected by this instruction will be connecting. dest-host either is a hyphen, -, which matches all hosts, or consists of the host's IP address, followed by one of the following suffixes:

  - ▪ /n — Network match: match all hosts on the network identified by ip-address.

  - ▪ /s — Subnetwork match: mask the host portion of ip-address, and leave the subnetwork and network portion.

- ◆ /h — Host match: match this host alone.

- ◆ dest-port gives the port on dest-host affected by this instruction. Ports can be identified by number, by a range of numbers, or by service name; a hyphen, -, indicates all ports.

- ◆ userlist names one or more users who are explicitly covered by this instruction.

- ◆ proxylist names the host or hosts through whose SOCKS server the SOCKS-ified clients will connect to the outside world. If no host is identified, the SOCKS library uses the host:port set in environmental variable SOCKS5_SERVER.

EXAMPLE CONFIGURATION FILE A SOCKS configuration can be quite complicated. However, basic configuration is simple. Consider the following example:

```
# Proxy cmd    dest-host      dest-port       userlist
  proxylist
noproxy -      192.168.1.0/n  -
socks5  -      -              -
```

This example has two instructions:

◆ The instruction `noproxy` tells the SOCKS library that all connections to any host on network `192.168.1.0` should be made directly rather than through the SOCKS server. Recall that `192.168.1.0` is the address that we gave to our local intranet; therefore, this instruction tells the SOCKS library not to use proxying when connecting to any machine on the local intranet. The hyphens indicate that this instruction affects any command connecting to any port.

◆ The instruction `socks5` tells the SOCKS library that any connection by any command, to any port, on any host (other than those on network `192.168.1.0`) should go through the SOCKS server. The SOCKS server's host and port are not identified explicitly; rather, the value set in environmental variable `SOCKS5_SERVER` is used, and if that variable is not set, the default value compiled into the SOCKS library is used.

Thus, the two instructions tell SOCKS to use proxying when clients connect to hosts outside the local intranet, and not to use proxying when connecting to hosts on the local intranet – a simple and effective configuration.

INSTALLING SOCKS-IFIED APPLICATIONS

The SOCKS package comes with numerous common networking utilities that have been modified to use SOCKS. Each has had an `r` prefixed onto its name, to indicate that it has been SOCKS-ified; for example, `rarchie` is the SOCKS-ified version of `archie`, `rtelnet` is the SOCKS-ified version of `telnet`, and so on.

To use the SOCKS-ified versions of these clients instead of the usual, non-SOCKS-ified versions, do the following:

1. Copy each application into directory `/usr/local/bin`.

2. Change the name of each application to match the name of the utility that it is superseding: for example, rename `/usr/local/bin/rtelnet` to `/usr/local/bin/telnet`.

3. Edit file `/etc/profile`, and change the definition of the environmental variable `PATH` so that directory `/usr/local/bin` appears first. This ensures that users execute `/usr/local/bin/telnet` (the SOCKS-ified version) rather than `/bin/telnet` (the non-SOCKS-ified version).

4. Finally, rename the original utility, so that it cannot be invoked accidentally.

For example, to use the SOCKS-ified version of `telnet`:

```
mv $(which telnet) $(which telnet).orig
cd /usr/local/bin
mv rtelnet telnet
```

After you do this, the `telnet` command you invoke should be the SOCKS-ified one.

SOCKS-IFYING APPLICATIONS

As we mentioned earlier, the SOCKS package includes numerous standard applications that have been modified to use the SOCKS client library. If, however, you want to run under SOCKS an application that is not included as part of the SOCKS package, you can use script `runsocks`. Script `runsocks` dynamically relinks an application to use the SOCKS library.

To put this method into standard practice, do the following:

1. Move the original command, to get it out of the way:

```
mv $(which command) $(which command).orig
```

where `command` names the command you want to run under `runsocks`.

2. Use a text editor to write a brief shell script that uses `runsocks` to call the original command:

```
#!/bin/sh
exec /usr/local/bin/runsocks command.orig $*
```

This concludes our brief introduction to SOCKS. For more information on this most useful package, see the references at the end of this chapter.

This also concludes our discussion of how to let the systems on your intranet directly access the outside world. You should be able to choose the method that best suits your needs and preferences.

We now move on to the final topic in our discussion of coupling your intranet with the outside world: setting up your own domain-name service.

SOCKS AND WINDOWS 95

SOCKS libraries are also available with Windows 95. You need to download the `sockscap` package from the SOCKS Web site, previously listed, and follow the instructions there for SOCKS-ifying clients.

If the only application that you want to SOCKS-ify is Netscape, you do not need the `sockscap` package, because SOCKS has support built in. The menu path is as follows: Edit → Preferences → Advanced → Proxies → Manual proxy → socks = socks.myexample.com:1080.

◆ Edit

◆ Preferences

◆ Advanced

- ◆ Proxies
- ◆ Manual proxy
- ◆ socks = socks.myexample.com:1080

For a fuller description of interfacing Linux and Windows 95, see Chapter 9.

Domain Name Service

People are better at remembering names than numbers. Thus, you need to establish a system with which humans can translate the names of each machine in your intranet into its IP address – and vice versa.

Much of the work of building and maintaining an intranet involves maintaining this system of recording and distributing your machines' names and IP addresses. In this section, we discuss the methods by which you can maintain such a system.

Hosts File versus DNS

In the early days of the Internet, name service consisted of a master `hosts` file that named every host on the Internet. Occasionally, each host used `ftp` to download this file. Clearly, this method is inadequate now: the Internet is simply too large and changes too rapidly.

As the Internet grew, this method gave way to DNS, which distributes the work to the owners of the different domains. As we described in Chapter 1, DNS divides the name space into *zones*. The work of recording and distributing information about the hosts within a zone can be delegated to servers distributed throughout the network. To convert a name to an address, you simply send a query to the correct server – or rather, to one of the correct servers. The server sends you the answer, if it knows it, or forwards the query to a better-informed server, if it knows of one. In either case, you eventually end up with a definitive answer: either the IP address that you seek, or an answer indicating the name cannot be translated into an IP address.

DNS and hand distribution of a `hosts` file differ principally in their scope and how they distribute responsibility.

The method of using file `/etc/hosts` is limited in scope: it can comfortably handle only a few systems. If the file does not contain a host's address, no higher authority exists that a host can consult to find the address. Also, this method assumes that the network's administrator (or the administrators of the individual hosts) are responsible for maintaining the completeness and the accuracy of the information in the file.

DNS is broader in scope: in theory, a well-configured DNS system should encompass all systems on your intranet, and give access to information about every system on the Internet. A well-configured DNS system also places responsibility for maintaining addressing information solely on the shoulders of the intranet's DNS server, instead of giving each host on the intranet responsibility for maintaining its own addressing information.

As a rule of thumb, if you have a small, static intranet, then distributing a hosts file should be adequate for your purposes. If, however, you have an intranet of more than five hosts, or if the hosts on your intranet change their configuration – in particular, if any of your intranet's hosts are laptop machines that may be receiving IP addresses dynamically – then you should at least consider setting up DNS.

We introduce the file /etc/hosts in Chapter 6, so we do not discuss it here. In the rest of this section, we discuss the details of setting up and running domain-name service. We start with the basics of DNS, and then progress to setting up an example system.

How DNS Works

We describe in Chapter 1 how DNS works internally. The following discussion reviews what we discussed in Chapter 1, but reorganizes it somewhat to emphasize what you must know to configure DNS correctly.

THE DOMAIN-NAME SPACE

The Internet organizes its domain-name space into a tree. The root domain of the domain-name space is the '.' domain.

Domain names resemble the UNIX/Linux file system: both are tree structures, and both are built from a single root entity. A couple of differences exist, however. A file's full path name is read from left to right, while an Internet domain name is read from right to left. A file's name uses the backslash, /, as its separator and to name its root directory, whereas an Internet domain name uses a dot . for the same purpose. However, if you think of a domain name as being analogous to a file name, you will not be too far off the mark.

DOMAINS AND SUBDOMAINS   Domains like com, net, and de are subdomains of the root domain. Because these are *top-level* domains, we usually don't bother adding to these domain's names the trailing dot of the root domain (for example, com.). However, we sometimes talk about *fully qualified domain names*, which is simply a fancy way of referring to the full name of a domain, including the dot that identifies the root domain (for example, com. is the fully qualified version of the com domain). This is important because often you must use fully qualified domain names as you set up DNS.

In the domain-name system, the unit of space is called a *zone*. Each zone encompasses all the names within a tree of the domain-name space. For example, the zone of domain com. encompasses all names that end in .com, while the zone of domain whitehouse.gov. encompasses all domain names that end in whitehouse.gov — that is, all hosts that comprise the domain whitehouse. Each zone is responsible for maintaining information about itself and the hosts that comprise it.

The zones that are children of a particular zone can delegate their authority to another zone's server. In the case of the Internet, the zones com, net, and edu, which are children of the root domain, are delegated to the server maintained by the InterNIC. By custom, children of these zones are delegated to corporations and individuals. For example, control of the zones ibm.com and digital.com are delegated to IBM and Digital Equipment Corporation, respectively. Our fictitious domain myexample.com is also a zone and it could be delegated to someone. If myexample.com were delegated to you, it would be your responsibility to ensure that a server is available for names within myexample.com. If you were directly connected to the Internet, this would mean setting up three zones. We'll discuss what these three zones are a little later in this chapter.

VARIETIES OF SERVERS

The two varieties of domain-name servers are the following:

◆ *The primary name server* holds the definitive database that translates host names into IP addresses. Each zone must have exactly one primary name server.

◆ *Secondary name servers* periodically copy the primary server's database. Secondary servers back up and assist the primary server: they reduce the load on the primary server, and provide name service when the primary server is down or otherwise not available.

Domain-name servers also have attributes. The most common attribute is *forwarding*, which refers to the server's practice of sending to a better-connected server all the requests that it cannot answer itself.

If your organization is small and you have only one machine directly connected to the Internet, you can run that machine as a name server and forward all name-translation queries to another server.

ANSWERING QUERIES

Domain-name servers fulfill *translation request queries* (or *queries*, for short).

The software that generates queries is called the *resolver library*. This library is linked into every client and server that performs TCP/IP networking, regardless of the operating system it is running under – Linux, Free BSD, Windows, and so forth.

The basic function of the resolver is to accept the name of a host and return its IP address. To do this, the resolver library generates a DNS query and sends it to a DNS server. Depending on how the name is structured and how the server is configured, the resolver will return either an answer to the query, the address of a server that is better able to answer the query, or the answer it received from a recursive request to another server that it thinks is better able to answer the query.

If an answer could be found, that answer is either authoritative or nonauthoritative:

◆ An answer that comes from a domain-name server's zone database is *authoritative*. An authoritative answer can come only from a primary or secondary domain-name server for that domain's zone.

◆ Domain-name servers store in a cache the answers to all queries executed within a given period of time – typically within the last few hours or days. It does this so that it does not have to retrieve the same information from the same server again and again. When a domain-name server retrieves an answer from its cache rather than obtaining the answer from a zone's primary or secondary domain-name server, that answer is *nonauthoritative*. An answer is labeled *nonauthoritative* to warn the user that the name may have changed since the server cached it.

STRUCTURING DNS ON YOUR INTRANET

If you decide to use DNS on your intranet, you must set up one primary name server. If your network is large or has many users, you should also create one or more secondary name servers. The secondary servers will provide coverage in case you need to take down the primary server – for example, to do maintenance.

We recommend that you set up your primary domain-name server on your intranet's host that is principally responsible for providing networking services to the other hosts. In myexample.com, this host is thor, so we will set up the primary DNS server on it.

We also recommend that you set up a secondary domain-name server on your intranet's gateway machine. Because this machine communicates directly with the Internet, its domain-name server will build up a large cache of names and IP addresses, and therefore be able to respond quickly to requests to resolve off-site zones, without having to continually forward queries to domain-name servers on the Internet. In myexample.com, the gateway host is heimdall, so we will set up a secondary domain-name server on it.

Table 8-1 shows the domain-name servers that we will set up for our example network, myexample.com.

TABLE 8-1 **DNS SERVERS FOR** myexample.com

Name	IP Address	Type of Host	Type of Server
thor	192.168.1.1	Ordinary	Primary
odin	192.168.1.2	Ordinary	None
baldur	192.168.1.3	Ordinary	None
heimdall	192.168.1.100	Gateway	Secondary
loki	192.168.1.101	PPP Server	None

IMPLEMENTATION OF DNS

Domain-name service under Linux is implemented in the form of a package called bind (Berkeley Internet Name Daemon). This package consists of the name-server daemon named, and a set of utilities for debugging problems with domain-name service.

Currently, two versions of this daemon are in circulation: version 4.9.x and version 8.x.x. In this section, we describe version 4.9.x, which is the older version.

CONFIGURING NAMED   The name-server daemon named performs the work of domain-name service: it receives a query, and either returns the information requested, or forwards the query to a domain-name server that is better equipped to answer that query and then returns the reply to the requester.

To configure named, you must create or modify the following files:

◆ /etc/named.boot, whose instructions perform basic configuration of the server.

◆ A set of db files, which describe the zone and its hosts. named reads these files to answer queries.

Much of the rest of this section describes how to set up these configuration files.

THE NEXT STEP

This concludes our brief review of how DNS works. In the rest of this section, we describe how to do the following:

◆ Configure a primary domain-name server.

◆ Configure a secondary domain-name server.

◆ Configure hosts to use the newly created domain-name service.

◆ Turn on DNS.

◆ Use debugging tools to check and debug the configuration of your domain-name service.

We discuss each topic in turn.

Configuring the Primary Server

We first discuss how to configure the primary domain-name server for your intranet.

As we previously mentioned, configuring a primary domain-name server involves editing the following configuration files:

◆ `named.boot` – This file performs basic configuration of `named`.

◆ db files – These files hold the information about the domain that is propagated by the primary server.

We discuss each in turn.

CONFIGURING /ETC/NAMED.BOOT

Configuration file `/etc/named.boot` holds the directives that set the basic configuration of the domain-name server `named`.

This file can be quite complicated, so we walk you through an example of how to configure this file. The following code gives the configuration file for the primary domain server for `myexample.com`, which runs on host `thor` (`192.168.1.1`):

```
;-----------------------------------------------
;         /etc/named.boot
;         Master DNS configuration file of primary DNS server for
;         myexample.com., running on thor.myexample.com
;
directory          /etc/namedb
;-----------------------------------------------
;         This daemon provides primary nameservice for myexample.com
;         and all the reverse domains that it encompasses.
;
primary       myexample.com.                    db.myexample.com
primary       1.168.192.in-addr.arpa.           db.192.168.100
;-----------------------------------------------
;         Every instance of named must provide reverse information
;         for the localhost address
;
primary       0.0.127.in-addr.arpa              db.127.0.0
;-----------------------------------------------
;         You must provide the mapping of names to addresses for
;         the root servers so the root servers can provide us with hints
```

```
;          for other domains. Our situation is also somewhat special as
;          our primary server will be forwarding only and this server
;          will cache outside requests as well as provide secondary
;          service for our domain.
cache            .                              db.cache
;─────────────────────────────────────────────────────────
;          For security, let only DNS servers on the intranet map the
;          network. Letting crackers ``map'' your network through DNS
;          is a bad idea:
xfernets         192.168.1.0
;─────────────────────────────────────────────────────────
;          Forwards unresolvable requests to secondary server running
;          on 192.168.1.100 (that is, heimdall, the gateway machine):
forwarders       192.168.1.100
; End of file (/etc/named.boot)
```

To begin, a semicolon marks the beginning of a comment. The header comment in this file tells us what this file contains – in this instance, the DNS configuration for the primary domain-name server for domain myexample.com.

This file contains four types of directives:

◆ directory – Names the directory in which named stores its files. The directory should be on a file system that has lots of space; this is particularly true of the secondary server that runs on the gateway machine, because it will cache lots of information that it downloads from the Internet.

◆ primary – States that this server is the primary server for a given domain, and names the database file that holds the authoritative information for this domain.

◆ xfernets – Identifies the hosts to which the primary server can download its database: in this example, any of the hosts on our example intranet 192.168.1.0. This directive is designed to prevent crackers from learning about the structure of your intranet simply by downloading your primary server's database.

◆ forwarders – Identifies the host or hosts to whose domain-name server the primary server should forward queries that it cannot resolve on its own. In this example, the primary server will forward queries to the secondary server that runs on host 192.168.1.101 (heimdall), which is our intranet's gateway.

The following subsections discuss each directive in more detail.

PRIMARY DIRECTIVE   As the preceding list indicates, the directive primary names a domain for which this instance of named is the primary domain-name server.

File `named.boot` for our primary domain-name server contains three instances of this directive. The directive

```
primary          myexample.com.          db.myexample.com
```

says that this server is the primary server for domain `myexample.com.` (note the fully qualified name), and that the information about `myexample.com.` resides in file `db.myexample.com.`

Likewise, the directives

```
primary          1.168.192.in-addr.arpa. db.192.168.1
primary          0.0.127.in-addr.arpa.   db.127.0.0
```

do the same for domains `1.168.192.in-addr.arpa` and `0.0.127.in-addr.arpa`. Now, you probably are asking yourself where these strange zones came from. These records are for *reverse domain-name lookups* — translating a numeric IP address into its corresponding name. This is the basis for the authentication scheme of the `r*` commands, such as `rlogin` (which we introduced in Chapter 7). Also, some FTP servers perform a reverse domain-name lookup to determine whether they will grant you service. Address `1.168.192.in-addr.arpa.` refers to the local intranet, and `0.0.127.in-addr.arpa.` refers to the loopback device on the local host. We discuss the `in-addr.arpa.` zone in more detail later in the chapter.

CACHE DIRECTIVE   Directive `cache` preloads the name server's database with answers to certain queries. This is used almost exclusively to preload the domain-name server with the names and addresses of the domain-name servers for the root domain, so that our zone's primary domain-name server can find names in other domains besides our own.

This directive has the following syntax:

```
cache domain file-name
```

`zone` names the zone whose information is cached. This almost always is '.', for the present zone.

`file-name` names the file that identifies the domain-name servers for the Internet's root domain.

For example, the `cache` directive in our example `named.boot`

```
cache            .                          db.cache
```

states that the directive applies to the present zone, and that the information is stored in file `db.cache`.

We discuss writing hints in some detail later in the chapter, when we introduce named's db files.

XFERNETS DIRECTIVE   Directive xfernets restricts the dissemination of information about your zone. A name server's network address must be listed in the xfernets directive before that name server will be allowed to download the full set of information about your domain.

If you do not use this directive, your domain-name server will download zone information to anyone who asks. This is important, because you don't want crackers to get a map of your intranet from your DNS servers with one command.

xfernets has the following syntax:

```
xfernets ip-network-address [...]
```

where ip-network-address gives the IP address of a network to which you will download zone information. You can name an indefinite number of networks with this directive.

FORWARDERS DIRECTIVE   Finally, directive forwarders names the host to which the domain-name server forwards queries that it cannot resolve itself.

This directive takes the following syntax:

```
forwarders ip-address
```

For example, directive

```
forwarders        192.168.1.100
```

tells the primary domain-name server to forward queries that it cannot resolve to the DNS server on host 192.168.1.100, which is our intranet's gateway host. This server will retrieve the answer from its cache or interrogate another domain-name server on the Internet, and then return the answer.

The directives in file named.boot appear complicated, but they really are quite straightforward – once you grasp what each is trying to do.

Now we discuss the database files that actually describe our domain.

db FILES

The information about a zone is stored in a set of db files. These files are stored in the directory named by named.boot's directive directory.

DB RECORDS   Each db file consists of records. Each record either helps to configure how the domain-name server behaves, or holds information that the domain-name server will use to answer queries.

Each record within a db file has the following format:

```
object-name [time-to-live] class record-type [parameters]
```

♦ `object-name` names the entity that this record describes. It can be a service, a host name, or an IP address. In many cases, this field can be skipped.

♦ `time-to-live` indicates how long the information in this record will be applicable. Again, this field often can be skipped.

♦ `class` gives the class of hosts to which this record applies. The only class currently implemented is `IN`, which stands for Internet.

♦ `record-type` gives the type of record this is.

♦ `parameters` gives the parameters – the data – required by this type of record. Some types of records do not require any parameters.

These records may be puzzling to you at first glance; therefore, we look in some detail at each type of record.

SUITE OF DB FILES   When you set up a primary domain-name server, you must create four `db` files, as follows:

1. A master lookup file for the zone. This file maps the zone's host names to their corresponding IP addresses.

2. A master reverse-lookup file for the zone. This file maps the zone's IP addresses to their corresponding host names.

3. A lookup file for the local host.

4. A lookup file for accessing information about the root domain.

The domain-name server knows which files contain this information, because they are named by directives in file `named.boot`:

♦ The files that hold the master lookup file for the zone, the master reverse-lookup file for the zone, and the lookup file for the local host are named by `primary` directives. In the version of `named.boot` that we prepared for our example intranet, these directives read:

```
primary        myexample.com.          db.myexample.com
primary        1.168.192.in-addr.arpa. db.192.168.1
primary        0.0.127.in-addr.arpa.   db.127.0.0
```

◆ These directives state that file db.myexample.com is the master lookup file for the zone myexample.com., that file db.192.168.1 is the master reverse-lookup file for zone 1.168.192.in-addr.arpa., and that file db.127.0.0 is the lookup file for zone 0.0.127.in-addr.arpa. (which always describes the local host).

◆ The lookup file for accessing information about the root zone is named by the cache directive. In our example version of file named.conf, the cache directive reads as follows:

```
cache              .                                db.cache
```

◆ This directive states that file db.cache is the lookup file for accessing information about the root domain.

As with file named.boot, a db file and its instructions can be quite complicated — or at least appear to be at first glance. Therefore, we discuss each of these four db files in turn, and discuss the records that each contains.

MASTER LOOKUP FILE   The master lookup file for a zone is the most important of the db files distributed by the primary domain-name server. named loads its name-to-address conversion database directly from this file.

The following code provides the syntax for db.myexample.com, which is the master database file for domain myexample.com:

```
;
;       Master domain name file for myexample.com
;
@               IN SOA thor.myexample.com. heimdall.myexample.com. (
                980102000         ; Serial number YYMMDD###
                43200             ; Refresh frequency: twice per day
                3600              ; Retry rate: refresh each hour
                172800            ; Time to expire: two days
                86400)            ; Time to wait: one day
;
;       Nameservers in our domain
;
                IN NS             thor.myexample.com.
                IN NS             heimdall.myexample.com.
;
;       Mail servers in our domain
;
                IN MX 10          heimdall.myexample.com.
;
; thor is the main server on the network. It provides pop, www, news,
; and DNS for the network.
;
thor            IN A              192.168.1.1
```

```
pop                IN CNAME        thor.myexample.com.
www                IN CNAME        thor.myexample.com.
nntp               IN CNAME        thor.myexample.com.
news               IN CNAME        thor.myexample.com.
ns1                IN CNAME        thor.myexample.com.
;
; heimdall is the gateway to other networks.
;
heimdall           IN A            192.168.1.100
gw                 IN CNAME        heimdall.mydomain.com.
smtp               IN CNAME        heimdall.mydomain.com.
socks              IN CNAME        heimdall.mydomain.com.
www-proxy          IN CNAME        heimdall.mydomain.com.
ns2                IN CNAME        heimdall.mydomain.com.
;
; "A" records for other ordinary hosts in myexample.com. None
; provides services to other hosts.
;
odin               IN A            192.168.1.2
baldur             IN A            192.168.1.3
loki               IN A            192.168.1.101
;
; "A" record for local host's loopback device
;
localhost          IN A            127.0.0.1
```

db.myexample.com contains records that describe domain myexample.com.

This may seem to be a very large file for such a small intranet; after all, myexample.com has only five hosts. However, db.myexample.com must hold a record that describes each service provided by each host, and the hosts in this domain provide a large number of services: one host provides FTP, mail, news, company-wide Web, and name services; a second host is a gateway to the Internet that provides proxying and outbound mail services; and the third host is a terminal server into which outside sales staff can dial.

db.myexample.com contains five types of records:

- ◆ SOA — Source of authority
- ◆ NS — Name server
- ◆ MX — Mail exchanger
- ◆ A — Address
- ◆ CNAME — Canonical name or alias

We look at each in turn.

SOA record

An SOA (source of authority) record sets the source of authority for a zone in the Internet name space. An SOA record must be the first record in any zone-database file. This record specifies several parameters about the zone.

Let's look at the SOA record given in `db.myexample.com`:

```
@                       IN SOA thor.myexample.com. odin.myexample.com. (
                        980102000      ; Serial number YYMMDD###
                        43200          ; Refresh frequency: twice per day
                        3600           ; Retry rate: refresh each hour
                        172800         ; Expire in two days without refresh
                        86400)         ; Default time to live
```

This record says that the source of authority for `myexample.com.` (note trailing '.') is the machine `thor.myexample.com`.

The SOA record is special in two ways:

◆ First, you can use @ at the beginning of the line. This special character copies the name of the zone from file `named.boot`.

◆ Second, you can extend this record beyond one line, by enclosing it in parentheses.

The parameters specified in the SOA record control the following:

◆ *Serial number* – Secondary name servers use this value to check whether to reload a zone from a primary server. If this serial number differs from the serial number of the file that a secondary server has in its cache, the secondary server reloads the zone from the primary server. For this reason, changing the serial number every time you change the zone file on the primary server is vital: this is the only way for the secondary servers to know that the zone's configuration has changed.

◆ *Refresh frequency* – The number of seconds that a secondary server must wait before it again looks at the primary server to see whether the zone file has changed. In this example, refresh is 43,200 seconds (12 hours).

◆ *Retry period for refreshes* – If a refresh fails, for whatever reason (for example, the primary domain-name server was down), this parameter sets the time that the secondary server must wait before it again attempts to refresh its copy of the zone-definition file. In this example, secondary servers must wait 3,600 seconds (one hour) before again attempting a refresh.

◆ *Time to expire* – How long to keep a set of records on hand if they cannot be refreshed. This time is given in seconds. If no successful refresh happens within this time (in seconds), all of that zone's data is thrown away. In this example, records expire in 172,800 seconds (48 hours).

◆ *Time to wait* – How long to wait before dropping a record if a primary server cannot be contacted. This applies to records that do not have an explicit time-to-live field. This parameter is not intended so much for secondary servers as it is for outside servers that access this information. In this example, a server must wait 86,400 seconds (24 hours).

NS record

The NS record gives the *authoritative name server* for a domain, which must be primary or secondary for the domain, and must load the domain information during the boot process rather than building it up as a cache.

Omitting the name of the domain here and instead specifying NS records right after the SOA records is a matter of style. You should list all the name servers for your zone in NS records after the SOA record.

The following gives the NS records for myexample.com:

```
        IN NS        thor.myexample.com.
        IN NS        heimdall.myexample.com.
```

These directives name two domain-name servers in our local zone: one running on thor (the primary domain-name server, which we are now configuring), and one on heimdall (the secondary domain-name server, whose configuration we describe later in the chapter). Note that we use the fully qualified domain name for each host.

MX record

An MX record names a *mail exchanger*, which supports the mail system in case the primary machine specified by a mail address, myexample.com, cannot be contacted – for example, because it is down or not connected to the Internet.

File db.myexample.com has one MX record:

```
        IN MX 10        heimdall.myexample.com.
```

This states say that mail for myexample.com. should be sent to heimdall.

The number that precedes each address is a *precedence*. When a db file has more than one MX directive, the mailer contacts the hosts these directives name in the order of their precedence, from lowest precedence to highest.

A record

An A record translates a host's name into its IP address. For example,

```
thor            IN A            192.168.1.2
```

sets the IP addresses for host thor. Because we did not fully qualify the domain name by ending it with a period, named will append onto thor the name of the domain, as set by the SOA record.

db.myexample.com contains one A record for each host in domain myexample.com, including the loopback device used by each host.

CNAME record

A CNAME record gives a nickname to a host. These records give you some flexibility in setting up your network and moving things around to accommodate future growth.

File db.myexample.com has numerous CNAME records. The following example declares that www is a nickname for thor.myexample.com, because our Apache Web server runs on this host:

```
www             IN CNAME        thor.myexample.com.
```

Hosts on our intranet can address their Web requests to server www and they will be resolved correctly. If, in the future, we decide to shift our Web server to another machine, we simply change this CNAME definition, and requests to www continue to be resolved correctly – the users on our intranet will not know that they're talking to a different host, nor should they care.

Adapting the master lookup file

When you're setting up DNS on your intranet, you should adapt this example file to suit your intranet's needs and structure:

1. Rename the file to reflect the domain name of your intranet.

2. Modify the SOA record to name the hosts that provide domain-name service on your intranet. Set the serial number to a reasonable value that you can track – the date and time makes a good serial number. The time values given in our example are useful defaults, although you may want to change them to suit your particular needs.

3. Modify the NS records to name the name servers in your intranet.

4. Change the MX records to name the hosts that provide mail service on your intranet.

5. Change the A records to name the hosts on your intranet and give their IP addresses.

6. Finally, change the CNAME records to give the appropriate nicknames to the hosts on your intranet. You are not required to give any CNAME records, but as we previously mentioned, nicknames for hosts are a real convenience to the users on your intranet.

This concludes our discussion of our master lookup file for zone db.myexample. com. Next, we explore the master reverse-lookup file for this domain.

Master reverse-lookup file

The master reverse-lookup file for a zone holds the information needed to do reverse lookups – that is, to translate the IP addresses in a zone back into the names of the hosts.

File db.192.168.1 gives reverse-name lookups for the hosts in myexample. com. This zone's primary domain-name server reads this database file when a query gives an IP address and requests the name of a host that corresponds to this address.

You may be asking yourself, if DNS is designed to look up names through zones, how does it look up a number? After all, an IP address has no zone information in it.

To solve this problem, the designers of bind created a zone that exists solely to map IP addresses into names – called the in-addr.arpa. zone. Then, they created a method of mapping an IP address into a name in the in-addr.arpa space, and a record for converting names in the in-addr.arpa space into names in the regular domain space (com, org, net, edu, and so forth).

To convert an IP address into a name in the in-addr.arpa space, the domain-name server reverses the numbers, appends a dot, ., and inserts the string in-addr.arpa.. Why reverse the numbers? An IP address becomes more specific as you read from left to right, but a name becomes more specific as you read from right to left. For example, IP address 192.168.1.4 maps to name 4.1.168.192.in-addr.arpa. in the in-addr.arpa space.

A database record of type PTR (*pointer*) associates a name in one zone with a name in any other zone. Database file db.192.168.1 holds the reverse-lookup records for domain 1.168.192.in-addr.arpa, and as you would expect, it consists almost entirely of PTR records that map names in the in-addr.arpa zone to names in the local zone. Here is the syntax for database file db.192.168.1:

```
;-------------------------------------------------
;       Reverse name lookup for hosts on network 192.168.1.0 in
;       zone myexample.com
;
@       IN SOA  thor.myexample.com. heimdall.myexample.com. (
                980102000       ; Serial number YYMMDD###
                43200           ; Secondaries refresh twice per day
                3600            ; Retry failed refresh each hour
                86400           ; Expire in one day
                86400)          ; Minimum TTL
;       Nameservers for this domain
```

```
            IN NS    thor.myexample.com.
            IN NS    heimdall.myexmaple.com.
;           Hosts in this domain
1           IN PTR   thor.myexample.com.     ; Master server for the
  network
2           IN PTR   odin.myexample.com.     ; Ordinary host in this
  network
3           IN PTR   baldur.myexample.com.   ; Ordinary host in this
  network
100         IN PTR   heimdall.myexample.com. ; Gateway to the internet
101         IN PTR   loki.myexample.com.     ; PPP dial-in server
```

The SOA record in this file is the same as in db.myexample.com. The source of authority is heimdall and the name server is thor.

PTR record

As we promised, PTR records are abundant in the preceding code. We dissect one here:

```
1           IN PTR      thor.myexample.com.
```

As we noted previously, a PTR record associates a name in one zone with a name in another zone. In this example, the name in the default zone is given as 1. named uses the rules we previously described to expand this name into the host's fully qualified name in the in-addr.arpa zone — in this example, 1.1.168.192.in-addr.arpa.. The second argument in this record links name 1.1.168.192.in-addr.arpa. with the name thor.myexample.com. (both fully qualified).

Thus, this record lets named translate a reverse-lookup query for the host with IP address 192.168.1.1 into the correct host name — in this case, thor.myexample.com.

Adapting the master reverse-lookup file

When you set up domain-name service on your own intranet, you can adapt the preceding example to suit the needs of your intranet:

1. Rename this file to reflect the IP address you give to your intranet.

2. Change the NS records to name the hosts on your intranet that offer domain-name service.

3. Change the PTR records to reflect the IP addresses and names of the hosts in your intranet.

This concludes our discussion of the master reverse-lookup file. We next discuss two files that are very different in scope: one describes the lookup device on the local host (db.127.0.0), while the other (db.cache) describes the root domain.

LOOKUP FILE FOR THE LOCAL HOST   File db.127.0.0 defines the localhost device for each host in this domain:

```
; ──────────────────────────────────────────────
;       /etc/namedb/db.127.0.0
;       Name service database for the localhost address. This has to
;       be present for all files and should never change, Hence the
;       values in the SOA record.
@               IN SOA beast.myexample.com.
  postmaster.myexample.com. (
                        960101000       ; Serial number YYMMDD###
                        604800          ; Refresh once per week
                        86400           ; Retry refresh each hour
                        1209600         ; Expire in two weeks
                        1209600)        ; Minimum TTL
                IN NS   thor.myexample.com.
                IN NS   heimdall.myexample.com.
1               IN PTR  localhost.myexample.com.
; End of file: /etc/namedb/db.127.0.0
```

The file for the local host will always be named db.127.0.0, because the localhost driver always uses this IP address. This file serves all the hosts that use this machine as a name server.

Because this information almost never changes, the SOA record has very long times in it.

When you set up domain-name service for your own intranet, you can easily adapt this file to meet your needs: simply modify its NS records to give the names of the host or hosts that provide domain-name service on your intranet.

LOOKUP FILE FOR THE ROOT ZONE   Finally, file db.cache holds information — also called *hints* — about how to retrieve domain-name information about the root domain '.'.

The following gives an example of db.cache:

```
; ──────────────────────────────────────────────
;       namedb/db.cache — name server hints for the root domain.
;       Current nameservers for the root domain can be found by
;       looking at any up-to-date server on the and asking for the NS
;       records for the domain '.'. This should return at least one
;       of the root servers. If you set that server to be your server
;       under nslookup and ask it again (and it actually is one of the
;       root servers) then you repeating the query will make a list of
;       all of the root servers.
;       Nameservers for the root domain as of 01/15/98
;
.
                        99999999 IN NS          e.root-servers.net
                        99999999 IN NS          c.root-servers.net
                        99999999 IN NS          f.root-servers.net
                        99999999 IN NS          d.root-servers.net
```

```
                               99999999 IN NS      a.root-servers.net
                               99999999 IN NS      b.root-servers.net
                               99999999 IN NS      g.root-servers.net
                               99999999 IN NS      i.root-servers.net
                               99999999 IN NS      d.root-servers.net
;
;           root Name server addresses.
;
a.root-servers.net             99999999 IN A       198.41.0.4
b.root-servers.net             99999999 IN A       128.9.0.107
c.root-servers.net             99999999 IN A       192.33.4.12
d.root-servers.net             99999999 IN A       128.8.10.90
e.root-servers.net             99999999 IN A       192.203.230.10
f.root-servers.net             99999999 IN A       192.5.5.241
g.root-servers.net             99999999 IN A       192.112.36.4
h.root-servers.net             99999999 IN A       128.63.2.53
i.root-servers.net             99999999 IN A       192.36.148.17
```

In theory, you can put into db.cache directives to load hints for any zone; however, restricting your hints to the root domain is best, which is what we have done here.

In this example, the first half of the file is filled with NS records that name hosts that maintain domain-name servers – in this case, nine hosts that are defined by the NIC to service the entire Internet. Each is given a time-to-live of 99999999 – in effect, a time-to-live of infinity.

The second half of the file is filled with A records that translate the name of each host identified in the preceding code into its corresponding IP address. Again, each record is given an infinite time-to-live.

With the hints in this file, the primary server can directly interrogate the NIC's domain-name servers for information about nearly any zone on the Internet – either how to reach that zone, or at least how to reach a server that can tell us something more about that zone. Did we mention that without these hints you will not be able to load names from any zone outside of your own? This is because the hints provide a way to get to the root servers, and the root servers can get everywhere else.

This concludes our discussion of how to configure the primary server. We now discuss how to configure the secondary server.

The information in this example works for all zones on the Internet. When you set up domain-name service on your intranet, you can copy this file without modification.

Alternative Domain-Name Systems

The example given above works for all zones on the Internet – or, to be more accurate, for all of the zones managed by the InterNIC. As we noted in Chapter 1, the InterNIC does not have a monopoly on domain-name registration; at least one other group, which calls itself the AlterNIC, has set up an alternate system of top-level domains, and is soliciting Internet users to register their secondary domains with it.

If the AlterNIC gains in popularity, you may wish to support its top-level domains as well as those managed by the InterNIC. To do so, you must add the AlterNIC's domain-name servers to the table of hints in db.cache.

For information on the AlterNIC and its domain-name service, see its Web page at http://www.alternic.net.

This concludes our discussion of how to configure the primary domain-name server. Next, we discuss how to configure a secondary domain-name server.

Configuring the Secondary Server

Now that we have discussed how to configure the primary domain-name server, the next step is to configure a secondary domain-name server. This task is not nearly as complex as configuring the primary domain-name server, principally because you do not have to prepare nearly as many db files.

We first discuss how to configure file /etc/named.boot for the secondary server, and then briefly describe the db files used by the secondary server.

CONFIGURING /etc/named.boot

As a reminder, the secondary domain-name server for our example intranet, myexample.com, runs on the intranet's gateway machine, heimdall, which has IP address 192.168.1.100.

The following code gives the configuration file for our secondary domain-name server:

```
;----------------------------------------------
;          /etc/named.boot
;
;          DNS configuration file for secondary server at
;          myexample.com.
;
directory          /etc/namedb
;----------------------------------------------
;          Provide primary nameservice for myexample.com and all the
;          reverse domains that it encompasses.
;
secondary          myexample.com.                    192.168.1.1
  db.myexample.com
secondary          1.168.192.in-addr.arpa.           192.168.1.1
  db.192.168.1
;----------------------------------------------
;          Every name server must provide reverse information for the
;          localhost address.
;
primary            0.0.127.in-addr.arpa              db.127.0.0
;----------------------------------------------
;          This server provides the mapping of names to addresses for
;          the root servers so the root servers can provide us with hints
;          for other domains. Our situation is also somewhat special as
```

```
;          our primary server will be forwarding only, and this server
;          will cache outside requests as well as provide secondary
;          service for our domain.
cache                .                                    db.cache
;─────────────────────────────────────────────
;          Only transfer bulk information to our nets for security.
;          Letting crackers map your network through DNS is a bad idea.
xfernets           192.168.1.0
; End of file (/etc/named.boot)
```

Most of the directives in this file should be familiar to you from our discussion of the primary server. However, this file does contain one new directive: `secondary`. We now look at this directive in a little more detail.

SECONDARY DIRECTIVE   Directive `secondary` states that this instance of `named` is a secondary server for a given zone. This directive has the following syntax:

```
secondary zone ip-address-list backup-file
```

The keyword `secondary` indicates that this server is a secondary server.

`zone` names the zone for which this server is a secondary domain-name server.

`ip-address-list` names the hosts that this server periodically polls for information about this zone. The server polls the domain-name servers on the hosts whose addresses appear in this list, until it finds one that responds. This process is called *zone refresh*; we discuss this in detail later in the chapter.

`backup-file` names the file that holds the backup copy of zone information about `zone`.

For example, file `named.boot` for the secondary domain-name server that is running on `heimdall` has two `secondary` directives, as follows:

```
secondary        myexample.com.                     192.168.1.1
  db.myexample.com
secondary        1.168.192.in-addr.arpa.            192.168.1.1
  db.192.168.1
```

The first directive states that this server is a secondary server for zone `myexample.com.`, that it polls the domain-name server on host `192.168.1.1` for information about this zone, and that it keeps its backup information about this zone in file `db.myexample.com`.

The second directive is the `in-addr.arpa` analogue of the first: it states that this server is the secondary server for zone `1.168.192.in-addr.arpa`, that it polls the domain-name server on host `192.168.1.1` for information on this zone, and that it keeps its backup information in file `db.192.168.1`.

THE ZONE REFRESH PROCESS   When the time comes to refresh the zone, a secondary server polls the domain-name server on each host whose IP address appears in the `secondary` directive.

When the domain-name server on one of the hosts on that list responds to your secondary server's query, the secondary server compares the serial number in the polled server's SOA record with the serial number that the polling server has in its SOA record. If the serial numbers differ, the polling domain-name server replaces its file of zone information with a copy that it downloads from the polled server.

The interval between polls is controlled by the *refresh* field in the SOA record. If a poll fails, the secondary server retries the poll at the interval specified in the *retry* field. If a successful poll hasn't happened by the time specified in the *expire* field, the secondary server dumps its zone information; it cannot fulfill queries until it successfully polls another server and retrieves an up-to-date file of zone information.

In most situations, you should list only the primary server in the IP address list, to keep old data from propagating through in the caches of the secondary servers. If you decide to list secondary servers in your IP list, you should make sure that the primary is the first server consulted for zone transfers, and the secondaries serve as backups, to be polled only if the primary is down for an extended period of time.

db FILES

The `db` files that you must configure for the secondary server are considerably fewer than those maintained by the primary server: in effect, only `db.127.0.0` and `db.cache`. Both files are identical to those used by the domain's primary server.

The secondary server will also maintain a number of `db` files on its own. These hold information that is downloaded from the primary server, and from other domain-name servers around the Internet. Because the secondary domain-name server maintains these files on its own, you do not need to delve into them.

This concludes our discussion of how to configure the secondary domain-name server. Next, we describe how you can configure a host to use your newly established domain-name service.

Configuring Hosts to Use DNS

So far, we have shown you how to configure your domain-name servers. However, one important question remains to answer: how do I get my hosts to use this new service?

The answer to this question again lies in the configuration files. In this case, we need to modify two files on all hosts that we want to use DNS: `/etc/resolv.conf` and `/etc/host.conf`.

The first file to modify is `/etc/resolv.conf`. This file names the domain that this host is in, and gives a list of name servers that it can contact to resolve queries. It looks like this:

```
domain          myexample.com
search          thor.myexample.com
nameserver      192.168.1.1
nameserver      192.168.1.100
```

This file has the following three directives:

◆ domain — Sets the host's domain for name searches. Names presented for searching without a trailing dot (names that are not fully qualified) have this name appended to them automatically. For example, if you ask DNS to search for host thor, DNS translates the name to thor.myexample.com before it performs the search.

◆ search — Specifies additional domains to search. The preceding example forces the name server to look up all hosts in domain thor.myexample.com, in addition to those in the domain myexample.com.

◆ nameserver — Gives the IP address of the machine whose name server is to be used. The preceding example shows two nameserver directives: one for the machine with address 192.168.1.1 (thor, which runs the primary domain-name server), and the other for the machine with address 192.168.1.100 (heimdall, which runs our secondary domain-name server). This form is appropriate for all machines except thor and heimdall themselves: because these hosts are each running a domain-name server, they should specify the localhost interface first (that is, 127.0.0.1) and the other server second.

Finally, you need to set the order of sources from which the host looks up domain-name information. File /etc/host.conf determines the order in which sources are searched. For example:

```
order bind, hosts
multi on
```

Directive order sets the order in which this host searches sources of domain information. In the preceding example, DNS (bind) is used first; then file /etc/hosts. The act of making a name server doesn't make the /etc/hosts file go away. In fact, you can still look up names in it — the host will use DNS first, and then look up the name in /etc/hosts if DNS fails for any reason.

If you have set up DNS on your intranet, we recommend using it first, and the hosts file second. In either case, we suggest you keep as few entries in /etc/hosts as possible, to help eliminate configuration bugs.

Turning on DNS

At this point, you have configured your intranet's DNS servers, configured each host on your intranet to use your intranet's domain-name service and servers, and have configured your ordinary hosts to use DNS. The time has come to turn on the daemon `named` and test it.

The easiest way to turn on `named` is to log into a system on which you have configured a DNS server and invoke `named` from the command line:

```
/usr/sbin/named -d 2
```

This command invokes `named` with the debug option turned on, so that you can get detailed information about any errors that the daemon encounters. `named` writes its debugging output into file `/var/tmp/named.run`.

REREADING CONFIGURATION FILES

When you change one of `named`'s configuration files, you must force `named` to reread them, so that it uses the new information to reconfigure itself properly. To force `named` to reread its configuration files, type the following command:

```
named -b
```

EDIT /etc/rc.d/rc.inet2

After you have everything straight, you should edit file `/etc/rc.d/rc.inet2` on each Linux workstation on which you can configure a domain-name server, so that the workstation starts up `named` automatically whenever you reboot it.

This change is straightforward: simply insert the following instructions into `/etc/rc.d/rc.inet2`:

```
# Start the NAMED/BIND name server.
if [ -f ${NET}/named ]; then
  echo -n " named"
  ${NET}/named
fi
```

You may find that your copy of `/etc/rc.d/rc.inet2` already has this code in it, but commented out. If this is the case, simply uncomment the lines.

This concludes our discussion on how to configure and invoke domain-name service on your intranet. Next, we discuss how to use the `bind` package's tools to check and debug your domain-name service.

Checking and Debugging DNS

Now that we have discussed how to set up DNS, we will review two tools, `nslookup` and `host`, that you will use often when you try to debug your name server's setup:

◆ `nslookup` returns the addresses of hosts, and offers debugging options that enable you to watch the process as it happens.

◆ `host` is a simpler version of `nslookup`.

We discuss each in turn.

nslookup

Testing performed by using `nslookup` is, at its most basic, very simple: `nslookup` simply uses the resolver library as an application would, and then prints the results of the query in a form that a human being can read.

`nslookup` offers two modes of operation: *interactive mode*, and *noninteractive*, or *command-line, mode*. Everything you can do with `nslookup`'s command-line options, you can also do interactively, so we leave the discussion of `nslookup`'s command line to its manual page.

To invoke `nslookup` in interactive mode, simply type **nslookup** with no command-line options. `nslookup` presents its prompt `>`; in response, you can type one of `nslookup`'s interactive commands. The most commonly used commands are the following:

◆ `name` – Query and show results for domain `name`.

◆ `exit` – Exit `nslookup`.

◆ `server`, `lserver` – Change the domain-name server being interrogated.

◆ `set [parameter]` – Set `parameter`, or show the parameters that are already set.

◆ `ls` – List all the records in a given domain.

We discuss each in turn.

LOOK UP A NAME   If you type a host name at `nslookup`'s command-line prompt, `nslookup` attempts to translate that name into an IP address.

For example, if a user on system `heimdall` invoked `nslookup`, then typed `heimdall` at `nslookup`'s prompt, she would see:

```
Server:  localhost.myexample.com
Address:  127.0.0.100
```

Because `heimdall` is the local host (the host that our user is logged into), `nslookup` returns information about the local host. If, however, our user typed `heimdall.myexample.com` at `nslookup`'s prompt, she would see:

```
Name:    heimdall.myexample.com
Address:  192.168.1.100
```

If a query is taking longer than you would like, you can abort it by typing
Ctrl+C.

Please note that nslookup is stupid about its input: if it does not recognize as a
command something that you type at its command-line prompt, it assumes that
what you typed is a host name, and tries to resolve it. In other words, it treats legitimate host names and typographical errors exactly the same. For example, if our
user typed quit instead of exit, nslookup would look for a host named quit, and
then display the following:

```
Server:  localhost.myexample.com
Address:  127.0.0.1
*** localhost.myexample.com can't find quit: Non-existent
 host/domain
```

COMMANDS SERVER AND LSERVER   Commands server and lserver change the
default server that nslookup uses. You must type the command, followed by the
name of the server that you now want to make the default server.

For example, if our user on system heimdall.myexample.com typed command

```
lserver thor
```

she would see:

```
Default Server:  thor.myexample.com
Address:  192.168.1.1
```

nslookup will now use thor as its default server, instead of the localhost (in
this case, heimdall).

If you type commands server or lserver without an argument, nslookup
reverts to the default server.

The difference between server and lserver is the host that nslookup uses to
look up the address of the server to which you want to change: server uses the
current default server, whereas lserver uses the server that nslookup was initially
using when it started up. This is important if you happen to set the default server to
a machine that is not running named. Consider the following nslookup session:

```
> server baldur
Default Server:  baldur.myexample.com
Address:  192.168.1.3
> odin
Server:  baldur.myexample.com
Address:  192.168.1.3
*** baldur.myexample.com can't find odin: No response from server
> server thor
*** Can't find address for server thor: No response from server
> lserver thor
```

```
Default Server:  thor.myexample.com
Address:  192.168.1.1
```

In this example, we set the server to baldur, a host that is not running named. Because it's not running named, it cannot get the IP address of a server when we try to undo the mistake; thus, when we try to look up the IP address of host baldur, nslookup replies that it cannot find this host. When we try to use command server to get us out of this pickle, we will fail, again because nslookup could not find the host thor, to which we try to change. Command lserver gets us out of this, by reverting to the original default server – in this case, heimdall, which is running a domain-name server.

Please note that if command lserver does not get you out of a situation like this, you can always specify the host to use by IP address rather than name.

COMMAND SET   nslookup's command set changes one of the resolver's parameters.

For example, the resolver looks up A records by default. However, let's assume that you are having trouble delivering mail to inetcorp.com. In this case, the A records won't help us; instead, we need an MX record so that we can see which host is responsible for taking mail for inetcorp.com. This is handled by the MX type of record. The resolver's parameter querytype sets the type of record that the resolver retrieves; therefore, we should use command set to change this parameter from A to MX that nslookup searches:

```
> set querytype=mx
> inetcorp.com
Server:  localhost.myexample.com
Address:  127.0.0.1
Non-authoritative answer:
inetcorp.com preference = 30, mail exchanger = ns0.inetcorp.com
inetcorp.com preference = 10, mail exchanger = smtp.inetcorp.com
inetcorp.com preference = 20, mail exchanger = gw.inetcorp.com
Authoritative answers can be found from:
inetcorp.com nameserver = gw.inetcorp.com
inetcorp.com nameserver = ns0.inetcorp.com
inetcorp.com nameserver = nic.near.net
ns0.inetcorp.com     internet address = 172.16.1.87
inetcorpmail.lss.inetcorp.com     internet address = 172.16.2.94
gw.inetcorp.com     internet address = 172.16.1.41
nic.near.net    internet address = 192.52.71.4
```

This result tells us that the preferred mail exchangers for inetcorp.com are smtp.inetcorp.com, gw.inetcorp.com, and ns0.inetcorp.com, in that order.

This is the first query that we've shown for a zone that we don't manage – this changes the answers somewhat. Note that nslookup qualifies the answers as nonauthoritative, and then gives us the name servers from which authoritative answers can be found. This is saying: *The answers given here are from* named*'s* *cache and so may have changed since I last looked them up. If this isn't good enough, here's a source from which you can get the real McCoy.*

If you need the authoritative answer, you can then use the command `server` or `lserver` to set your default name server to one of those listed as returning authoritative answers for `inetcorp.com`, and then reexecute the query.

COMMAND LS   `nslookup`'s command `ls` lists all the records in a zone. This is most useful for inspecting your domain, and making sure that you have everything set up correctly on a primary server.

The syntax for `ls` is as follows:

```
ls [options] domain [> filename]
```

`options` specifies the record types from one of the following:

- `-a` — List canonical names and aliases.

- `-h` — List CPU type and operating system.

- `-s` — List well-known services.

- `-d` — List all records.

- `-t type` — List records of a given `type` (for example, `A`, `CNAME`, or `MX`).

`domain` specifies the domain you want to list. Note that `ls` will not work if your current server is not authoritative for the domain you are trying to list, nor will it work if the zone's owner has used the command `xfernets` to forbid zone transfers to your address.

Many times, the information that `ls` lists will scroll down the screen too quickly to read. You can control this by redirecting the output of the zone transfer into a file and then using the commands `less` or `more` to view that file's contents. (Please note that in some distributions of Linux, command `more` is broken. If this is the case, we suggest that you substitute command `less` in its place.)

This concludes our brief description of how to use `nslookup` as a debugging tool. `nslookup`'s greatest strength is that it uses the same code to translate names as your applications do in practice. You can be reasonably sure that the answer you get with `nslookup` is the same answer your application is getting. In most cases, you will use the `name` lookup feature to convert a name to an IP address.

The Host command

Command `host` is a simpler alternative to `nslookup`.

In its most commonly used form, `host` returns the address of any host you give it as a parameter. For example, the command

```
host thor
```

on our example intranet returns the following:

```
thor.myexample.com has address 192.168.1.1
```

host can also translate aliases. For example, the command

```
host smtp
```

on our example intranet returns the following:

```
smtp.myexample.com is a nickname for heimdall.myexample.com
heimdall.myexample.com has address 192.168.132.100
```

host can also look up names when given an IP address. For example, the command

```
host 192.168.1.1
```

on our example intranet returns the following:

```
Name: thor.myexample.com
Address: 192.168.1.1
Aliases:
```

Finally, if you give host a domain name, as we did earlier in one of our nslookup examples, it returns the MX records for that domain. For example, the command

```
host inetcorp.com
```

returns the following:

```
inetcorp.com mail is handled (pri=10) by smtp.inetcorp.com
inetcorp.com mail is handled (pri=20) by gw.inetcorp.com
inetcorp.com mail is handled (pri=30) by ns0.inetcorp.com
```

You can even use host to change the server and the list domains. However, because the command line is your only interface, serious debugging with host can be tiring.

host has many options. A quick scan of its manual page will help you to decide how you can best use this command.

TESTING DNS

The worst way to test your name server is to put it up and let your users complain when things don't work.

One test strategy is the brute-force approach: that is, use `host` or `nslookup` to interrogate each domain-name server about each host on your intranet, and confirm by hand that each name server returns the correct address for each name and the correct name for each address in your domain.

A better way is to have `named` do this for you, because `named` has a way to do this built into it:

♦ Each process in UNIX can receive signals asynchronously. Each signal tells the process that some event has occurred — that a new configuration is available, for example, or that it's time to execute a graceful shutdown. We described signals when we introduced daemons in Chapter 7.

♦ When `named` receives the signal `INT` (interrupt), it copies its database and cache into file `/var/tmp/named_dump.db`. The following is the easiest way to do this:

```
kill -INT $(cat /var/run/named.pid)
```

You can then examine the file `/var/tmp/named_dump.db` to see the results, and confirm that the domain-name server returns the correct name for each host name, and the correct name for each IP address.

Please be warned that if this server has a cache and has been running for a while, sifting out the records for your domain may be difficult.

Summary

This chapter discusses how to configure one of the Linux workstations on your intranet so that it can act as a gateway to the Internet for all machines on your intranet.

First, we described techniques whereby all machines on your intranet can exchange data with hosts on the Internet through a single IP address. Two such methods are presented: IP masquerading and SOCKS. The former method is easier to set up, and is included with the standard Linux kernel. The latter method is harder to set up, as it must be done one application at a time; however, it is more secure, and allows an administrator to monitor activity through the gateway more easily.

Finally, we described how to set up domain-name service (DNS) on your intranet. The configuration of DNS can be rather complicated; however, this section describes the files used to configure DNS, and the types of records each can hold.

Part IV

Advanced Topics

Chapter 9

Connecting Windows 95 to Linux

IN THIS CHAPTER

- ◆ Preliminary concerns
- ◆ Installing Ethernet onto a Windows 95 machine
- ◆ Basic Windows 95 configuration
- ◆ Installing and configuring Samba
- ◆ Accessing Windows 95 files from Linux
- ◆ Windows 95 networking commands

IN THIS CHAPTER, we describe how to connect a machine that is running the Windows 95 operating system to an intranet that is built around the Linux operating system.

Linux comes with tools that enable a user of Windows 95 to use Linux resources transparently: in particular, she can browse and read files from a Linux file system, and browse and use printers that are plugged into a Linux box. Likewise, tools are available that enable a Linux user to access files from Windows 95, and even mount Windows 95 file resources onto her file system.

At first glance, it appears politically incorrect for a book entitled *The Linux Network* to discuss Windows 95. After all, we Linux users are attracted to Linux because we want to go places that Microsoft can't take us.

However, we discuss linking Windows 95 and Linux for one simple reason: Windows 95 boxes sit on the desks of many users in enterprises that want to use Linux as a network server. In particular, many small businesses and schools run Windows 95 in order to run proprietary office-management or educational software. For these enterprises, Linux can be extremely helpful, particularly as a network server that links these Windows 95 machines and gives them a gateway to the Internet. This is particularly true when the enterprise cannot afford (or is wary of) an expensive, proprietary solution, such as using Windows NT Server.

The combination of Linux server and Windows 95 clients can help enterprises gain the advantages of true TCP/IP networking without replacing their Windows 95 machines or retraining users.

And who knows? Maybe some of those users will discover the advantages of using Linux as a desktop operating system, and *really* start going places!

Some Preliminary Concerns

In this chapter, we describe the network configuration shown in Figure 9-1.

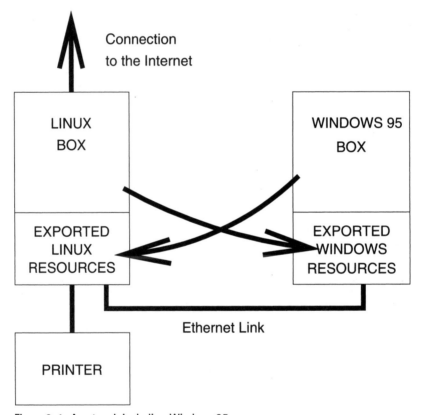

Figure 9-1: A network including Windows 95

Windows 95 boxes and Linux boxes share the network in the following manner:

♦ The Linux and Windows 95 machines are connected via Ethernet. Twisted-pair Ethernet and thin-coax Ethernet work equally well.

♦ A Linux workstation serves as the network's gateway to the Internet.

♦ The Windows 95 boxes access resources on the Linux workstation. In particular, the Windows 95 boxes can browse and access printers that are plugged into the Linux box, browse and access files on the Linux box's disks, and mount Linux directories as network drives.

♦ The Linux workstation can browse and access files on the Windows 95 box.

In this chapter, we also help you configure Windows 95 so that it is more "network-friendly." In particular, we introduce the Windows 95 networking commands NET and NETSTAT, and discuss how to use these commands to help Windows 95 behave a little more rationally.

NetBIOS and SMB

Before we plunge into the thicket of explanations, we must first deal with one topic: the networking protocols used by Windows 95, and how they interact with TCP/IP.

NETBIOS

The first networking cards for the IBM PC were devised by IBM itself. This was in the mid-1980s, when TCP/IP and the Internet were confined to universities and laboratories. To manage networked PCs, IBM invented its own protocol: the *Network Basic Input/Output System (NetBIOS)*.

Over time, IBM's networking cards were pushed out of the marketplace by faster, cheaper Ethernet hardware, but IBM chose to use its NetBIOS protocol as the basis for networking under its OS/2 operating system, which it commissioned Microsoft to write. As part of that deal, Microsoft licensed NetBIOS technology from IBM. Microsoft then used NetBIOS to implement networking for its Windows line of products, including Windows for Workgroups, Windows 95, and Windows NT.

Much of your work in making Windows 95 and Linux interact over the same network involves bridging NetBIOS and TCP/IP, so you will find knowing something about how NetBIOS works helpful.

NAMES AND WORKGROUPS   In brief, NetBIOS is roughly equivalent to IP. However, it differs from IP in that it identifies each host not with a number, but with a name. NetBIOS has no notion of classes of networks, or of domain-name resolution (although some attempt has been made to fill this last void).

Hosts on a NetBIOS network are organized into groups – or, to use Microsoft-speak, a *workgroup*. A workgroup is roughly the equivalent of an IP network: the hosts in a workgroup are known to each other by name, and can address each other by name.

An extension to NetBIOS, called the *NetBIOS Extended User Interface* (or *NetBEUI* – a fine example of IBM's nested acronyms) lets each host change its name at will, as long as it does not attempt to use a name that has already been taken by another host in the workgroup. Names are taken on a first-come, first-served basis: the first machine within a workgroup that takes a particular name gets to keep it. No central repository of names exists – no NetBEUI equivalent of a domain-name server; rather, machines communicate their names to each other by broadcasting them over the network.

A NetBEUI-based network is easy to set up: just name your workgroup, give a name to each machine, and *voilà!*, your machines can talk to each other. However, this ease of setup is purchased at the price of scalability: the larger the network, the more time each machine spends processing the names broadcast by the other machines in the workgroup.

FROM WINDOWS TO LINUX   Since the mid-1980s, commercial firms have been writing code that bridges NetBIOS/NetBEUI with TCP/IP, for the following two reasons:

◆ To let NetBIOS-based networks take advantage of TCP/IP scalability

◆ To give NetBIOS-based networks the ability to plug themselves into the Internet

Windows 95 comes with software to bridge NetBIOS and TCP/IP, and a large portion of this chapter is taken up with the details of configuring this bridge. This process is easier if you can keep the following points in mind:

◆ NetBIOS identifies each host by a *name*. TCP/IP identifies each host by a *number* – but it also lets hosts be identified by name, as a mnemonic for the user. The TCP/IP host name and the NetBIOS host name do not have to be the same, but you will find life to be much easier if you assign one – and only one – name to each machine on your intranet, and use that name for both TCP/IP and NetBIOS.

◆ NetBIOS assigns a name to its workgroup. TCP/IP also assigns a name to a group of computers, called a *domain*. Again, the NetBIOS workgroup name and the TCP/IP domain name are entirely separate – they do not have to have anything to do with each other. However, you again will find life to be much easier if you use the same name for your NetBIOS workgroup and your local domain.

The fact that two networking protocols coexist on one Windows 95 machine can be confusing. However, with a little thought and care, you can bridge TCP/IP and NetBIOS without difficulty.

SMB

Just to make life a little more interesting, the Windows and OS/2 family of operating systems use a second protocol, called the *Server Message Block* (*SMB*) protocol, to share resources among machines. SMB is roughly equivalent to NFS (which we introduced in Chapter 7), although in some ways SMB is more flexible.

With SMB, a machine can make its files and printers available to other machines in its workgroup. The administrator can tune the SMB interface to make all of a machine's resources available to the workgroup, or open up some resources to the workgroup while reserving other resources for that machine's exclusive use.

Users of the machines within a NetBIOS workgroup can identify themselves by an identifier and a password, which must be unique throughout the workgroup. SMB can use this information to further control access to resources: for example, to make some files available to selected users and deny them to other users.

SMB OR NFS?   Making resources on your Linux machine available to users on your Windows 95 machines is very useful. For example, the Linux machine can be used as a central repository of files, and as a printer server.

The following are two approaches to making Linux resources available to Windows 95:

♦ You can teach Windows 95 to use Linux-style resource-sharing. This requires that you install software – usually an NFS package – onto each Windows 95 box.

♦ You can teach Linux to use Windows 95-style resource-sharing. This requires that you install an SMB package onto your Linux workstation.

We prefer the latter approach – teaching Linux to deal with Windows 95 – for the following reasons:

♦ Teaching Windows 95 to deal with Linux means installing and configuring a software package on each Windows 95 box on your intranet. This is difficult and time-consuming. Further, because you must purchase a separate license for each Windows 95 box, it can be expensive.

♦ Teaching Linux to deal with Windows 95 means installing one package onto your Linux server, and configuring it to deal with all of your Windows 95 boxes at once. Obviously, installing one package onto one machine is easier than installing a package onto many machines.

♦ Most importantly, an excellent package that implements SMB under Linux is available for free. This package, called *Samba*, does an excellent job of making Linux resources available to Windows 95 boxes. Samba is easily installed and configured, and it won't cost you a cent.

♦ The Samba package comes with a command, called `smbclient`, that enables you to use an FTP-like text interface to work with SMB resources on Windows 95 boxes. Linux comes with a package, called `smbfs`, that enables you to mount Windows 95 file resources onto your Linux file system. These resources give you access to the files on the Windows 95 boxes, to use or administer, as you see fit.

The Rest of This Chapter

The rest of this chapter shows you how to integrate Windows 95 and Linux, in the following steps:

1. Install an Ethernet card into your Windows 95 box.

2. Perform basic configuration of NetBIOS and TCP/IP on the Windows 95 box, so that the Windows 95 box can communicate with both your intranet and the Internet. We discuss configuring Microsoft Exchange so that Windows 95 users can download electronic mail from a Linux server and upload mail to it. We also discuss using some networking applications under Windows 95, so that your Windows 95 boxes can access the Internet via your Linux gateway.

3. Install and configure Samba on your Linux box, so that users of Windows 95 can use selected directories on your Linux box, and spool jobs to a printer plugged into your Linux box. We also show how to configure Windows 95 so that Linux directories and printers are available for browsing.

4. Use `smbclient` to access files on Windows 95 systems.

5. Set up `smbfs` to mount Windows 95 file resources onto your Linux file system.

6. Finally, we discuss some Windows 95 commands that will help you manage networking under Windows 95.

And this said, we now begin our work.

Installing Ethernet onto a Windows 95 Machine

The first step to adding a Windows 95 box to your local intranet is to install an Ethernet card into it. This job is pretty simple, but it must be done carefully.

If your Windows 95 box came with Ethernet preinstalled on it, then you have nothing further to do: skip to the next section.

If you are installing the card yourself, then you have four tasks ahead of you:

1. Select the card.

2. Physically install the card.

3. Configure the card – set the base address and the interrupt that it uses.

4. Install the Windows driver for the card.

Selecting, physically installing, and configuring the card are the same under Windows 95 as under Linux. For information on these tasks, see Chapter 2.

One task you must perform under Windows 95 that you did not perform under Linux is installing the MS-DOS or Windows driver for the card. Most brands of cards, even the cheap ones, come with a utility that walks you through the process of installing the driver. To find this utility, put the floppy disk that came with the card into the Windows 95 box's floppy-disk drive; then use Windows Explorer to check its contents. If you see a file called SETUP or INSTALL, click it; this probably is the utility you need to set up the card and install the driver. The utility will walk you through the steps for configuring the card and installing the driver.

If you cannot find a setup utility for this Ethernet card, check the documentation that comes with the card; it should tell you how to install the driver by hand. Usually, this involves copying a file onto your hard disk, and then typing some information into file CONFIG.SYS. Unfortunately, we cannot be more specific, because this process varies from one manufacturer to another.

After you configure the card, reboot your Windows 95 system, so that Windows 95 can detect the Ethernet card.

Basic Windows 95 Configuration

In this section, we show you how to perform a basic setup on your Windows 95 box so that it can work with other machines on your intranet. This task involves the following steps:

1. Configure Linux so that it includes the Windows 95 box in the intranet that it manages.

2. Configure Windows 95 so that it can use TCP/IP via Ethernet to communicate with your Linux box.

3. Configure Microsoft Exchange – the Windows 95 mail utility – so that it can exchange mail with your Linux system.

4. Try out Windows 95 applications that use networking. These include the ordinary utilities, such as `ping`, `telnet`, and `ftp`, and the Netscape Navigator Web browser.

We discuss these topics in turn.

Configuration of Linux

Before you begin to configure a Windows 95 box, you must first enter some basic information about it into your Linux machine. By preparing the Linux box first, you can use the Windows 95 box to communicate with your Linux system almost immediately, and test whether the Windows 95 box is configured correctly.

Configuring the Linux box involves four steps:

1. Enter basic information about the Windows 95 box: its name and IP address.

2. Assign a login and password to each user who is using Windows 95.

3. Configure IP masquerading to recognize a datagram from each Windows 95 box and handle it appropriately.

4. Configure POP3 service.

We discuss each topic in turn.

ASSIGN NAMES AND ADDRESSES
The first step is to assign a name to each Windows 95 box on your system. Each name that you assign should be unique to your intranet. Also, you should think up a name for your local workgroup. We strongly suggest that you give the work-group the same name as your domain. Once you have thought up the names, jot them down. You need them throughout this process of networking your Windows 95 boxes.

If you have not already done so, the next step is to assign an IP address to each Windows 95 box. Do so as we describe in Chapter 6.

Enter the name of each machine and its IP address into file `/etc/hosts`, as we describe in Chapter 6.

ASSIGN USER LOGINS
The user of the Windows 95 box must use the same login identifier and password on the Windows 95 box that she uses on the Linux box. Unfortunately, no simple way exists to coordinate logins and passwords between Windows 95 and Linux. We suggest you do the following:

1. Use the command **newusers** to create a login for each Windows 95 user. (If you are unfamiliar with newusers, use the command **man newusers** to read its manual page.) Use a standard convention for assigning login identifiers — for example, the user's first initial and last name.

2. Bring each user, in turn, to the Linux box, and use the command **passwd** to let the user set her own password. Tell the user most solemnly to remember her login identifier and password.

3. Bring the user back to her Windows 95 box and have her set her Windows 95 login and password, as follows:

4. Click the Start button in the lower-left corner of the Windows 95 screen.

5. When the Start menu appears, click Shut Down.

6. When the window titled Shut Down Windows appears, click the button labeled *Close all programs and log on as a different user.*

7. Click the button labeled Yes.

8. When Windows 95 reboots, have the user log in by using the newly assigned login identifier, and the password set on the Linux box.

You should do this immediately after the user has set her Linux login and password — if you delay, the chances are good that it will either not be done or not be done properly.

You, the network administrator, should also log in on each Windows 95 box that you will be administering, using your standard Linux login identifier and password. You need to do this when you configure the Windows 95 box to work with your intranet.

The user should use her Linux-compatible login and password from now on. Please remember, too, that if for any reason the user needs to change her login or password under one operating system, she must change it under the other operating system as well.

CONFIGURE IP MASQUERADING

Recall from Chapter 8 that two ways to configure IP masquerading are available:

◆ You can set it up for all boxes on your intranet.

◆ You can set it up for some individual machines on your intranet, but not others.

If you used option 1, you do not need to perform any further configuration: when you plug a Windows 95 box into your intranet and assign it an IP address on that network, IP masquerading works automatically for it.

If, however, you used option 2, you must add a line of the following form to file `/etc/rc.d/rc.inet2`:

```
ipfwadm -F -a m -S ipaddress/32 -D 0.0.0.0/0
```

where `ipaddress` is the IP address (in dot notation) of the Windows 95 box that you are plugging into your network. You should also `su` to the superuser `root` and execute this command from the command line. You need to do this only once; hereafter, the command is executed automatically whenever you reboot your Linux system.

CONFIGURE POP3 SERVICE

If you want your Windows 95 users to download mail from the Linux server, then you must enable the POP3 server on your Linux box. POP (Post Office Protocol) reads the mail from an individual user's mailbox and forwards it to her. A POP3 daemon, called `in.pop3d`, is included with Linux.

Configuration of the POP3 daemon is simple: you simply turn it on. To do so, `su` to the superuser `root` and do the following:

◆ Make sure that the following lines in file `/etc/services` are *not* commented out:

```
pop3        110/tcp          # POP version 3
pop3        110/udp
```

◆ Make sure that the following line in file `/etc/inetd.conf` is *not* commented out:

```
pop3  stream  tcp  nowait  root  /usr/sbin/tcpd /usr/sbin/in.pop3d
```

Then, restart the `inetd` daemon, as we describe in Chapter 3.

SHADOW PASSWORDS   One "gotcha" that you should be aware of is that the POP3 daemon, as compiled under Slackware, assumes that you have shadow passwords installed. If you chose not to use shadow passwords when you installed Slackware, the POP3 daemon will not work correctly — it will always fail when the user enters her password, because it will look for the password in the file `/etc/shadow` instead of `/etc/passwd`.

The only solution to this problem is to obtain the sources to the POP3 daemon and recompile the program. If you are not familiar with C programming, ask your local "guru" to do this for you.

One commonly distributed implementation, by programmer Katie Stevens, is in archive `pop3d-1.00.4.tar`. This should compile correctly out of the box; just make sure that the `Makefile` has the `CFLAGS` set as follows:

```
CFLAGS = -O6 -DLINUX
```

Makefile must *not* have the constant SHADOWPWD set.

This creates an executable named pop3d. To install this executable, su to the superuser root; then type the following command:

```
mv pop3d /usr/sbin/in.pop3d
```

With this, you have prepared your Linux box to interact with Windows 95. We perform a more complex configuration on the Linux box when we install the Samba server; but for now, the Linux box can interact on a rudimentary level with Windows 95.

The time has come to configure Windows 95 for TCP/IP networking.

Configure Windows 95

The first and most important task is to configure Windows 95 so that it can communicate via Ethernet with the other machines on your intranet. This is a fairly complicated process; we walk you through it step by step.

BEGIN CONFIGURATION

At this point, we assume that the Windows 95 user's login and password are set correctly on both the Windows 95 and Linux boxes. Begin configuration of networking, as follows:

1. Click the Start button, in the lower-left corner of the Windows 95 screen. When the Start menu appears, move the mouse pointer to the entry labeled Settings; when that pop-up menu appears, click the entry labeled Control Panel.

2. When the Control Panel window opens, double-click the Network icon. This opens a window labeled Network, into which you enter the information needed to exchange information with your network. Figure 9-2 shows this window.

   As you can see in Figure 9-2, three tabs appear at the top of the Network window:

   ■ The Configuration tab controls physical access to the network: you tell it which hardware you have and which protocol you are using, and Windows 95 installs its drivers for that physical configuration. This is roughly — very roughly — equivalent to the network-access tier of TCP/IP.

   ■ The Identification tab controls how you identify your system to the network. It is into this tab's screen that you type this box's IP address.

■ Finally, the Access Control tab lets you control how users on other systems have access to this machine's files and printers.

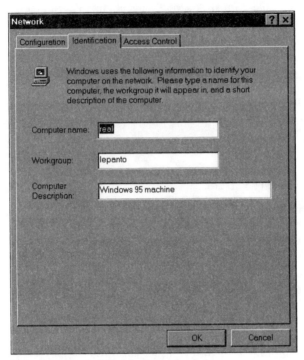

Figure 9-2: Control Panel's Network window

We discuss each tab's screen in turn.

THE CONFIGURATION SCREEN

You see the Configuration screen when you click the Configuration tab in the Control Panel's Network window.

To configure your physical network, you must enter information about three "pieces" of the network:

- ◆ The Client, which is the software through which you communicate with the network.

- ◆ The Adapter, which (in effect) describes the Ethernet card with which your system is plugged into the network.

- ◆ The Protocol, which sets the networking protocol with which this machine will communicate with the local intranet.

Actually, a fourth piece exists to configure, the Services, which describes what services you want to make available on this machine to users on other machines in the network, and how you want to control access to those services. This part of the configuration is not necessary to getting the Windows 95 machine "on the air," so we discuss it later in the chapter when we describe how to access Windows 95 services from within Linux.

To add a client, adapter, or protocol, click the Add button, which is just below the panel that lists the installed network components. When you click this button, Windows 95 opens a window titled Select Network Component Type. Figure 9-3 shows this window.

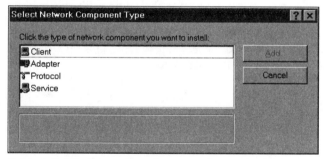

Figure 9-3: Window used to select type of network component

This window displays an entry for Client, Adapter, and Protocol (as well as Service). We discuss these three components in turn.

SELECTING A CLIENT   The first step is to select the client you will use. To do so, click the Client icon in the Select Network Component Type window, and then click the Add button. Windows 95 opens its Select Network Client window, as shown in Figure 9-4.

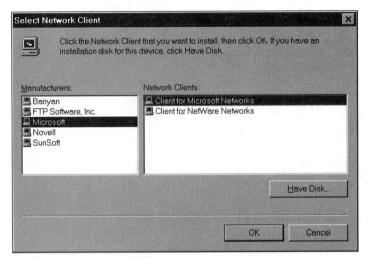

Figure 9-4: Window used to select network client

We assume that you want to use the Microsoft client for Microsoft networks. In the field on the left, click the entry labeled Microsoft; then in the field on the right, click the entry labeled Client for Microsoft Networks. Then click the OK button. This client should already be present on your Windows 95 system. If for some reason it is not, Windows 95 prompts you for a disk; place your Windows 95 CD-ROM into the CD-ROM drive, and then click Have Disk; Windows 95 should then install the client properly.

After you make your selection, Windows 95 should close the Network Client window automatically. If it does not, click the X box in the upper-right corner of the window to close the window. This returns you to the Control Panel's Select Network Component Type window.

SELECTING AN ADAPTER   Selecting the adapter probably is the trickiest part of attaching a Windows 95 box to your network. This principally is due to the fact that you must know ahead of time which type of Ethernet card you are using. We assume that the Ethernet card has already been installed on your machine, and has been configured.

To select the adapter (the Ethernet card) for your Windows 95 box, click the Adapter icon in the Select Network Component Type window, and then click the Add button. This brings up the Select Network Adapters window, as shown in Figure 9-5.

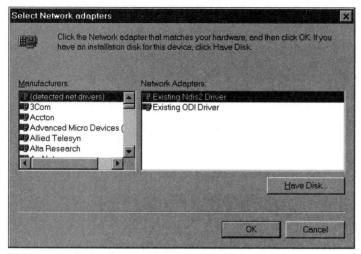

Figure 9-5: Window used to select network adapter

This window has two scroll fields in it. The one on the left is labeled Manufacturers; this lists the manufacturers of Ethernet cards whose drivers are included with Windows 95. The scroll field on the right is labeled Network Adapters; this lists the models of Ethernet cards for which Windows 95 has drivers. If you click an entry in the Manufacturers field, Windows 95 displays in the Network Adapters field the models of that manufacturer's cards for which Windows 95 has a driver.

Fortunately, Windows 95 can sense what hardware and drivers are installed on the computer; so if a driver has already been installed for your Ethernet card, Windows 95 likely has discovered it. If it has, you will see an entry at the top of the Manufacturer for (detected net drivers). If you see this, click it; the Network Adapters field should then display an entry for the driver you installed into the Windows 95 box. Click it; then click the OK button. Windows 95 will use the driver you installed earlier, and then return you to the Select Network Component Type window.

If you did not install a driver for the Ethernet card, or if Windows 95 did not find it, you can select a driver from among those that come with Windows 95. To select a driver, do the following:

1. Scroll through the Manufacturers field until you find the company that made your card. Click it.

2. Scroll through the entries in the Network Adapters field until you see the model of your card. Click it.

3. Click the OK button. Windows 95 may ask you to put the Windows 95 CD-ROM into your CD-ROM drive, so that it can copy onto your hard disk the driver you selected.

If you are not sure who manufactured your Ethernet card, or what model it is, check the documentation that came with your card. If you are using a clone, then use the driver for the manufacturer and card that the clone is mimicking. One hint: if the clone says that it is compatible with an NE2000 or NE1000, the driver's manufacturer is Novell/Anthem, and the network adapter (driver) is NE2000 Compatible or NE1000 Compatible, respectively.

You can also install a driver from this screen. To do so, pop into your floppy-disk drive the disk that has the driver; then click the Have Disk button. Windows 95 then walks you through the process of finding the driver and installing it onto the machine's hard disk.

SELECTING A PROTOCOL   The last step in this phase of configuration is to select the protocol. Windows 95 supports numerous different protocols – TCP/IP, Novell Networks, and so on. You can also install various different implementations of *protocol stacks*. We have found that Microsoft's TCP/IP stack, which is shipped with Windows 95, is adequate, so we install it.

To do so, click the Protocol icon in the window Select Network Component Type. Windows 95 opens its window Select Network Protocol, as shown in Figure 9-6.

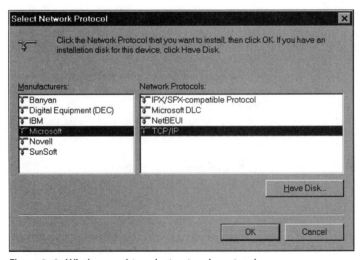

Figure 9–6: Window used to select network protocol

This window resembles the Network Adapter window, in that it has two scroll fields: the field on the left lists manufacturers, and the field on the right lists products. To install the Microsoft TCP/IP protocol, do the following:

1. In the left scroll field, click the entry for Microsoft.

2. In the right scroll field, click the entry for TCP/IP.

3. At the bottom of this window, click the OK button.

Windows 95 may need to retrieve these bits from its CD-ROM. If it prompts you to place the Windows 95 CD-ROM into the CD-ROM drive, do so; then follow the prompts Windows 95 gives you. Windows 95 should then return you to the Select Network Component Type window.

REMOVE OTHER SOFTWARE   At this point, you have installed the client, the adapter, and the protocol that you want. Click the Cancel button to close the Select Network Component Type window. This returns you to the Network window.

In some circumstances, advanced users of Windows 95 may want to use multiple protocols or adapters. However, for most users, having multiple adapters or protocols installed onto the Windows system simply creates problems. Thus, the next step is to remove the clients, adapters, and protocols that you will not be using:

1. For each of the clients, other than the one labeled Microsoft Networks, click its icon and then click the Remove button.

2. For each of the adapters, other than the one you have just selected, click its icon and then click the Remove button.

3. For each of the protocols, other than the ones labeled TCP/IP or NetBEUI, click its icon and then click the Remove button.

At this point, you have installed the software that Windows 95 will use to communicate with your intranet and, in particular, with your Linux box. We still have to configure this software — or, to use Windows-speak, to *set its properties*. However, before we get to that, one task remains that we must perform: set the NetBIOS identity of the Windows 95 box.

THE IDENTIFICATION SCREEN
The next step is to set your Windows 95 box's NetBIOS name and workgroup. Click the Identification tab, which is at the top of the Network window. This brings up the window shown in Figure 9-7.

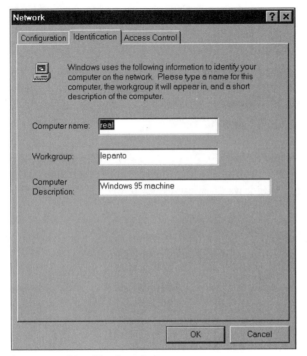

Figure 9-7: Identification window

To give your computer an identity, do the following:

1. In the field labeled Computer Name, type the name you earlier gave
   to this Windows 95 box. This name must be unique to the NetBIOS
   workgroup of which this machine is a member. Please note that you
   could give the same machine one name under a NetBIOS workgroup and
   a different name under a TCP/IP network; however, we find that this is
   confusing and no advantage is gained by doing so. Therefore, use the
   same name that you assigned to this machine in your Linux box's file
   /etc/hosts.

2. In the field labeled Workgroup, type the name you selected earlier for the
   Windows 95 workgroup to which your local Windows 95 boxes will
   belong. All of the Windows 95 machines on your intranet should be part
   of the same workgroup. Again, you could use one name for your local
   workgroup and another for your TCP/IP domain; however, you probably
   are better off using the same name for both. Therefore, enter the name of
   your local domain.

3. Finally, in the field labeled Computer Description, type a brief description
   of this machine.

After you enter an identity for the Windows 95 box, click the Configuration tab, located at the top of the Network window. This returns you to the Windows 95 Network configuration window, as shown in Figure 9-2. We now set the properties of the network components that we have just installed.

SETTING PROPERTIES

Now that we have selected the Windows 95 network components, and have set the Windows 95 box's NetBIOS name and workgroup, we must configure – or *set the properties of* – the components we have just installed. We discuss this task for each component in turn.

CLIENT PROPERTIES   To set the client's properties, enter the Control Panel's Network window. Click the icon labeled Client for Microsoft Networks (the top icon in the Network components window); then click the Properties button. Windows 95 opens the configuration window for this client, as shown in Figure 9-8.

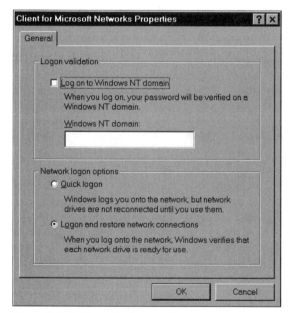

Figure 9-8: Setting client properties

The top of the window asks about logon validation. Do not click this on, as we presently have no way to validate a Windows 95 logon through Linux.

The bottom of the window asks whether network connections should be established automatically when this user logs onto the system. If the user will be mounting her Linux home directory as a network drive, click the lower button. This tells Windows 95 to automatically mount network drives when this user logs into

Windows 95. We show you later in this chapter how to mount a Linux directory as a network drive.

After you finish, click the OK button. This returns you to the Network window.

ADAPTER PROPERTIES   The Adapter Properties window enables you to confirm Windows 95's configuration of your Ethernet card. The contents of this screen will vary, depending upon the make of Ethernet card that you are using. In this section, we show the configuration of a cheap NE2000 clone.

The bad news in this process is that you must have some detailed information about your Ethernet card: the type of driver you want to use (if more than one is available), the interrupt it uses, and the base address it uses. (We hope that you jotted down the interrupt and base address when you configured the card, as we suggested in Chapter 2.) The good news is that Windows 95 does a good job of detecting the configuration of almost every brand of Ethernet card, so in all probability, you just have to confirm what Windows 95 already knows.

To enter the Adapter Properties window, click the icon for your adapter, and then click the Properties button. This brings up the Adapter Properties window, as shown in Figure 9-9.

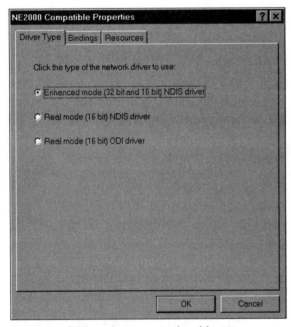

Figure 9-9: Setting adapter properties: driver type

This window has three tabs at the top: one for Driver Type, one for Bindings, and one for Resources. Driver Type is topmost, as Figure 9-9 shows.

The Driver Type tab enables you to select the type of driver you want to use for this card. We suggest that you not change what Windows 95 has selected by default, unless you know the drivers well and have a reason to override the Windows 95 default selection.

The next step is to check the bindings – that is, which network protocol is used to interact with this Ethernet card. Click the Bindings tab. The Properties window now appears, as shown in Figure 9-10.

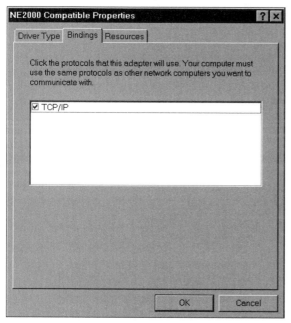

Figure 9–10: Setting adapter properties: bindings

If you have installed only one protocol, it should be clicked, as Figure 9-10 shows. If you have installed more than one protocol, click the one that is labeled TCP/IP. If you do not see an entry for TCP/IP, something went wrong when you added the TCP/IP protocol: click the Cancel button to return to the Network screen, and again install this protocol as we described earlier in this chapter.

After you bind the Ethernet card to a protocol, you must confirm the hardware resources that the Ethernet card uses. To do so, click the Resources tab. The Resources screen appears, as shown in Figure 9-11.

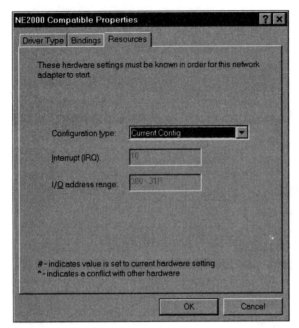

Figure 9-11: Setting adapter properties: resources

You must confirm two settings: the interrupt (IRQ) number with which the computer communicates with this Ethernet card, and the base address of memory that this card uses to exchange data with the computer.

The screen shows the current configuration, which Windows 95 has read from the card itself. You should confirm, from the notes you kept during configuration, that these values are correct. If they are, and no setting is marked with an asterisk, you have nothing else to do. However, you may encounter one of two error situations:

◆ The resources are not as you set them. Windows 95 usually does not somehow read the resources incorrectly from your Ethernet card, but this has been known to happen. In this instance, you can describe the resources to Windows 95.

◆ The resources are displayed correctly, but one or both values is marked with an asterisk, which indicates that this resource is also used by another peripheral device. Such a *resource conflict* means that neither peripheral device can work correctly. In this case, you must reset the resources in this screen to something that Windows 95 finds palatable; then, go back and configure your card to use these settings.

To reset the Ethernet card's resource settings, do the following:

1. Click the arrow button to the right of the field labeled Configuration Type, and select the entry for Basic Configuration 0. When you do so, the fields labeled Interrupt and I/O Address Range are no longer grayed out: you can now change the information in them.

2. Click in the field that is in error, and then use the arrow buttons at the right of the field to reset the field to its correct setting. If you are resetting a resource because Windows 95 found a conflict with another peripheral device, be sure to set the resource to a value that can be handled by your Ethernet card — most Ethernet cards recognize only a few interrupts and base addresses. Check the documentation that came with your card to find the settings that this card recognizes. Also, if you are resetting the resources due to a conflict, be sure to write onto your log sheet the new settings that you enter.

After you finish, click the OK button. This returns you to the Network screen. If you reset the resource settings for your Ethernet card because the old settings had a conflict, you must now reconfigure your Ethernet card so that its settings match those that you just set in the Resources window.

One last configuration task remains: configuring TCP/IP.

PROTOCOL PROPERTIES   The final set of properties are those for the protocol — in this case, for TCP/IP. This is the most complicated set of properties to enter, but it should have no surprises for you.

To enter properties, enter the Network window (if you are not there already). Click the TCP/IP icon, and then click the Properties button. Windows 95 brings up its TCP/IP Properties window, as shown in Figure 9-12.

Six tabs are displayed across the top of this window. These are labeled, respectively, Bindings, Advanced, DNS Configuration, Gateway, WINS Configuration, and IP Address. You need to enter information into each of these tabs, so we go through them next, one at a time.

IP Address tab

The IP Address tab enables you to set the IP address of this Windows 95 computer. If its screen is not uppermost on the TCP/IP Properties window, click that tab. The screen should now appear, as shown in Figure 9-12.

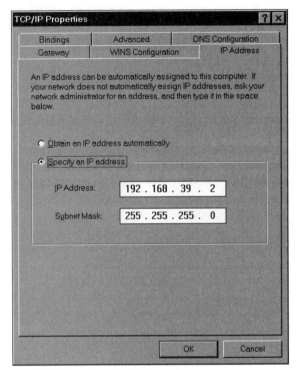

Figure 9-12: TCP/IP Properties window

You should set the IP address explicitly, rather than obtain an IP address automatically. To do so, click the button labeled Specify an IP Address.

Then, in the field labeled IP Address, enter the IP address that you earlier assigned to this Windows 95 box. You have to enter the four bytes of the address separately; use the mouse to click the subfield for the octet that you want to enter, and then type the byte. If the value is three digits long, the cursor will jump automatically to the next byte's subfield.

Then, type the mask into the field labeled Subnet Mask. If, as we suggested, you selected one of the Class-C network addresses for your intranet, type mask 255.255.255.0, as shown in Figure 9-12.

This concludes entering the IP address. However, do *not* click the OK button — that will return you to the Network window. Instead, continue your configuration of TCP/IP by entering information about your intranet's gateway.

Gateway

The next step is to enter the address of the machine that is your intranet's gateway to the Internet. To do so, click the tab that is labeled Gateway; the TCP/IP Properties windows appears, as shown in Figure 9-13.

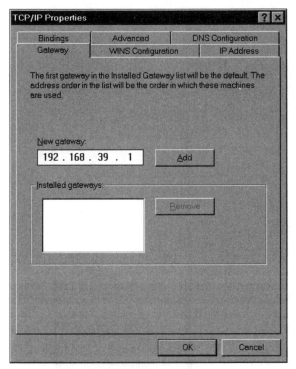

Figure 9-13: Gateway address

To add the IP address of the Linux machine that is your intranet's gateway to the Internet, click the Add button, and then type the IP address into the field labeled New Gateway.

You can enter more than one gateway. Windows 95 accesses gateways in the order in which you enter them.

After you enter your gateway machine's IP address, do *not* click the OK button – we still have some more work to do on this screen before we are finished.

Bindings

The next step is to bind the networking protocol to the client protocol. To do so, click the Bindings tab. You see a screen that resembles Figure 9-14.

Because we have selected only one client – Client for Microsoft Networks – only that client should appear on this screen; and it should be clicked by default. If you selected more than one client, click the entry for the Microsoft Networks client. If you selected only one client but for some reason it does not have a check mark in the little box to the left of its entry, click its entry to bind it explicitly to the TCP/IP protocol.

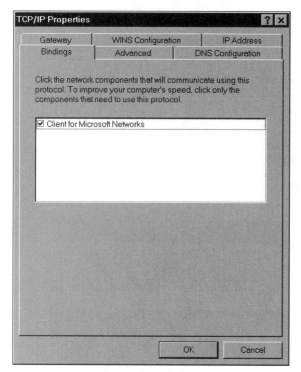

Figure 9-14: Bindings configuration

The next step is to configure domain-name service (DNS).

DNS configuration

To configure DNS, click the tab that is labeled DNS Configuration. The screen should now resemble what you see in Figure 9-15.

You can either disable or enable DNS. Click the button labeled Enable DNS.

Next, you must enter the TCP/IP name of this machine, and the name of the domain. As we mentioned earlier, this name should be the same as the machine's NetBIOS name, although it does not have to be.

To enter the TCP/IP name of the machine, click the field labeled Host, and then type the name you have given to this Windows 95 box. To enter the name of the TCP/IP domain, click the field labeled Domain, and then type the name of your intranet's domain.

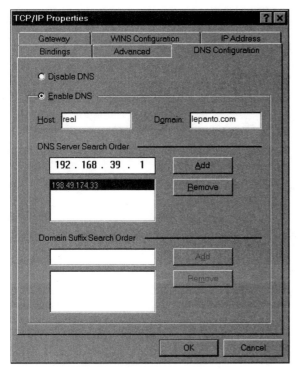

Figure 9-15: DNS configuration

The next step is to enter the IP addresses of the machines that the Windows box will access for domain-name service. If you have set up domain-name service on your Linux box, then enter its IP address. You should also enter the IP address of any other machine that provides DNS and that can be accessed through your gateway machine – for example, your Internet provider's DNS machine. This will enable Windows 95 programs that access the Internet, such as Netscape Navigator, to find IP addresses directly from your Internet provider, rather than always having to go through the medium of your Linux workstation.

One last point: Windows 95's implementation of TCP/IP can also use a `hosts` file, into which you can type the names and addresses of frequently accessed machines – in particular, the names and addresses of the machines on your intranet. We discuss this file a little later in this chapter.

Advanced Configuration

The Advanced Configuration window lets you fine-tune some properties of TCP/IP networking. Most properties of TCP/IP networking do not require advanced tuning, so when you click the Advanced tab, the screen probably will resemble what is shown in Figure 9-16.

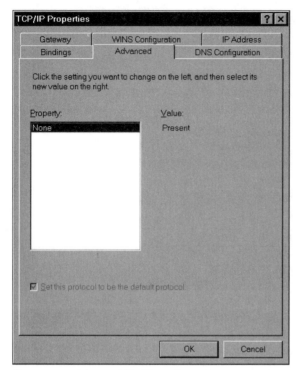

Figure 9-16: Advanced TCP/IP configuration

In almost every instance, this screen will have nothing for you to do.

WINS Configuration

Finally, you must configure the Windows Internet Naming Service (WINS). Click the tab labeled WINS Configuration. The screen should resemble Figure 9-17.

WINS is a Windows service that translates NetBIOS machine names directly into IP addresses. This feature is useful only if your intranet has on it a Windows NT box that is running the WINS service.

In most instances, you should simply disable WINS. To do so, click the button labeled Disable WINS Resolution.

REBOOT   You are finished configuring the TCP/IP protocol. Click the OK button at the bottom of the TCP/IP Properties window. This returns you to the Control Panel's Network window.

And, with the configuration of the TCP/IP properties, you have finished installing and configuring networking on the Windows 95 box. Click the OK button at the bottom of the Network window.

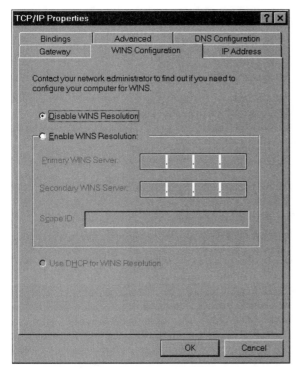

Figure 9-17: WINS Configuration window

Windows 95 stores the configuration information you have entered. It then may tell you that it must reboot for the configuration to take effect; if it does, click the button labeled Reboot Now.

After the system reboots, you should be running TCP/IP on your Windows 95 box. The next step is to test whether it actually works.

TESTING AND TROUBLESHOOTING
Now that all configuration is done, the time has come to test the Windows 95 box's configuration. We first test connectivity to other machines on the intranet, and then check connectivity to the Internet.

CONNECTING TO YOUR INTRANET   To check connectivity to your intranet, we use the familiar program `ping` to ping another system on the intranet. Do the following:

1. Click the System button. When the System menu appears, click the entry for Programs. On the Programs menu, click the entry for MS-DOS Prompt. This opens an MS-DOS window.

2. In the MS-DOS window, type the command **ping ipaddress**, where
ipaddress is the IP address of your Linux box. If networking is
configured correctly on your Windows 95 box, you should see something
like what is shown in Figure 9-18.

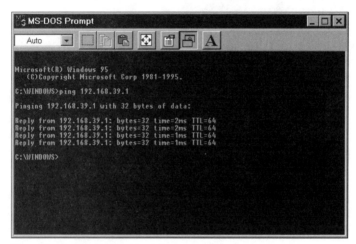

Figure 9-18: Pinging the Linux box

If you do see this, then congratulations! You now have TCP/IP networking set up
on your Windows 95 box, and it is communicating with your Linux box via
Ethernet.

If ping does not work, then something is malconfigured. Sometimes, ping
returns an error message that helps diagnose the problem:

◆ The error message Bad command or file name indicates that Windows
95 cannot find the command ping. This indicates that Windows 95 did
not install its TCP/IP software correctly. (When Windows 95 installs
TCP/IP, it also installs the TCP/IP clients ping, ftp, and telnet as part of
the package.) In this case, go back to Control Panel and again install the
TCP/IP software, as we described earlier.

◆ The error message Request timed out indicates that ping cannot reach
the IP address that you typed – or the machine that has that address on
the other end somehow cannot reply to the Windows 95 box. Check that
you correctly typed the Linux workstation's IP address.

CONNECTING TO THE INTERNET   At this point, we assume that you can `ping` the other machines on your intranet, and, therefore, TCP/IP is correctly installed and configured on the Windows 95 box. The next step is to test whether the Windows 95 box can connect automatically to the Internet.

As we explain in Chapter 8, the design of the ICMP host-to-host protocol (which `ping` uses) means that a `ping` datagram sent by your Windows 95 box to the Internet is not returned to the Windows 95 box. This is a limitation of IP masquerading — not a major limitation, but it exists nonetheless. Thus, to test the Windows 95 box's connectivity to the Internet, we must use an application that uses the TCP or UDP host-to-host protocol; in this example, we use the Windows 95 implementation of the familiar program `ftp` to connect to the FTP site at the Library of Congress.

To do so, open an MS-DOS window, and then type:

```
ftp ftp.loc.gov
```

If all goes well, Windows 95 will dispatch an FTP datagram to your Linux gateway machine. The Linux machine, in turn, should detect that it is outward bound, and do the following:

1. IP masquerading should give your Windows 95 session its own port.

2. `diald` should dial your Internet provider and connect to a modem hooked into your provider's machine (if you are not connected already).

3. The Linux workstation then opens a PPP connection with the Internet and starts passing datagrams between your Windows 95 box and the FTP server at the Library of Congress.

All this should take place automatically, and within a few seconds of your issuing the MS-DOS `ftp` command. What you see in your MS-DOS windows should resemble Figure 9-19.

You can log in as **anonymous**. Use the login on your Linux workstation as your password. And now, from the Windows 95 box, you can begin to examine the catalogues of the Library of Congress — one of the world's great libraries.

At this point, any problem you see probably is due to malconfiguration on the Linux workstation. Make sure that `diald` and IP masquerading are set up correctly, as we described in Chapter 8.

Figure 9-19: ftping to the Library of Congress

DEFINE C:\WINDOWS\HOSTS

To this point, we have been typing IP addresses into our MS-DOS commands. We could have used host names, but only if we had set up domain-name service (DNS) on our Linux machine – if we had not typed them, every time your Windows 95 box needed to find the IP address of a machine on your intranet, it would have tried to access your Internet provider's domain-name server, which would needlessly dial the modem – and wouldn't work anyway (as your Internet provider's domain-name server has no idea what IP addresses you have assigned to the machines on your intranet).

Fortunately, a way around this difficulty exists. When Microsoft implemented TCP/IP under its Windows family of operating systems, it adhered fairly closely to the Berkeley UNIX standard. This included using the standard Berkeley configuration files services and hosts. These files can be edited with a text editor to change the behavior of TCP/IP under Windows 95.

You will never need to edit services; however, you can edit hosts and insert the names and IP addresses of the hosts on your intranet. Thereafter, TCP/IP under Windows 95 will resolve those host names into their IP addresses automatically, without requiring the assistance of a domain-name server on your Linux workstation. For once, Microsoft did not monkey with an established standard, so you can use one common hosts file throughout your intranet – on Linux workstations and Windows 95 boxes alike.

To edit hosts, use the Wordpad program under Windows 95 to edit file C:\WIN-DOWS\HOSTS. As with file /etc/hosts under Linux, each line on this file describes one machine: the first entry on each line should be the machine's IP address, and all subsequent entries should be the machine's various names. Comments begin with a pound sign, #. Figure 9-20 shows an example of one such edited hosts file.

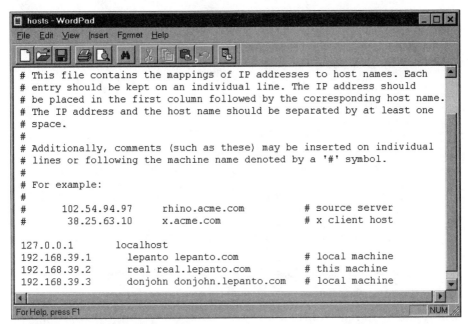

```
# This file contains the mappings of IP addresses to host names. Each
# entry should be kept on an individual line. The IP address should
# be placed in the first column followed by the corresponding host name.
# The IP address and the host name should be separated by at least one
# space.
#
# Additionally, comments (such as these) may be inserted on individual
# lines or following the machine name denoted by a '#' symbol.
#
# For example:
#
#      102.54.94.97      rhino.acme.com           # source server
#       38.25.63.10      x.acme.com               # x client host

127.0.0.1        localhost
192.168.39.1        lepanto lepanto.com          # local machine
192.168.39.2        real real.lepanto.com        # this machine
192.168.39.3        donjohn donjohn.lepanto.com  # local machine
```

Figure 9-20: Edited hosts file

As always, the first entry should be for localhost. Subsequent entries should be for the other machines on the intranet, including this Windows 95 box itself.

When you edit this file, be absolutely sure that you save the file in Text mode. If you do not — that is, if any formatting information is embedded in the file — the TCP/IP networking programs will not be able to read it, and may in fact react rather gracelessly.

Later in this chapter, we show you how to distribute a common hosts file to all the Windows 95 boxes on your intranet.

MAIL: FORMATTING MICROSOFT EXCHANGE

Microsoft Exchange is the mailer that is included with Windows 95. You can configure Microsoft Exchange to download mail from your Linux box via the Linux box's POP3 server, so that the Windows 95 user can read her mail without having to log into Linux.

Microsoft Exchange will access the Linux server's POP3 daemon to download mail to the Windows 95 box, and it will use the Linux server's SMTP daemon to upload mail from the Windows 95 box. We described earlier in this chapter how you can turn on the POP3 daemon; for information on how to turn on the SMTP daemon, see Chapter 5.

Before we begin this process, three points should be made:

◆ Importantly, we must again emphasize that the Windows 95 user should use the same login and password under Windows 95 that she has under Linux. This enables Windows 95 and Linux to exchange data that belongs to that user much more easily.

◆ More importantly, Microsoft Exchange is designed to work with the NetBIOS networking protocol. You must go through some gyrations to get it to work correctly with a TCP/IP-based operating system, such as Linux or any other UNIX-based server. Other vendors offer Windows 95 mailers that are designed to work with TCP/IP; for example, Netscape Communicator includes a mailer that requires minimal configuration.

◆ Finally, please note that if a user attaches a file to a mail message composed with Microsoft Exchange, that software encodes it in a proprietary format that can be read only by Microsoft Exchange. If your user wants to be able to mail files to users who are using a variety of mailers, she should *not* use Microsoft Exchange.

However, Microsoft Exchange does have one advantage: If you have Windows 95, you already have a copy of Exchange. And, despite the preceding caveats, it works. So, let us proceed with our description of configuration.

INSTALL MICROSOFT EXCHANGE   If you do not see the Inbox icon on the Windows 95 desktop, then Microsoft Exchange was not installed when Windows 95 was installed onto this PC. If this is the case, you must now install it, as follows:

1. Place the Windows 95 CD-ROM into the machine's CD-ROM drive. Wait patiently until the machine finishes playing the Microsoft jingle.

2. Click the Start button. When the Start menu appears, click the entry for Settings; when that menu appears, click the entry for Control Panel.

3. In the Control Panel window, click the icon labeled Add/Remove Programs.

4. In the Add/Remove Programs Properties window, click the tab labeled Windows Setup.

5. In the Windows Setup screen's Components field, click the entry labeled Microsoft Exchange; then click the OK button.

Windows 95 should install Microsoft Exchange automatically. If it asks you any questions about how you want to configure the software, select the default configuration. This process should not take very long; when it has finished, remove the Windows 95 CD-ROM from the machine's CD-ROM drive, replace it in its sleeve, and put it away safely.

INSTALL TCP/IP MODULE   One last task must be performed before you can use Microsoft Exchange with Linux: you must obtain a copy of the shared-library file `minet32.dll`, which implements Internet mail for Windows 95.

Unfortunately, this file is not part of the base Windows 95 release as distributed to PC manufacturers when Windows 95 first appeared (although it may now be part of the default Windows 95 release).

To download this file, do the following:

1. Using a Web browser, access the following site:

`http://www.microsoft.com/windows95/info/system-updates.htm`

2. In this window, click the entry labeled *Internet Mail Service for Windows 95 Release/Update*. You may need to scroll down the window for a bit before this entry appears.

3. Follow the instructions for installing this shared library. Be sure to install it into folder `C:\WINDOWS\SYSTEM`.

This concludes the preliminaries. Now you are ready to configure Microsoft Exchange.

CONFIGURE MICROSOFT EXCHANGE   To begin configuration of Microsoft Exchange, click the Inbox icon on your desktop. The Microsoft Exchange template will appear. Microsoft Exchange will try to make connection with a server; when it does not find one (as it will not, because a server is not yet configured), it complains that something is wrong. Click the box that tells it to continue working.

Microsoft Exchange then displays a window labeled Inbox—Microsoft Exchange. Click the entry labeled Tools in the menu at the top of the window. When the Tools drop-down menu appears, click the entry labeled Options. This opens the Options window, through which you can configure Microsoft Exchange. The Options window has six tabs, as shown in Figure 9-21.

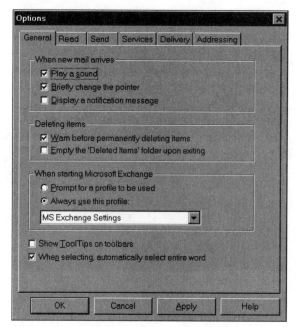

Figure 9-21: Microsoft Exchange's Options window

To configure Microsoft Exchange to exchange mail with your Linux machine, do the following:

1. Click the Services tab at the top of the Options window. This opens a screen like that shown in Figure 9-22.

2. In the scroll field, you should see an entry for Internet Mail, as shown in Figure 9-22. If you do not, then you must add it. To do so, click the Add button. This opens a window labeled Add Service to Profile, as shown in Figure 9-23.

3. Click the entry for Internet Mail. (If you do not see an entry for Internet Mail in this window, then something went wrong when you installed the Internet-mail module onto your system. Try installing it again, and try rebooting your system, as well.)

4. After you click Internet Mail, click the OK button. The Add Service to Profile window closes, and you should see Internet Mail listed in the Options window.

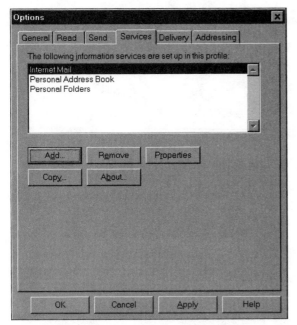

Figure 9-22: Option Windows' Services screen

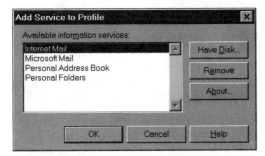

Figure 9-23: Add Service to Profile window

5. If you also see an entry for Microsoft Mail in the Options window, click it; then click the Remove button. This prevents Microsoft Exchange from being confused by having more than one mail-protocol module "visible" to it.

6. Now, you must set the properties for the Internet-mail module: click the entry for Internet Mail, then click the Properties button. Windows 95 opens its Internet Mail window, as shown in Figure 9-24.

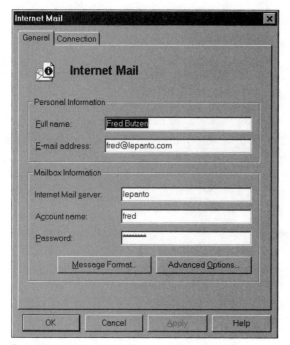

Figure 9-24: Internet Mail's general configuration

This window has two tabs at the top. The General tab enables you to enter information about the user whose mail will be downloaded to this machine. Configure it as follows:

1. In the field labeled Full Name, type the full name of the user whose mail will be downloaded.

2. In the field labeled E-mail Address, give the user's e-mail address on your Linux box. This should be the user's Linux login identifier plus the name of your Linux box as it is known to the Internet.

3. In the field labeled Internet Mail Server, give the name of your Linux machine, as you set it in the Windows 95 hosts file. If you have not put any entries into the Windows 95 hosts file, then enter the Linux machine's IP address, as it is set on your intranet.

4. In the field labeled Account Name, give the user's Linux login identifier.

5. Finally, in the field labeled Password, type the user's password for her Linux account.

6. Next, click the Connection tab, which opens a screen similar to Figure 9-25.

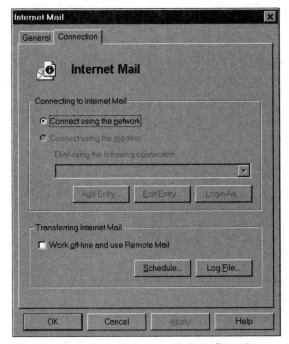

Figure 9-25: Internet Mail connection configuration

Click the button labeled *Connect using the network*, which is located at the top of this window.

And with this, you have configured Microsoft Exchange to use Internet mail.

TEST THE CONFIGURATION   To test the configuration, shut down Microsoft Exchange, and then restart it. It may prompt the user to re-enter her login identifier and password; then it will connect with the Linux server, and finally declare itself ready.

If you still see an error message at this point, then something went wrong with the configuration. The error message may give you a hint as to what the problem is.

If you do not see an error message, then the connection probably is configured correctly.

To test the connection, the user should try sending a mail message to herself. She should be sure to use her full e-mail address, as set on the Linux machine. The message should be uploaded to the Linux machine; the user can then download the message back to the Windows 95 box. In a moment, an entry for it should appear in Microsoft Exchange's box.

If the message appears, then congratulations! Your Windows 95 user can now exchange mail with your Linux server – and by extension, with the entire Internet.

Windows 95 Applications

Windows 95 comes with numerous standard programs as part of its TCP/IP package. In Chapter 4, we introduced the Linux versions of these programs. On the whole, the Windows 95 implementations adhere to established standards, and thus behave the same as do their Linux analogues. However, the Microsoft implementations do differ from the versions shipped with Linux in terms of what command-line options they recognize, so we review them briefly here.

PING: CHECK NETWORK CONNECTION

Earlier in this chapter, we used the command ping to check whether a Windows 95 box could access other machines on the intranet. This useful little program is the quickest and easiest way to check whether a network is active or another machine is "on the air."

The Windows 95 implementation of ping works exactly like its Linux analogue. The basic command line is also the same as with the Linux implementation: ping *hostname*, where *hostname* names the host to ping. However, the command-line options that the Windows 95 version of ping recognizes differ somewhat from those recognized by the Linux version:

- ◆ -f — Fragmentation: set the "don't fragment" flag in the transmitted datagram.

- ◆ -l *bytes* — Send a datagram that is *bytes* large.

- ◆ -i *ttl* — Set the "time to live" field in the datagram to *ttl*.

- ◆ -n *number* — Transmit *number* datagrams. The default is 4.

- ◆ -r *count* — For *count* hops, record the route that a datagram follows. The route is printed on the screen when the datagram is echoed back to its host of origin.

- ◆ -t — Ping until interrupted. This is the default under Linux, but an option under Windows 95. Under the MS-DOS shell, type **ctrl + C** to interrupt a command.

- ◆ -w milliseconds — Wait milliseconds before timing out. For example, the command

```
ping myexample -w 5000
```

tells ping to ping system myexample, and to wait five seconds before timing out.

FTP: UPLOAD OR DOWNLOAD FILES

The command `ftp` uses the TCP/IP File Transfer Protocol (FTP) to upload files to a remote site, or download files from it. The Windows 95 implementation of `ftp` works almost exactly as does the implementation used under Linux.

To invoke `ftp` under Windows 95, open an MS-DOS window, and then type the command **ftp** *host*, where *host* gives the name or IP address of the host with which you want to exchange files. After `ftp` connects with *host*, you can use its commands to control the exchange of files, as described in Chapter 4.

One useful task for `ftp` is to download a copy of the `hosts` file from your Linux machine to the Windows 95 machine. Figure 9-26 shows an `ftp` session in which the `hosts` file is downloaded.

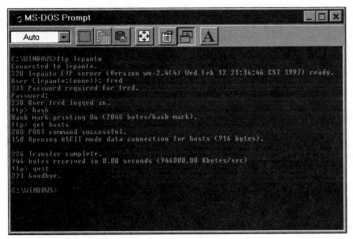

Figure 9-26: Downloading hosts file via ftp

Please note that Slackware, by default, compiles the `ftp` server to use shadow passwords. If you did not install shadow passwords on your Linux server, you must recompile the `ftp` server on your Linux machine so that it does not use shadow passwords.

TELNET: TERMINAL SESSION

The program `telnet` gives you a virtual terminal with which you can log into UNIX-based computers on the network and run a normal terminal session.

You can invoke the program as you do the Linux version we described in Chapter 4: type **telnet** *host port*, where *host* gives the name or IP address of the host to which you want to connect, and the optional argument *port* gives the number of the TCP or UDP port to which you want to connect.

The Windows 95 implementation of telnet differs from the Linux implementation in that the Windows 95 implementation opens a window on the Windows 95 desktop, rather than working through the console or an xterm window. The commands at the top of the window (File, Edit, and so forth) give you access to the standard Windows 95 menus. You can also use the menus to set such features as the type of terminal to emulate, the size and typeface to use on the display, and the display's background color. (By the way, we strongly urge you to stick with the default typeface if you are going to telnet to run any programs that use a curses interface.)

Figure 9-27 shows the beginning of a telnet session, in which the user typed the command telnet myexample into the Run entry of the Start menu.

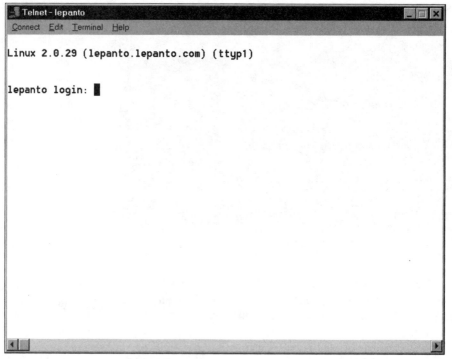

Figure 9–27: telnet session under Windows 95

One limitation of telnet under Windows 95 (unlike telnet when run through an xterm window) is that you have little control over the size of window you can use: you have a 24-line window or a 25-line window, and that's about it. Another problem that we've noticed is that, unless your Windows 95 box is a fairly souped-up model, the scrolling in the telnet window may well be unacceptably slow.

WEB BROWSER: NETSCAPE NAVIGATOR

Many other network-based programs are available for Windows 95 that enable you to communicate with either your Linux machine or other hosts around the Internet. However, one is particularly useful: the Netscape Navigator Web browser.

Netscape Navigator under Windows 95 works largely as it does under Linux. The principal differences are those that result from the differences in desktops: under Linux, Netscape Navigator uses the Motif desktop, whereas under Windows 95, it uses the Windows 95 desktop. Thus, the layout of buttons and menus differ somewhat between the two editions; however, their functionality and behavior are largely the same.

You can download an evaluation copy of Netscape Navigator from Web site `http://www.netscape.com`. Your copy of Windows 95 may have come with a copy of Microsoft's Internet Explorer preinstalled (as we write this chapter, the Justice Department is suing Microsoft over this practice); but you may want to consider downloading (and purchasing) Netscape Navigator for your Windows 95 machine, for the following reasons:

◆ Netscape Navigator works across a wide range of platforms, including both Linux and Windows 95. Internet Explorer, on the other hand, works just on Windows 95. Having all users use the same Web tools makes training users — and moving users from one operating system environment to another — much easier.

◆ The tools included in the Netscape Communicator package are designed to work with TCP/IP, rather than with the obsolete IBM/Microsoft NetBIOS protocol. This means that Communicator's tools are much easier than Microsoft's to configure for working with the Internet. For example, compare our earlier description of configuring Microsoft Exchange to work with your intranet with Netscape Communicator's mailer, which works without requiring any configuration at all. Clearly, this saves you time and stress.

◆ Finally, the Netscape corporation has been extraordinarily supportive of Linux: Netscape makes the full range of its tools available for Linux, despite the fact that it probably loses money on the effort. We think that "turn-about is fair play": as Netscape has supported Linux, we think that, all else being equal, the Linux community should support Netscape.

This concludes our discussion of using networking programs to connect Windows 95 with your intranet.

Conclusion

This concludes our discussion of the basic configuration of TCP/IP networking under Windows 95. By this point, you should have TCP/IP networking installed on your Windows 95 machine, and be able to exchange information with both your intranet's Linux machine and other hosts on the Internet.

In the next section, we move to advanced topics, in particular, letting Windows 95 machines mount a Linux directory as a network drive, and letting Windows 95 spool jobs directly to a printer that is plugged into your Linux machine. We also introduce Samba, the free package that makes this magic happen, and one of the extraordinary software packages that has been pleasurable to work with.

Samba

Samba is a package written by Andrew Tridgell, an Australian programmer, assisted by various people from around the world. It is available for free, under the terms of the GNU Public License. Samba implements the NetBIOS and SMB protocols under various flavors of UNIX, including Linux.

By installing Samba onto your Linux host, you can make printers and selected directories available to Windows users. A user can mount a Linux directory as a network drive, browse it, write files into it (including .exe files), and edit or execute files – just as if the directory were sitting on the user's C drive. Samba also handles the details of translating a Linux file system to Windows 95 – the fact that the Windows 95 and Linux file systems are completely different is of no concern to the user, as Samba transparently handles the details of translating bits from one file-system format to the other.

Samba is included as part of the standard Slackware release. We show you how to compile it, install it, and use its basic configuration.

Some Terminology

At the beginning of this chapter, we briefly discussed the NetBIOS, NetBEUI, and SMB protocols, which are the basis for networking under the Windows family of products. Before we continue, we must define two more terms that come from the Microsoft lexicon:

♦ A *share* is a resource that a machine makes available via SMB to the other machines in its workgroup. A share can be a printer, or a portion of a disk. A disk share names a directory and the files in it. You can set permissions on a disk share: either read-only, or read, write, and delete.

◆ A *service* is a share available on a given machine. For example, if Windows 95 machine `thor` makes the disk-share `msoffice` available to the other machines in its workgroup, then that share can be addressed as the service `\\thor\msoffice`. Please note the syntax of naming a service: `\\machinename\sharename`.

We speak of shares and services throughout the rest of this chapter. That said, we now describe how to install and configure Samba.

Install Samba onto Linux

The installation of Samba has three steps:

1. Compile the sources.

2. Copy the compiled bits into the appropriate places on your system.

3. Configure Samba.

We discuss each in turn.

COMPILING SAMBA

You need to recompile Samba on your Linux machine. If you are new to Linux and have never compiled an application, don't panic – it's really quite easy. The steps of compilation are as follows:

1. Copy the sources onto your Linux machine.

2. Modify the `Makefile`.

3. Compile.

We walk you through these steps one by one.

FIND AND COPY THE SOURCES

Your first step is to find a copy of the sources.

Copying from Slackware release

If you are using Slackware, use the command `su` to assume the identity of the superuser `root`. Then, pop into your CD-ROM drive the second CD that came with your Slackware release (the one that holds sources), and mount it. (If you do not yet know how to mount a CD-ROM, check your Slackware book.) Use the **cd** command to enter the following directory:

`/cdrom/networking/samba`

where directory *cdrom* is the name of the directory onto which you mounted the CD-ROM's file system. Type the following command:

```
cp samba-1.9.15p8.tgz /usr/src
```

By the time you read this, the name of the archive may have changed a little, to reflect that Slackware has installed a later release of Samba. The directory /usr/src, into which you are copying the archive, is the default place for storing sources, including the sources of your Linux kernel. If you are storing sources elsewhere, copy the Samba archive into that directory instead.

cd into directory /usr/src, and then execute the following command to extract files from the archive:

```
tar xvzf samba-1.9.15p8.tgz
```

This creates a directory called samba-1.9.15p8, and copies the source files into it.

Copying from the Web

If you do not have the Slackware release, you can download a copy of the Samba sources from site:

```
http://samba.anu.edu.au
```

Store the archive in the place where you usually store sources (usually directory /usr/src).

Extract the files from the archive, as just described.

MODIFY THE MAKEFILE   Now that you have obtained a copy of the sources, you must compile them. If you have not done this before, don't be intimidated: it's quite easy.

To begin, enter the directory in which the Samba sources are located — probably /usr/srcsamba-1.9.15p8, although this name may be a little different, depending upon where you store your source files and the release of Samba that you have. Once in the Samba directory, cd to directory source, which actually holds the source files.

Now, use a text editor to edit the Makefile, as follows:

   ◆ At the top of the make file are some entries that set the base directory that Samba uses:

```
# The base manpages directory to put the man pages in
# Note: $(MANDIR)/man1, $(MANDIR)/man5 and $(MANDIR)/man8 must
  exist.
MANDIR = /usr/local/man
```

```
# The directories to put things in. If you use multiple
# architectures or share the samba binaries across NFS then
# you will probably want to change this layout.
BASEDIR = /usr/local/samba
BINDIR = $(BASEDIR)/bin
LIBDIR = $(BASEDIR)/lib
VARDIR = $(BASEDIR)/var
```

By default, Samba stores its configuration file and executables in directory /usr/local/samba. If you prefer to use another directory, modify the macro BASEDIR to the directory you want to use. You should not change this default unless you have a clear reason for doing so.

◆ Uncomment one of the sets of instructions for the Linux operating system:

```
# Use this for Linux with shadow passwords
# contributed by Andrew.Tridgell@anu.edu.au
# add -DLINUX_BIGCRYPT if you have shadow passwords but don't have
 the
# right libraries and includes
# FLAGSM = -DLINUX -DSHADOW_PWD
# LIBSM = -lshadow
# Use this for Linux without shadow passwords
# contributed by Andrew.Tridgell@anu.edu.au
# FLAGSM = -DLINUX
# LIBSM =
```

One set of instructions is for Linux with shadow passwords, and the other is for Linux without shadow passwords. Uncomment the appropriate pair of lines — that is, the lines that define macros FLAGSM and LIBSM. (If you are new to make, a comment is a line that begins with a pound sign, #. To uncomment a line, remove # from its beginning.)

◆ Make sure that the instructions for all other operating systems are commented out. Clearly, Samba works under a great variety of UNIX systems.

COMPILE   After Makefile is properly edited, type the command **make**. This command automatically guides the compilation of the programs in the Samba package. Compilation may take a while, depending on the speed of your system.

You should see no errors. If an error occurs with make, be sure that you did not damage Makefile when you edited it. If an error occurred with the cc command that make invokes, cd to the Samba doc directory and check files INSTALL.txt and samba.faq for hints about diagnosing the error and fixing it.

INSTALL SAMBA

After the program compiles cleanly, the next step is to copy the compiled Samba bits into their proper places on your Linux system. To do so, re-enter the Samba source directory, su to the superuser root, and then type the command:

```
make install
```

make automatically copies the executables into their proper places on your system. This command also copies the Samba manual pages into the appropriate places, so that you can read them by typing the command **man**.

Configuring Samba

Now that Samba is compiled and installed on your system, you must configure it. This job has two steps:

1. Configure how your system turns on Samba.

2. Configure Samba itself, by editing its configuration file.

We discuss each task in turn.

TURNING ON SAMBA

The following are the two ways that you can tell Linux to invoke Samba:

◆ Through the master networking daemon inetd

◆ As a standalone daemon

Running Samba as a standalone daemon is a little easier, and the performance will be a little better. However, we think that running Samba through inetd is preferable: the loss in performance is hardly noticeable (unless your Linux machine is servicing quite a few Windows 95 boxes) and it spares your Linux box from being burdened with yet another daemon.

Please note that you can run Samba either through inetd or as a standalone daemon – but you must *not* do both.

We first discuss how to configure inetd to invoke Samba; then, we describe how to run Samba as a standalone daemon.

RUNNING SAMBA THROUGH INETD   To run Samba through inetd, do the following:

1. Edit file /etc/services so that it includes the following entries:

```
# NETBIOS Name Service
netbios-ns    137/tcp
netbios-ns    137/udp
# NETBIOS Datagram Service
```

```
netbios-dgm   138/tcp
netbios-dgm   138/udp
# NETBIOS session service
netbios-ssn   139/tcp
netbios-ssn   139/udp
```

> `/etc/services` may already have these entries: check to make sure
> before you modify this file.

2. Modify file `/etc/inetd.conf` to contain the following entries:

```
netbios-ssn stream tcp nowait  root /usr/local/samba/bin/smbd smbd
netbios-ns dgram udp wait root /usr/local/samba/bin/nmbd nmbd -
  Gmygroup
```

`inetd.conf` will not likely already contain these entries; however, it may well
have similar entries that are commented out. `mygroup` gives the name of your
Windows 95 machines' workgroup. If you have chosen to store the Samba binaries
in a directory other than the default directory `/usr/local/samba`, replace
`/usr/local/samba` with that directory's name.

RUNNING SAMBA THROUGH STANDALONE DAEMONS   To start up Samba as a
standalone daemon whenever you reboot Linux, `su` to the superuser `root`, and then
use a text editor to type the following commands into the end of file
`/etc/rc.d/rc.inet2`:

```
echo "Starting the Samba daemons ..."
/usr/local/samba/bin/smbd -D
/usr/local/samba/bin/nmbd -D
```

If you have chosen to install Samba into a directory other than
`/usr/local/samba`, name that directory instead.

Make sure that you don't change this file's permissions when you edit it – it
should still be executable.

And that's all there is to it. Now, we discuss the most difficult topic: the Samba
configuration file.

EDIT THE SAMBA CONFIGURATION FILE

When Samba first comes up, it reads the configuration file `smb.conf`. The
script that installed the compiled Samba bits did *not* install a copy of the Samba
configuration file; instead, you must build this file and install it into the appropriate directory.

Samba has many options and features, most of which are beyond the scope of
this book; however, we walk you through the process of modifying `smb.conf` so
that each user on a Windows 95 machine can mount her home directory on
the Linux machine as a network drive, and use the Linux box's `lp` queue to print
documents.

EDIT THE DEFAULT SMB.CONF   Among the files in the Samba archive that you
downloaded to your system is a directory named `examples/simple`. This directory
contains a file called `smb.conf`; and, as its location suggests, it contains a simple
example configuration for Samba. As with many things in life, the simplest
approach is the most useful, so we use that example to introduce configuration of
Samba — and modify it slightly to make it even more useful.

To edit this file, first cd to directory `examples/simple`. Because the first rule of
successful tinkering is to save all the parts, make a backup copy of file `smb.conf`.

Use your favorite text editor to open `smb.conf`. The file begins as follows:

```
; Configuration file for smbd.
; ===================================
; For the format of this file and comprehensive descriptions of all
 the
; configuration option, please refer to the man page for
 smb.conf(5).
;
; The following configuration should suit most systems for basic
 usage and
; initial testing. It gives all clients access to their home
 directories
; and allows access to all printers specified in /etc/printcap.
```

As its name implies, the sample configuration file contains numerous example
configurations. A comment begins with a semicolon ';'. The definition of a resource
resembles that used in a Windows `.ini` file: the resource name is give in square
brackets, and is followed by more definitions, each of which is indented.

The sample `smb.conf` file defines three resources:

- ◆ A `global` resource

- ◆ A `file` resource, which makes available to each Windows 95 user her
  Linux home directory

- ◆ A `printer` resource, which makes available to each Windows 95 user all
  printers plugged into the Linux box

We review each of these resources in turn.

Global resource

The `global` resource sets some definitions that are common to all resources. The
example `smb.conf` sets the `global` resource as follows:

```
[global]
    printing = bsd
    printcap name = /etc/printcap
    load printers = yes
    guest account = pcguest
;   This next option sets a separate log file for each client. Remove
```

```
;   it if you want a combined log file.
    log file = /usr/local/samba/log.%m
```

This resource defines the following values:

♦ `printing` – Names the software that your system uses to manage printing. The default is `bsd`, which is the standard printing software used under Linux and many other varieties of UNIX.

♦ `printcap name` – Gives the name of the `printcap` file that your machine uses. Samba reads this file to learn which printers are available on your system; for this reason, if your Linux system uses printing software that does not use a `printcap` file, you must create a `printcap` file for Samba to read. (For details on how to do so, see the document `INSTALL.txt`, which comes with the Samba sources.). The default for this definition is `/etc/printcap`, which is also the default under Linux.

♦ `load printers` – Sets whether printer resources should be made available to Windows users. The default is `yes`.

♦ `guest account` – Sets the name of a guest account. This account can be used by Windows users who do not have a login on the Linux machine, but who may need to get access to some Linux resources; for example, printer resources.

♦ `log file` – Lets you establish a separate log file for each Windows 95 user who will be accessing resources on your Linux machine.

Do not change the definitions for `printing`, `printcap`, and `load printers`, unless you need to correct something in them – and nothing should need to be corrected if you use the default Linux installation.

Be sure to check whether the account named in the definition `guest account` actually exists. To check whether a given account exists, check file `/etc/passwd`. The usual practice is to have a guest account named `guest` rather than `pcguest`; if your Linux system has such an account, change the definition of `guest account` from `pcguest` to `guest`. If your system has not defined a guest account, use command `useradd` to create one. (For details on how to use `useradd`, see its manual page.)

You may also want to comment out the `log file` entry, unless you plan to review each user's log file regularly. To comment out the entry, just insert a semicolon before it.

Home-directory resource

Resource `homes` makes each Windows 95 user's Linux home directory available to her.

The default version of `smb.conf` defines this resource as follows:

```
[homes]
    comment = Home Directories
    browseable = no
    read only = no
    create mode = 0750
```

This resource defines the following values:

◆ `browseable` – Lets the user browse her home directory, using the Windows 95 Browse button. The default is to set this to `no` – the user cannot browse her home directory. We suggest that you change this to `yes`, to turn on browsing.

◆ `read only` – Make the directory read-only: do not let the user write any files into this directory, or modify any files that already exist in this directory. By default, this is set to `no` – the user is granted permission to write and modify files in her home directory.

◆ `create mode` – When the user creates a file in this directory, give it permission of `0750`: that is, make it readable and executable by the user and members of the user's group, and make it writable by the user. You may want to change definition `create mode` to `0754`, which makes files readable by other users.

Printer resource

Resource `printers` makes the Linux box's suite of printers available to Windows 95 users:

```
[printers]
    comment = All Printers
    browseable = no
    printable = yes
    public = no
    writable = no
    create mode = 0700
```

Samba does not give access to the printer hardware itself. Rather, it gives the Windows 95 user access to the printer-management software that is built into your Linux system. As we see later in this chapter, a Windows 95 user can issue Windows-style commands to manipulate the printer queue on your Linux box; Samba interprets that request and issues the appropriate printer-management command under Linux.

This resource defines the following values:

◆ `browseable` — Lets the user see the Linux printer queue when she clicks the Browse button in the Windows 95 print screen. By default, this is set to `no` — the user cannot browse printers. We suggest that you change this to `yes`, so that printers can be browsed.

◆ `printable` — This must be set to `yes`, or files spooled to the printer queue will not be printed.

◆ `public` — When set to `yes`, this definition permits any Windows 95 user to print a file, regardless of whether she has a login on the Linux system. The default is `no` — only users who are identified to the Linux system have permission to print files.

◆ `writable` — When set to `yes`, this definition lets Windows 95 users directly write files into the directory owned by the print-spooling software. The default is `no` — files can be written into the spooling directory only by the spooler itself.

◆ `create mode` — Documents spooled to the Linux printer queue are given permissions of `0700` — readable, writable, and executable by the owner alone.

INSTALL AND TEST SMB.CONF   After you make these modifications, copy `smb.conf` into directory `/usr/local/samba/lib`. If you installed Samba into a directory other than `/usr/local/samba`, copy `smb.conf` into that directory's `lib` subdirectory instead.

The Samba package comes with a program, called `testparm`, that tests a Samba configuration file for problems. To invoke this program, type the command **/usr/local/samba/bin/testparm**. (Again, if you installed Samba into a directory other than `/usr/local/samba`, use that directory name instead. `testparm` reads your installed configuration file and tests it for errors. If all is well, you should see a printout that resembles the following:

```
Load smb config files from /usr/local/samba/lib/smb.conf
Processing configuration file "/usr/local/samba/lib/smb.conf"
Processing section "[homes]"
Processing section "[printers]"
No path in service printers - using /tmp
Loaded services file OK.
Press enter to see a dump of your service definitions
```

When you press Enter, `testparm` displays a detailed description of the resources you have made available via the SMB and NetBIOS protocols.

If file `smb.conf` has an error or problem, `testparm` will diagnose it for you. Try correcting the error in the installed copy of `smb.conf`, and then run `testparm` again. Continue until `testparm` runs cleanly.

When `testparm` runs cleanly, you have finished installation of Samba. But one task remains: tell Windows 95 about your newly created SMB server.

CREATE LMHOSTS   Windows 95 has three ways to convert a NetBIOS name into an IP address:

- ◆ Issue a request to a Windows Internet Name Server (WINS) server. A WINS server has a database that connects a NetBIOS name with its IP address.

- ◆ Read file `C:\WINDOWS\LMHOSTS`.

- ◆ Broadcast a request to all hosts on your intranet, asking a host with a given NetBIOS name to identify itself.

We have not set up a WINS server on our intranet; and continually broadcasting name-resolution requests can be very inefficient. Therefore, we will create an `lmhosts` file on our Windows 95 machine.

To do so, use a text editor on your Windows 95 box to edit file `C:\WINDOWS\LMHOSTS`. For each host, enter the host's IP address and NetBIOS name. For example, our Windows 95 box's `lmhosts` file has the following entry:

```
192.168.39.1     myexample
```

where `myexample` is the name of our Linux box.

Be sure to use a text editor to create this file – or, if you are using a word processor, use text mode to save it. Otherwise, your Windows 95 networking software will not be able to read it.

Copy this file onto each Windows 95 machine on your intranet.

Please note that an `lmhosts` file can be quite complicated; for example, you can embed an instruction in an `lmhosts` file that automatically reads a centrally located `lmhosts`. If you are interested, these options are documented in file `C:\WINDOWS\LMHOSTS.SAM` on your Windows 95 box.

Now comes the moment of truth: seeing whether Samba runs.

TURN ON AND TEST
To start up Samba, simply reboot your Linux system.

To test whether Samba is working, type command:

```
/usr/local/samba/bin/smbclient -L hostname
```

where *hostname* gives the name of your Linux workstation. (Note that Samba automatically uses the TCP/IP name of your local host as its NetBIOS name.) This command lists all resources that Samba has made available on your machine; for example, when we type command

```
/usr/local/samba/bin/smbclient -L myexample
```

we see the following:

```
Server time is Tue Oct 28 06:15:07 1997
Timezone is UTC-6.0
Domain=[myexample] OS=[Unix] Server=[Samba 1.9.15p8]
Server=[myexample] User=[fred] Workgroup=[myexample]
  Domain=[myexample]
        Sharename       Type        Comment
        ---- -          -- -         ---- -
        fred            Disk        Home Directories
        homes           Disk        Home Directories
        IPC$            IPC         IPC Service (Samba 1.9.15p8)
        lp              Printer
        printers        Printer     All Printers
This machine has a browse list:
        Server                  Comment
        ---- -                  ---- -
        MYEXAMPLE               Samba 1.9.15p8
```

If you see something like this listing, then congratulations! You now have Samba working on your Linux system. If you do not, then read the following; you may find some helpful hints for fixing what went wrong.

DEBUGGING   This subsection describes some of the problems that can arise with Samba, and suggests how to fix them.

Connection refused

If you see the message

```
connect error: Connection refused
```

then the Samba executables are not available.

If you are running Samba as standalone daemons, make sure that they are running: Type the command **ps -ax | grep smbd**. If you do not see a process for smbd, then start up smbd and nmbd, as previously described, and then try again.

If you are running Samba through inetd, check whether smbd and nmbd are correctly described in file /etc/inetd.conf. If they are not, insert these entries into the file, as we described earlier, and then restart the inetd daemon. If these entries are already in the file, again try restarting the inetd daemon, to force it to reread its configuration file.

Unfriendly server

If you see an error message like this:

```
Session request failed (0,0) with myname=MYGROUP destname=MYHOST
Unspecified error 0x0
Your server software is being unfriendly
```

then `inetd` could not run one of the two Samba programs named in file `/etc/inetd.conf`. This can have a couple of causes:

◆ Samba is not installed correctly — Make sure the Samba executables are installed into the directory named in file `/etc/inetd.conf`. For example, if the entries in `inetd.conf` for Samba read:

```
netbios-ssn stream tcp nowait root /usr/local/samba/bin/smbd smbd
netbios-ns dgram udp wait root /usr/local/samba/bin/nmbd nmbd -
  Gmygroup
```

then make sure that executable programs `smbd` and `nmbd` exist in directory `/usr/local/samba/bin`.

◆ `smb.conf` is not installed correctly — Samba will not run properly if `smb.conf` is not in the directory named in the `Makefile` you used when you compiled Samba. Remember, you must install `smb.conf` by hand — the command `make install` does not do it for you. `smb.conf` must be copied into the directory `lib` under the Samba root directory (the default is `/usr/local/samba`). Look at the `Makefile` with which you compiled Samba, and check the value for macro `BASEDIR`. If you did not copy `smb.conf` into directory `lib` under `BASEDIR`, then copy it there and try again.

Bad user account

If you see an error message of the form `Bad password`, the guest account with which you are accessing your Linux system is not correctly defined. Make sure that the account named in the `guest account` definition of the `global` resource actually exists. Further, make sure that it does *not* have a password set.

This error can also occur if Samba is not compiled to handle passwords in the same way as your system does: if your system uses shadow passwords, Samba must be compiled to use them; whereas if your system does *not* use shadow passwords, Samba must be compiled to *not* use them. Make sure that Samba has been compiled correctly, as we described earlier.

FURTHER TESTING

If you've gotten this far, then it appears that Samba is installed correctly onto your Linux system. Now, let's switch back to the Windows 95 box and see whether we can talk to the Linux server from there.

To test the connection, open an MS-DOS window and type the command:

```
net view \\myserver
```

where *myserver* names your Linux box. The command should display the shares available to you on your Linux box. For example, when we type the command **net view \\myexample**, we see:

```
Shared resources at \\MYEXAMPLE
Sharename     Type          Comment
- - - - - - - - - - - - - - - - - - - - - - - - - - - - - - - -
fred          Disk          Home Directories
homes         Disk          Home Directories
lp            Print
printers      Print         All Printers
The command was completed successfully.
```

This assumes that you are using the same login and password under Windows 95 as you do under Linux.

IF PROBLEMS PERSIST

If you have tried the preceding tests and you cannot get them to work correctly, the Samba package includes the following documents that will be helpful to you:

◆ Document INSTALL.txt describes installation of Samba in much more detail than we have gone into here. It may describe a situation on your Linux system that users of our default Slackware release will not have to face.

◆ Document DIAGNOSIS.txt walks you through a far-reaching set of diagnostic tests. It may describe a test that will help you diagnose the problem on your system.

◆ Document samba.faq holds frequently asked questions about Samba. You may find your problem described in there.

◆ The manual page for smb.conf describes every definition that Samba recognizes. You may find some helpful hints there on how to configure Samba to work best with your intranet. This page was installed into your Linux box's set of manual pages, so to read a formatted version of this page, type the command **man smb.conf**.

All of these documents are in directory docs, under the directory into which you installed the Samba source files.

If you get this far, congratulations! Your Linux box and your Windows 95 box are now exchanging data via the SMB protocol. Now, let's switch back to your Windows 95 box and do some more configuration, so that your Windows users can take advantage of what Samba offers.

CONNECTING A NETWORK DRIVE

One of the more attractive features of the Samba/Windows 95 interaction is that a user can mount her home directory on the Linux box as a network drive under Windows 95 – as, say, Windows 95 drive E. Thereafter, when she wants to use a Windows 95 application to work with a file that is in her Linux home directory, she can use the Windows 95 `Open File` and `Save File` features to read the file from drive E, as if it were physically on her Windows 95 box.

It is easy to mount a user's home directory as a network drive on a Windows 95 machine, as follows:

1. Click the My Computer icon. This usually is in the top of the Windows 95 screen. This opens the My Computer window, as shown in Figure 9-28.

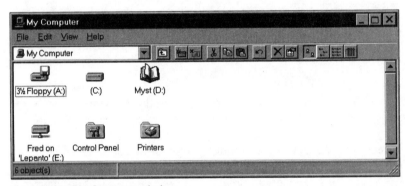

Figure 9-28: My Computer window

2. Click the second icon from the left on the toolbar – the icon that vaguely resembles a disk drive and has a little green "sparkle" in its upper-left corner. This is the icon immediately to the right of the "manila folder" icon. This icon opens the Map Network Drive window. (If the My Computer window does not display the toolbox, use the View menu to display it.) Figure 9-29 shows the Map Network Drive window.

This window consists of two text fields and a check box:

◆ The upper field, which is labeled Drive:, displays the letter of the next available drive – physical or network.

◆ The lower field, which is labeled Path:, lets you type in or select the directory on your Linux machine that you want to mount as a Windows 95 drive.

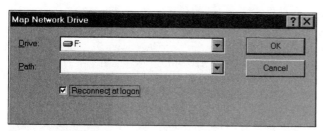

Figure 9-29: Map Network Drive window

With regard to assigning a drive, usually the default displayed in the Drive: field is acceptable. However, to select a drive other than the default, click the down-arrow button at the right of the field. This displays a scroll list from which you can pick the letter you want to assign to the drive you are mounting.

With regard to entering the path of the drive, you can either type its name or click the down-arrow button to select it from the list of Linux directories that Samba has made available to you:

1. To select a directory from the list, click the down-arrow button, and then use the mouse to click the appropriate directory. The directories available to you for mounting will vary, depending on how you configure Samba. The default configuration of Samba, which we described a little earlier in this chapter, lets you access only your home directory on your Linux system. Thus, when you click the down-arrow button, you see two paths: one that gives the name of your home directory (for example, fred or chris), and another that names directory homes. Both identify your home directory on your Linux box.

2. To type the drive you want, just type its name. The format is \\hostname\directoryname. Please note that you do *not* use the path name of the directory; for example, the path to user fred's home directory on machine myexample is \\myexample\fred — *not* \\myexample\home\fred. If you type the name of a directory that is not visible to you — either because you lack permission or because it does not exist — Windows 95 displays an error message.

If you want to have the drive remounted automatically whenever you log into Windows 95, click the check box labeled Reconnect at logon. This is at the bottom of the Map Network Drive pop-up window.

Please note that the preceding will not work unless you use exactly the same login identifier and password under Windows 95 as you do under Linux.

USING THE COMMAND NET USE   Using the control-panel interface is simple and effective; however, it does have a drawback: writing the interaction with a wizard into script is difficult. If you will be modifying multiple Windows 95 machines, you may find it helpful to have a single MS-DOS command that you can copy into a file, download to all the target machines, and then run to configure all the machines at once. Remember, too, that some people find a command-line interface to be superior to a graphical interface: after all, we switched from hieroglyphics to a phonetic alphabet many years ago, for the simple reason that the alphabet is a more efficient and more accurate way to encode information.

The MS-DOS command NET gives you a command-line interface to practically all of Windows 95's networking features. You can write a NET command into a script (or .bat file), and then execute it repeatedly on all the machines you want to configure.

We discuss NET throughout the rest of this chapter; in brief, the NET command is typed into an MS-DOS window. It uses subcommands, each of which takes arguments.

To use NET to mount a directory on your Linux machine as a network drive, do the following:

1. Click the Start button; when its menu pops up, click Programs, and when *its* menu pops up, click the entry labeled MS-DOS Prompt. This opens a text window into which you can type MS-DOS commands.

2. Type the command **NET USE** *drive*: *host**homedirectory*. For example, to mount user fred's home directory on Linux machine myexample as drive K:, type the command:

```
NET USE K: \\myexample\fred
```

Please note once again that you do not type the path of your home directory — only its name (or to be more precise, the name of the user whose home directory you want to use). Note, too, that for this command to work, you must use the same login identifier and password under Windows 95 as you use under Linux.

NET gives you a command-line interface to practically all the Windows 95 networking features. A summary of NET appears at the end of this chapter.

Printer Sharing

You can use Samba to give Windows 95 access to a printer that is plugged into a Linux box. You can mount the printer as a resource — in effect, you can assign it a virtual printer port on your machine, and Windows 95 users can use it just as they use a printer that is directly plugged into the Windows 95 box.

We should note that, in its default configuration, Samba does not give Windows 95 access to a physical printer. Rather, Samba gives Windows 95 access to the printer *queue* on your machine – in most instances, the queue that is managed by your Linux machine's command lp. If lp redirects print jobs to a physical device that is plugged into another Linux box on your network (as we describe in Chapter 7), this will be invisible to Windows 95: it will think that it is directing its print jobs to a printer that is plugged into another Windows 95 box.

Before we continue, one caveat must be noted. The following descriptions assume that you are using the default configuration for Samba, and the default configuration for Samba assumes that you are using the Berkeley commands to manage your printing queues – in particular, the print-manager daemon lpd. (Please do not confuse this with the print command lp, which – confusingly enough – is an entirely separate entity.) Slackware and almost every other release of Linux installs the Berkeley commands by default. If you do not know what commands are being used to manage your printing queue, chances are that you are using the Berkeley commands. But if you run into a problem, be sure that printing is configured correctly on your system, and that the daemon lp is up and running.

Having said that, two ways that you (or an ordinary Windows 95 user) can mount a network printer are available: by using the Windows 95 Add Printer Wizard, or by using the MS-DOS command NET USE. We discuss each in turn.

USING THE ADD PRINTER WIZARD
To invoke and use the Add Printer Wizard, do the following:

1. Click the Start button, in the lower-left corner of the Windows 95 screen.

2. When the Start menu appears, click the entry labeled Settings.

3. When the Settings menu appears, click the entry labeled Printers. This opens a pop-up window that is titled Printers. This window holds one icon for each printer that is connected to the Windows 95 box, and it also has an icon that is labeled Add Printer, with which you can add another printer to the machine's set of printers. Click the icon that is labeled Add Printer.

4. When you click the Add Printer icon, Windows 95 invokes its Add Printer Wizard, which walks you through the process of adding a printer. We describe each of the wizard's screens in turn:

5. The first window (Figure 9-30) contains some descriptive information. Click the button labeled Next>.

Figure 9-30: Add Printer Wizard: information screen

6. The next window (Figure 9-31) asks you to choose whether the printer is a local printer (a printer that is plugged directly into the Windows 95 box), or a network printer (a printer that is plugged into another computer, and that is accessed over the network). Click the radio button labeled Network Printer, and then click the button labeled Next>.

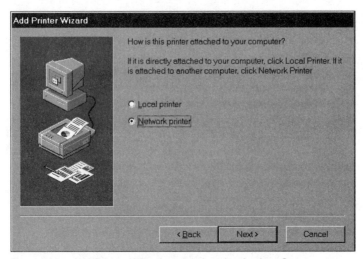

Figure 9-31: Add Printer Wizard: network or local printer?

7. The next window (Figure 9-32) asks you to enter information about the network printer. In the field labeled *Network path or queue name:* you can type the name of your Linux machine and its queue; however, you probably will find it easier to click the Browse button, and let the wizard worry about getting the syntax of the queue name correct. When you click the Browse button, the wizard opens a window that displays all the machines on your network that have made services available to this Windows 95 box. You should see an icon for your Linux workstation; click it.

8. When you click the icon for your Linux box, you will see an entry for the Linux box's printer queue (by default, the queue managed by the Linux printer-command 1p). Click the icon for 1p, and then click the OK button. The wizard closes the browse window, and then displays the network path of your Linux box's 1p queue in the Network Path field. For example, if your Linux box is named myexample, you will see the path \\MYEXAMPLE\1p in the Network Path field. Click the button labeled Next>.

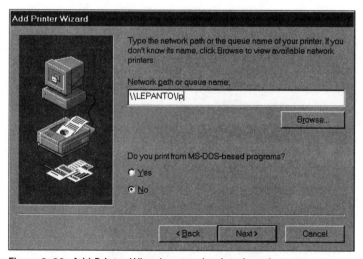

Figure 9-32: Add Printer Wizard: network printer's path

9. The next window (Figure 9-33) asks you to select the manufacturer and model of the printer you are using. This helps Windows 95 to load the driver for this type of printer. Windows 95 comes with drivers for nearly every kind of popular printer, and you can also load a custom driver, if you need one. The printer-driver window consists of two scroll lists: the list on the left lists manufacturers of printers, the one on the right lists the machines that the selected manufacturer builds. Click the appropriate manufacturer in the left scroll list, and then click the appropriate model in the right scroll list. For example, if you have a Hewlett-Packard LaserJet IIP with a PostScript cartridge in it, you would click HP in the left scroll list, and HP LaserJet IIP PS Cartridge in the right list. After you make your selection, click the OK button. If Windows 95 does not have a driver for this printer already installed, it may prompt you to place your Windows 95 CD-ROM back into the CD-ROM drive, so that it can read the driver from the disk. If your printer is not described in the list, and you have a floppy disk that has that printer's driver on it, click the Have Disk button, and follow the wizard's directions. After you select the printer that is plugged into your Linux box, click the Next> button.

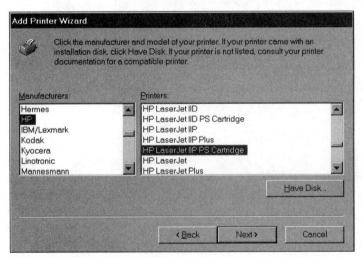

Figure 9-33: Add Printer Wizard: select the printer's manufacturer and model

10. If in the previous window you selected a type of printer for which Windows 95 has already installed a driver, you can either keep the current driver or replace it with a new driver. We recommend that you always keep the current driver; this option is the default. To keep the current driver, simply click the Next> button.

11. The next window (Figure 9-34) lets you name the printer. The field labeled Printer Name displays a default name for the printer; however, you can type another, more descriptive name if you prefer (for example, **Linux Printer**). At the bottom of the window are two radio buttons that enable you to tell Windows 95 to use this printer as the default printer. If you want Windows 95 programs to use this printer by default, click the Yes button; the default is No. After you enter the printer's name and click the appropriate radio button, click the Next> button.

12. The next window asks whether you want to print a test page. You should do so, just to confirm that everything is working correctly. After it has dispatched the test page, the wizard asks whether the page printed correctly. If it did not, the wizard makes some suggestions to correct the problem. If problems occur, log into your Linux box and try to print something, to ensure that no problem exists on the Linux side: make sure that the lp daemon is running, and make sure that the printer is turned on and is connected correctly. When the printer is working to your satisfaction, click the Finish button, which indicates that you are finished with this installation.

Figure 9-34: Add Printer Wizard: name the printer

A new icon for the printer you have just installed should appear in the Printers window. You can now use this printer to print jobs from your Windows 95 applications (for example, Microsoft Word), just like any printer that is plugged directly into your Windows 95 box.

USING THE COMMAND NET USE

As we described earlier, the command NET is a simple and powerful MS-DOS command that gives you a command-line interface to manipulating nearly all of Windows 95's networking features. To use NET to add a printer to a Windows 95 system, use its subcommand USE, as follows:

1. Click the Start button; when its menu pops up, click Programs, and when *its* menu pops up, click MS-DOS Prompt. This opens a text window into which you can type MS-DOS commands.

2. Type the command **NET USE LPT port:** *host**printerqueue*. port gives the name of a parallel port (real or virtual) onto which you want to mount the printer queue; this always takes the syntax LPT (for "line printer"), followed by a single-digit number. Be sure not to use a parallel port for which a printer is already described, or Windows 95 will be hopelessly confused. *host* names the computer whose queue you want to mount as a network printer. *printerqueue* names the printer queue being mounted as a network printer; for a Linux machine, this is always the printer queue lp. For example, to mount the printer queue lp on Linux machine myexample as virtual parallel port LPT3, use the following command:

```
NET USE LPT3: \\myexample\lp
```

You can also use the NET command to manage a printer queue on the remote machine. The command NET PRINT lets you suspend the printing of a job, resume the printing of a job, or kill a print job. For details on how to use NET USE or NET PRINT, see the summary of the NET command that appears at the end of this chapter.

And with that, we conclude our discussion of configuring Windows 95 to access Linux resources.

Accessing Windows 95 Files from Linux

Up to this point, we have discussed how a Windows 95 user can access Linux resources. However, the flip side to this coin is letting a Linux user access Windows 95 resources, particularly Windows 95 files.

Linux comes with two methods with which you can access files on a Windows 95 box:

♦ The command `smbclient`, which is part of the Samba package. This command uses a text interface like that of the command `ftp` (introduced in Chapter 4). It is not as slick as a Windows 95 graphical interface, but it gets the job done. `smbclient` commands can be used in a shell script, to perform such tasks as automatically backing up Windows 95 files to disk or tape.

♦ `smbfs`, which is an interface to SMB files that works directly within the kernel. By using `smbfs`, plus its associated tools `smbmount` and `smbumount`, you can mount an SMB resource directly onto your Linux file system and use ordinary Linux commands (such as `cp`, `mv`, and `tar`) to manipulate its files.

In this section, we first discuss how to make Windows 95 file shares accessible to Linux users via the network. Then we introduce `smbclient` and `smbfs`.

Making Windows 95 Files Accessible

Before you can begin to work with Windows 95 file shares from under Linux, you must make them visible to the workgroup of which the Linux box and the Windows 95 box are a part. The following walks you through this rather convoluted process.

TURN ON SERVICES
The first step in this process is to tell Windows 95 to inform its workgroup of its services, as follows:

1. Click the Start button. Move the mouse pointer to the Settings entry in the Start menu. When the Settings menu appears, click the entry for Control Panel.

2. In the Control Panel window, click the Network icon (as shown in Figure 9-2).

3. Click the button labeled File and Print Sharing (Figure 9-35).

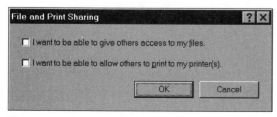

Figure 9-35: The File and Print Sharing button

4. Click the box labeled *I want to be able to give others access to my files*; then click the OK button to close the File and Print Sharing window.

5. In the Network window's area that shows installed network components, you should see an entry labeled *File and printer sharing for Microsoft Networks*. Click the OK button in the Network window. Windows 95 will prompt you that you must reboot Windows 95 for the changes to take effect. Click the button to reboot immediately.

MAKE DIRECTORIES ACCESSIBLE

After the Windows 95 box reboots, it has its file-sharing service turned on. The next step is to make file shares (directories) available to another machine in the workgroup:

1. Click the icon labeled My Computer, which is on the Windows 95 desktop. This opens the My Computer window (Figure 9-28).

2. Click the icon labeled (C:). This opens a window that displays the directories in the Windows 95 file system on the C drive. Figure 9-36 shows this window.

Figure 9-36: Directories on C drive's file system

3. Click the directory that you want to make available to the workgroup as a file share. Then, click the File entry on (C:) window's menu bar. When this drops down, click the entry for Properties.

4. When the Properties window opens, click the Sharing tab, as shown in Figure 9-37.

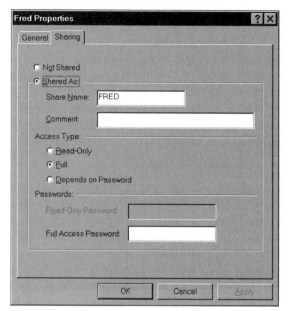

Figure 9-37: Sharing a directory

Fill in the window as follows:

1. Click the button labeled Shared As.

2. Under the Access Type entry, click the button that sets the level of access you want to give on this directory: Read-Only, Full, or Depends on Password.

3. If you click Read-Only, you can enter a password into the field labeled Read-Only Password. If you enter a password into this field, the user who wants to access the files in this directory from the Linux box must enter this password before she can read a file. If you do not enter a password into this field, no password is required to read the files in this directory.

4. If you click Full (give read, write, and delete permissions in this directory), you can enter a password into the field labeled Full Access Password. If you enter a password into this field, the user who wants to access the files in this directory from the Linux box must enter this password before she can manipulate a file. If you do not enter a password into this field, no password is required to manipulate the files in this directory.

5. If you click Depends on Password, you must enter a password into both the Read-Only Password and the Full Access Password fields. Windows 95 will use the password the user enters to grant the degree of permission. Be sure you enter a different password into each field.

6. Click the OK button. The icon for this directory will change to one that has the unofficial Microsoft logo at its bottom (that is, a hand extended palm-up), which indicates that this directory's files can be shared.

Repeat these steps for each directory whose contents you want to open as a file share to the other machines in the workgroup.

And with this, your Windows 95 machine is ready to share its resources with the other machines on your intranet, including your Linux machine. Next, we discuss the Linux tools with which you can read Windows 95 files from your Linux box.

smbclient

smbclient, a utility that is part of the Samba package, enables you to manipulate files on selected resources: read, copy, insert, or delete them. smbclient uses a command-line interface that resembles that of the networking command ftp — although with some important differences, as you will see.

To use smbclient, you must first have compiled and installed Samba, as previously described, and configured the Windows 95 box to interact with your Linux box. smbclient itself requires no special configuration.

smbclient is described fully by its manual page, which is part of the Samba package. The following describes some of the more commonly used options.

INTERROGATING A WINDOWS 95 BOX

The following command-line options to smbclient help you to retrieve information from the Windows 95 box with which you want to work:

◆ -L *windows95box* — Lists the shares that the Windows 95 box makes available to the Linux box. *windows95box* gives the Windows 95 box's NetBIOS name. For example, if a user on Linux box myexample wants to find out what services Windows 95 box thor makes available, she would type command:

```
smbclient -L thor
```

smbclient returns a listing that resembles the following:

```
Server time is Sat Oct 11 08:11:04 1997
Timezone is UTC+8.0
Server=[THOR] User=[] Workgroup=[MYEXAMPLE] Domain=[MYEXAMPLE]
Sharename      Type      Comment
- - - - -      - -       - - - -
FRED           Disk
IPC$           IPC       Remote Inter Process Communication
MSOFFICE       Disk
WINDOWS        Disk
This machine has a browse list:
Server                   Comment
```

```
_ _ __-                  _ _ _-
MYEXAMPLE                   Samba 1.9.15p8
THOR               .      Windows 95 machine
```

The first two lines of the listing give the current time and the time zone. The phrase UTC+8.0 means the time zone that is eight hours behind UTC (Greenwich) time — the Central Standard Time zone.

The next line names the Windows 95 box (the server that the Linux box is interrogating), its NetBIOS workgroup, and its TCP/IP domain.

The next lines list the shares that the Windows 95 box makes available to its workgroup. Shares FRED, WINDOWS, and MSOFFICE are file shares — directories whose contents (both files and subdirectories) can be manipulated by users who are on other machines in the workgroup. Share IPC$ describes interprocess communication. This share, like all shares that end in $, is not available to users.

Finally, the smbclient printout describes the machines that thor can browse: in this case, the Linux box myexample, through its Samba server, and thor itself.

◆ -I *ip_address* — Give the IP address of the Windows 95 box to connect to. *ip_address* gives the IP address, in dot format. If you do not use this option, but simply identify the Windows 95 box by its NetBIOS name, smbclient tries to locate the Windows 95 box by broadcasting a request that it identify itself. You should use this option if, for some reason, your smbclient is having trouble resolving the NetBIOS name of the Windows 95 box into its IP address.

◆ -U *username[%password]* — Name the user who is interrogating the Windows 95 box. Optionally, you can attach a password to the user's name; they must be separated by a single % character, with no spaces. For example, to interrogate the Windows 95 box as user fred whose password is mypassword, use the option -U fred%mypassword. If you do not use this option, smbclient uses the value of the environmental variable USER as the name of the user who is interrogating the Windows 95 box, and prompts you to type a password; obviously, this default works only if the user who is interrogating the Windows 95 box also has a login on that box, and under the same name. Please note, by the way, that if you *do* embed a user's name and password in a script, be very careful to limit who has permission to read the file that holds this script; otherwise, a malevolent user will be able to gain access to a Windows 95 machine's file shares, and possibly damage them.

INTERACTIVE USE OF SMBCLIENT

After you learn which shares a Windows 95 box makes available, you can use smbclient to work with those shares interactively. To work interactively with a

Windows 95 share, invoke `smbclient` as follows:

```
smbclient '\\windows95box\share'
```

where *windows95box* gives the NetBIOS name of the Windows 95 box with which you'll be working, and `share` names the share you'll be manipulating. For example, earlier we used the command

```
smbclient -L thor
```

to discover the shares that the Windows 95 machine `thor` has made available to the other machines in its workgroup, and to discover that among these shares is the directory `MSOFFICE`. So, to interactively work with the files in directory `MSOFFICE` on machine `thor`, we use the command `smbclient '\\thor\msoffice'`. Please note that `smbclient` automatically shifts the name of a share into uppercase letters, as Windows 95 expects. Note, too, that we enclose the name `\\thor\msoffice` in apostrophes (also called single quotes) so that the backslashes are not interpreted by the Linux system's shell; if you do not, `smbclient` will fail with the error message `Not enough '\' characters in service`.

If you do not use the `-U` option to name the user who asks to manipulate the Windows 95 share, `smbclient` reads the Linux shell's environmental variable `USER` for the name of the user to pass to Windows 95, and then prompts you for the password.

After you connect with the Windows 95 machine, `smbclient` displays the prompt `smb: \>`. The backslash character `\` indicates that you are working with that file share's root directory; if you change directories within this file share, `smbclient` includes the name of this directory in its prompt. You can use any of the following commands to work with the contents of the file share:

- `cd [directory]` — Change to *directory* within the file share. If you use `cd` without an argument, `smbclient` prints the name of the directory you are now in. `smbclient` includes in its prompt the name of the directory with which you are now working.

- `del [pattern]` — Delete all files in the current directory that match *pattern*. A *pattern* can include letters and the wildcard characters `*` and `?`. For example, the command `del a*` deletes all files in the current directory that begin with the letter a. Please note one difference from the Linux shell: the wildcard character `?` matches any single character, or no character at all. Thus, if the current directory contains files `foo` and `foo.bar`, the command `del foo?*` will delete both `foo` and `foo.bar`, whereas under the Linux shell, only file `foo.bar` would be deleted.

- `dir [pattern]` — List all files that match *pattern*. A *pattern* can include the wildcard characters `*` and `?`. If you do not give a *pattern*, this command lists all files in the directory.

◆ `exit` – Close the connection with the Windows 95 box, and exit from `smbclient`.

◆ `get windowsfile [linuxfilename]` – Copy file `windowsfile` from the Windows 95 box into your local directory on the Linux box. If optional argument `linuxfilename` is given, file `windowsfile` is renamed `linuxfilename` on the Linux box. Please note that this command retrieves one, and only one, file from a Windows 95 box. To retrieve multiple files, use the command `mget`.

◆ `lcd [linuxdirectory]` – Change the current local directory – the directory that you are using on the Linux machine – to `linuxdirectory`. Files retrieved from the Windows 95 box will be written into the new current directory. If you use this command without an argument, `smbclient` prints the name of your current Linux directory.

◆ `mget pattern` – Copy multiple files from the Windows 95 box to the Linux box. The files to be copied must match `pattern`, which can include the wildcard characters * and ?. For example, to copy all C source files from the Windows 95 share to the Linux box, use the command `mget *.c`.

◆ `mkdir directory` – Create `directory` on the Windows 95 box. The new directory is created in the directory you happen to be in on the Windows 95 box.

◆ `mput pattern` – Copy multiple files from the Linux box onto the Windows 95 box. The files being copied must match `pattern`, which can include the wildcard characters * and ?. For example, to copy all files from the current directory on the Linux box into the current directory on the Windows 95 box, use the command `mput *`.

◆ `prompt` – Toggle whether `smbclient` asks for your approval before it copies a file via the commands `mget` or `mput`.

◆ `put linuxfile [windowsfilename]` – Copy the file `linuxfile` from the current directory on the Linux box into the current directory on the Windows 95 box. By default, `linuxfile` retains its name under Windows 95; however, the optional second argument to `put` renames `linuxfile` to `windowsfilename`.

◆ `recurse` – Toggle recursion for the commands `mget` and `mput`. When recursion is turned on, `mget` and `mput` search for files that match a given `pattern`, not only in the current directory, but also in all directories that lie below the current directory. For example, with recursion turned on, the command `mget *` will copy every file from the Windows 95 share into the current directory on the Linux box.

◆ `rmdir` *directory* — Remove *directory* from the Windows 95 box. This command fails if *directory* contains any files.

This concludes our brief introduction to command `smbclient`. For a more detailed discussion, see its manual page.

SMBTAR: BACK UP WINDOWS FILES

The command `smbtar` is a shell script that uses `smbclient` to copy files from a Windows 95 share, and archives them via the Linux command `tar`.

The following describes `smbtar`'s most commonly used options:

◆ `-s` *windowsbox* — Back up files from machine *windowsbox*.

◆ `-x` *share* — Back up files from *share*. For example, command

```
smbtar -s thor -x msoffsice
```

backs up all files in file share (that is, directory) `msoffice` on the Windows 95 box `thor`.

◆ `-p` *password* — Use *password* when connecting to the Windows 95 box.

◆ `-u` *user* — Assume the identity of *user* when backing up files. If this is not set, `smbtar` uses your current login identifier to identify itself to the Windows 95 box.

◆ `-t` *output* — Write the archived files to *output*. This can be the name of a file or device. For example, command

```
smbtar -s thor -x foo -t /dev/fd0
```

copies all files from share `foo` on Windows 95 box `thor` onto the floppy-disk device `/dev/fd0`. (This assumes that your Linux system grants you permission to write to this physical device.) If this option is not used, `smbtar` archives files into file `tar.out` on the Linux box.

◆ `-n` *filename* — Back up only the files that are younger than file *filename* on the Windows 95 box. For example, if file `myfile` was last modified on November 19, 1997, then the command

```
smbtar -s thor -x msoffice -n myfile
```

will back up all files that reside in directory `msoffice` on machine `thor` and that were created after November 19, 1997.

◆ -r — Restore files from an output file back into a share. The share into which files are restored is not necessarily the same one from which they were first backed up. For example, the commands

```
smbtar -s thor -x firstshare -t tmp.tar
smbtar -s thor -x secondshare -t tmp.tar
```

archive all files in service \\thor\firstshare into file tmp.tar, and then copy them from that file into service \\thor\secondshare. This assumes that you have appropriate permissions in both firstshare and secondshare.

For a fuller description of smbclient and its options, see the manual page for smbclient. To view this page, type the Linux command **man smbclient**.

smbfs

smbclient is a useful program, particularly for performing routine administrative tasks, such as backing up files. However, Linux also offers a technique with which you can work directly with Windows 95 files: smbfs.

smbfs is a block of code that manipulates an SMB file resource as if it were a file system, just like the ISO-9660, ext2, or MS-DOS file systems. When smbfs is compiled into your Linux kernel, you can mount a Windows 95 file resource onto your Linux file system, and then use Linux commands, such as mv, cp, and tar to manipulate the Windows 95 files directly, just as if they were on your Linux box's hard disk.

COMPILING smbfs

As we mentioned, smbfs is compiled directly into your Linux kernel. In fact, when we built our default networking kernel in Chapter 3, we included smbfs.

If you are not sure whether smbfs is part of your kernel, check file /usr/src/linux/.config, and look for an entry that reads:

```
CONFIG_SMB_FS=y
```

If you do see this entry, smbfs is already in your kernel. If it is not and you want to add it, simply reconfigure your kernel as we described in Chapter 3; and when you see the question

```
SMB filesystem support (to mount WfW shares etc..) (CONFIG_SMB_FS)
  [Y/m/n/?]
```

type y. Then recompile and install the kernel as usual.

smbmount AND smbumount

smbfs requires a special version of the commands mount and umount to mount or unmount a Windows 95 file resource. These commands, called smbmount and smbumount, are part of a package of smbfs utilities called ksmbfs.

Before you go any further, check your system to see whether commands smbmount and smbumount already reside on your system. If they do not, you can obtain a copy via FTP from the following URL:

```
ftp://ftp.debian.org/debian/stable/source/otherosfs/ksmbfs_2.0.1.ori
  g.tar.gz
```

By the time you read this book, a later version may be available.

Copy the archive into directory /usr/src; then use the command

```
tar xvzf ksmbfs_2.0.1.orig.tar
```

to de-archive and decompress the files. Then cd into directory ksmbfs-2.0.1.orig, and type the commands:

```
make
make install
```

That's all there is to it.

MOUNTING A WINDOWS 95 RESOURCE

To mount a Windows 95 resource, use the command smbmount. Like the command mount, it takes two arguments: the resource you want to mount, and the name of the directory onto which you want to mount the resource.

As with commands mount and umount, only the superuser root can use smbmount and smbumount. The Windows 95 disk resource must already have been exported to other machines in its workgroup, as we described earlier in this chapter.

For example, to mount the exported file resource windows on Windows 95 machine thor onto Linux directory /win95, use the following command:

```
smbmount //thor/windows /win95
```

The Windows 95 box will prompt you for your Windows 95 password; enter it. That's all there is to it. When you type the command

```
ls /win95
```

you will see the contents of the Windows 95 directory windows, just as if it were on your Linux machine's hard disk. You can now use your standard Linux commands to work with these Windows 95 files.

To unmount the Windows 95 file resource, use the command `smbumount`. This command differs a little from the standard command `umount`, in that you give the name of the directory to unmount, not the device. For example, to unmount the Windows 95 file resource mounted onto directory `/win95`, type the command:

```
smbumount /win95
```

As you can see, `smbfs` is a much more powerful way to work with Windows 95 than is `smbclient`. However, `smbclient` is still useful, particularly in administrative scripts that run in the background.

And with this, we conclude our discussion of how to access Windows 95 files from within Linux.

Windows 95 Networking Commands

Windows 95 (and Windows NT) come with two text-based commands that you can use to manage networking:

◆ `NET` — Perform many common networking tasks.

◆ `NETSTAT` — Give a summary of what the network is doing at this moment.

It may seem incongruous that a book titled *The Linux Network* should detail Windows 95's networking commands. However, one of the goals of this book is to help you establish an intranet that can include many different types of machines, not just those that run Linux; and if you are going to be interfacing Linux with Windows 95, you will be better able to do your job if you have some familiarity with the Windows 95 networking commands.

We introduce each command in turn.

NET: Manage Networking

The Windows 95 command `NET` performs many networking tasks. It works in a line-oriented manner. `NET` is one of the most important — and under-documented — commands that come with Windows 95. In the words of Tom Yager, this is a "command so powerful that just understanding it can get you a raise (or a job, if you don't have one)."

This command executes several subcommands. Each subcommand, in turn, can take any number of arguments. The following list includes the subcommands and their arguments. If an argument is in square brackets, it is optional; if two arguments are separated by a vertical-bar character, |, you can pick one argument or the other, but not both.

♦ NET CONFIG [/YES] — Display the current workgroup settings. Argument /YES tells NET not to prompt you for information or to confirm its actions.

♦ NET DIAG [/NAMES | /STATUS [machinename]] — Show diagnostic information about the network. This command uses the Microsoft Network Diagnostics facility, running on either the machine into which you type this command or another Windows 95 or Windows NT machine on the network. NET DIAG is not of much use if you are not familiar with the Microsoft Network Diagnostics. NET DIAG can take either of two arguments:

♦ /NAMES — Name a machine that is running the Microsoft Network Diagnostics program. If you do not enter a machinename that is running diagnostics, the current machine runs diagnostics.

♦ /STATUS — Name the machine about which you want to see diagnostic information. If you do not enter a machinename, NET DIAG prompts you to enter the name of the machine whose status interests you.

♦ NET HELP [sub-command | errornumber] — Print information about how to use the NET command or one of its subcommands. If used without an argument, this command prints a summary of all the NET subcommands. Argument subcommand tells it to print detailed information about subcommand. For example, to print a summary of how to use the subcommand DIAG, type **NET HELP DIAG**. Another way to get information about a command is to type the command with the argument /?. For example, to see information about the command NET HELP, type **NET HELP /?**. Argument errornumber prints information about error errornumber.

♦ NET INITIALIZE [/DYNAMIC] — Load protocol and network-adapter drivers without binding them to Protocol Manager. Optional argument /DYNAMIC loads the Protocol Manager dynamically. This is useful with some third-party networks to resolve memory problems.

♦ NET LOGOFF [/YES] — Break the connection between your computer and the shares it is using on another machine. Optional argument /YES tells the command to run without prompting you to approve what it does.

♦ NET LOGON [user [:password | ?]] [/DOMAIN:name] [/SAVEPW:NO] [/YES] — Add a user to a workgroup. If you invoke this command without arguments, it prompts you for the name of the user and her password, and then adds the user to the workgroup. You can also invoke this command with the following arguments:

♦ *user* :*password* — *user* gives the user's name; it can be no more than 20 characters. The optional *password* can be no more than 14 characters. A *password* of ? tells the command to prompt you for a password. If you give no *password*, this user's access will not be protected by a password.

♦ /DOMAIN:*name* — Add *user* to workgroup *name*. If you do not use this argument, this subcommand adds *user* to the current workgroup.

♦ /SAVEPW:NO — Do not create a password-list file for *user*.

♦ /YES — Run without prompting you to approve what it does.

♦ NET PASSWORD [*machinename*] [*nowpassword* [*newpassword*]] — Change the password with which you gain access to computer *machinename*. *nowpassword* and *newpassword* give your current password and your new password, respectively.

♦ NET PRINT *machinename* *printer* | *port* [*job* /PAUSE | /RESUME | /DELETE] [/YES] [/YES] — Display information about a print queue, or manipulate a print job. When used without the argument *job*, this command shows the status of that print job. This command recognizes the following arguments:

♦ *machinename**printer* — *machinename* names the machine whose print queue you want to manipulate. *printer* names the particular print queue you want to manipulate. To get information about the print queue on a Linux box into which a printer is plugged, use the command \\\\linuxbox\\lp. For example, if a Windows 95 box accesses a printer on Linux box myexample via Samba, use the command

```
NET PRINT \\myexample\lp
```

to see information about myexample's print queue.

♦ *port* — The name of the parallel port (for example, LPT1 or LPT2) whose printer you want information about. Use this command only for a printer that is plugged directly into the Windows 95 box.

♦ *job* /PAUSE | /RESUME | /DELETE — Manipulate a print job on the specified print queue. *job* gives the number of the print job. Options /PAUSE, /RESUME, and /DELETE, respectively, pause the printing of a job, resume the printing of a paused job, and remove a job from the print queue (or aborts the printing of a job).

♦ /YES — Run without prompting you to approve what it does.

Please note that if the Linux box whose queue is being manipulated has exported a print job to another Linux machine (via the printcap instruction rm), none of these commands will work as intended. Rather, they will work – but because the print jobs were exported, they will not be examining the printer queue on the machine that is actually executing the print jobs (that is, the machine to which the jobs were exported). Therefore, if you intend to give Windows 95 users the power to manage print jobs on the Linux machine that is printing their work, you should install Samba on the machine that is actually printing the jobs, and have the users spool jobs to that machine directly. This configuration is a little more difficult to set up, but it gives your Windows 95 users the power to manage their printing jobs properly.

♦ NET TIME [*computer* | /WORKGROUP:*groupname*] [/SET] [/YES] – This subcommand reads the time from a given machine. You can either display the time, or synchronize your computer's clock with the time as retrieved from that machine. This command recognizes the following arguments:

  ♦ *computer* – The name of the computer whose time you want to read.

  ♦ /WORKGROUP:*groupname* – Read the time from the time server of the Windows workgroup *groupname*.

  ♦ /SET – Set your computer's clock to the time read from the *computer* or *groupname*.

  ♦ /YES – Run without prompting you to approve what it does.

Please note that if your Linux machine is set to Greenwich time and uses the TIMEZONE environmental variable to convert system time to local time (which is the default), setting the Windows 95 box's system time to the Linux box's time will give you some strange – and probably unwelcome – results.

♦ NET USE – Connect to, or disconnect from, a share, or display information about shares to which the Windows 95 box is connected. When this subcommand is invoked without arguments, it shows the shares to which this Windows 95 box is connected. It takes a number of arguments as follows:

♦ NET USE [drive: | *] [*computer\directory* [*password* | ?]] [/SAVEPW:NO] [/YES] [/NO] – This subcommand lets you mount a property on another machine as a network drive on the current Windows 95 machine. Such a drive can be accessed through its letter, just like the Windows 95 C drive (the hard disk) or D drive (the CD-ROM drive). This form of the subcommand recognizes the following arguments:

  ♦ *drive* is the letter to assign to this drive. A * tells Windows 95 to use the next available letter.

◆ *computer* names the computer whose directory you will be mounting as a network drive. This may be a Linux machine, or another Windows 95 machine. *directory* names the directory being mounted as a network drive. Note the use of backslashes in naming the directory.

◆ *password* assigns a password to this connection. A ? tells Windows 95 to prompt for the password.

◆ /SAVEPW tells Windows 95 to save this password. /SAVEPW:NO tells it not to save the password.

◆ /YES automatically replies yes to all prompts. Contrary to this, /NO automatically replies no to all prompts.

◆ NET USE [*port:*] [*computer**printer* [*password* | ?]] [/SAVEPW:NO] [/YES] [/NO] — This subcommand mounts a printer on another machine as a shared printer. *port* names the parallel (LPT) port name you assign to a shared printer. For example, to mount the lp print queue on Linux machine myexample as parallel port LPT3, use the command:

```
NET USE LPT3: \\myexample\lp
```

◆ NET USE *drive*: | *computer**share* /DELETE [/YES] — Unmount *share*, which is on machine *computer*.

◆ NET USE *port*: | *computer**printer* /DELETE [/YES] — Unmount *printer*, which is on machine *computer*.

◆ NET USE * /DELETE [/YES] — U-mount all currently mounted shares.

◆ NET VIEW [[*computer*] | [/WORKGROUP:*groupname*]] [/YES] — This subcommand gives a summary of the available shares. When invoked without arguments, it displays the servers that are in the current workgroup. When invoked with argument *computer*, it shows the resources available on machine *computer*; for example, command

```
NET VIEW \\myexample
```

shows all the shares available on machine myexample. When invoked with argument /WORKGROUP:*groupname*, it shows the servers that make resources available within workgroup *groupname*. Argument /YES tells Windows 95 to execute this command without prompting you for information or to confirm actions.

NETSTAT: Get Networking Status

Command NETSTAT gives a text-oriented way to observe activity on the network into which a Windows 95 box is plugged.

When invoked without an argument, this command prints a summary of all active connections on the network. Otherwise, NETSTAT can be invoked with one of the following arguments:

- -a – Summarize all connections and listening ports. Normally, NETSTAT does not show server-side connections.

- -e – Summarize activity on the Ethernet network. This option can also be combined with the option -s.

- -n – Summarize all active connections, just as if you invoked NETSTAT without an argument, except that NETSTAT displays the IP address of each server, instead of its name.

- -p *proto* – Show the connections made for the protocol *proto*, which can be either udp or tcp. This argument can also be used with argument -s, in which case proto can be udp, tcp, or ip.

- -r – Show the routing table.

- -s – Summarize activity, arranged based on protocol. By default, this option shows statistics for TCP, UDP, and IP. This option may be combined with option -p to select one or another protocol.

In addition to the preceding arguments, you can specify an *interval*, which tells NETSTAT to redisplay selected statistics every *interval* seconds. To stop the display of statistics, press Ctrl-C.

Summary

In this chapter, we presented how to integrate a Windows 95 box into your Linux-based Ethernet. With proper configuration and the correct software installed on your Linux workstation, Windows 95 and Linux can work together almost seamlessly on your intranet.

To begin, the chapter first discussed the networking protocols used by Windows 95, in particular the NetBIOS and SMB protocols.

The chapter then discussed hardware issues, in particular, how to install an Ethernet card into a Windows 95 box, and how to connect it physically into your intranet. It then discussed how to configure your Windows 95 box so that it recognizes and uses the Ethernet card, and so that it can use the TCP/IP protocols to communicate with the rest of your intranet. Finally, we discussed how to configure mail on your intranet so that a Windows 95 user can send and receive mail: how to set up a POP3 server on your Linux box, and how to set up the Microsoft Exchange MUA to download and upload mail to your Linux workstation

We then discussed software that can be installed onto your Linux workstation so that Linux and Windows 95 can exchange resources. The Samba package makes Linux disk and printer resources available to Windows 95 boxes, and the SMBFS file system lets you mount and manipulate Windows 95 resources as if they were directly mounted onto your Linux file system.

Finally, we discussed in depth the Windows 95 command NET, which is most helpful in configuring and managing networking on a Windows 95 box.

Chapter 10

Security

IN THIS CHAPTER

- ◆ Encryption
- ◆ ssh – the secure shell
- ◆ Principles of security

To conclude this book, we discuss the often-vexing subject of security. As you open up your intranet to the Internet at large, you must be aware that among the many folk roaming Cyberspace, vandals are lurking who delight in trashing insecure systems, and thieves will steal sensitive information (such as credit-card numbers and passwords) and use it to hurt you.

In a sense, perfect security is easy to achieve: simply unplug your modem and lock the door. However, that security comes at too high a price: the whole point of the exercise, after all, is to attach your machine into the Earth's Cyberspace. You want to devise a security scheme that will let in your friends and keep out your foes, and let your friends do only what you permit them to do.

Unfortunately, as recent cracker-attacks on the Pentagon and the CIA have shown, devising a security scheme that will fight off a determined attack forever is extremely difficult, if not impossible. In this form of warfare, as in all others, offense is always a step ahead of defense. However, you can take steps that will fend off the casual vandal and the amateur thief. You owe it to yourself to do nothing less: after all, having your system trashed by a cracker is bad enough, but having it trashed by some bumbling cracker-wannabe just rubs salt into the wound.

In this chapter, we discuss the following topics:

- ◆ Encryption – This section gives brief introductions to the varieties of encryption commonly used to secure data. These include strong encryption and public-key encryption.

- ◆ ssh – This secure shell and its tools use strong encryption to allow remotely located systems to exchange data securely.

- ◆ Principles of security – The disciplines you should practice day-in and day-out to keep your intranet secure.

That said, let's get started.

Encryption

Encryption is the ancient technique of hiding information in plain sight. A person who reads an encrypted message cannot interpret it unless he possesses some special item of information, also called a *key*, which translates the encrypted information into common language. In theory, as long as the key is kept secret, the information within an encrypted message also remains secret.

In this section, we briefly discuss two complementary methods of encryption: *strong encryption* and *public-key encryption*. We also briefly describe the RSA encryption package.

Strong Encryption

Strong encryption is stronger than the 40-bit encryption maximum that can be exported from the United States under U.S. law. In theory, strong encryption cannot be broken easily, even by a supercomputer. (We say "in theory" because the National Security Agency may have developed techniques for doing so that – for obvious reasons – it hasn't seen fit to tell us about.)

Public-Key Encryption

Public-key encryption is a type of asymmetric encryption. *Asymmetric encryption* is a system in which you encrypt your message with one key, and the recipient decrypts it with a mathematically related, but different key.

What makes public-key encryption "public" is the fact that knowledge of the key that is used to encrypt the message does not reveal how to decrypt the message. Thus, you can hand out the public key to anyone who wants to send an encrypted message to you, but only you can decrypt and read the messages encrypted with the public key.

As we have discussed elsewhere in this book, the "pretty good privacy" (PGP from Network Associates) package uses a form of public-key encryption to transmit a session key for a message. The session key is generated at random and then used to encrypt the message. Thus, a PGP-encoded message includes two pieces of information:

♦ The message encrypted with a private key or symmetric encryption system, such as 3DES, Blowfish, or Idea.

♦ The session key used to encrypt the message in an encrypted form, using the RSA public-key cryptographic system.

To decrypt a PGP-encrypted message, you must first use your private key to decrypt part 2, get the session key and encryption system. PGP can use any of the previously mentioned algorithms. Next, you use the session key and cryptographic algorithm to decrypt part 1. The program that we are about to describe, ssh, uses this method, but with a twist – instead of using the session key to encrypt one message, the session key encrypts the entire contents of a TCP session with a strong encryption method, such as IDEA. Packets transmitted between client and server can be intercepted by a cracker, but will be totally useless to her, because she won't have the session key needed to decrypt it.

ssh, the Secure Shell

ssh stands for *secure shell*. It is a package that uses strong encryption to enable users to create sessions on your Linux or other UNIX machines from a remote site. By using strong encryption, ssh significantly enhances the security of both the *authentication process* (determining that a user really is who he says he is) and the session itself.

In this section, we describe how you can install and configure ssh on your Linux workstation, and then we briefly discuss how to use ssh to secure communications among machines.

The security in this package is so much better than that of telnet or the r* commands that we recommend you install it and use it to access Linux systems, whenever possible, on your local area network or remotely across the Internet. In particular, ssh is useful if your users are plugging themselves into your intranet from remote locations – say, from laptop computers that your users carry on the road.

Before we begin our description of how to install and use ssh, we should note that, because ssh is designed to allow access to your Linux system from other systems, this discussion obviously is not relevant to you if you have only one host that you want to access. If you have only one standalone Linux workstation, then this section of the chapter probably holds little to interest you. However, if you have multiple hosts, or your ISP is forward-looking enough to support ssh on its shell machine, or you want to use the network infrastructure you have built to share information with another business or individual, then you should read on.

Getting and Installing ssh

Getting and installing ssh is easy. Currently, the latest version is 1.2.22, and it is distributed by FTP at URL:

```
ftp://ftp.funet.fi/pub/unix/security/login/ssh/ssh-1.2.22.tar.gz
```

If you are within the United States, you also need to get the RSA Reference Library (version 2).

This is available at URL:

```
ftp://ftp.funet.fi/pub/crypt/cryptography/asymmetric/rsa/rsaref2.
  tar.gz
```

To use ssh, you must download it from the URL previously listed. Put the archive in a place that you can remember, in case you ever need to look at its documentation. (The usual place to store sources under Linux is /usr/local/src, although no rule says that you must put sources there.) To extract files from the archive, type the command

```
tar xvzf ssh-1.2.22.tar.gz
```

You should see the following, or something very much like it:

```
ssh-1.2.22/
ssh-1.2.22/COPYING
ssh-1.2.22/rfc-pg.c
ssh-1.2.22/RFC
ssh-1.2.22/RFC.nroff
ssh-1.2.22/make-ssh-known-hosts.pl
ssh-1.2.22/install-sh
ssh-1.2.22/server_config.sample
ssh-1.2.22/config.h.in
ssh-1.2.22/acconfig.h
ssh-1.2.22/config.sample
ssh-1.2.22/host_config.sample
```

and so on.

tar lists the names of the files as it extracts them. When it's done and you see your shell prompt again, use cd to enter the directory that tar created for the source distribution.

As with any software for your Linux machine, familiarizing yourself with the installation and operation procedures that the software uses is a good idea. This is especially true of security software. The ssh distribution has two files that you should read—sooner rather than later: README and INSTALL.

If you are in the United States, you also need to extract the RSA Reference Library by executing the following command:

```
tar xvzf /usr/local/src/rsaref2.tar.gz
```

Then, type the following command to configure ssh to use the RSA Reference Library:

```
./configure —with-rsaref
```

The option —with-rsaref is required, for legal reasons, in the United States: the RSA algorithms are patented here, and under the agreement, you cannot use any free implementation of RSA except the one that RSA distributes freely. You will see something like the following:

```
creating cache ./config.cache
checking host system type... i486-unknown-linux
checking cached information... ok
checking for gcc... gcc
checking whether the C compiler (gcc  ) works... yes
checking whether the C compiler (gcc  ) is a cross-compiler... no
checking whether we are using GNU C... yes
checking whether gcc accepts -g... yes
checking for POSIXized ISC... no
checking for getspnam... yes
checking for pw_encrypt... no
checking for pw_encrypt in -lshadow... yes
checking whether to enable pw_encrypt... no
checking that the compiler works... yes
checking if the compiler understands -pipe... yes
checking whether to enable -Wall... no
checking return type of signal handlers... void
```

and so on.

Outside the United States, you need to configure the software only with the following command:

```
./configure
```

You will see something like the following:

```
creating cache ./config.cache
checking host system type... i486-unknown-linux
checking cached information... ok
checking for gcc... gcc
checking whether the C compiler (gcc  ) works... yes
checking whether the C compiler (gcc  ) is a cross-compiler... no
checking whether we are using GNU C... yes
checking whether gcc accepts -g... yes
checking for POSIXized ISC... no
```

and so on.

The configuration script will now check hundreds of aspects of your system, and then set up the rest of the process for building ssh.

When the configuration process is done and you have a prompt again, compile the software by typing the command make.

After compilation is finished, you can install the software by running command make install. You should see something like the following:

```
umask 022; if test '!' -d /usr/local; then \
  mkdir /usr/local; fi; \
```

```
if test '!' -d /usr/local; then \
  mkdir /usr/local; fi; \
if test '!' -d /etc; then \
  mkdir /etc; fi; \
if test '!' -d /usr/local/bin; then \
  mkdir /usr/local/bin; fi; \
if test '!' -d /usr/local/sbin; then \
  mkdir /usr/local/sbin; fi; \
```

and so on.

This takes some time as make creates a host key for your machine and installs default configuration files into directory /etc.

After this is complete, the software is installed and you only need to make arrangements to start it up at boot time. Normally, you would invoke a program like ssh through inetd, but ssh has to manage authentication information on the fly before the connection starts, so it must run as a standalone daemon. The README file mentions how to change this, but the change loosens the security a lot, so we prefer to use the default.

To start ssh at boot time, you only need to add the line

```
/usr/local/sbin/sshd
```

to the end of file /etc/rc.d/rc.local.

That's all there is to it. Now we discuss the more interesting topic of how to use ssh.

Using ssh

ssh is simple to use. The package includes six commands:

- ssh
- slogin
- scp
- ssh-agent
- ssh-add
- ssh-keygen

You can use ssh-keygen to create a new public-key – private-key pair. You should do this once before you start to use the program, and thereafter whenever you have reason to believe that your current key pair has been compromised in any way.

ssh, slogin, AND scp

Commands `ssh`, `slogin`, and `scp` work like their counterparts `rsh`, `rlogin`, and `rcp`. Whereas command `rlogin heimdall` attempts to log you into the account with your current user name on host `heimdall`, `slogin` does the same, but with a couple of twists:

If `heimdall` is running the daemon `sshd`, and the connection can be authenticated, then the entire session will be encrypted. This will make it difficult, if not impossible, for someone who is using a "packet sniffer" to intercept and read your datagrams to steal information.

As a convenience, if the `DISPLAY` variable is set on your connection, `ssh` will also establish an encrypted pipe back to your X Window server, so that you can start X applications from the remote server on your display. Because this connection is compressed and encrypted, it is slower than the connection that you would get if you used the `xauth` program to exchange tokens, as you would with the `r*` commands. However, if your applications are mainly text-based, like `xterm` or `xemacs`, or if your connection is over Ethernet, then you will hardly notice the difference in speed, and this will be a benefit that you'll want to take advantage of.

Likewise, `ssh` and `scp` do the same things as their `r*` counterparts. For example, command

```
ssh remotesystem command
```

runs a command on the remote machine with its standard output redirected from your terminal. Likewise, command

```
scp localfile remotesystem:remotefile
```

copies a file from the local machine to the remote machine.

Again, in each of these cases, the connection between the local and remote machines is encrypted for security.

ssh-keygen

Command `ssh-keygen` generates random numbers that you can use as keys. For example, when you type the command `ssh-keygen`, you see something like the following:

```
Initializing random number generator...
Generating p:  ...................++ (distance 256)
Generating q:  ...........................................++
 (distance 1238)
Computing the keys...
Key generation complete.
```

When you generate a key pair, `ssh` will prompt you for its location. The default suffices for all normal applications, so you can just hit Enter at this prompt:

```
Enter file in which to save the key (/home/csh/.ssh/identity):
```

Next, ssh asks you to protect your private key with a pass-phrase. This phrase can be as long as you like, and all characters are significant, so you should take advantage of it. In the following example, each typed letter is represented by an asterisk:

```
Enter passphrase: *****************************************
Enter the same passphrase again:
                  ***************************************
Your identification has been saved in /home/csh/.ssh/identity.
Your public key is:
1024 33 12135556769923999968866850...
Your public key has been saved in /home/csh/.ssh/identity.pub
```

Be sure to remember your pass-phrase exactly.

When you are done, ssh-keygen saves your private and public keys, and prints your public key on the terminal. In the future, any time ssh needs to use your private key for authenticating a session, it will prompt you for this pass-phrase.

RSA AUTHENTICATION

The reason you set up and use key pairs is to enhance the security of the ssh commands. When you generate a key pair, the private key is used to decrypt data coming to your machine, and the public key is used to encrypt during the authentication phase. Giving away the public key only allows an attacker to encrypt messages to you, nothing more.

ssh can use these split keys as a method of authentication. It works like this:

◆ At the start of the connection, ssh tells the sshd server the public key that it wants to use for authentication.

◆ The server checks to see whether the user has previously granted access to the account with this public key. If so, sshd generates a large, random message and encrypts it with the key.

◆ The encrypted random message is sent to the ssh client, which decrypts the message with the user's private key. This generates a block of data.

◆ The client computes a hash from this data and returns it to the sshd server.

◆ The sshd server computes a hash using the same function as the client on the original random message.

◆ It compares the hash that it computed from the original random number, to the hash computed by the client. These two will match only if the client could correctly decode the message.

◆ If the two hashes are equal, then the authentication is accepted and the session is allowed.

You should notice that this form of authentication relies on matching public and private keys. DNS and host IP addresses don't have to be trusted — in fact, they aren't even needed — so this works from a host that receives a different IP address each time it connects to your intranet.

Furthermore, no sensitive information is exchanged during the authentication process. This makes ssh more secure than rsh, which relies on DNS to convert numbers to names, and much more secure than telnet, which exchanges sensitive information (the user name and password) in clear text during the authentication process.

Finally, if the RSA authentication process fails, ssh can default to the host/IP-based authentication model that rsh uses, or even simply ask for a password over the encrypted connection.

SENDING YOUR KEY TO ANOTHER COMPUTER

To prepare another computer for RSA authentication, you must send it the proper public key.

During authentication, the ssh server sshd scans the file ~/.ssh/authorized_keys for public keys that should be permitted access to this user's account. When you created the key pair with ssh-keygen, it put the private part of the key in the file ~/.ssh/identity, and the public part of the key in the file ~/.ssh/identity.pub. To grant access, you must have the public key listed in the remote account's file ~/.ssh/authorized_keys.

To set up authentication for a new account, do the following:

1. First, create a .ssh directory for the remote account. You can use ssh to do that. You will be prompted for a password, but the connection will be encrypted, so you needn't worry. For example:

```
ssh heimdall "mkdir ~/.ssh; chmod 700 ~/.ssh"
csh's password:
```

2. Next, add your public key to the account's authorized_keys file. The following command will do that, again prompting you for a password:

```
cat ~/.ssh/identity.pub | ssh heimdall "cat > ~/.ssh/authorized_
  keys"
csh's password:
```

Note that the quotation marks on these commands are needed to keep the local shell from expanding the directories specified with the ~, and to keep the shell from redirecting the output into a local file in the `cat` command.

ssh-agent AND ssh-add

Commands `ssh-agent` and `ssh-add` are useful in X Window environments in which you establish sessions on multiple workstation ends, each of which has a different key pair. `ssh-agent` sets up a simple repository-and-retrieval system for multiple private keys. `ssh-add` prompts the user for a password, if necessary. If the password is entered correctly, it adds the key to the repository.

During the authentication phase, the `ssh` client can use any key in the repository. You are prompted for a password only if the `sshd` server cannot authenticate with one of the keys from the client's repository.

To work, `ssh-agent` must be the parent of all the processes that use the repository. This is usually arranged by having `ssh` start your window manager. Normally, the last line in your `.xsession` or `.xinitrc` file will start a window manager, like this:

```
exec fvwm95
```

To use `ssh-agent`, simply modify the last line of your `.xsession` file to read:

```
exec ssh-agent fvwm95
```

From any `xterm` started by your window manager, the command `ssh-add` will prompt you for your password, if necessary, and add the identity to the repository:

```
ssh-add
Need passphrase for /home/csh/.ssh/identity
 (csh@heimdall.myexample.com).
Enter passphrase:
Identity added: /home/csh/.ssh/identity (csh@heimdall.myexample.com)
```

From now on, any operation with `ssh` that needs to authenticate with the key `csh@heimdall.myexample.com` will be able to do so without prompting you for a password.

Review

The preceding section describes how to install and use `ssh`, and goes a little into the details of how `ssh` works and why it is more secure than `telnet` or the `r*` commands.

However, `ssh` is capable of many things, and we have only scratched the surface of what it can do.

The documentation for the `ssh` package is a good source of information for anyone who needs to securely transfer information from one computer to another.

Principles of Security

In these days, in which everyone is trying to connect their computers and networks to the Internet, computer and network security is a hot topic.

If we've done our job with this book and you've done yours in working with your Linux system, you now have a computer network, possibly connected to the Internet, either part-time through a dial-up link or full-time through a leased line. This provides access outbound – your users can now get information from the World Wide Web, or they can use `telnet` or `ftp` to connect to servers throughout the world.

Of course, in doing this, you've also provided access *into* your network to every other computer connected to the Internet. Like any endeavor worth doing, this entails risk. As administrator for your intranet, you are also *de facto* security administrator, and the users of your intranet expect that you take reasonable steps to control security risks.

At this point, we want to insert a disclaimer. This chapter is only a start. UNIX and Internet security is a field that deserves a book of its own, and we realize that we cannot do it justice in just one chapter; but we do want to inform you of what you need to think about. Your security problems are simplified by the fact that your connection to the Internet is probably low-speed or intermittent. If this isn't your situation, you should skip ahead to the recommended readings. Pick one book on UNIX security and another on firewalls. You need to understand both UNIX security and firewalls, to secure your network properly, and as you can see, these aren't topics that we can fit in one book, much less one chapter.

Categories of Attack

The first, most important step to devising defenses against attack is to consider how your enemies will attack you. So, we first discuss methods of attack; then we discuss devising defenses against those attacks. From a security standpoint, two broad categories of attack exist that you need to guard against: unauthorized access and denial of service. *Unauthorized access* is any access that you do not want to happen on your network. *Denial of service* is an attack that denies authorized users access to some or all of the service that they should be able to access from your network.

We discuss each form of attack in turn.

Unauthorized Access

Unauthorized access can happen from either outside your network or within it.

The obvious example of outside access is a determined system cracker who gains access to your Linux server and downloads a copy of your latest bid on a consulting project. A less-obvious example is a user on your intranet who cruises to an inappropriate Web site and seriously offends another worker within your organization by displaying inappropriate material. (The definition of "inappropriate" we leave to your imagination.) Both events can be equally devastating to your company.

Your network being in your home doesn't exempt you from security problems. If you use a dual-boot Windows 95 and Linux system when you connect to the Internet, or if you have a dedicated Linux box that connects to the Internet as a proxy for a Windows 95 network, you should regard all the files on all the machines connected to the Internet to be at risk to system crackers. If you use financial applications, such as Microsoft Money or Quicken, you can wind up in serious trouble, because the data encryption used in these applications is usually weak, yet these files are "up for grabs" to any cracker who can break into your Linux system.

In brief, by connecting your network to the Internet, you've opened up the possibility for a large number of people to access any data from any machine on your network — and not all of those people are well-intentioned. Also, we are sure that not every Internet site contains material appropriate for the younger members of your household.

All of these situations amount to access problems. Most of them are fairly simple to fix.

SECURITY STANCES

Before you can solve access problems, you must decide on a security stance for your site. Only two choices are available here: you can make it your rule either that "all access that is not expressly permitted is denied," or that "all access that is not expressly denied is permitted."

Security managers usually prefer the first option, which is called *default-deny* for short. Security managers like this approach because it causes no surprises when a new service on the Internet is found to have a major security exploit attached to it.

On the other hand, users appreciate the second rule, the *default-permit* stance, because it puts the least amount of restriction on the user, and she can go on doing whatever she likes until you discover that it's insecure. The problem with default-permit, of course, is that you may discover a new service is insecure only after it causes a security problem at your site.

UNAUTHORIZED ACCESS INBOUND

Protecting against inbound unauthorized access is simplified by the fact that, to access anything, you have to cooperate with the system cracker by providing a service. If you look back to our discussion of `inetd.conf` in earlier chapters, you will see that `inetd` is the main method of providing access to services for outside machines. When looking from the perspective of unauthorized access, the services you provide from your Linux box really fall into two categories: services where the daemon is started by `inetd`, and services that are provided by standalone daemons.

Your Linux box comes with an excellent method of controlling access to inbound services that are started from `inetd`, called *TCP wrappers*. Unfortunately, if the service cannot be started from `inetd`, you cannot use TCP wrappers with it; but, as we will see, most services in this category have their own access-control lists.

Access Controls

If your organization is like most others, your users are the weakest link by far in the chain that makes up your security system.

Make no mistake about it – a malicious user is your worst nightmare – she has keys to the office and access passwords for many, if not all, of your systems. Thankfully, you probably won't have to deal with this problem. Although some of the things that your users do may seem malicious, they are probably done out of ignorance.

To combat these problems, you should share as much information as you can about how to use the various aspects of the system. Telling your users what you are doing, and why, is always a good idea. We cannot emphasize this enough when it comes to setting passwords.

PASSWORDS

Good passwords are a requirement for any system to be secure. Most preliminary attacks against your machine will be information-gathering attacks. In particular, the system cracker is after information about your network. The most valued piece of information he can get is your password file.

In an older UNIX system, file `/etc/passwd` named each user, and contained a cryptographic hash of each user's password. At login time, the password the user typed was passed through the same hash function that was used when the password was first written into the file. The result of the login-time hash was compared to the hash saved in `/etc/passwd`; if they were the same, access could be safely granted.

The fatal flaw in this process was that file `/etc/passwd` contained information useful to various commands, and these commands could not function without access to the information. Thus, access to `/etc/passwd` had to be left fairly relaxed, and so getting hold of users' encrypted passwords used to be a simple matter.

By itself, this wouldn't be a great problem, but the encryption system used to hash the passwords wasn't particularly strong. The range of different passwords wasn't very large, and to make matters worse, most users used a small subset of the range. Finally, delays were added to the encryption, because without the delay, it operated too quickly. Someone soon figured out a way to remove the delay and apply the hashing algorithm to a dictionary, and then compare the results to what was stored in the password file. If the dictionary contained your password, then this method would find it. So the *modus operandi* for crackers was as follows:

1. Obtain the password file.

2. Apply the hash function to each entry in a dictionary and compare the results to each hash in the password file.

3. A match indicates that you can use the word from the dictionary as the password for the account in the password file.

The encryption is DES, which isn't "weak," but the key is restricted to eight printable characters, which only yields 56 bits of key information. To make matters worse, a common practice was to use a password made up of only lowercase letters, which further restricts the key space from 56 bits to a little more than 38 bits.

Modern UNIX systems, Linux included, use a more evolved method for protecting the password file. This method is based on the fact that only the login program itself needs to read a user's password. The other programs needed other information and forced the use of less-strict access controls on the /etc/passwd file. The solution to this problem is to remove the hashed passwords from the /etc/passwd file and put them in a file that only protected programs can access. This system is called *shadow* passwords.

You should not make the mistake of assuming that shadow passwords are a panacea. Any program that authenticates users through the shadow password file (such as ftpd or qpopper) is a danger, because if it is forced to core dump, the core dump will contain pieces of the password file, if not the entire password file. If other insecurities on the system allow users to download the core dump, the user can use a binary editor to snip out the binary file and run crack against it. Furthermore, the underlying hash function is still DES, and the key space is still only 56 bits long. Thus, this method of protection has only made obtaining the password file harder for a cracker. If a cracker can get your shadow password file, he can still run a dictionary-based attack on it.

A common attack today is to get a program that reads the shadow password file to a state where the file has been read, and then feed it bad input and force it to crash. This crash writes out a file for debugging purposes, called a *core dump*. Now, the cracker's problem is easier. He simply needs to read the resulting core file. If the cracker is lucky, some password information was in the buffer of the program before it crashed.

After the cracker has your password file or a fragment of it, she can use tools commonly available on the Internet to figure out the correct password from the hash. The simplest is the *brute force* method: the cracker encrypts a large file of words and phrases that are popularly used as passwords (names of popular movies and televisions shows, popular media characters, common given names, and so on). If one of the encrypted terms matches an entry in the stolen password file, then bingo! the cracker knows that user's password. The cracker can now masquerade as that user to penetrate and undermine your intranet.

A truly determined cracker can do some detective work on you and your users to find public facts about you – the names of your spouse and children, your car's license-plate number, your driver's license number and Social Security number – and check whether you have used any of these as your password. If you have, then watch out – that cracker has just stolen your identity.

When it comes to picking passwords, we are reminded of an incident that occurred in the early 1960s, when a bank in Chicago installed a password system on its mainframe computer. Each user had to pick a three-digit number to use as a password. However, the bank quickly abandoned this scheme when it discovered that more than half of the men at the bank picked "007" as their password. As this story shows, a good password should be easy to remember but difficult to guess:

- ◆ Avoid single words like your name, your spouse's name, your dog's name, and so on.

- ◆ Avoid alphanumeric information that a cracker can easily find out about you, such as the license-plate number of your car. If you want to make a good password, concatenate two words with a number or punctuation mark.

- ◆ Avoid names or phrases that are popular in the media. For example, `Titanic` and `KateWinslett` are poor choices of passwords.

- ◆ Use upper- and lowercase letters in your password.

- ◆ Use easily remembered misspellings or phonetic spellings.

- ◆ Scatter punctuation marks and numerals randomly throughout your password.

For example, a good password for an animal lover would be:

```
1Dog,2Kat
```

Of course, that now is not a good password because we have printed it in this book.

Another approach is to use an easy-to-memorize phrase, such as a line from a favorite song or poem, particularly if it's not in English. One last thing to be aware of with passwords is the fact that even with shadow passwords, releases of Linux that predate release 2.0 still only consider significant the first eight characters of a password. This means that the password:

```
ABCEDFGHIJKLMN
```

is exactly the same as:

```
ABCDEFGH
```

Finally, after your users have gone to the trouble to secure your system with good passwords, they shouldn't blow it by writing down the password or sharing it with anyone else – not even with you. You must emphasize this to your users, or the following may happen:

◆ They will choose poor passwords that are easily guessed.

◆ They will write down their passwords where an unknowing person, such as a security guard, can be tricked into giving away the password to an ersatz system administrator over the telephone. They will unwittingly give them away to someone who claims to be the system administrator.

If you don't believe the third problem, try actually sending the forged mail from Chapter 5; of course, change the reply-to address so you get responses.

TCP Wrappers

TCP wrappers work through the `inetd` daemon. The wrapper intercepts the inbound service request before the daemon is started. It checks some parameters of the connection; if the connection passes all criteria, then TCP wrappers allow it to proceed; otherwise it drops the connection.

This mechanism is enough to protect against most casual attacks. However, if a cracker can gain access to a machine that you are not blocking, or can trick your machine into thinking that she should be allowed access, then TCP wrappers will fail.

SETTING UP TCP WRAPPERS

TCP wrappers is controlled by two files: `/etc/hosts.allow` and `/etc/hosts.deny`.

These files contain access-control lists. The `hosts.allow` file names hosts and services that are allowed to establish connections to your machine. The `hosts.deny` file names hosts and services that are denied access to your machine.

When determining whether to accept a connection, TCP wrappers first consults `hosts.allow`. If the host/service pair is listed there, then the connection is allowed to proceed. If it is not, TCP wrappers then checks `hosts.deny`. If the host/service pair is found in the `deny` file, the connection is dropped.

If TCP wrappers gets to the end of the `deny` file without matching, the connection is accepted. *You must understand that this amounts to TCP wrappers using a default-permit rule if you don't explicitly change the configuration.*

The format for rules in the `hosts.accept` and `hosts.deny` file is the following:

```
daemon-list: host-pattern : shell-command
```

Like most UNIX configuration files, you can add written comments by preceding them with a # character.

For example, to deny the machine `evil.crackers.org` access to your `telnetd` server, you simply add the line

```
in.telnetd: evil.crackers.org
```

to file `/etc/hosts.deny`.

If you want to use TCP wrappers to implement a default-deny status for inbound connections from the Internet, you must add the line

```
ALL: .mydomain.com
```

to file `/etc/hosts.allow`, and add the line

```
ALL: ALL
```

to the end of file `/etc/hosts.deny`. ALL is a special token that matches any daemon when specified for the daemon part, and any host when used for the host part.

The host pattern `.myexample.com` matches any host on any subdomain of `myexample.com`. Several ways exist to grant this permit status, however, and you are well advised to know the differences. All of the following lines allow access to any host on `myexample.com`, which we assume corresponds to a network address of `192.168.1.0` with a netmask of `255.255.255.0`:

```
# Matches all hosts that DNS finds in mydomain.com. This is
# subject to DNS spoofing attacks
ALL: .myexample.com
# The ``LOCAL'' token matches all hosts without a period in
# them. This is good if you  have no sub domains from your
#  main domain but again is subject to DNS spoofing.
ALL: LOCAL
# You can match numeric IP addresses by specifying them ending
# with a period. Any number that you don't specify here will be
# wildcarded. IP addresses have the added advantage that they
# are slightly more difficult to spoof.
ALL: 192.168.1.
# You can also match Numeric addresses by specifying them in
# network-ip/net-mask format like this. Again, IP addresses have
# the added advantage that they are slightly more difficult
# to spoof.
ALL: 192.168.1.0/255.255.255.0
```

All of the preceding examples match the domain that you've seen described in this book, and would be suitable for inclusion within file `/etc/hosts.allow`.

After you make these modifications to the TCP wrappers files, you can change the access that others have to your network on an *ad hoc* basis. For example, if you have a friend that is going to do some consulting work on your network, you can allow him access to `telnet` and `ftp` by adding the following lines:

```
in.telnetd: friend.consulting.com
in.ftpd: friend.consulting.com
```

The rules for TCP wrappers are really a small language on their own, and many more options than we have described here are available. We recommend that you look at the manual page for this package.

Services That Don't Start with inetd

We cannot describe a case for each daemon that does not rely on `inetd` to start up. You should know that valid reasons exist for why a service might not go through `inetd`. For example, the daemons that run the secure shell service, `sshd`, and `apache` do not start this way, because simply too much startup overhead is required for them to work if started by `inetd`. As we have seen, `ssh` itself comes with a strong authentication system, so TCP wrappers isn't needed; but other standalone daemons and clients that lie outside the control of TCP wrappers may cause trouble. Note that, barring extraordinary situations, `apache` doesn't need this protection.

Unauthorized Access Outbound

Restricting outbound access is a more difficult problem. Your mechanism needs to be able to distinguish good sites from bad, and that is a value judgment at which computers are simply not very good.

However, if you choose to implement your outbound access using SOCKS, you have a built-in method for logging and even restricting access to selected sites on the Internet.

Determining what is good and what is bad, and tabulating an access-control list is up to you; but SOCKS at least provides the mechanism whereby you can lock out sites known to be inappropriate and – just as important – log and monitor all connections to all sites. It gives an alternative between all and nothing.

If you use IP masquerading for outbound access, you should read on before going to get the SOCKS distribution, however.

If you stuck to the configuration from Chapter 8 when you set up SOCKS, then you set up a default-deny status for inbound connections and a default-permit status for outbound connections. Whereas default-permit is bad for inbound access, it's generally acceptable for outbound services. After all, you built your network to allow outbound access in the first place. But as the number of users on your intranet grows, you may discover, and find inappropriate, that a person in your office is accessing the `www.crackertricks.com`. If you have implemented SOCKS, you can simply modify the original `/etc/socks.conf` file:

```
# File: /etc/socks5.conf — A socks5 config file for a dual homed
  server
#
#                       Src              Dst              Src  Dst
#Action Auth    Cmd     addr             addr             Port
  Port
permit  -       -       192.168.1.0/n    -                -    -
# Allow inbound connections to the ssh daemons on all hosts via
  socks but
# deny anything else.
permit  -       -       -                192.168.1.0/n    -    22
deny    -       -       -                -                -    -
by adding deny lines as follows:
deny    -       -       -                .crackertricks.com -  -
```

Like TCP wrappers, SOCKS reads this file in order, so your outbound-deny rules must appear before your permit rules. So the final file, with comments, looks like this:

```
# File: /etc/socks5.conf — A socks5 config file for a dual homed
  server
#
#                       Src              Dst              Src  Dst
#Action Auth    Cmd     addr             addr             Port
  Port
# Outbound deny rules go first. Add any sites that you feel
# should not be contactable from this network to this
# list. Shrink or grow this list as needed.
deny    -       -       -                .crackertricks.com -  -
# If it's not on the list above then assume it's okay.
permit  -       -       192.168.1.0/n    -                -    -
# Allow inbound connections to the ssh daemons on all hosts via
  socks but
# deny anything else.
permit  -       -       -                192.168.1.0/n    -    22
deny    -       -       -                -                -    -
```

You can see that SOCKS uses the same trick as TCP wrappers by allowing you to specify just the network part of the address. In this case, we specified the name, because determining a blank IP address to deny is usually a bit harder. It's easier with your network, because it's *your* network.

One other good thing about SOCKS is that it uses syslogd to log each site to which it connects. If you have a user who is persistent about attempting outbound access to unauthorized sites, SOCKS will log each and every connection attempt. You can review the contents of the log periodically to figure out how you need to update the access-control list.

We have found, too, that telling users that their connections are logged goes a long way toward getting users to police themselves. For example, you can inform your users about the login on the startup page of their Web browser:

```
Welcome to the World Wide Web at International Widget Corporation.
 Although we realize that a little light-hearted fun on company time
 — e.g., viewing the "Exploding Strawberry Pop Tarts" from Yahoo's
 Useless Web pages — can be a morale booster, some sites on the
 Internet have content of a nature that is inappropriate for viewing
 at work, because your fellow workers will find it threatening or
 offensive. We know that you will be responsible enough to avoid
 these sites, but we do wish to inform you that the Web sites you
 visit are logged and monitored. Thank you for your cooperation.
       John Lizardo — System Administrator
       International Widget Corporation
```

The next time an employee is tempted to browse www.vilepornography.com on company time, his knowing that the session is being logged and monitored may be enough to give him pause.

We must emphasize that locking out all sites that may give offense to one or another of your company's employees is practically impossible. However, you should at least exercise due diligence to stop your company's computers from being used as tools of harassment.

If you use IP masquerading instead of SOCKS to give the machines on your intranet access to the Internet, you don't have as easy a method of blocking or monitoring outbound access. Although it's beyond the scope of this book, you should know that the IP masquerading package is based on the IP firewall package designed for filtering packets. Using a combination of masquerading and firewalling to provide access to some, but not all, services on the Internet should be possible. For more information on this, see the manual pages on command ipfwadm.

Denial of Service

Denial of service is an easier attack to perform than unauthorized access. Fortunately, many crackers consider a plain denial-of-service attack to be unsporting — rather like stealing a child's milk money. However, a denial-of-service attack can be useful to a cracker if she has a spoofing attack running against another machine and she is spoofing you. For example, if the cracker is spoofing mail from your site, she may shut down mail on your site so that real mail will not appear from your site to "blow her cover."

Unfortunately, some denials of service are simply by-products of the fact that you are providing a service in the first place. If you put a mail server on the Internet, a cracker can flood your machine with so much mail that it can do little else. This may happen if a spammer chooses your system's SMTP server for bouncing her spam onto the Internet; or a well-intentioned but misguided person may do this to punish your system for some vile spam that was spoofed as coming from your mail server. On the good side, most of these attacks have a lifetime: eventually, the cracker gets tired and moves on to someone else, and because no real access occurred, you haven't lost much.

However, defects present in the implementation of Linux and networking can create a situation where a denial of service can cause a machine to reboot, or worse. These attacks generally are aimed at a flaw in the design or implementation of a networking service. The only defense against these attacks is to monitor the Linux security news groups to see what flaws your fellow administrators have uncovered, and then upgrade to the latest stable or development kernel that has a patch that fixes the attack.

Summary

To conclude this primer on the Linux network, we discuss security.

To begin, we present some background information on encryption: what it is, and how it works.

We then discuss ssh, the secure shell. ssh uses strong encryption, so that remote users can connect to workstations on your intranet without worrying about having their session spoofed or their data intercepted.

Finally, we discuss the principles of security: What security consists of, and strategies for setting up and enforcing security on your intranet. These include enforcing the use of passwords, using TCP wrappers to limit which resources are made available to which categories of users, and monitoring internal users. We emphasize that security not only consists of protecting the network against unauthorized penetration, but also requires protecting your organization against unauthorized or inappropriate use of the computer facilities to harass personnel.

Appendix A

About the CD-ROM

The CD-ROM that accompanies this book contains – in addition to the latest release of Slackware Linux – copies of the more useful configuration files described in this book.

Directory `config.files` contains configuration files described in Chapters 3, 5, and 7:

- `sendmail.cf` – Standard configuration file for `sendmail`.

- `smtp-direct.cf` – `sendmail` configuration file that uploads mail directly to the recipient's machine.

- `smtp-relay.cf` – `sendmail` configuration file that uploads mail to a relay machine.

- `smtp.cf` – `sendmail` configuration file that sends outgoing mail via SMTP.

- `uucp.cf` – `sendmail` configuration file that sends outgoing mail via UUCP.

- `test.html` – A brief HTML file to test whether Apache is working.

- `ppp-on.password` – A PPP connection script that uses login-and-password authentication.

- `ppp-on.pap` – A PPP connection script that uses PAP authentication.

- `ppp-on-dialer.password` – A PPP dialer script that uses login-and-password authentication.

- `ppp-on-dialer.pap` – A PPP dialer script that uses PAP authentication.

Appendix B

References

The following references gives sources in which you can find more information on the topics discussed in *The Linux Network*. We have organized the references on a chapter-by-chapter basis, to make it easier for you to find a reference on a particular topic.

Chapter 1

Many sources offer information about networking in general, and TCP/IP networking in particular. The following references give a few that we have found to be particularly useful:

W. Richard Stevens: *TCP/IP Illustrated*, volume 1: *The Protocols*. Reading, Mass., Addison-Wesley Publishing Co., 1994. W. Richard Stevens has written some of the most important and influential books on TCP/IP and how to program it. His series *TCP/IP Illustrated* is without equal – thorough, clearly written, and filled with useful examples. Highly recommended.

W. Richard Stevens: *TCP/IP Illustrated*, volume 2: *The Implementation*. Addison-Wesley Publishing Co., 1995.

W Richard Stevens: *TCP/IP Illustrated*, volume 3: *TCP for Transactions, HTTP, NNTP, and the UNIX Domain Protocols*. Addison-Wesley Publishing Co., 1996.

Michael Santifaller: *TCP/IP and NFS: Internetworking in a UNIX Environment*, translated by Stephen S. Wilson. Reading, Mass., Addison-Wesley Publishing Co., 1991. This is a good general reference on TCP/IP networking, with emphasis on the *network file system* (NFS) protocol.

Craig Hunt: *TCP/IP Network Administration*. Sebastopol, Calif., O'Reilly & Associates, Inc. 1991. This is a standard book on administering TCP/IP. It is tailored for Sun's Solaris operating system rather than Linux. A good reference volume, especially for persons who will be administering a complex network.

Olaf Kirch: *The Linux Network Administrators' Guide*. This document again is aimed at persons who administer complex networks, but its early chapters also cover the fundamentals of TCP/IP. It is freely available at Web site `http://sunsite.unc.edu/LDP`. An edition has been published by O'Reilly & Associates, Inc.

The Linux Bible. San Jose, Calif., Yggdrasil Computing Inc., 1997. This volume reprints much of the freely available documentation for Linux, including Olaf Kirch's *Linux Network Administrators' Guide* and "howtos" on various networking topics, including Ethernet and serial ports. These documents give a wealth of information about networking under Linux. As we proceed through this book, we will point you to specific documents that give detailed information on specific topics being discussed.

Steven Baker's Net Worth column runs monthly in the magazine *UNIX Review.* Mr. Baker is deeply knowledgeable on networking topics, and writes well. His columns from 1992 and 1993 discuss many of the basic issues we presented here. To our knowledge, these columns have not been reprinted in book form, but you may find them archived in the library of a local university. The following columns are of particular interest to beginners:

◆ January 1992: Introduction to the ARPA "layer cake"

◆ February 1992: History of the Internet. The physical layer of a network

◆ March 1992: The IP layer. Useful RFCs

◆ April 1992: IP addressing and classes

◆ May 1992: From IP address to physical address: ARP and RARP

◆ July 1992: Site and domain names; name servers

◆ August 1992: Domain-name service

◆ November 1992: Routing

The "horse's mouth" for TCP/IP programming is the TCP/IP protocols themselves. These protocols are, of course, written for persons who are intimately familiar with computers and programming; however, the protocols are lucid and may be read with some value even by beginners. All of these documents, though copyrighted, are freely available. The *InfoMagic Standards CD-ROM* (Pennington, NJ, InfoMagic, 1993) reproduces all of the Internet TCP/IP RFCs, plus many other standards that are beyond the scope of this book. You can also freely download all RFCs from Internet site http://www.internic.net/ds/dspglintdoc.html.

The following lists the RFCs that are most relevant to the topics discussed in this chapter:

◆ RFC768: The User Datagram Protocol (UDP)

◆ RFC791: The Internet Protocol (IP)

◆ RFC793: The Transmission Control Protocol (TCP)

◆ RFC826: The Address Resolution Protocol (ARP)

- ◆ RFC903: The Reverse Address Resolution Protocol (RARP)

- ◆ RFC1055: The Serial Line Internet Protocol (SLIP)

- ◆ RFC1171: The Point to Point Protocol (PPP)

- ◆ RFC-INDEX: An index of all RFCs

Domain names are changing continually; and as we mentioned earlier, the system of top-level domains is being reorganized as this book is being written. The set of country domains (for example, .us for the United States) is defined by document ISO-3166, written by the International Organization for Standards. This document is not freely available; however, for a summary, see Internet site ftp://ftp.ripe.net/ripe/docs/iso3166-codes. Document RFC1480 defines the US domain in detail; it, like the other RFCs, is available from Internet site http://www.internic.net/ds/dspg1intdoc.html.

If you are interested in writing programs that interact directly with TCP/IP software, one book is most useful: *UNIX Network Programming*, by W. Richard Stevens (Englewood Cliffs, NJ, Prentice-Hall Inc., 1990). This volume assumes that you are an experienced programmer who is thoroughly familiar with C. However, Stevens' explanation of the concepts that underlie networking and the TCP/IP protocols, though brief, may be useful even to non-programmers. (And yes, this book also makes a cameo appearance in the movie *Wayne's World II*.)

Finally, for more information on the Internet in general, check out Internet site http://www.internic.net. This is the home Web site for the InterNIC and offers a wealth of information about the Internet, its governing bodies, and Internet-related activities. This site also contains information about registered domains.

Chapter 2

For detailed information on Ethernet cards – and in particular, on the Ethernet hardware that is compatible with Linux – see the Linux Ethernet HOWTO, which is available from the Internet at site:

http://sunsite.unc.edu/LDP/HOWTO/Ethernet-HOWTO-1.html

For more information on using serial ports under Linux, see the Linux Serial HOWTO, which is available from the Internet at site

http://sunsite.unc.edu/LDP/HOWTO/Serial-HOWTO-1.html

For information on mgetty and related programs, see:

http://www.leo.org/~doering/mgetty/index.html

For more information on the InterNIC – and in particular, to submit a request for an Internet domain – check out the InterNIC's Web page at site:

```
http://www.internic.net
```

Chapter 3

Chapter 3 discusses topics that are specific to Linux. Therefore, the principal source of additional information is the documents that describe the Linux system itself. These documents can be downloaded from Internet site:

```
http://www.linux.org/info/index.html
```

◆ To look further into compiling the Linux kernel, check the Linux Kernel HOWTO. For detailed information on any given sub-system that is being compiled into the kernel, check the documents in directory /usr/src/linux/Documentation. These documents are included as a standard part of the Linux kernel sources.

◆ For further information on the networking configuration files, see the files themselves. They contain comments that explain their contents and lay out in somewhat more detail than we give here.

◆ For information on the configuration commands ifconfig and route, use the man command to view their manual pages.

◆ For more information on the scripts rc.inet1 and rc.inet2, you should read these files. They contain comments that explain their actions. In particular, script rc.inet2 will describe what networking features it turns on and which it does not.

◆ For more information on pppd, use the command man to view its manual page. This manual page also gives information on pppd's configuration files. Unfortunately, script ppp-on-dialer is very specific to your Linux system and to your ISP, so there is not much more information available.

◆ For more information on diald, see the documentation that comes with its sources. In particular, the manual page for diald-examples is helpful in explaining the rather convoluted syntax of diald's configuration files.

Chapter 4

`ftp`, `ncftp`, `telnet`, and `trn` are venerable programs for which not a great deal of information is available for beginners. However, you may find the following to be helpful:

◆ The manual page for each program is helpful. The writing is not always the clearest, but the pages are complete. To view them, use the `man` command.

◆ An FAQ (that is, a document of frequently asked questions) has been compiled for each program. Most FAQs have been collected together, and can be downloaded from the Internet easily; for details, check Web site `http://www.faqs.org`.

The following RFCs are also relevant:

◆ RFC 959 describes the File Transfer Protocol (FTP). This is particularly helpful, in that it defines all of the messages returned by an FTP server.

◆ RFC 854 describes the TELNET protocol.

◆ RFC 977 describes the Network News Transfer Protocol (NNTP).

`lynx` comes with a wealth of documentation, including a full tutorial. To access this document, simply invoke `lynx`, then press `h` to display its help screen. You can select the tutorial from that screen and either read it or print it.

Libraries of books have been written on the subjects of HTML and Web browsers. You may find the following sources of information to be helpful.

◆ The Hypertext Transfer Protocol (HTTP) is defined in RFC 1945 (version 1.0) and RFC 2068 (version 1.1).

◆ The Hypertext Markup Language (HTML) is defined and is being extended by the World Wide Web Consortium (W3), which includes many of the computing world's most influential organizations. To freely download the W3 publications that define HTML and describe its future directions, check URL `http://www.w3.org/WWW/TR`.

Chapter 5

The best source of information about SMTP is its definition in RFC 821, written by Jonathan B. Postel. This document is available from the NIC's Web site; look for document STD10.

For a good summary of UUCP, you should check out *Using and Managing UUCP*, by Ed Ravin, Tim O'Reilly, Dale Dougherty, and Grace Todino (Sebastopol, Calif, O'Reilly & Associates, Inc., 1996). This book combines material from two earlier books, *Using UUCP and Usenet* and *Managing UUCP and Usenet*, by the same authors, which were two of O'Reilly's original Nutshell books. It has been updated to cover Taylor UUCP.

If you are interested in receiving mail via UUCP, be sure to check the ISPs in your locale. Two ISPs to our knowledge offer UUCP mail service at a relatively low price:

- Ripco Communications, Chicago (http://www.ripco.com)

- Connix Communications, Middlefield, Connecticut (http://www.connix.com). Connix also offers news feeds via UUCP.

With regard to sendmail, two books stand out:

- *sendmail*, by Bryan Costales and Eric Allman, second edition (Sebastopol, Calif., O'Reilly & Associates, Inc., 1997).

- *sendmail Desktop Reference*, by Bryan Costales and Eric Allman (Sebastopol, Calif., O'Reilly & Associates, 1997).

sendmail Desktop Reference is designed so that knowledgeable users can look up information quickly. *sendmail* is more tutorial, and is designed to lead you down the twisty, tortuous path of sendmail's design and configuration. These books contain information about sendmail at a level of detail that you should be afraid exists. If you ever have to do any complex mail routing, sendmail is the program and these are the books.

Chapter 6

For more information on using Ethernet under Linux, see document:

http://sunsite.unc.edu/pub/Linux/docs/HOWTO/Ethernet-HOWTO

Wiring information came from the 1997 Siemon Company Catalogue. You can get a copy of this from:

`http://www.siemon.com`

The material that pertains to wiring standards TIA/EIA 568A is under:

`http://www.siemon.com/standard.html`

There is also an interesting section on home cabling options under:

`http://www.siemon.com/homecable/homecable.html`

Please note that much of the hardware described here looks nice, but is expensive.
For more information on the arguments that can be passed to the kernel, see document:

`http://sunsite.unc.edu/pub/Linux/docs/HOWTO/Kernel-HOWTO`

For a good summary of how to pass to the kernel via arguments to `lilo`, see document:

`http://sunsite.unc.edu/pub/Linux/docs/howto/mini/LILO`

Finally, if you are interested in *Also Sprach Zarathustra*, we warmly recommend the 1954 recording by Fritz Reiner and the Chicago Symphony Orchestra (RCA Victor 09026-61494-2), which is reissued on CD as part of RCA's Living Stereo series. This classic performance by one of the great conductors of the 20th century was beautifully remastered for CD by John Pfeiffer, using the original analog recording equipment. Play it loud!

Chapter 7

`inetd`, `ftpd`, and `telnetd` are well described by their manual pages. `inetd` is also discussed by the Linux how-to document; to download a copy, check out Web site `http://www.linux.org`.

Apache comes with a wealth of documentation in HTML format. The documentation is packaged with the archive of Apache sources; or to view the Apache documentation interactively, check out Web site `http://www.Apache.org`.

For what we think is a pretty good summary of how to build CGI scripts and Java applets, see *The Linux Database*, by Fred Butzen and Dorothy Forbes (New York, MIS:Press, 1997). The emphasis is on building scripts and applets that interact with a relational database, but you can use its descriptions with more garden-variety scripts and applets as well.

For a thorough description of NFS and other systems of sharing resources across a network, we recommend *TCP/IP and NFS: Internetworking in a UNIX Environment*, by Michael Santifaller (Reading, Mass., Addison-Wesley Publishing Co., 1991).

For information on printing under Linux, see best source of information is the Linux printing how-to. This, too, is available at URL `http://www.linux.org`.

Many, many books have been published on the X Windows System. We have found two to be particularly helpful:

◆ *The Joy of X* by Neil Mansfield (Reading, Mass., Addison-Wesley Publishing Co., 1993). This does an excellent job of explaining the complex architecture of the X Window System.

◆ *The X Window System in a Nutshell* edited by Ellie Cutler, Daniel Gilly, and Tim O'Reilly (Sebastopol, Calif., O'Reilly & Associates, Inc., 1992). This is a fine handbook and reference to the X Window System, its commands, and its library calls (should you ever feel the urge to program in X).

Finally, if you are interested in thorough and erudite (and often hilarious) definitions of commonly used computer terms, see *The Computer Contradictionary*, second edition, by Stan Kelly-Bootle (Cambridge, Mass., The MIT Press, 1995). *Highly recommended.*

Chapter 8

The best information on IP masquerading that we have found has been prepared as part of the Linux documentation project:

◆ The IP Masquerading Mini-howto, by Ambrose Au. This is a condensation of the full IP masquerading "howto" document. It is well organized and clearly written, and makes this topic accessible even to beginners. It is available at URL:

`http://www.linux.org/help/minihowto.html`

◆ The IP Masquerading FAQ. This document presents questions about IP masquerading that are asked frequently. It describes problems that are encountered frequently, as well as some that occur only rarely. It is available at URL:

`http://www.linux.org/help/faq.html`

These documents are updated continually, so we suggest that you take the time to retrieve the latest edition, rather than just using the ones included with your Linux release.

For more information on firewalls, we suggest that you read two manual pages in particular:

◆ The manual page `ipfw` gives a good general discussion of what a firewall is, and how it works.

◆ The manual page for the command `ipfwadm` summarizes this command, and goes into some detail on how to configure and tune a firewall.

With regard to SOCKS, the best source of information is the documentation that is included with the package. You can download the documentation from the Internet sites referred to in the section on SOCKS.

For more information on the secure shell `ssh`, which we mentioned briefly in this chapter, see William LeFebvre's article "The Secure Shell," which appeared in the September 1997 issue of *UNIX Review*. The article gives a good summary of `ssh`, and gives you a taste of how it would work in your intranet.

Finally, for a thorough discussion of DNS and `bind`, we recommend *DNS and BIND* by Paul Albitz and Cricket Liu (Sebastopol, Calif., O'Reilly & Associates, Inc., 1996), now in its second edition. This book is a typical O'Reilly production: readable, well organized, and thorough.

Chapter 9

Many, many, many books have been written about Windows 95. Some are even worth reading. For the general public, the book that probably is most helpful is Andy Rathbone's *Windows 95 for Dummies* (Foster City, Calif., IDG Books Worldwide, 1995). Don't let the title fool you – Linux users are no dummies, but this book is a fine introduction to Windows 95 and its maze of twisty passages, all a little different. In particular, it will be most helpful to the Windows 95 user who will be using your intranet.

For a good general introduction to the NetBIOS and SMB protocols, see Steven Baker's article "Serve up Microsoft networking on UNIX" (*UNIX Review*, August 1997, pp. 15-22).

Microsoft has invested a great deal of effort in supporting and extending the SMB protocol. For Microsoft's view of SMB, see site:

`ftp://ftp.microsoft.com/developr/drg/SMB.TXT`

Two RFCs deal with the interaction between NetBIOS and TCP/IP:

◆ RFC 1001 describes how to encapsulate NetBIOS within TCP/IP.

◆ RFC 1002 describes NetBIOS naming conventions. It also describes the structure of a NetBIOS name server (what Microsoft calls a WINS).

For more information on Samba, see the following URLs:

- `http://samba.anu.edu.au` — Home page for Samba

- `http://samba.anu.edu.au/cifs/docs/what-is-smb.html` — Richard Sharpe's primer on SMB. This page also offers links to other SMB-related resources on the Internet.

- `http://samba.anu.edu.au/samba/docs/faq/sambafaq.html` — The Samba FAQ. A copy of this document is included with the Samba sources, but it is continually being extended and revised. If you run into a problem with Samba, your first step should be to secure the most up-to-date copy of this FAQ.

Finally, for more information on the Windows command NET, see the article "Taking command of Windows, part II", by Tom Yager (*UNIX Review*, November 1997, pp. 33-42). The author discusses its use in real-world scenarios, particularly as an aid to integrating UNIX and Windows NT; but much of his discussion also applies to Windows 95.

Chapter 10

A great deal has been written about encryption techniques. One good source of information is the Web site of the National Security Agency, at `http://www.nsa.gov`. The NSA is the ultra-secret agency that is in charge of electronic intelligence. This site includes some fascinating descriptions of the cryptographic side of the Cold War.

The history of cryptography is a fascinating story in itself. For a history of this subject, we warmly recommend *The Codebreakers* by David Kahn (New York, Macmillan, 1967). This book ends where the computer era of computer encryption begins, but it is very strong on the human story of encryption and codebreaking, particularly the U.S. Navy's *Magic* project, which broke the Japanese diplomatic and naval codes, and the British *Ultra* group's breaking of the German "Enigma" codes, which were instrumental in the Allies' victory in World War II.

For a thorough description of the PGP package, see *PGP* by Simpson Garfinkel (Sebastopol, Calif., O'Reilly & Associates, Inc., 1995).

For more information on the secure shell `ssh`, see William LeFebvre's article "The Secure Shell in the September 1997 issue of *UNIX Review*. The article gives a good summary of `ssh`, and gives you a taste of how it would work in your intranet.

For information on security and firewalls, we recommend two books: *Practical Unix and Internet Security*, by Simson Garfinkel and Gene Spafford (Sebastopol, Calif., O'Reilly & Associates, Inc., 1996), and *Building Internet Firewalls*, by D. Brent Chapman and Elizabeth D. Zwicky (Sebastopol, Calif., O'Reilly & Associates, Inc., 1995). Both of these books contain lots of practical information about securing UNIX and Linux machines that will connect to the Internet. The book on firewalls describes the art protecting yourself from the Internet once you have connected to it.

Finally, the up-to-the-minute nature of mailing lists and news groups makes them an especially good source of information on security. For example, at the beginning of March 1998, a small group of crackers decided to exploit an IP fragment-handling defect in the Windows 95 and NT TCP/IP stack. The defect causes NT to hang and if the machine is not configured to reboot itself after a kernel crash, the machine will stay in this state until someone reboots it. It's believed that this attack began in the early morning of Monday, March 1, 1998. Thousands of machines were affected. People who subscribe to the BugTraq mailing list were aware of the problem by noon of the same day. You can view the Bugtraq list archives at:

```
http://www.geek-girl.com/~bugtraq
```

You can subscribe to the list by sending an e-mail with only the words "subscribe bugtraq" in the body to `listserv@netspace.org`.

Finally, if Usenet news is more to your liking, you can find UNIX security information in the groups:

- `Comp.security.unix`
- `Comp.security.firewalls`
- `Comp.security.ssh`

Index

A

continued

continued

continued

IDG BOOKS WORLDWIDE, INC.
END–USER LICENSE AGREEMENT

READ THIS. You should carefully read these terms and conditions before opening the software packet(s) included with this book ("Book"). This is a license agreement ("Agreement") between you and IDG Books Worldwide, Inc. ("IDGB"). By opening the accompanying software packet(s), you acknowledge that you have read and accept the following terms and conditions. If you do not agree and do not want to be bound by such terms and conditions, promptly return the Book and the unopened software packet(s) to the place you obtained them for a full refund.

1. License Grant. IDGB grants to you (either an individual or entity) a nonexclusive license to use one copy of the enclosed software program(s) (collectively, the "Software") solely for your own personal or business purposes on a single computer (whether a standard computer or a workstation component of a multiuser network). The Software is in use on a computer when it is loaded into temporary memory (RAM) or installed into permanent memory (hard disk, CD-ROM, or other storage device). IDGB reserves all rights not expressly granted herein.

2. Ownership. IDGB is the owner of all right, title, and interest, including copyright, in and to the compilation of the Software recorded on the disk(s) or CD-ROM ("Software Media"). Copyright to the individual programs recorded on the Software Media is owned by the author or other authorized copyright owner of each program. Ownership of the Software and all proprietary rights relating thereto remain with IDGB and its licensers.

3. Restrictions on Use and Transfer.

   (a) You may only (i) make one copy of the Software for backup or archival purposes, or (ii) transfer the Software to a single hard disk, provided that you keep the original for backup or archival purposes. You may not (i) rent or lease the Software, (ii) copy or reproduce the Software through a LAN or other network system or through any computer subscriber system or bulletin-board system, or (iii) modify, adapt, or create derivative works based on the Software.

   (b) You may not reverse engineer, decompile, or disassemble the Software. You may transfer the Software and user documentation on a permanent basis, provided that the transferee agrees to accept the terms and conditions of this Agreement and you retain no copies. If the Software is an update or has been updated, any transfer must include the most recent update and all prior versions.

4. **Restrictions on Use of Individual Programs.** You must follow the individual requirements and restrictions detailed for each individual program in Appendix A, "About the CD-ROM," of this Book. These limitations are also contained in the individual license agreements recorded on the Software Media. These limitations may include a requirement that after using the program for a specified period of time, the user must pay a registration fee or discontinue use. By opening the Software packet(s), you will be agreeing to abide by the licenses and restrictions for these individual programs that are detailed in Appendix A and on the Software Media. None of the material on this Software Media or listed in this Book may ever be redistributed, in original or modified form, for commercial purposes.

5. **Limited Warranty.**

   (a) IDGB warrants that the Software and Software Media are free from defects in materials and workmanship under normal use for a period of sixty (60) days from the date of purchase of this Book. If IDGB receives notification within the warranty period of defects in materials or workmanship, IDGB will replace the defective Software Media.

   (b) IDGB AND THE AUTHORS OF THE BOOK DISCLAIM ALL OTHER WARRANTIES, EXPRESS OR IMPLIED, INCLUDING WITHOUT LIMITATION IMPLIED WARRANTIES OF MERCHANTABILITY AND FITNESS FOR A PARTICULAR PURPOSE, WITH RESPECT TO THE SOFTWARE, THE PROGRAMS, THE SOURCE CODE CONTAINED THEREIN, AND/OR THE TECHNIQUES DESCRIBED IN THIS BOOK. IDGB DOES NOT WARRANT THAT THE FUNCTIONS CONTAINED IN THE SOFTWARE WILL MEET YOUR REQUIREMENTS OR THAT THE OPERATION OF THE SOFTWARE WILL BE ERROR FREE.

   (c) This limited warranty gives you specific legal rights, and you may have other rights that vary from jurisdiction to jurisdiction.

6. **Remedies.**

   (a) IDGB's entire liability and your exclusive remedy for defects in materials and workmanship shall be limited to replacement of the Software Media, which may be returned to IDGB with a copy of your receipt at the following address: Software Media Fulfillment Department, Attn.: *The LINUX Network*, IDG Books Worldwide, Inc., 7260 Shadeland Station, Ste. 100, Indianapolis, IN 46256, or call 1-800-762-2974. Please allow three to four weeks for delivery. This Limited Warranty is void if failure of the Software Media has resulted from accident, abuse, or misapplication. Any replacement Software Media will be warranted for the remainder of the original warranty period or thirty (30) days, whichever is longer.

(b) In no event shall IDGB or the authors be liable for any damages whatsoever (including without limitation damages for loss of business profits, business interruption, loss of business information, or any other pecuniary loss) arising from the use of or inability to use the Book or the Software, even if IDGB has been advised of the possibility of such damages.

(c) Because some jurisdictions do not allow the exclusion or limitation of liability for consequential or incidental damages, the above limitation or exclusion may not apply to you.

7. **U.S. Government Restricted Rights.** Use, duplication, or disclosure of the Software by the U.S. Government is subject to restrictions stated in paragraph (c)(1)(ii) of the Rights in Technical Data and Computer Software clause of DFARS 252.227-7013, and in subparagraphs (a) through (d) of the Commercial Computer – Restricted Rights clause at FAR 52.227-19, and in similar clauses in the NASA FAR supplement, when applicable.

8. **General.** This Agreement constitutes the entire understanding of the parties and revokes and supersedes all prior agreements, oral or written, between them and may not be modified or amended except in a writing signed by both parties hereto that specifically refers to this Agreement. This Agreement shall take precedence over any other documents that may be in conflict herewith. If any one or more provisions contained in this Agreement are held by any court or tribunal to be invalid, illegal, or otherwise unenforceable, each and every other provision shall remain in full force and effect.

Every month *Linux Journal* brings subscribers the most complete news and information on what the powerful Linux operating system can do. This includes Linux news, tips, features and reviews which you cannot find anywhere else. Our coverage of kernel changes, programming tools, and product releases is unparalleled.

■ Keep up on the latest Linux technology news
■ Read comprehensive reviews on Linux merchandise
■ Find answers in our Best of Technical Support column
■ Get involved with the Linux community
■ Increase your technical knowledge
■ Receive *LJ*'s Annual Buyer's Guide FREE with your subscription

Return this coupon and you will automatically receive a free issue of Linux Journal, compliments of

M&T Books
The Linux Network

By subscribing today, you will save over 60% off cover price.

	2 YEARS	1 YEAR
US	❏ $39	❏ $22
CAN/MEX	❏ $49 (USD)	❏ $27 (USD)
Elsewhere	❏ $64 (USD)	❏ $37 (USD)

Please allow 6-8 weeks for processing

NAME _____

COMPANY _____

ADDRESS _____

CITY _____ STATE _____ POSTAL CODE _____

COUNTRY _____ E-MAIL _____

TELEPHONE _____ FAX _____

❏ Visa   ❏ MasterCard   ❏ American Express   ❏ Check Enclosed

CREDIT CARD # _____ EXPIRES _____

SIGNATURE _____

Detach and return this coupon:

Linux Journal
PO Box 55549
Seattle, WA 98155-0549

http://www.linuxjournal.com
PH 888-66-LINUX
FAX 206-782-7191

my2cents.idgbooks.com

Register This Book — And Win!

Visit **http://my2cents.idgbooks.com** to register this book and we'll automatically enter you in our fantastic monthly prize giveaway. It's also your opportunity to give us feedback: let us know what you thought of this book and how you would like to see other topics covered.

Discover IDG Books Online!

The IDG Books Online Web site is your online resource for tackling technology — at home and at the office. Frequently updated, the IDG Books Online Web site features exclusive software, insider information, online books, and live events!

10 Productive & Career-Enhancing Things You Can Do at www.idgbooks.com

- Nab source code for your own programming projects.

- Download software.

- Read Web exclusives: special articles and book excerpts by IDG Books Worldwide authors.

- Take advantage of resources to help you advance your career as a Novell or Microsoft professional.

- Buy IDG Books Worldwide titles or find a convenient bookstore that carries them.

- Register your book and win a prize.

- Chat live online with authors.

- Sign up for regular e-mail updates about our latest books.

- Suggest a book you'd like to read or write.

- Give us your 2¢ about our books and about our Web site.

You say you're not on the Web yet? It's easy to get started with IDG Books' *Discover the Internet*, available at local retailers everywhere.

CD-ROM Installation Instructions

The CD-ROM that accompanies this book includes Slackware 3.5, as well as a few networking tools.

For basic installation instructions for Slackware 3.5, insert the disk in your CD-ROM drive and locate the files README35.TXT and INSTALL.TXT.

To install the networking tools included on the CD, click the appropriate icon.

For a complete listing and description of the software on the CD-ROM, see Appendix A, "What's on the CD-ROM."